BACK IN B

Born in California, Gerard DeGroot is Professor
of Modern History at the University of St
Andrews. He has written many books on
various aspects of twentieth-century history,
most recently *The Seventies Unplugged*. He
regularly contributes to national newspapers
both in Britain and in the USA.

GERARD DEGROOT

Back in Blighty

The British at Home in World War One

VINTAGE BOOKS
London

Published by Vintage 2014

2 4 6 8 10 9 7 5 3 1

First published by Longman in 1996 under the title *Blighty*.
This is a fully revised and updated edition

Vintage
Random House, 20 Vauxhall Bridge Road,
London SW1V 2SA

www.vintage-books.co.uk

Addresses for companies within The Random House Group Limited
can be found at: www.randomhouse.co.uk/offices.htm

The Random House Group Limited Reg. No. 954009

A CIP catalogue record for this book
is available from the British Library

ISBN 9780099582229

The Random House Group Limited supports the Forest Stewardship
Council® (FSC®), the leading international forest-certification
organisation. Our books carrying the FSC label are printed on FSC®-
certified paper. FSC is the only forest-certification scheme supported
by the leading environmental organisations, including Greenpeace.
Our paper procurement policy can be found at:
www.randomhouse.co.uk/environment

Printed and bound by Clays Ltd, St Ives plc

*To my wonderful students at the University of St Andrews:
your charm, razor wit and phenomenal intelligence have been
a great joy for three decades.*

Contents

Acknowledgements

We are grateful for permission to reproduce the following copyright material:

'The General' and part poems 'Suicide in the Trenches' and 'The Rank Stench' by Siegfried Sassoon are copyright © Siegfried Sassoon and included by kind permission of the Estate of George Sassoon; part poems 'Perhaps' and 'To My Brother' by Vera Brittain are included by permission of Mark Bostridge and T.J. Brittain-Catlin, Literary Executors for the Vera Brittain Estate 1970; part poem 'Recruit from the Slums' by Emily Orr are copyright © Emily Orr from 'The Harvester of Dreams', Burn & Oates, included by permission of Bloomsbury Publishing Plc; 'The Dancers' from *Clown's Houses* by Edith Sitwell is reprinted by permission of Peters Fraser & Dunlop (www.petersfraserdunlop. com) on behalf of the Estate to Edith Sitwell.

War memorial fund poster copyright © Mary Evans Picture Library; British food rationing poster copyright © Illustrated London News Ltd / Mary Evans Picture Library; 'Knitted Comforts for Men on Land and Sea' pamphlet copyright © Barbara Smith; John Bull pamphlet copyright © George Simmers; Glasgow war poster © CSG CIC Glasgow Museums and Libraries Collection: The Mitchell Library, Special Collections, Libraries, Information and Learning; 'The Win-the-War Cookery Book' pamphlet copyright © Beth Wilmshurst.

Every effort has been made to trace and contact copyright holders prior to publication. If notified, the publisher undertakes to rectify any errors or omissions at the earliest opportunity.

Introduction

History books reveal as much about the present as they do about the past. Because our perspective on the past is shaped by what concerns us today, history is a fluid, ever-changing thing. Thus, back in the 1960s, hope and progress seemed everywhere apparent. Historians working during that decade, undoubtedly affected by the prevalent mood of optimism, gazed backwards upon the previous half-century of British history and perceived a great ferment of progress fired by the catalyst of war. According to the accepted narrative, the struggle for survival in two world wars pushed women towards emancipation, governments towards social responsibility and workers towards solidarity. A 'deluge' of social and political change resulted.

Or so it seemed. Back in 1996, I challenged the 'war and social change' school of history when I published *Blighty: British Society in the Era of the Great War*. In the introduction to that book, I wrote that, from my own perspective at the end of the twentieth century,

> change does not seem as profound, nor progress so direct. Politics is still dominated by the party of conservatism and tradition. Even Mrs Thatcher's brief period of radicalism seems to have been absorbed and contained by her party. There is a striking similarity between the individuals who

dominate politics today and those who dominated during the Great War. (Even some of the names are the same.) Despite a century of 'progress' in education and social welfare, the vast majority of working-class children leave school early and the vast majority of middle class children go on to university. The arguments which were used to constrain women within the sphere of the home remain popular to this day. Those women who manage to pursue a career still receive lower pay for equal work and find advancement severely restricted.

Sixteen years after writing that book, I still stand by this thesis. I do not believe that the Great War brought forth a deluge of social and political change. I still think that the striking feature of British experience in the twentieth century is the way progress has been contained by a smothering blanket of tradition. As I wrote back then: 'One can never ignore the deep worship of the past which exists within the British psyche. Britain is a very old country and . . . a country which wants to remain old.'

I am nevertheless aware of how *Blighty* was shaped by my own experience growing up as an academic and writer in Thatcher's Britain. The 1980s were acrimonious times, and I immersed myself in their strife. The emotions inspired by the battles of that decade spilled on to the pages of my book. Reading it now, it seems an excessively strident work, with subtlety smothered by my own hard-edged political certainty.

The assumptions I adhered to in the 1990s are now difficult to defend. Politics, thanks to the contradictions of the Blair years, seems less susceptible to easy verdict. Party labels are no longer convenient short cuts to judgement; there is wisdom, idiocy and iniquity on both sides of the political divide. More importantly, I'm reminded of something Bill Clinton said recently with regard to the distorting effect of political belief:

'the problem with any ideology is that it gives the answer before you look at the evidence. So you have to mold the evidence to get the answer that you've already decided you've got to have.' Applying that wisdom to the writing of history, it seems that if political agendas are discarded, a much more interesting, nuanced and accurate account of the past should emerge.

I had these thoughts firmly in mind when I recently offered *Blighty* to Vintage, with an entirely new version in mind. I wanted not simply a new edition, but a new book, built on the foundation of the 1996 volume. *Blighty* was written for my students at the University of St Andrews, and others studying the Great War at school and university. It was a textbook, though one which students found enjoyable to read. This new book, intended for a wider readership, has been freed from the formulaic restraints typical of a textbook. The chapter structure is similar to *Blighty*, but there's hardly a sentence from the old book that remains the same. The research has been updated to take advantage of the impressive scholarly work that has been carried out since 1996 and of the wealth of primary sources that have been made available. What results is, I think, a more well-informed account, but also one which is less sanctimonious and po-faced than the book previously published.

This new book is intended, quite simply, to be an account of a fascinating time when the British faced up to the challenge of a mammoth war. With the volume lowered on my own political animosity, I've found that I've become much more sensitive to the nice little stories that emerge from this era. There are certainly political lessons to be drawn, but they should not obscure what is still an incredibly moving tale of how a nation adapted to the strains of total war, while at the same time desperately trying to retain as much as possible from a glorious past. After over three decades of teaching and writing about the Great War, I find that it is the creative adaptability and heroic resilience of the British people that shines most brightly from this tragedy of war.

This is a social history of Britain in the Great War, crafted for the general reader. I delve into politics only where it is necessary to make sense of social change. I accept that an economic perspective is necessary to the understanding of social change, but I have tried to keep the economic analysis to a minimum in order to maintain the dramatic thrust. As with any book, the process of writing leaves one depressed at what has to be left out in order to keep the length manageable. In truth, this book is just a sampler of a strange and wonderful world that existed one hundred years ago. So much of that world will seem bizarre, but the core beliefs that drove a people towards victory should be rather familiar. Times change, but attributes like duty, sacrifice, heroism, devotion and love are constants. The British did not want war, but when it came, they fought with extraordinary courage and dedication. The Great War revealed a nation at its best. As Ralph Waldo Emerson said in 1847: 'This aged England sees a little better on a cloudy day; in storm of battle and calamity she has a secret vigour and a pulse like a cannon.'

Part One

Going to War

Chapter 1

A Lovely War

On the evening of 4 August 1914, a huge crowd gathered outside Buckingham Palace. When the King and Queen appeared on the balcony, a crescendo of shouts, whistles and applause erupted. The atmosphere resembled that of a jubilee or royal wedding. On this occasion, however, the merriment was inspired by Britain's declaration of war. The crowd cheered madly the approaching cataclysm.

According to contemporary commentators, over the previous year a fog had blanketed Britain, shrouding vision and smothering good sense. Winston Churchill recalled 'a strange temper in the air' which rendered aggression appealing. Echoing that theme, the political activist Mary Agnes Hamilton observed how her friends 'seemed always to be waiting for something from outside which was going to decide what they thought. It was appalling, but it was there. They sat and watched it coming as they might have sat and watched a thunderstorm approach.' Rejecting the weather metaphor, the pacifist historian Caroline Playne preferred instead that of a virulent epidemic:

the thoughtful, no less than the others, were under the spell of an immense crowd infection ... in the hot dog-days of 1914. The desire went out from the more primitive-minded, those to whom force made a supreme appeal – militarists, chauvinists, imperialists. The mental contagion – it was a contagion, something more immediate than a suggestion – swept down the mindless, expectant, half-frightened, wondering crowds, and ... swept down progressives, earnest people, intelligent people as well. But these last had to sublimate motives, to idealise, to call evil good, to invent specious pretexts for following on with the multitude.

Metaphors of weather or illness suggest inevitability. In such a scenario, ordinary people lose agency and are overwhelmed by events. Inevitability suggests in turn a clear path, a sequence leading inexorably towards doom. Thus the *Manchester Guardian*, looking back from the vantage point of 12 November 1918, remarked: 'The idea of humanity receded in favour of the state, freedom gave way to discipline and organisation, right to the strong hand, reason to passion, and self-restraint to ambition ... It began to be felt that things could not last as they were. The piled-up armaments were like vast electric accumulators awaiting their discharge.' The words are beautiful, but the reasoning is suspect. Clarity of direction is always easy to discern in hindsight. At the time, the path to war did not seem particularly obvious, nor was enthusiasm for it the predominant feeling.[1]

According to the scenario peddled by Hamilton, Playne and others, the British convinced themselves that war was not only tolerable, but beneficial. By welcoming war, they rendered it more likely. The pathogens of war fever, it seems, could be found in every organ of society. Thus the education system – or, specifically, the public schools – encouraged false sentimentality, turning the spirit of the playing field into martial obsession. Militaristic youth movements produced boys eager not just to drill but to fight. The popular press and 'invasion novels' encouraged a paranoiac fear of Germany, while West End plays warned of a population gone soft. Meanwhile, anguish over suffragettes, militant trade unionism and Irish republicanism supposedly encouraged a tendency to look outwards for distraction. An embattled government consequently saw war as a welcome escape from internal strife, a chance to unite a fractured country. Even the weather played a part: an unusually warm summer caused either restless tension, carefree complacency or primal aggression, depending on the commentator's point of view.

Some elements in this grand *mise en scène* have factual grounding, others are gossamer fantasy. Since we know that war did break out, the factors that hastened its advent seem obvious while those that militated against it dissolve into insignificance. We ignore, for instance, the tremendous popularity of Norman Angell's pacifistic book *The Great Illusion*, which argued that war was economically absurd. Or the enormous progress in international cooperation, especially in banking, transportation and communication. Or the worldwide interest in the Olympic movement. Or the civility which the Hague Conferences of 1901 and 1907 contributed to international relations. Or the proliferation of pacifist groups. Or the reverence for Germany among British intellectuals and businessmen. On the day war was declared, Sir Edward Goschen, the British Ambassador to Berlin, remarked to his German colleagues upon the ironic 'tragedy which saw the two nations fall apart just at the moment when the relations between them had been more friendly and cordial than they had been for years'. That was not diplomatic hyperbole. In many ways, Europe had become, by 1913, a continent at peace with itself. A British businessman could travel from country to country without need of passport and could cash a cheque with ease in Berlin, Budapest, Paris or Vienna. Had war not materialised, historians would today point to these phenomena as clear harbingers of a glorious age of peace.[2]

Furthermore, it is misguided to presume (as so many do) that a bellicose people can propel a nation to war. In every country, the foreign office is the most undemocratic of government agencies; foreign ministers revel in their isolation from the hoi polloi. Before 1914, the British Foreign Office preferred that the public should remain ignorant of international affairs; it intentionally avoided opportunities to explain its policies. In any case, governments go to war not because of mysterious forces swirling in the ether but for purely pragmatic reasons. While politicians will usually hesitate before committing a nation to a decidedly unpopular war, no amount of 'war fever' will drive a government towards a war that is not in the national interest. Thus the explanation for why Britain intervened in 1914 should begin with high diplomacy.

By 1914, nearly a century had passed since British soldiers had fought in Western Europe. During that time Britain led the world in industrial output and amassed the largest empire in history. That she was able to avoid war against her European rivals is testimony to skilful diplomacy and to the strength of her navy. At least as far as European power politics was concerned, Britain was a peaceable kingdom. Granted, she was an aggressive imperial power, but her aggression was carefully directed. The numerous imperial 'wars' during the nineteenth century were essentially police actions fought to ensure imperial stability. Two points deserve emphasis: firstly, it was not Britain's inclination to intervene in a continental war. Secondly, her peaceful tendencies meant that she was militarily weak.

'We are attempting to maintain the largest Empire the world has ever seen with armaments and reserves that would be insufficient for a third-class power', the War Office official Sir Henry Brackenbury complained in 1899. Around the same time, the Liberal statesman Lord Rosebery described a worrying scene of Britain 'so lonely in these northern seas, viewed with so much jealousy, with such hostility, with such jarred ambition by the great empires of the world, so friendless among nations which count their armies by embattled millions'. Vulnerability was compounded by the fact that the problem seemed devoid of solution. Stated simply, Britain could not respond to weakness by becoming strong. There were too many demands on the public purse to make possible a meaningful expansion of military forces. Nor did the people desire a fortress nation.[3]

Splendid isolation no longer seemed splendid. 'So long as you are isolated,' the Colonial Secretary Joseph Chamberlain asked in 1898, 'can you say that it is not possible, can you even say that it is not probable, that some time or another you may have a combination of at least three Powers against you?' That threat was compounded by the need to protect a far-flung empire. Imperial possessions, once a symbol of British strength, were now an indication of vulnerability. The only conceivable response to this predicament was diplomatic. As the new century began, the government sought allies, the very thing that Britain had carefully avoided for over eighty years. The ideal of Pax Britannica – of standing aloof – was cast aside and Britain went looking for friends.[4]

The first significant overture was directed toward Japan, with whom an alliance was signed in 1902. Britain agreed to stand aside in a war confined to Russia and Japan, but promised to support Japan if Russia was joined by another European power. The agreement gave Japan the confidence to pursue expansion at Russia's expense, even, as it happened, to the point of war. While the agreement obviously benefited Japan, the British were concerned only with the gain to themselves – namely Japan's agreement to steer clear of British possessions in East Asia. This allowed Britain to protect that area without massive military commitment. Even more important was the effect upon Russia. The British surmised that preoccupation with an ambitious Japan would curb Russia's aspirations in India and the

Persian Gulf. Neutralisation of this threat would in turn allow Britain to reduce her naval commitments in East and South Asia and redeploy them in more vulnerable European waters. This was all terribly cynical, but foreign policy is seldom an expression of principles.

Next came France. From a twenty-first-century perspective, the Entente Cordiale of 1904 seems natural, given Anglo–French cooperation in two world wars. At the time, however, it was a radical departure. The British and French had, after all, nearly come to blows during the Fashoda crisis six years earlier. Tempers had not significantly cooled. Thus there was very little that was *cordiale* about the entente. The agreement was simply amoral pragmatism: both sides sought to protect imperial interests through compromise with a rival. Specific areas of competition were addressed, in particular Morocco and Egypt, but cordiality was not supposed to extend to the European continent. In other words, this was not meant to be an anti-German alliance. Unfortunately, France thought otherwise; she saw the entente as a way to isolate Germany. The agreement reveals both the naivety of British diplomacy and the dangers of pacts inspired by desperation. At the price of stability in Africa, Britain was sucked into the European vortex.

By 1898, the biggest threat to the British Empire was not France, nor Germany, but Russia – or so it seemed. 'A quarrel with Russia anywhere, about anything, means the invasion of India,' the prominent Conservative Arthur Balfour warned in 1901. The Committee of Imperial Defence seriously doubted the army's ability to defend India against a determined Russian onslaught, a prospect that also frightened the Viceroy, Lord Curzon. 'As long as we rule India we are the greatest power in the world,' he argued. 'If we lose it we shall drop straight away to a third-rate power.' The massive Russian army (potentially 3,600,000 men) was a problem, but even more daunting was the fact that Russia was virtually invulnerable to British naval might. The Anglo-Russian convention of 1907 resolved this predicament satisfactorily for the British, but at the cost of drawing Britain even deeper into European affairs.[5]

A hat-trick of agreements had buttressed the Empire, but had also produced a complex web of entanglements. These agreements are more important stepping stones towards British intervention in August 1914 than are any of the episodes of Anglo-German antagonism before the war, such as the naval rivalry, the Kruger telegram, the Agadir crisis, or the Berlin–Baghdad railway. Nevertheless, it might be asked, if Britain was inclined to address vulnerability with diplomacy, why did she not forge a pact with Germany? Some politicians, including the Chancellor David Lloyd George, certainly favoured an agreement. An essential motivating factor was, however, missing: the *raison d'être* of British foreign policy was to neutralise rivals and Germany was not a rival. Britain's concerns were mainly imperial, Germany's mainly continental. Since these interests did not intersect, there was little to offer in a bargain. Germany was the one European power with whom Britain could co-exist in relative harmony.

Most Britons mistakenly saw the Empire as symbolic of British supremacy. In truth, it was like an early Victorian stately home: a grand facade obscured a ramshackle structure plagued by poor design, inadequate maintenance and internal rot. Supposedly secure imperial markets had encouraged complacency, with the effect that Britain's industrial lead was steadily eroded by more dynamic entrepreneurial nations – in particular, Germany, Japan and the United States. Germany surpassed British steel production during the 1880s; the United States a decade later. Costs of defending and administering the Empire steadily outstripped profits from it. Nor was it still performing its most important function: that of a dependable trading community. As time passed, Europe superseded the Empire as Britain's main focus for trade. Between 1880 and

1900, exports to Europe increased by 23 per cent, imports from Europe by 27 per cent. Even more worrying was the fact that imports exceeded exports by approximately five to three. In other words, regardless of those entangling alliances, Britain was dangerously dependent upon continental producers.

The British had long pretended detachment from Europe, yet that comfortable sense of indifference had become an illusion. The new reality was felt most profoundly in the pit of British stomachs. As war approached, Britain produced only one third of the food she ate. In 1900, 50 per cent of meat consumed, 65 per cent of dairy products and 80 per cent of wheat was imported. Granted, not all these imports came from Europe, but that was not the point. Britain, an island nation, was dangerously vulnerable to the weapon of hunger (i.e. blockade) even though she possessed the greatest navy in the world. Furthermore, the Royal Navy offered little protection against an even greater threat: that of one hostile power or group of powers gaining hegemony over Europe. If that were to happen, Britain might find herself shut off from continental markets, whilst simultaneously threatened by an insurmountable military power.

Chickens came home to roost immediately after the assassination of Archduke Franz Ferdinand on 28 June 1914. At first, the crisis seemed insignificant – another example of Balkan beastliness. As the days passed, however, it became rudely apparent that this was a pan-European affair and that a European war would indeed be Britain's war. The Foreign Office official Sir Eyre Crowe provided a devastating analysis of Britain's predicament: 'Should this war come and England stand aside, one of two things must happen: (a) Either Germany and Austria win, crush France and humiliate Russia . . . What will be the position of friendless England? (b) Or France and Russia win. What would then be their attitude towards England? What about India and the Mediterranean?' Agreeing with Crowe, Sir

Arthur Nicolson, ambassador to Russia, complained that some colleagues in government did not understand that splendid isolation was no longer reality. 'So many people regard the maintenance of the equilibrium of Europe as merely an abstract principle, for the support of which it is not worth firing a shot, and they do not understand that were the Triple Entente broken up we should be isolated and compelled to do the bidding of the Power which assumed the hegemony of Europe.' The July crisis revealed the cruel implications of those agreements that had been designed to protect the Empire: neither Russia nor France would be inclined to behave themselves in India or Africa if Britain let them down in Europe. Even more important, Britain could not stand aside while the war produced a dominant European power – either Germany or France – determined to exploit British vulnerability.[6]

Having painted herself into a corner, Britain declared war on 4 August 1914. The *Manchester Guardian* had previously argued that there were no grounds for a declaration; it seemed inconceivable 'that this country could be dragged into the horrors of a general European war, although she has no direct interest in it and is admittedly bound by no treaty obligations to take part'. What the paper chose to ignore was that the conflict was about empires, capitalism, trade and food, not about democracy, honour or civilisation. Cynical motives were, however, purified when Germany invaded poor little Belgium. 'What one can't get over is the lack of all feeling of decency in trampling down a gallant little country whose misfortune it is to stand between the aggressor and her prey,' wrote Georgina Lee. A middle-class housewife, Lee defined ordinary in the sense that she oozed Englishness from every pore. The only thing that made her extraordinary was that she kept a war diary and wrote in it her day-to-day observations on the turmoil of war. These were recorded with impressive sensitivity and considerable eloquence. She will figure large in this book because she was the perfect barometer of how ordinary people felt about the war. Historians, who pay too much attention to the unusual, have failed to appreciate the worth of Lee's mundane recollections. Her reactions to the invasion of Belgium are a case in point: if Lee was outraged, it is fair to say that so too were the vast majority of Britons.[7]

Brave little Belgium

With the 'rape' of Belgium, a war of markets quite suddenly became a war of morals. Granted, attacking France via the Belgian route made strategic sense for the Germans. That strategy had, however, the unfortunate side effect of arousing the righteous indignation of the British people, an enemy the Germans unwisely discounted. When Goschen saw the German Chancellor Theobald von Bethmann-Hollweg for the very last time on 4 August, the latter complained that Britain was going to war 'just for a word – "neutrality" . . .

just for a scrap of paper Great Britain was going to make war on a kindred nation who desired nothing better than to be friends with her'. Goschen feigned insult, arguing that it was 'a matter of "life and death" for the honour of Great Britain that she should keep her solemn engagement to do her utmost to defend Belgium's neutrality'. One can easily imagine the scene: a proper English gentleman preaching earnestly about principles that were in fact immaterial. Britain did not need the rape of Belgium to justify a declaration of war, but that violation made declaring war so much easier. Without it, the Liberal government would probably have split and the people would have argued issues of justice. Once defenceless Belgium was invaded, however, doubts dissolved. The war became just, righteous, noble, even holy. On 6 August, Prime Minister Herbert Asquith confidently told the Commons: 'I do not believe any nation ever entered into a great controversy . . . with a clearer conscience and a stronger conviction that it is fighting, not for aggression, not for the maintenance even of its own selfish interest, but . . . in defence of principles . . . vital to the civilisation of the world.' The British, who like nothing better than a cause, suddenly had a moral justification for a war that was in fact unavoidable.[8]

Referring to the Triple Entente, Asquith claimed that Britain had 'a solemn international obligation, an obligation which, if it had been entered into between private persons in the ordinary concerns of life, would have been regarded as an obligation not only of law but of honour, which no self-respecting man could possibly have repudiated'. That was nonsense. Britain had no obligations, moral or otherwise, to Russia or France. A little over a year earlier, the Prime Minister had admitted as much when he denied that Britain 'was under any obligation . . . which compels us to take part in any war'. A genuine alliance might in fact have deterred German belligerence. That, however, was distasteful to the British, who were still pretending to abhor binding commitments. In truth, the only obligation Britain felt was to herself. Self-preservation was her moral purpose. Survival, however, depended upon France, so helping the French was essential. As Bethmann-Hollweg sneered: 'England drew the sword only because she believed her own interests demanded it.' On that score, he was absolutely right.[9]

In popular imagery, Belgium became an abused child or a wounded puppy deserving of sympathy and support. In truth, the country was a cold strategic interest. Britain's long-established commitment to her neutrality, formalised in 1839, arose from a calculated acceptance of the fact that trade with the continent required that a friendly (or at least neutral) power should control the ports of Ostend and Zeebrugge. The importance of the two ports was subsequently demonstrated by the enormous damage caused to British shipping by German submarines operating out of them during the Great War and by Britain's costly (but futile) attempts to capture them.

Images were nevertheless important to the British sense of self. Because of the invasion of Belgium, Germany was instantly transformed from a modern, civilised nation to a slavering, militaristic beast – a dragon that St George would slay. A war of markets became a war of ideals. On 19 September 1914, Lloyd George told a Queen's Hall audience:

We have been living in a sheltered valley for generations. We have been too comfortable, too indulgent, many, perhaps, too selfish. And the stern hand of Fate has scourged us to an elevation where we can see the great everlasting things that matter for a nation; the great peaks we had forgotten – Duty and Patriotism, clad in glittering white, the great pinnacle of Sacrifice pointing like a rugged finger to Heaven.

That was, of course, tripe, but the British are fond of tripe. It was precisely because the British had lived in sheltered valleys (or rather empires) that they were still naive enough to convince themselves that values like honour, duty and patriotism mattered between industrial powers.[10]

'Germany tried to bribe us with peace to desert our friends and duty,' the *Daily Mirror* argued. 'But Great Britain has preferred the path of honour.' The war was now a crusade, the British noble knights. Their war was fundamentally an act of preservation. Britain fought to protect the values that underlay her greatness. Germany, it was argued, promoted mad, irresponsible modernism which would upset the stable world order – too much *Sturm und Drang*. She needed to be taught a lesson in British moderation. Popular images, exaggerated though they were, had a core of truth. British culture was proudly old-fashioned, German culture modern and progressive. Yet while culture – or *Kultur* – was often mentioned in righteous tones, it was not the real issue at stake. Britain felt a comfortable fondness for the past, but was not bent on an anti-modernist crusade, since such a crusade contradicted British liberal tolerance. She is instead best seen as a massive ocean liner ploughing through turbulent seas without change of speed or direction. Her conservatism harmonised perfectly with her foreign policy – she was the epitome of solid, respectable, rather boring stability. Her position at the pinnacle of the world order convinced her that she had nothing to gain from change. The illusion that prestige and power could be protected by standing still was enormously attractive.[11]

Strange as it seems, the common people, who would have been the beneficiaries of progressive reform, generally mirrored this conservatism. There are few more conservative groups than the British working-class, who tolerate their own subjugation by indulging in fantasies of national greatness. While some workers were attracted to radicalism of various sorts, most were suspicious of change. Their pride in empire, the monarchy and British tradition was immense; most believed, despite their poverty, that they were superior to workers elsewhere in the world. Gradual enfranchisement had encouraged illusions of political empowerment, without fostering wild dreams of a new Jerusalem. Evidence suggests that ordinary people did indeed feel threatened by rampant German modernism. Germany did not seem to pose an existential threat, but rather a more subtle risk to the social and political order – a destabilising of the status quo. One soldier told his parents in October 1914 that 'we should remind ourselves that it is our great privilege to save the traditions of all centuries behind us. It's a grand opportunity, and we must spare no effort to use it, for if we fail we shall curse ourselves in bitterness every year that we live and our children will despise our memory.' Lloyd George's Queen's Hall speech was specifically calculated to appeal to this same romantic sentiment, as was wartime propaganda which played heavily on the English rural idyll, a sturdy symbol of tradition. To the urban industrial worker that idyll might have been as familiar as the surface of the moon, but the ideals it evoked were deeply cherished. [12]

The Pied Piper Lloyd George

One essential characteristic of a noble war was that it should be fought in a civilised manner, according to accepted rules, like rugby or cricket. Since British society equated games with war, it naturally approached war as if it was a game. Evidence that this delusion survived into the war can be found in a letter to *The Scotsman* in January 1915 in which a British soldier described an aerial dogfight involving one German pilot pitted against sixteen French and British. What made the spectacle so wonderful was that the German escaped unscathed. 'And we gave him a great cheer,' the correspondent wrote, 'for the odds were against him, and he must have been a great chap.' The British believed they were fighting a good game and papered their lives with colourful, heroic stories to reinforce that belief. The *Daily Mail*, for instance, once recounted an allegorical tale of fraternisation between British and German soldiers during a cold winter in the trenches. Soldiers began by trading pleasantries across no-man's-land, then threw tobacco and chocolates to their adversaries and ended by joining in a jolly snowball fight. Inevitably, perhaps, the amiable exchange ended when a German, resorting to form, put a rock in a snowball which injured one Tommy in the eye. Clearly, the Germans did not know how to play the game.[13]

This rather jolly approach to war militated against hating Germans. It is difficult to generalise about popular attitudes, but it appears that in the pre-war period anti-German feeling was not as rampant as might be expected. The Anglo-German naval rivalry resembled not the deadly arms race of the Cold War, but instead a rugby match between two closely matched schools. Rates of ship construction were presented in newspapers like football league tables. This sense of good-spirited competition annoyed Sir Charles Hardinge, Permanent Under Secretary at the Foreign Office, who complained in 1909 that 'Public opinion in England has not as yet grasped the danger to Europe of Germany's ambitious designs.' While bigotry towards Teutons was not completely absent, in most cases it was safely hidden beneath a veneer of British tolerance. As will be seen, once the war began, the veneer cracked and venom seeped through, especially on the home front, where it was fostered by propaganda. Before August 1914, however, Germany was widely admired, certainly more so than the French 'ally', a much more dependable object of hatred.[14]

It is therefore misguided to claim, as many have done, that 'invasion literature' – books like *The Riddle of the Sands*, *The Invasion of 1910* and *The Battle of Dorking*, and plays like *An Englishman's Home* – was responsible for inspiring anti-German feeling in the decades before the Great War. Granted, the literature was popular and the enemy was usually German. The intent was to provide warning of an impending threat and thus to provoke fear of Germany, but that does not explain its appeal. The pre-war generation, like today, had a healthy interest in espionage literature. Since thrillers are always more credible if the bad guy is believable, linking the fictional enemy to a contemporary adversary provided a useful element of reality that enhanced the drama.

The British belief in a righteous mission made them formidable. Few, in fact, welcomed war. In stark contrast to the scene at Buckingham Palace described at the start of this chapter, a crowd on Hampstead Heath taking advantage of the warm Bank Holiday weather seemed in sombre mood. 'It was obvious,' a reporter concluded, 'that the idea of war was distasteful to all.' Yet that which is distasteful can be stoically endured if it also seems necessary. The unifying effect of the conflict can be seen in the reaction of the *Daily News*. Staunchly anti-interventionist during the July crisis, it quickly brought itself into line after the declaration: 'We have said our last word of controversy . . . Being in, we must win.' The MP Will Crooks told a Labour fete: 'we have fought for peace to the last moment, but if war has got to come, you and I must shoulder the burden'.[15]

Victory would not only protect the world from what Germany represented, it would also restore a sense of propriety to Britain, after a period in which traditional values had seemed under threat. 'I'm anxious that England may act rightly', Rupert Brooke confessed to his friend Edward Marsh in July 1914. The arch-imperialist Lord Milner hoped that the war would force into being stronger government, leading in turn to a reinforced empire, a more formidable military and a disciplined society. War, he thought, would 'ring out the feud of the rich and poor'. The ideal of empire would smother the class struggle and 'ancient forms of party strife'. In this sense, the war seemed to offer an escape from the pre-war turmoil caused by the Irish, the trade unions and the suffragettes, turmoil which had seemed to portend an age when old values were trampled asunder. Thus it would be a purgation, a return, a renewal. 'A sour, soiled, crooked old world [was] to be rid of bullies and crooks and reclaimed for straightness, decency, good nature,' recalled the journalist C. E. Montague. For Brooke, soldiers marching to war were like 'swimmers into cleanness leaping/Glad from a world grown old and cold and weary'. Britain would win because her noble values would inevitably prove triumphant. 'How could I be left behind?' wrote Alfred Pollard on 8 August. On that day he left his insurance office and ran as fast as he could to a recruiting office.[16]

'We are in for it at last,' wrote Georgina Lee in her diary. 'But there is not one of us in the country who is not thankful at heart that the great fight is to take place at last.' That was an exaggeration, but the general sentiment was accurate. A war about economics and European hegemony had been transformed into one about values, culture, good form, clean living, respect for the past and caution towards the future. The prevalent mood placed severe limits upon the change which war could possibly inspire. The British went to war in defence of the past. They feared change, resisted it for as long as possible and, when it became inevitable, tried to contain it within a cocoon of tradition. They wanted not to transform the world, but to return it to the certainties of the Victorian age, certainties undermined since the turn of the century. They would fight not for something new, but for something gloriously old.[17]

Chapter 2

Gentlemen and Amateurs

Sarah Macnaughtan was in many ways a typical middle-class Englishwoman, for whom social convention had long been an obstacle to meaningful pursuit. For a brief period, the war, by making all labour valuable, gave her purpose. The conflict provided an opportunity to be quintessentially British. 'God knows, we are full of faults', she wrote in early 1915. 'But the superiority of the British race to any other that I know is a matter of deep conviction with me.' Most Britons shared her certainty and sense of purpose. That explains their confidence, despite the fact that they were woefully unprepared for war. They felt assured that their superiority would pull them through, allowing them to improvise a war machine. The ability to muddle through was as British as a bulldog.[1]

In August 1914, Britain's standing army was a tenth the size of Germany's. The Germans also had access to a vast reservoir of trained reserves, while the British did not. Though Britain boasted that its all-volunteer force was uniquely professional, there was cold comfort in that assertion. 'Professional' in this case described the relationship between the soldier and the army: soldiers were careerists, not conscripts. 'Professional' did not mean highly trained; these soldiers were well drilled, but woefully ignorant of modern war. The army was like an antique fire engine: spotless, shiny and in perfect working order, but useless at putting out big fires.

In superficial ways, the army mirrored Edwardian society. The rigid class structure that separated gentry from workers also divided officers from men. Officers were educated in the same public schools that produced the elite of civilian society. Thus a common belief system linked the officer class with their peers in the civil service, politics, the judiciary and the church. That, however, is where similarities ended. In fact, the army was a hothouse of conservatism more reactionary than civilian society. Progressive trends evident in ordinary life were resisted within the military, because officers considered themselves guardians of tradition.

Further down the social scale, the army bore little resemblance to the parent society. Enlisted men were not representative of the working-class, but were rather a distorted offshoot. Ordinary soldiers tended to be vagabonds who could find no place in civilian life: recruits from the bars and brothels of city slums or the human detritus produced from the shrinkage of the agricultural sector. This separation between army and society was more pronounced in Britain than in other European countries precisely because the army was a volunteer force. In France and Germany, conscription meant that recruits were drawn from all walks of life. Since Cromwell's time, the British had been suspicious of a large standing army, which explains in part their resistance to compulsion. This also demonstrates why the army became a closed caste – ignored and often despised by wider society. Soldiers complained that they were often denied admission to bars and theatres. When his Winchester headmaster learned of Archibald Wavell's intention to join the army, he protested to Wavell's father: 'I do not think that you need take this extreme step, since I believe that your son has sufficient brains to make his way in other walks of life.' The mother of the future Field Marshal Lord Robertson, upon hearing of his enlistment, wrote: 'I would rather bury you than see you in a redcoat.'[2]

Thus, the pre-war army was an institution, rather like the police, which was recognised as essential but seldom loved. Imperial wars inspired romantic fantasies about brave, noble warriors, but *real* soldiers were pariahs. The army nevertheless performed an immensely valuable function. By keeping the Empire quiet, it encouraged a false sense of security – commonly known as Pax Britannica. In this way the British were able to ignore world affairs and concentrate on their day-to-day lives. Few yearned for a vast army like that of Germany, which might become too powerful or politically ambitious. Satisfaction, however, bred complacency. Ignoring the army proved an expensive luxury. By 1914, Britain found herself with a force ridiculously ill-suited to the task which confronted it.

Complacency seemed affordable because of the sense of well-being provided by the Royal Navy. That Britain ruled the waves was a cliché but not a myth. As an island nation with a formidable navy, Britain enjoyed genuine security at least until the advent of the bomber. True, the idea of Pax Britannica, which held that Britain could remain aloof from European affairs, was a fallacy, since she grew ever more dependent upon continental markets. Nevertheless, Britain did not feel *physically* threatened by Germany or France. Neither invasion nor blockade troubled the minds of ordinary people.

The role of the Royal Navy was therefore to protect Britain and the Empire from invasion, a task it performed well. The army's role was that of an imperial police force designed to deal with colonial rebellions. During Queen Victoria's reign, it performed this function in 72 separate campaigns, usually successfully, but not always conspicuously so. Success inspired a small-war mentality that impeded the serious study of military science. Fought in exotic places against unpredictable enemies, these small skirmishes seemed to contradict classical principles of war. Their lessons could therefore be safely ignored – or so it seemed. The army instead held to Napoleonic principles that remained sacred despite all the technological developments that had occurred since Waterloo. This shortcoming was exacerbated by the country's reluctance to plan for war. The prejudice against a large standing army went hand in hand with an aversion to strategic planning. Both, it was felt, reeked of militarism. Thus Britain was the very antithesis of a militaristic society before 1914 since it determinedly avoided preparing for war, preferring instead an army of improvisers. Stated differently, Britain was quite happy to muddle through.

This rather casual approach impeded professionalisation. British commanders took a simplistic view of success: victories in small colonial wars came about when disciplined soldiers performed like the automatons they were trained to be. Failure, on the other hand, occurred when discipline broke down. Senior officers therefore perceived little need to develop new tactics to suit new weapons. The large wars of the nineteenth century – including the Franco-Prussian War and American Civil War – were studied only to the extent that they reinforced classical maxims. Thus, at the Staff College, great emphasis was given to Stonewall Jackson's cavalry campaigns but not to Ulysses Grant's battles of attrition. Likewise, lessons about modern firepower arising from the Franco-Prussian War were largely ignored. Launcelot Kiggell, Commandant of the Staff College and later Chief of Staff of the British Expeditionary Force (BEF), expressed a typical attitude: 'History proves . . . that in all ages the moral has been to the physical as three is to one. Courage, energy, determination, perseverance, endurance, the unselfishness and discipline that make combination possible – these are the primary causes of all great successes, and in turning our thoughts to new guns or rifles or bayonets, we too often forget the fact.'[3]

In truth, the moral only prevails if the physical will allow.

In her small wars, Britain won because she had the better guns, rifles and bayonets and because her soldiers were usually of superior physical conditioning. It was therefore easy to be brave. What the British seemed loath to accept was that their morale resulted not from superior character, but was instead a manifestation of more advanced development in comparison to her colonies. The obsession with moral qualities exacerbated a tendency to discount technology. The confidence inspired by small wars would prove a thin shield against a superbly trained continental army supplied with modern weaponry.

Colonial campaigns were usually dominated by a single commander who imposed his will upon the campaign, or failed to do so. This encouraged the belief that good generalship was solely a question of character, not a skill learned through studying war. Small wars gave birth to large heroes who mistakenly assumed that they could succeed without the help of a professionally trained staff. The campaigns also created the impression amongst the public that war was a distant adventure, of little relevance to everyday life. Casualties were always small (especially compared to those of the enemy), victory usually inevitable. All this reinforced the tendency to ignore the army, except to the extent that it provided excellent raw material for adventure stories read by public school boys. It also encouraged the judging of campaigns only by their outcome, not their cost. Neither the army nor the government nor the people asked whether the investment brought appropriate return. Victory was the only measurement of success.

Officers were supposed to be gentlemen, not professionals. Courage and honour were valued far more than knowledge or ability. Leadership was assumed to be an attribute of birth, not something to be learned. Because he was a gentleman, the officer was beyond reproach; he operated according to a code of practice universally accepted but never subjected to critical analysis, and underwent no periodic reviews of his performance. Those who studied the science of war were considered suspicious, since genius could not be learned and overt ambition seemed abhorrent. Until 1871, a system of purchase governed entry into the army and subsequent promotion. The abolition of that system did not bring about a meritocracy, since the new criteria for selection remained as restrictive as the old. The officer was still judged and promoted according to highly personalised standards relating to his birth, his bearing, his accent, the school he attended, the clubs he joined and the way he looked on a horse. In 1891, all 373 Sandhurst entrants came from just 55 prestigious public schools and universities. Since 'good' public schools placed heaviest emphasis upon classics and athletic prowess, Britain built her army from men who could conjugate Latin verbs and kick a ball into touch.[4]

The influence of wealth was not as overt as had prevailed under the purchase system, but was still significant. In the late Victorian period, a middle-class male required an income of at least £700 per year to support himself in a style appropriate to his aspirations. Since only around 280,000 of the 7,000,000 households in Britain could have afforded such a sum, the pool of potential officers was very small, especially since that pool also provided politicians, diplomats, clergy and other persons of influence. Membership of a regiment required that the officer be able to afford mess expenses and other costs; the more prestigious the regiment, the higher these were. One major expense was recreation, something essential to advancement. Careers were often built on the impressions made at lavish parties. Prowess in field sports – particularly polo and shooting – was a prerequisite of the gentleman-officer. Expenses increased at each stage of promotion. These costs undoubtedly deterred many who might otherwise have considered a military career and discouraged able but less affluent officers from seeking promotion.

The army was therefore a reflection of wider society, but a

distorted one. Class stratification was rigid and opportunities for the self-made man rare. In 1912, 59 per cent of officers were middle class, 32 per cent landed gentry and 9 per cent aristocracy. While the middle-class officer may have been in the majority, his status was inevitably low. In the period up to 1914, the proportion of aristocrats of the rank of major general and above was two and a half times that of their distribution within the rest of the officer corps. In fact, as the army as a whole became more middle class, the upper classes became even more dominant within it. Field Marshal Lord Robertson, who entered the army as a private, was the most significant intruder into this highly closed caste. But, as he readily admitted, his was an exceptional case; before 1914, only about four or five officers per year were promoted from the ranks.

A competitive examination was supposed to assess the soldierly qualities of officer candidates. This caused problems, however, since examinations usually favour the intelligent, and the army was more interested in character than intellect. During the Victorian period, the army discovered that otherwise promising candidates from the better public schools were finding the entrance exam too difficult. It was therefore dumbed down in order to protect those who possessed the desired social characteristics. Two compulsory subjects, mathematics and English, had to be taken along with three options. Among the latter, the classics paper was weighted three times more heavily than the other options, which meant that, in order to pass, the candidate was virtually forced to choose classics as an option. The emphasis upon Latin and Greek arose from the assumption that a solid grounding in classics was the mark of a gentleman, and gentlemen made the best officers. Crammers made a lucrative career from helping wealthy dullards to pass.

In the late Victorian period it became increasingly important for the ambitious officer to be a Staff College graduate. This did not, however, mean that intellect had become more important in the selection of leaders. Each year, 30 officers were admitted to the college after a competitive entrance examination. The army quickly discovered that officers from the relatively plebeian artillery and engineers performed best at the exam, which posed a problem. Since those branches were more technologically orientated than the infantry or cavalry, they attracted intelligent men keen to study their craft – in other words, not the type considered to make good senior commanders. As a result, a quota of six artillerymen and engineers per year had to be enforced, because if the competition had been fair, these officers would have secured almost all the places. On occasion, the army resorted to admitting cavalry and infantry candidates who had failed the exam rather than increase the intake from the artillery and engineers. In effect, the army was rewarding ignorance.

The instruction officers received at the college remained antiquated, even as late as 1914. This deficiency was exacerbated by the fact that the army had yet to decide the actual purpose of a general staff. The very idea of staff officers – professionals trained to advise commanders and plan campaigns – contradicted the army's steadfast belief in inspired leadership and individual genius. The college also encouraged a dangerous assumption that 'normal' war (the kind fought against other developed nations) was short, predictable and won through decisive attack – as Napoleon had demonstrated. This in turn reinforced the assumption that inspired leadership and morale were more important than tactical organisation, logistical planning or technological might. No wonder, then, that the army still placed such high importance on recruiting officers of good pedigree.

The elitist character of the army is illustrated by the dominance of the cavalry within it. During the Great War, both commanders-in-chief of the BEF (Sir Douglas Haig and Sir John French), all the chiefs of staff and five of nine army commanders were cavalrymen. Yet the cavalry made up less than one tenth of the army's total personnel, and was itself virtually obsolete. The cavalry was like 'old money': a socially pure group untainted by the technological advance of warfare and the consequent rise of the middle-class technicians. Because cavalry engagements occurred at close quarters – man to man – the cavalryman was thought to embody the gentlemanly qualities that were so highly prized. The cavalry's dominance of the army's higher echelons impeded the adjustment to modern war.

If the officers in the Victorian army were society's elite, the enlisted men were its dregs. A Royal Commission, reporting in 1867, concluded that men enlisted 'for want of work, pecuniary embarrassment, family quarrels, etc.'. The Superintendent of Recruiting admitted that the richest source for 'volunteers' was the public houses, adding, 'you must go where you can find the material'. The situation did not markedly improve over subsequent decades; soldiering remained the last resort of the destitute. The pay in 1892 was 1s. 2d per day, minus 4½d for rations. At that time a British agricultural worker made 13s. to 15s. per week and US Army privates earned the equivalent of 1s. 9d per day with free meals, in real terms twice as much. Poverty inevitably affected health standards. For most of the Victorian period the death rate for enlisted men, excluding wars, was double the national average.[5]

The Duke of Cambridge, Commander-in-Chief of the Army from 1856 to 1895, stubbornly argued that 'There is . . . a time for change; and that is when it can be no longer resisted.' The senior officers who would command in the Great War grew up in the Duke's army and inherited his thinking. Conformity was prized and reform aroused suspicion. Nevertheless, between the end of the nineteenth century and the advent of war in 1914, two events did shake the ramparts of tradition. The first was the Boer War of 1899–1902, a massive embarrassment for the army and the country as a whole. The second event, the

Haldane Reforms, arose out of the fears aroused by the South African war.[6]

After British troops were repeatedly humiliated during the first few weeks of the Boer War, the nation began to question whether the army was adequate even for its limited role of policing the Empire. Sir Redvers Buller, Commander-in-Chief in South Africa, was hastily replaced by Britain's favourite general, Lord Roberts, who brought with him as Chief of Staff Herbert Kitchener. A more methodical approach ensued, eventually resulting in the capture of Pretoria on 5 June 1900. That, however, was not the end. The Boers resorted to guerrilla warfare, and again the British struggled to find an answer. Over 450,000 troops fought for nearly three years, at a financial cost of £200 million and a personal loss of 22,000 dead, to defeat a Boer force that numbered fewer than 50,000.

The war's lessons were widely misunderstood. After Buller was sacked, Roberts fought the war in a familiar way (namely short, effective and mobile), thus seeming to confirm the Staff College orthodoxy. (The guerrilla phase, judged an anomaly, was ignored.) The cavalry interpreted one insignificant but nonetheless dramatic charge prior to the relief of Kimberley as proof of its continued importance. Since the war seemed otherwise atypical, its hard lessons were discounted. British officers failed to appreciate the effectiveness of machine guns, nor did they draw appropriate lessons from the way entrenched Boers employing concentrated fire could hold up an attack. The Boer fondness for trenches was in fact seen as evidence of their lack of breeding – gentlemen did not hide in a hole. The Boer War should also have taught the British that a determined population, mobilised for war, could endure for a very long time. As far as the Boers were concerned, this was a total war, a conflict in which the full resources of the military and civilian population are mobilised. In such a war, victory comes not just on the battlefield, but also through defeating the will of the enemy population. As with the other lessons, however, this one was ignored because it seemed a weird war.

While the army learned little from the Boer War, the government became obsessed with the debacle. Nearly all available troops had been sent to South Africa, leaving Britain and the rest of the Empire virtually undefended. When the government tried to replenish its forces, recruits were found wanting, not in spirit but in health. Around 70 per cent were rejected for failing to meet minimum health standards and in some poorer areas, nine out of ten were turned away. 'The want of physique,' the Director General of Army Medical Services pointed out, 'is not only serious from its military aspect, it is serious also from its civil standpoint, for if these men are unfit for military service, what are they good for?' Clearly, Pax Britannica had shaky foundations. If Britain could not easily defeat a small force of untrained farmers, how could she possibly cope with a huge continental army? Given the increasing importance of relations with Europe, the continental balance of power could no longer be ignored. Forced to confront her vulnerability, Britain began a frantic attempt to prepare for a European war.[7]

In conjunction with the new diplomatic initiatives discussed in the last chapter came a modernisation of Britain's military – a long and painful process. It fell to the Liberals to implement reforms after their election victory in 1906. That government is famous for a raft of social welfare measures which laid the foundation of the modern welfare state. What is seldom understood, however, is that the ambitious welfare programme was motivated not by compassion for the poor, but rather out of a quest for 'national efficiency' – crudely stated, the ability to fight a modern war. While these reforms were being pushed through, the government also addressed the problem of modernising the military. Although relations with Germany had worsened over the preceding decade, the German threat was not the primary focus of the new War Minister, Richard

Burdon Haldane. Rather, his two most important priorities were to create an efficient army within a strict budget of £28 million and to establish a reserve force in a country averse to conscription. Had Haldane genuinely intended to prepare for a continental war (as he later claimed), he would have pushed for larger army estimates and a compulsory service law. He would also have failed, since both were intolerable. Neither the government nor the country were prepared to accept the political and social implications of a continental strategy. Haldane achieved the best he could, but his reforms were, in truth, a political solution not a military one.

Haldane's reforms can be grouped into three areas. The first, the formation of a General Staff, fell far short of the German model. Instead, Britain ended up with an essentially administrative staff – a team of bureaucrats. A more ambitious solution was opposed both by the army and by influential civilians who feared a dangerously powerful military elite. The second area of reform involved creating an Imperial General Staff, which would allow the various colonial and dominion forces to fight harmoniously with those from Britain. This meant standardising weapons and training, and planning the mobilisation of imperial forces in the event of war.

The final area of reform was the most difficult to achieve, namely the organisation of army commands, the creation of a reserve and the formation of the BEF. The government wanted an adaptable army that could be easily mobilised and quickly expanded on the outbreak of war. A reserve was created by converting the old auxiliary units – Militia, Yeomanry and Volunteers – into a single force, renamed the Territorials. This amalgamation was stubbornly resisted by the old auxiliary units who were keen to preserve their cherished identity and reluctant to submit to regular army command. As a compromise, the Territorial and Reserve Forces Act, passed on 19 June 1907, stipulated that the Territorials would not be sent overseas without their permission. They were instead intended for home defence while the BEF fought on foreign soil.

The formation of army commands and the BEF proved easier. Before 1907, a proper expeditionary force did not exist. The army was merely a collection of diverse regiments with only one genuine corps, stationed at Aldershot. The Army Order of 1 January 1907 coordinated this disorganised mass into one cavalry and six infantry divisions, a force of 120,000 men capable of rapid mobilisation. This consolidation allowed the army to reach its maximum possible size within budgetary restraints. In fact, that meant an actual decrease in numerical strength. Some field batteries and infantry battalions were retired, but, significantly, the cavalry came through unscathed. The BEF, designed to be mobilised within 14 days, was essentially the force that went to war in 1914. It was certainly well organised, but it was unsuited to the task it would encounter in France and Belgium, since it was too small and could not be rapidly expanded. In addition, most of its commanders were incapable of the strategic and tactical improvisation which war would demand.

Some critics recognised that the army was woefully ill-suited to the dangers lurking. They came in two general types: those who doubted its quality, and those who ridiculed its size. Among the former was a small but vocal group who argued that failures in South Africa arose from an obsessive British faith in amateurism. One such critic, George Brodick, argued in *The Nineteenth Century* that 'The young Englishman of this great leisure class is no dandy and no coward, but he is an amateur born and bred, with an amateur's lack of training, an amateur's contempt for method, and an amateur's ideal of life.' Amateurs, according to Brodick, dominated politics, the civil and foreign service and the army. The young officer 'seldom takes his profession seriously, and is hardly encouraged to do so. There is little enough "shop" talked in mess rooms, and little real enthusiasm except for sporting and social amusements; military duties are . . . recognised by most as a "bore".[8]

The solution, Brodick declared, was not better organisation and education, but a different state of mind. As he pointed out, the remarkably successful Boer generals,

> while they were not professionals in training . . . were not amateurs in spirit. Having for their single object the defeat of the enemy, they were hampered by no rules of military etiquette and few scruples of military honour, exercising the utmost ingenuity and sparing no pains to inflict the greatest possible injury upon our troops with the least possible injury to themselves, allowing us to claim barren victories so long as their losses were much smaller, and retreating shamelessly for strong positions if by doing so they could draw us on to assault still more formidable positions in the rear.

The argument displayed extraordinary insight, especially bearing in mind what happened to British troops during the Great War. But, in a culture where amateurism was sacred, Brodick's complaints were never likely to receive serious consideration. A typical response was that of Sir Herbert Maxwell in the same journal: 'Every institution is known by its fruits; if these are sound there is not much to complain of in the trunk . . . My contention is that there are no signs of decay – no abatement of zeal – no withering of fidelity – in the public services.' Sadly, Maxwell's views prevailed, which limited the scope of reform. Haldane and his acolytes proved proficient at creating new bureaucracies, but they did not address the need for an entirely new ethos. As long as officers adhered to Napoleonic conceptions of war and British society reacted with suspicion to professionalism and planning, Britain would be ill-prepared for war.[9]

A more popular solution to perceived deficiencies was the cure-all of conscription. The National Service League, founded in 1902, called for compulsory military training for all able-bodied male citizens. Beyond the fact that it seemed an effective response to the German threat, the solution would also, it was argued, address problems of 'national efficiency' exposed by the Boer War. Soldiers would be brought to fitness before a conflict arose, though how this would be achieved without addressing the problem of poverty was not explained. National service was also seen as an effective antidote to the juvenile delinquency and social disorder which plagued inner cities, and to trade union unrest. According to conscription advocates, after a dose of military service, the worker would return to his factory with the 'alertness, the docility and the discipline' of the German working man.[10]

Under the patronage of Britain's favourite soldier, Lord Roberts, the League garnered considerable publicity before the war, and reached a peak membership of just under 100,000. Among its supporters were Robert Baden-Powell, founder of the Scouts, and some captains of industry, not to mention *The Times, Daily Mail, Observer, Daily Telegraph* and other papers. While 177 MPs of all parties supposedly backed the League, few did so enthusiastically. Despite all its efforts, including an average of 240 meetings per month in 1912, the League never became a mass movement and never came close to achieving its goal. It was opposed not only by liberals and the left, but also by conservatives who saw compulsion as thoroughly un-British. Senior army officers, among them Haig and Kitchener, argued that volunteers made more dependable soldiers. The League's failure provides yet more evidence of the unmilitaristic nature of pre-war British society.

The army's deficiencies were tolerable because the British remained confident that the Royal Navy would be their salvation. This sense of security did not, however, breed complacency; in the decade before the Great War, much energy was directed towards naval reform. Sir John Fisher, First Sea Lord from 1904 to 1910, pushed through improvements in officer training, the redirection of fleets to home waters, the scrapping of obsolete vessels and the creation of an active reserve. His most important effect, however, lay in the decision to build the dreadnought class of battleship. While these reforms were not directed towards Germany, being instead part of a normal modernisation programme, they were interpreted that way by Kaiser Wilhelm, who coveted a navy to rival the British. Thus began the Anglo-German naval race – a competition suited to the simplicities of the populist press. Seldom had there arisen an issue so perfectly suited to jingoistic passions. The logic of bigness smothered subtle issues of strategy. For the average Briton, safety lay in large ships.

The naval race was based on the uncritical assumption (derived from the writings of Captain Alfred Thayer Mahan) that political and economic hegemony came from mastery of the sea. That reductive notion was then rendered even more absurd by a tendency to concentrate on raw numbers of big ships, without sufficient attention to their strategic utility nor to the quality of the sailors who manned them. Dreadnoughts were built because it was assumed that future naval encounters would follow the classical pattern of massed forces meeting in a set-piece battle like two grand masters sitting down to chess. The humiliation of the Russian navy by the Japanese at the battles of Tsushima and Port Arthur had unfortunately encouraged that flawed notion. Behind it lay the same short-war mentality that gripped European armies. In fact, since the state of military technology militated against a short land war, a set-piece battle at sea was madness. No naval power (especially not an island nation) could risk the destruction of its entire fleet in one massive battle if the war was going to be long. With big battles unlikely, large ships should have become less important.

In a long war, the navy's role is to maintain a blockade, transport troops and protect merchant shipping, tasks best performed by considerably smaller ships than dreadnoughts. While this logic seems clear in retrospect, at the time it was blasphemy. The British people, their government and the Admiralty noticed that the Germans were eager for a race and responded by sprinting – without first determining the best direction to run. There was little the government could have done differently (even if it had understood the issues), given a rabid public fired by invasion stories, and newspapers shouting 'We want eight and we won't wait.' Britain, mesmerised by German battleship production, failed to notice that the Germans were also building lots of submarines, a much more ominous threat.

Despite all the attention given to reform, the army and navy that went to war in 1914 were remarkably similar to those mobilised in 1899. The Royal Navy had been superficially modernised, but it retained a faith in the patterns of ancient naval battles and, most of all, remained confident of its own invincibility. The army had been administratively restructured and was now capable of speedy mobilisation, but it was still essentially a Victorian army commanded by officers wedded to tradition. Britain had decided to stick with the status quo, rejecting the advice of those who wanted a larger or more professional military. Despite the setbacks in South Africa, confidence remained high; the British convinced themselves that they would be able to meet any crisis. Thus the military was shaped by both the insecurities and the egotism of Edwardian and Victorian Britain. The public's faith in the amateur ideal, its suspicion of large armies, its adherence to liberal conceptions of freedom and its belief in a capacity to muddle through gave Britain the forces she deserved.

In early 1914, war loomed on the western, rather than the eastern, horizon. The possibility that the army might be called upon to enforce Irish Home Rule frightened everyone, since no other issue tested the loyalty of the officer corps so severely. It was therefore something of a relief when war broke out in Europe, not Ulster. Nearly everyone assumed that it would be a short and glorious war, an opportunity not to be missed. Staff officers who should have stayed home to study the peculiar problems of this war instead rushed off to join the fray. And who could blame them? Unfortunately, the war they encountered was not the war they expected. After a brief period of mobility, stalemate descended like an impenetrable fog. War, contrary to all expectations, was static, costly, demoralising and long. It was also unexpectedly deadly: by the spring of 1915, the army of Victoria by way of Haldane was all but obliterated. A new army had therefore to be created. Britain's ability to muddle through would be tested as never before.

Chapter 3

Muscular Christians

On 1 May 1914, the regular army was nearly 11,000 men short of the size prescribed by the Army Order of 1907, proof of the population's lack of enthusiasm for military service. Four months later, after the outbreak of war, recruiting offices were swamped by a flood of volunteers too large to process. When Britain was forced to improvise, the people responded with alacrity. The men who came forward were, superficially at least, the perfect raw material for an army. From the public schools came potential officers of limitless zeal, unquestioning patriotism and enormous confidence. From the working-class came the perfect foot soldiers: deferent, fatalistic men who expected little from life and who often saw the army as their salvation. The 'rush to the colours' encouraged the impression that the British did indeed have a peculiar ability to muddle through any crisis.

In the autumn of 1914, R. C. Sherriff, author of *Journey's End*, applied for an officer's commission. The first question the adjutant asked was what school he had attended.

> I told him and his face fell. He took up a printed list . . .
> 'I'm sorry', he said 'but I'm afraid it isn't a public school'.
> I was mystified. I told him that my school, though small, was a very old and good one – founded, I said, by Queen

Elizabeth in 1567. The adjutant was not impressed. He had lost all interest in me. 'I'm sorry', he repeated. 'But our instructions are that all applicants for commissions must be selected from the recognised public schools and yours is not among them.'

Since the public schools had produced the gentlemen officers of the old army, they were naturally seen as the source for new recruits. Beyond mere custom, this was a pragmatic response. 'It was a rough method of selection,' Sheriff admitted, 'a demarcation line hewn out with an ax; but it was the only way in the face of emergency, and as things turned out, it worked.' By selecting public school boys, the army went for a known commodity: by this means, new officers would have a consistent standard of basic training and a belief system relevant to military service. On the eve of war, 150 schools and 20 universities had established Officer Training Corps. Thus the public school boy had rudimentary military instruction: he could handle a rifle and was familiar with basic drill. Furthermore, the boarding school environment – its strict social hierarchy, monasticism, discipline and austerity – was remarkably similar to army life.[1]

These environmental similarities do not alone explain the army's fondness for public school boys. Rather, what appealed most was the boy's character, supposedly suited to leadership in battle. In the latter half of the nineteenth century, the schools had shifted their emphasis from 'godliness and good learning' to a more vigorous and manly training suited to empire. Often referred to as muscular Christianity, this ideal was epitomised by Rugby School and its headmaster, Thomas Arnold. At Rugby, athletic prowess took precedence over intellectual development. In Arnold's vision, 'sport . . . would give a young man the body of a Greek and the soul of a Christian knight'. Boys were supposed to be muscular and

Christian, but the Christianity was beefed up to suit imperial aspirations. Sermons taught that Jesus, a virile carpenter, was appealingly masculine, not to mention holy. The Reverend C. H. Spurgeon argued:

> There has got abroad a notion, somehow, that if you become a Christian, you must sink your manliness and turn milksop ... Young men, to you I would honestly say that I should be ashamed to speak to you of a religion that would make you soft, cowardly, effeminate, spiritless, so that you would be mere naturals in business, having no souls of your own, the prey of every designing knave.

Manliness encompassed a raft of attributes including honour, duty, sacrifice and honesty – not just physicality. Good character was thought to be the product of a strong will, which was in turn the sign of a healthy mind. Since mental and physical health were inextricably linked, Victorians assumed that exercising the body strengthened the will. Studies of the Victorian public school have tended to judge these ideas bizarre, yet the schools were merely acknowledging a link which few question today. Furthermore, team sports do encourage discipline, self-sacrifice and teamwork – attributes of value in later life. One wonders in fact whether the preoccupation with exercise was any more pronounced than is the case today. The big difference was that before 1914, the ethic was confined to the upper classes (and to males) and was seen as a way for the young to become adults rather than for adults to stay young. If the Victorians went astray, it was only in allowing a good idea to become an obsession.[2]

The cult of the physical caused other aspects of the boy's development to be neglected. Between the 1850s and the outbreak of war in 1914, educators held that it was not necessary to exercise the mind with challenging intellectual problems if mind and character were being developed on the playing field. The army tended to agree. The *Field Service Regulations*, the officer's bible, stipulated that 'Success in war depends more on moral than on physical qualities' – in other words, the man, not his weaponry. 'Skill cannot compensate for want of courage, energy and determination.' Those qualities, it was felt, could best be developed on the playing field, not in the classroom. In 1902, the Assistant Commandant of Woolwich Academy argued that teaching cadets science narrowed their minds. 'Our great point is character, we care more about that than [science] subjects.'[3]

Such was the importance given to athleticism that the headmaster of Westminster School complained when 'boys who are not very good at games' joined his rifle corps because 'they are not so much respected'. H. H. Almond, headmaster at Loretto, argued that his school did not in fact need a corps if the boys played rugby. Since war came to be seen as a higher form of athletic contest, it followed that the best way to prepare for it was to play games. Boys' adventure stories began with the hero cutting a swathe through the rival school's defenders and ended with him doing the same to a horde of raving Dervishes. The theme is best illustrated in 'Vitaï Lampada', by the Poet Laureate Sir Henry Newbolt:

> The sand of the desert is sodden red,
> Red with the wreck of a square that broke;
> The Gatling's jammed and the Colonel dead,
> And the regiment blind with dust and smoke.
> The river of death has brimmed his banks,
> And England's far, and Honour a name,
> But the voice of a schoolboy rallies the ranks:
> 'Play up! play up! and play the game!'

A Marlborough college song had a similar message:

> Be strong, Elevens, to bowl and shoot,
> Be strong, O Regiment of the foot,
> With ball of skin or lead or leather,
> Stand for the Commonwealth together.

Equating war with games encouraged the assumption that both were played to a single set of rules. War was assumed to be civilised, fought by gentlemen and won by the morally pure. While the 'uncivilised' admittedly did not always play the game properly, it was assumed that war between cultured Europeans would be the purest form of combat and therefore closest to the ethics of the playing field. When Fisher suggested that poison gas and aerial bombardments might be employed in future wars he was ridiculed, since the tactics violated human decency. The British failure to prepare adequately for submarine warfare can in part be explained by a belief that civilised powers would never wage war by hiding beneath the surface of the sea.[4]

The qualities fostered on the playing field help to explain the behaviour of the young men who volunteered in 1914. One such was loyalty. By playing for a team, the boy learned to place the interests of the group before his own. Once developed, loyalty to the school or house was easily redirected to the regiment. It became instinctive; the individual did not question whether the institution deserved his devotion. Thus *The Times* praised school spirit as a force which encouraged boys to 'distrust individual intellects and do an unselfish job'. In this way, the emphasis upon loyalty worked against the exercise of reason, a phenomenon ably described by Lord Tennyson in 'The Charge of the Light Brigade':

> 'Forward, the Light Brigade!'
> Was there a man dismay'd?

> Not tho' the soldiers knew
> Some one had blunder'd:
> Theirs not to make reply,
> Theirs not to reason why,
> Theirs but to do and die:
> Into the valley of Death
> Rode the six hundred.

Loyalty was the enemy of intellect. To question was to doubt, and to doubt was poisonous. Blind devotion suited the army perfectly, since it did not actually want its junior officers to think for themselves.[5]

Another quality encouraged at the public schools was 'good form'. The concept wove together physical and moral attributes – form and content – leading to an inevitable confusion between the two. Beautiful manner and impeccable dress were symbolic of moral virtue, and a 'clean' soul – or, in the case of a soldier, an impressive uniform – suggested courage, honour, self-sacrifice and again loyalty. Some naval commanders were reluctant to carry out gunnery practice because the cordite made ships dirty. In the same way, army officers – obsessed with appearance – seldom carried rifles when attacking, preferring instead a gentlemanly pistol or, in some cases, a walking stick. In combination, loyalty and good form stifled insight and imagination, but that did not seem to matter since independent thought, because it seemed disruptive, was suspect. This way of thinking was first instilled in the public school, where young gentlemen learned to recite Plato beautifully in the original Greek, but gave little thought to what the words actually meant.

In *The Loom of Youth*, Alec Waugh (the elder brother of Evelyn) described the public school boy as 'easy-going, pleasure-loving and absolutely without a conscience ... he has learnt to do what he is told, he takes life as he sees it and is content'. No wonder, then, that these boys marched eagerly off to war. Jane

Harrison, then a Cambridge lecturer, was astonished at the reaction of students and dons to the call to arms: 'it came to me as something of a shock to find that many of them . . . went, not reluctantly, but with positive alacrity'. In her opinion, the obsession with teamwork and self-sacrifice produced a herd instinct which stifled creative thought and critical enquiry. The warriors of 1914 were 'driven by a thirst for primary sensations'; they sought to 'drown their individual consciousness in collective militancy'.[6]

In this sense, the war was not simply an opportunity to crush German militarism or to defend Britain, it also offered, in a more personal sense, a rare opportunity to experience spiritual rebirth by satisfying primal yearnings. In *Desmond's Daughter*, Colonel Paul Wyndham echoed a common sentiment when he described war as

> the great paradox, the greatest in human history. It spells horror, but it spells also heroism, which is possibly what commends it to most healthy minded men . . . Call it what you like, a terrible medicine or an intermittent eruption of evil; it is still, with all its horror and wastefulness, the Great Flail that threshes the wheat from the chaff. So, in the long run, it makes for the ethical advance of the race.

According to the historian David Newsome, the public schools, by trying to teach manly virtues through games-playing, 'fell into the opposite error of failing to make the boys into men at all'. He feels, rightly, that the 'code of living became so robust and patriotic in its demands that it could be represented as reaching in its perfection a code of dying'.

Standard reading among schoolboys was *The Hill*, by H. A. Vachell, published in 1905. In the novel, the headmaster of Harrow School devotes his final sermon of the year to the tale of Henry Desmond, an old boy who died on Spion Kop in South Africa. His was the perfect death:

> To die young, clean, ardent; to die swiftly, in perfect health; to die saving others from death, or worse – disgrace – to die scaling heights; to die and to carry with you into the fuller ampler life beyond, untainted hopes and aspirations, unembittered memories, all the freshness and gladness of May – is not that cause for joy rather than sorrow?

Vachell described an essentially prelapsarian ethos which worshipped virginal boys who died heroically before life's vicissitudes could pollute their spirit.

> I entreat you to consider that, if we have faith in a future life, we must believe also that we carry hence not only the record of our acts, whether good or evil, but the memory of them; and that memory, undimmed by falsehood or self-deception, will create for us Heaven or Hell ... I would sooner see any of you struck down in the flower of his youth than living on to lose, long before death comes, all that makes life worth the living. Better death, a thousand times, than gradual decay of mind and spirit; better death than faithlessness, indifference, and uncleanness.

Henry Desmond was important not for what he achieved but for what he symbolised. The boys of Harrow could do no better than to emulate his heroic sacrifice:

> To you who are leaving Harrow, poised for flight into the great world of which this school is the microcosm, I commend the memory of Henry Desmond. It stands in our records for all we venerate and strive for: loyalty, honour, purity, strenuousness, faithfulness in friendship. When

temptation assails you, think of that gallant boy running swiftly uphill, leaving craven fear behind, and drawing with him the others who, led by him to the heights, made victory possible. You cannot all be leaders, but you can follow leaders; only see to it that they lead you, as Henry Desmond led the men of Beauregard's Horse, onward and upward.

Death in fetid mud did not figure in Vachell's vision, nor did the slow agony of gas poisoning or the torture of artillery bombardment. The loyalty, courage, self-sacrifice and patriotism a boy learned at school were, without question, attributes relevant to soldiering. They enabled him to withstand hardships otherwise unendurable. Somewhere along the line, however, the schools lost sight of the fact that the object of war is not to die heroically, but to win. War is not a game.[7]

Believers in muscular Christianity thought that the working-class might benefit enormously from the sporting ethic. The initiative was not inspired by liberal benevolence nor by a desire to encourage social mobility. Rather, it was felt that a good dose of manliness might transform a feckless, unhealthy, slum boy into a worthy servant of empire. In October 1883, William Alexander Smith, Glasgow businessman, YMCA member and lieutenant in the Lanarkshire Volunteers, formed the first company of the Boys' Brigade in Hillhead. He had in mind an organisation that would keep boys suitably occupied during their early teens, when idleness might otherwise tempt them towards delinquency. Religion alone, Smith believed, could not achieve this purpose since it was too sedentary and effeminate to appeal to spirited slum boys. He regretted the way Sunday school teachers – invariably women – encouraged 'among boys an impression that to be a Christian means to be a "molly coddle"'. Smith's Brigade would offer something different: 'All a boy's aspirations are towards manliness, however mistaken his ideas may sometimes be as to what that manliness means. Our boys are full of earnest desire to be brave true men; and if we want to make them brave, true Christian men, we must direct this desire into the right channel . . . We must show them the manliness of Christianity.' In order to achieve this ideal, the Brigade would offer worldly and heroic Christian lessons, reinforced by the discipline and order of military drill and team games. The Brigade was one of the first voluntary movements to introduce working-class boys to organised sports, hitherto the preserve of the public schools. Smith envisaged that boys would talk 'to each other in the most perfectly natural way about the Company Bible-Class before all their comrades on the football field! That is of the very essence of the Boys Brigade, for it aims at taking up everything that should enter into healthy Boy-life, and consecrating it all to the service of Christ.'[8]

The Brigade was a remarkable success, so much so that it was soon widely copied. An impressive number of youth organisations were established, all combining religion, athleticism, manliness and military discipline. The Church Lads' Brigade, the Jewish Lads' Brigade, the Duty and Discipline Movement and the National Council of Public Morals competed to colonise inner-city neighbourhoods. The most famous and successful youth movement was, however, the Boy Scouts. Founded in 1908 by General Sir Robert Baden-Powell, it was yet another manifestation of the quest for national efficiency that followed the South African embarrassment. Baden-Powell, hero of Mafeking, went beyond the traditional games ethic, stressing instead the beneficial properties of life on the imperial frontier. 'Football is a good game,' he argued, 'but much better than it, better than any other game, is . . . man-hunting.' Scouting was an evangelical response to the problems associated with urban poverty, and, as such, typical of the tendency to blame those problems on character deficiencies rather than destitution. Boys from the slum would be turned into loyal citizens of the empire simply by taking them into the countryside, where they would learn the moral purity and discipline of the scout. The movement's bible, *Scouting for Boys*, explained how scouts would learn to emulate the 'pioneers, explorers and missionaries' who had built the Empire. Scouts were

> real men in every sense of the word, and thoroughly up on scout craft, i.e. they understand living out in the jungles, and they can find their way anywhere, are able to read meaning from the smallest signs and foot-tracks; they know how to look after their health when far away from any doctors, are strong and plucky, and ready to face any danger, and always keen to help each other. They are accustomed to take lives in their own hands, and to fling them down without hesitation if they can help their country by doing so.

In South Africa, the Boer soldier had proved himself the better scout. The war had underlined rather profoundly the social degradation caused by urbanisation in Britain. Baden-Powell was determined that the next war would find the country better prepared. 'Every boy ought to learn how to shoot and obey orders, else he is no more good when war breaks out than an old woman.' 'Be Prepared' was not simply a motto, but rather a very specific injunction: 'BE PREPARED to die for your country . . . so that when the time comes you may charge home with confidence, not caring whether you are to be killed or not.'[9]

The message of manliness and preparedness was further emphasised in the boys' literature of the time. A few of the authors, like Jules Verne and Rudyard Kipling, had genuine literary merit, but most were simply crude propagandists cashing in on the muscular Christianity fad. For those who got the formula right, there was a healthy income to be made. One such was George Alfred Henty, who produced two or three books a year between the early 1880s and 1914, with each edition selling around 150,000 copies. The novels kept to a strict formula: there was a magnificent manly hero, lashings of adventure, a sprinkling of suspense, an element of reality (books were often linked to actual conflicts) and an appropriately heroic climax: right always triumphed. Henty, an honorary vice president of the Boys' Brigade, was essentially Smith in book form: he recognised that boys were not likely to be attracted to the piousness which characterised juvenile literature of the mid Victorian period.

The *Boy's Own Paper* took the Henty formula and published it as an affordable weekly magazine (price: 1d) which, according to one survey, was read by two thirds of Britain's schoolboys. The magazine was started by the Religious Tract Society as a response to the 'penny dreadful' which, it was feared, tempted boys down un-Christian paths. At the peak of its popularity, the *Boy's Own Paper* sold over 50,000 copies per week, with each one probably passed among at least three boys. Contributors included Verne, Rider Haggard and the ubiquitous Henty.

It would be tempting to judge the popularity of the *Boy's Own Paper*, Henty, the Boys' Brigade, the Boy Scouts and similar manifestations of muscular Christianity as evidence of rampant militarism. The evidence seems compelling. Within two years of its establishment, the Boy Scouts claimed 100,000 members. Over 40 per cent of all male adolescents belonged to some kind of youth organisation by 1914. Haldane, defending plans for setting up officer corps in schools and universities, confessed to the Commons that 'you are not in danger of increasing the spirit of militarism there, because the spirit of militarism already runs fairly high'. If this was militarism, however, it was rather tame, especially in comparison to the mania that gripped German society before 1914. According to a widely accepted definition, genuine militarism requires the domination of government and society by military elites, a tendency to overvalue military power and, finally, the dissemination of military values into wider society. Britain failed to satisfy the first criterion and only partially satisfied the second (witness the lukewarm response to military preparedness and compulsory service). As for the third, it is true that military values were disseminated into wider society, but one needs to examine the motivation for doing so. The 'militarism' of the public schools, Boys' Brigade and *Boy's Own Paper* was not designed primarily to prepare Britain for war nor even to turn boys into soldiers. Its main aim was instead social control, not unlike the knee-jerk response of commentators who, in the 1980s, advocated national service whenever English football hooligans ran riot in Amsterdam, Stockholm or Munich. The Boy Scouts, in fact, was specifically designed to provide an alternative to the football ground, where there gathered 'thousands of boys and young men, pale, narrow-chested, hunched-up miserable specimens, smoking endless cigarettes, numbers of them betting, all of them learning to be hysterical as they groan or cheer in panic unison'. In that aim, it was unsuccessful.[10]

Military values were not, in any case, effectively disseminated. Granted, it is impressive that 40 per cent of boys joined youth organisations, but that does not mean they were successful at spreading the martial gospel. Wily, opportunistic young boys probably took what they wanted from these groups and ignored that which was distasteful. When the Boys' Brigade extended its recruitment beyond established church congregations, it found that new recruits were not persuaded to attend church regularly – they swallowed the muscular morsel but threw away the Christian wrapping. The salient point about the Brigade, the Scouts and the Henty novels was that they were fun. A bit of Christian indoctrination and some innocent military drill was probably a small price for the opportunity to play a good game of football on a real pitch with a real ball or the chance to read a cracking good story. Baden-Powell succeeded because, above all, he offered boys an adventure.

And what of the six out of ten boys who did not join youth movements? These were the very ones Smith and Baden-Powell were most eager to indoctrinate, namely the 'hooligan' element. In other words, the organisations were least successful among boys they most wanted to help. This was especially true of the Boy Scouts, which was seen as rather elitist. The problem was partially one of means; uniforms, outings and paraphernalia, no matter how well subsidised, cost money which the very poor did not have. Even the Boys' Brigade, though not as costly, mainly attracted boys who had already made a good start in life, from skilled working-class homes (or better), who went to church and were often apprenticed to a respectable trade. The 12th Earl of Meath, honorary president of the Dublin battalion of the Brigade, admitted in June 1902 that the Brigade was attractive only to the 'better-behaved lads, those who have already a desire for something better, [and] a tendency towards religious organisations'. It could 'never hope to obtain the rough lads from the great mass of the population'.[11]

Beyond these financial constraints, there seems to have been a distinct abhorrence of youth groups among lower-working-class boys. They saw uniformed youth movements for exactly what they were, namely methods of control. Thus a refusal to join was an expression of class solidarity. Rejection of these groups stretched occasionally to violence against boys who were members. 'Many a company in those ancient days was conscious of a highly organised underground movement whose purpose was to conduct a continuous guerilla campaign against the Boys' Brigade,' recalled one former member. 'Often was a drill parade conducted under a fusillade of stones and bricks.' Similar stories of violence abound. Members of the Catholic Boys' Brigade of South London chose to change into their uniforms at the meeting hall, so as to avoid being attacked en route.[12]

The urban wastrel also read a different type of magazine, if he read at all. The Henty books, at a shilling each, were beyond his means, and the *Boy's Own Paper*, at 1d per issue, could be afforded only by the better-off boys who joined the Brigade or the Boy Scouts. Those less fortunate read papers priced at ½d per issue, such as *The Union Jack* and *The Halfpenny Marvel*, precisely the sort of magazines that the *Boy's Own Paper* had been set up to replace. Frederick Willis recalled that 'a very distinct barrier' divided 'that section of society which had a penny to burn and that which had only a halfpence'. The cheaper magazines were not, however, totally devoid of the manly message. The Harmsworth weeklies *The Gem* and *The Magnet* published stories by Frank Richards about a fictional public school, Greyfriars, where sturdy heroes strutted. As Frank O'Connor recalled, boys of his background did not always absorb the moral lessons in these stories:

> I kept in training by shadow boxing before the mirror in the kitchen, and practised the deadly straight left with which the hero knocked out the bully of the school. I even adopted the public school code for my own, and did not tell lies, or inform on other boys, or yell when I was beaten. It wasn't easy, because the other fellows did tell lies, and told on one another in the most shameless way, and, when they were beaten, yelled that their wrists were broken, and even boasted of their own cleverness and when I behaved in the simple, manly way recommended in the school stories, they said I was mad or that I was 'shaping' (swanking), and even the teacher seemed to regard it as an impertinence.

The ideal world of the public school was for most boys simply too far removed from reality to inspire imitation. For the street-corner youth, to be manly meant to smoke, drink, swagger, lie and cheat. Fighting was performed not with boxing gloves but with fists – the dirtier the better. Muscular Christianity was supposed to be an antidote to hooliganism, yet for the dispossessed the hooligan was the real model of manliness.[13]

In early August 1914, Private Alfred Pollard, newly volunteered, was issued a rifle. He could hardly contain his excitement. 'I was armed. It was a weapon designed to kill. I wanted to kill.' Pollard had never realised that he possessed this desire. He was not a psychopath. He was just an ordinary insurance clerk overcome by an elemental emotion buried deep within him, an urge that war released and made legitimate. Britain built an army out of millions of men like Pollard.[14]

Desire was plentiful, but preparedness thin. The BEF was woefully ill-suited to a continental war. The soldiers were undoubtedly dedicated and brave, but there were too few of them. The regular army originally consisted of one cavalry and six infantry divisions. According to Haldane's plans, only four divisions were to be sent to France, but by various means, eight were eventually cobbled together. The formation of a Guards division and the substitution of Territorials for regular battalions in the colonies provided another four divisions, a total of twelve. Yet by December 1914, having suffered casualties of around 80,000, this force was at skeleton strength. Reserves had been completely exhausted, leaving the British hard pressed to hold their small section of the line around Ypres.

Strategic plans had assumed that a war in Europe would be short. Manly myths relied on the same assumption; in order for war to be glorious, it had to be brief and decisive. Within a week of the declaration, however, these preconceptions collided head-on with the realities of modern weaponry. It became obvious that the war would be long and would destroy men at a prodigious rate. Lord Kitchener, the newly appointed Secretary of State for War, decided that Britain should immediately attempt to raise an army in excess of one million men. With scant regard for the consequences, he tossed aside Haldane's plans, which stipulated that both the regular army and the Territorials would employ their individual recruiting mechanisms to expand as required in time of war. Kitchener decided instead to go his own way, trusting that his prestige would convince the rest of the country to follow him. In that respect he seems to have been a success. 'Our illusions as to the short duration of the war are rapidly vanishing,' wrote Georgina Lee on hearing of Kitchener's plans. 'Today we are being prepared for the probability of it lasting two years, perhaps more.'[15]

Kitchener was suspicious of the Territorials and therefore reluctant to send them to France. His misgivings were a mix of justifiable doubts and irrational prejudice. One genuine obstacle was that the force was intended for home defence, and the threat of invasion seemed real. Secondly, to send them overseas necessitated rewriting their conditions of service, which required their permission. In addition, since Territorials enlisted for just four years, extended to five in time of war, the force would inevitably shrink as time passed, not a pleasant prospect in a long war. Most important in Kitchener's mind, however, was the suspect quality of many Territorial units. In some, upwards of 20 per cent of troops were unfit for service. The 42nd Territorial Division was nearly at full establishment when it left Britain, but when it arrived in Egypt in September 1914, the commander, Sir John Maxwell, found 100 men technically blind, 1,500 riddled with vermin, one dying of Bright's disease and 'hundreds . . . so badly vaccinated they could hardly move'. It seemed that the division had 'picked up any loafer or corner boy they could find to make up the numbers'.[16]

Kitchener called the Territorials a 'Town Clerks' army' – mere hobbyists who played at soldiering. While he could not exactly ignore that they were the only trained reserve Britain possessed, he did not feel that they were remotely the solution to the country's need for a large army to fight on the continent.

He preferred instead to start from scratch with a New Army unencumbered by tradition, trained according to the demands of this war, enlisted for the duration and able to be sent where necessity dictated. This desire inspired Alfred Leete's famous poster showing the imposing figure of Kitchener pointing his finger and proclaiming 'Your Country Needs You'.[17]

As Kitchener predicted, the response was enormous. Between August 1914 and December 1915, 2,466,719 men enlisted, the largest volunteer army ever to be raised anywhere. This great rush to the colours might seem an enormously unselfish response by citizens of all classes to their country's call, but it must be stressed that there was no common will to serve. Only by examining the various motivations for volunteering can we understand the type of army which eventually evolved and the effect war had upon these citizen-soldiers.

The great mass of volunteers can be divided into two groups: those from the public schools who mostly became officers, and those from the rest of society who made up the ranks. Of the former, some historians have cynically argued that their willingness to volunteer is easily explained since they had most to lose if Britain was defeated. That, however, seems unfair. An explanation so heavily reliant upon self-interest does not do justice to a generation of boys so devoid of guile, so conditioned to believe in romantic notions of honour, glory and sacrifice. It has become a cliché to quote Rupert Brooke in this context, but this cliché is singularly appropriate. Brooke was extraordinary only in his eloquence; the emotions he described were commonplace:

> If I should die, think only this of me:
>   That there's some corner of a foreign field
> That is forever England. There shall be
>   In that rich earth a richer dust concealed;
> A dust whom England bore, shaped, made aware,
>   Gave, once, her flowers to love, her ways to roam,
> A body of England's, breathing English air,
>   Washed by the rivers, blest by suns of home.

Public school boys were raised to believe in chivalric values that were all the more potent because they had not been tested in the real world. Their phantasmagoric vision of war and patriotism is perfectly encapsulated in a pamphlet written by Canon J. H. Skrine of Merton College, Oxford:

> A lad ... knows that he stands between his mothers and his sisters, his sweetheart and his girlfriends, ... and the inconceivable infamy of alien invasion ... And he learns, as he can in no other way, the supreme lesson of physical cleanliness and self-respect, for has not his body, with

its faculties – its endurance and its lithesomeness and its proud contempt for pain – become one of the bricks that form the living wall of the land he loves?

War is not murder . . . war is sacrifice. The fighting and killing are not of the essence of it, but are the accidents, though the inseparable accidents; and even these, in the wide modern fields where a soldier rarely in his own sight sheds any blood but his own, where he lies on the battle sward not to inflict death but to endure it – even these are mainly purged of savagery and transfigured into devotion. War is not murder but sacrifice, which is the soul of Christianity.

Public school boys worshipped war but seldom actually fought. As a result, ethos was exaggerated into absurdity. Images of war came from Henty, Newbolt and Kipling, not from disabled veterans of Balaclava or Ladysmith. When old boys recounted war stories on school speech days, they told not of chaos and slaughter, but instead perpetuated myths of heroism and self-sacrifice, reconstructing a narrative divorced from reality. It was generally expected that war against a civilised European enemy would conform to that narrative, embodying all of the sublime values absorbed at school. Such a conflict was the ultimate embodiment of the public school culture: not a calamity, but a sacred rite of passage offered only to the fortunate. Graham Greene recalled the joy he and his brothers felt when victory did not come quickly: 'As long as the war continued, we might one day be involved and the world of Henty seemed to come a little closer.'[18]

'I adore war,' wrote the poet and archetypal public school boy Julian Grenfell after just one month of fighting. 'It's like a big picnic without the objectlessness of a picnic. I've never been so well or happy. No one grumbles at one for being dirty.' Muscular Christian values had been so well disseminated that

Grenfell could freely write of war in this way without being judged a lunatic. The novelist and critic Nicholas Mosley later explained that Grenfell's reference to dirtiness was 'meant physically, but psychologically it was relevant too. For the first time a generation brought up to be clean and bright and brilliant could, without guilt, be fierce and babyish and vile.' That is true to an extent, but for this generation there was nothing fierce, nor babyish, nor vile about war. The front may have been dirty, but it had a cleansing effect on the soul. Vachell, it will be recalled, compared death in war to the 'freshness and gladness of May'. The mud of Belgium seemed like baptismal water.[19]

Granted, a few iconoclasts had no truck with public school patriotism. J. B. Priestley was one such, yet he too answered Kitchener's call with alacrity. As he later explained, he was affected not by peer pressure, nor by patriotism, nor by Kitchener's magnetism, nor by great heroic visions, nor by anything 'rational and conscious'. Instead,

> I went at a signal from the unknown ... there came out of the unclouded blue of that summer, a challenge that was almost like a conscription of the spirit, little to do really with King and Country and flag-waving and hip-hip-hurrah, a challenge to what we felt was our untested manhood. Other men, who had not lived as easily as we had, had drilled and marched and borne arms – couldn't we?

Priestley described a common male condition; war brings out the latent soldier which lies within most men – the need to know if one has what it takes. Every generation feels that pull. Yet this conscription of the spirit was stronger in 1914 because hard reality had not yet vanquished war's romance. As much as he might have denied it, Priestley was a product of his age.[20]

Ordinary workers were actually freer than public school

boys to choose their fate, since they were less brainwashed by cultural conceptions of duty. Elite schools were, after all, prisons of expectation. The workers, in contrast, were not one monolithic mass, but two million separate individuals, each with different reasons for volunteering. The decision to enlist might have come because they were deferent, desperate, bored, or simply drunk. Many sought glory; others felt a duty. Some craved adventure and some simply did what they were told.

The concept of a 'rush to the colours' is in fact misleading, at least as it is commonly presented. Nearly 300,000 men enlisted in August 1914, many before Kitchener pointed his finger. The most productive recruiting period lasted from the final week of August to the second week of September. Thus, if there was a rush, it was over by the 9th. Fewer men enlisted in all of October than during the first four days of September. This is potently illustrated when one examines the army's height requirements. When the war began, the minimum standard was five feet three inches. On 11 September that was raised to five feet six inches in order to control the flow of recruits. Unbeknownst to the recruiters, however, by that stage the flow was already diminishing. On 14 November the army, realising its error, reinstated the original standard and even began investigating the possibility of 'bantam' units of men below five foot three. Short men had advantages, as a correspondent to *The Times* pointed out: 'besides lessening the size of the target for the enemy to hit, he requires shallower trenches'.[21]

It is commonly assumed that men rushed to enlist because they thought the war would be short and did not want to miss the chance of glory. While these sort definitely existed, a far larger number waited to see whether the need for volunteers was genuinely urgent. Rates and times of enlistment varied according to occupation and social standing, with men employed in the commercial sectors volunteering more readily than those in agriculture, manufacturing or transport. The young went more quickly than the old, perhaps understandably given that the latter were more likely to have pressing reasons for staying home. Often, economic circumstances made volunteering attractive. It is no coincidence that the high rate of enlistment in August and September corresponded with a temporary but dramatic rise in unemployment. Industries, frightened by economic uncertainty, reacted by cutting jobs at the outbreak of war, with nearly 500,000 men made redundant by the end of August, and many more forced on to part-time status. Since these men would not have had any idea how temporary their jobless state would be, it is understandable that they found a spell of soldiering attractive. Thus, the very first rush of recruits was dominated by the sort of men who had always volunteered for the army, namely the young, unskilled, unemployed and desperate. Taking advantage of the widespread destitution, the Local Government Board in Bristol instructed charities in August 1914 not to grant poor relief to able-bodied men of military age. Ninety per cent of relief recipients promptly enlisted. When, in November, war contracts brought new orders to Bristol's factories, the enlistment rate fell sharply.[22] Nevertheless, as with the recruits from the public schools, the worker's willingness to volunteer was conditioned by an assumption that the war would be neither long nor particularly deadly. As recruitment rates in 1915 demonstrate, volunteers would not have come forward so enthusiastically in the first few months had they been fully aware of the horrors of this interminable war.

The Bristol example shows that destitution was an important motivator only during the first two months. By the beginning of October, orders for munitions and supplies made employment plentiful, and in consequence, poverty ceased to be a motivation. One therefore needs to look elsewhere to explain why men from stable and essential jobs volunteered in significant numbers. 'Unemployment did not fill the ranks of Kitchener's Army, popular sentiment did,' the historian Jay

Winter insists. 'The protection of "little Belgium", the defence of the empire, the need to be seen to be doing one's military duty alongside the men of one's district or village: these may sound like outworn clichés today, but in 1914 they had force and substance in the minds of ordinary people.' The statement requires qualification, but is basically sound. Private Thomas Bickerton, for instance, recalled being drawn by 'The romance of it, the mystery and uncertainty of it, the glowing enthusiasm and lofty idealism of it: of our own free will we were embarked on this glorious enterprise, ready to endure any hardship and make any sacrifice, inspired by a patriotism newly awakened by the challenge of our country's honour. Nothing could have been more romantic'.[23]

In other words, after the first few months, popular sentiment became the main inspiration for joining. Words like duty and honour occur nearly as often in working-class diaries and letters as in those from the middle class. This is interesting because, strictly speaking, the workers were defending a social system that had not treated them well. Their willingness to serve certainly perplexed the pacifist poet Emily Orr:

> What has your country done for you,
>   Child of a city slum,
> That you should answer her ringing call
> To man the gap and keep the wall
> And hold the field though a thousand fall
>   And help be slow to come?
>
> . . .
>
> 'What can your country ask of you,
>   Dregs of the British race?'
> 'She gave us little, she taught us less,
> And why we were born we could hardly guess
> Till we felt the surge of battle press
>   And looked the foe in the face.'

What Orr's poem reveals is that the self-proclaimed defenders of the downtrodden seldom understand the working-class mentality. Prior to the war, class consciousness was increasingly expressed as industrial militancy. One might therefore assume that those willing to go on strike would also be reluctant to volunteer. This, however, betrays a fundamental misunderstanding of the worker's loyalties. The worker who despised his boss and distrusted his government usually still loved his country. Patriotism was, and remains, an expression of working-class consciousness. In other words, the question 'What has your country done for you?' seems not to have troubled the average worker. 'We had been brought up to believe that Britain was the best country in the world and we wanted to defend her,' Private George Morgan reflected. 'The history taught us at school showed that we were better than other people and now all the news was that Germany was the aggressors and we wanted to show the Germans what we could do.'[24]

Granted, patriotism is easily manipulated. Workers were a deferent, politically naive group gullible about threats to their nation. They were told that their country was in danger, that her cause was just and that plucky Belgium needed help. Leete's famous war poster was carefully constructed to play to their sentiments. Kitchener's pointing finger could hardly be ignored; the poster beckoned, commanded, threatened, cajoled and shamed all at the same time. Nevertheless, the message – YOUR COUNTRY NEEDS YOU – was one which the lowly worker would not often have heard. Seldom in the past had he been told that he was needed. The effect was profound. My nation needs ME.

Along with national loyalty, regional pride could also be tapped. The War Minister Lord Derby is commonly credited with the idea of 'Pals' battalions, units formed in a locality or among workers from a single factory or business. In fact,

Derby mainly lent prestige to the scheme; the proposal was the brainchild of War Office civil servants who set it in motion twelve days before Derby's formal announcement on 24 August. The very first Pals battalion, the 'Stockbrokers' of the Royal Fusiliers, began recruiting on the 21st. Whatever its origin, the idea was a stroke of genius – or so it seemed at first. It played on the herd instinct, one of the most effective motivators for volunteering, and at a stroke solved the problem of the need for group solidarity within a unit. In other words, men volunteered because their 'pals' were joining and automatically felt a sense of battalion identity that otherwise might have taken months to establish. A sample of the units illustrates the variety of constituencies from which they were drawn: 'Accrington Pals', 'Grimsby Chums', 'Glasgow Corporation Tramways', 'University and Public School Brigade', 'Tyneside Scottish', 'Tyneside Irish', 'Cotton Association', etc. Boys' Brigade and OTC units often formed the nucleus, as would athletes or supporters from local football, rugby or cricket teams. The consequences of this strategy were revealed when these units went into battle. If a Pals battalion found itself in the wrong place at the wrong time, the result could devastate the village from which it had sprung. Around 700 Accrington Pals went forth as one on the first day of the Battle of the Somme. Just twenty minutes later, 235 were dead and 350 wounded. When a rumour spread around Accrington that only seven men had survived the battle, an angry crowd surrounded the mayor's house, demanding explanation.

The same spirit of voluntarism which brought millions of men to recruiting centres was apparent in other sectors of society. Postmen switched to mufti and donated over 100,000 blue uniforms to the army. A dentist, Austrian by birth, but a naturalised British subject, offered to extract teeth free of charge from any man who volunteered. A man whose poor eyesight prevented his volunteering advertised for a tutor to teach him to knit. An injured airman who needed skin grafts wrote to *The Times* asking for donors. He received over fifty responses in one day. During November 1914, schoolchildren in Grangemouth were encouraged to bring a potato to school every day. Two tons of potatoes were collected for Belgian refugees. During 'Million Egg Week' in August 1915, 1,036,380 eggs were collected from private citizens for soldiers at the front. A charitable group hoping to establish a hospital in France advertised for the loan of a milk cow. Not only were a number of cows donated, but middle-class ladies volunteered as milkmaids and dairy appliance firms donated equipment. One mother, whose great misfortune it was to have no sons of military age, offered her two-year-old as a mascot to any regiment that would have him.[25]

Among the comfortable middle class, charitable organisations proliferated like dandelions in summer. The government itself received, unsolicited, £25 million in charitable donations during the first ten months of the war, an impressive sum given that during the same period income tax doubled and other taxes ate into disposable income. Every day the papers ran appeals for worthy causes, some rather imaginatively presented:

> Dogs and cats of the Empire! The Kaiser said: 'Germany will fight to the last dog and cat.' Will British dogs and cats give 6d each to provide a YMCA Soldiers Hut in France?

> Flashlight, a New Forest pony, appeals to all four-footed friends for donations towards an ambulance for wounded horses. She will gratefully acknowledge all money sent to her.

So profound was the charitable spirit (or at least the enthusiasm for collecting donations) that in March 1916 established charities demanded a system of licensing. Cases of fraud were not unknown, and so prolific were volunteers collecting donations on the streets that the public began to complain.[26]

I AM "TOBY" WHO IS NEVER SHUNN'D
SO WILL YOU HELP ME WITH THIS FUND.

Before 1914, those opposed to professionalisation and preparedness took refuge in the argument that the British ability to improvise quickly would carry the country through a crisis. The way Britain responded to the war certainly seemed to justify this confidence. The work of the Parliamentary Recruiting Committee is a case in point. The idea behind the PRC was to redirect political party constituency organisations into recruiting, thus making use of their local knowledge, access to halls, canvassing techniques, talents for public speaking and possession of voter lists. The PRC soon discovered profound similarities between campaigning and recruiting. Among its many activities, the group produced an estimated 54,000,000 posters, leaflets and other publications, in addition to organising 12,000 meetings and 20,000 speeches. Calls to volunteer were impossible to avoid; messages were emblazoned on taxis, printed on the back of London tram tickets and posted on every blank wall. When imagination was applied to recruiting, new schemes proliferated. In July 1915, for instance, the PRC joined with the Women's Emergency Corps in distributing leaflets among West End shoppers urging them to carry home their own parcels, in order to free delivery men for military service. The retired principal of a ladies' college offered her services as a nanny free of charge to any widower prevented from volunteering because of the need to look after his motherless children.[27]

Those who would not willingly jump were pushed into the military, with ever-increasing force. Government, press and the pulpit were not above using coercion and shame. A famous recruiting poster showed a humiliated father being asked by his children: 'Daddy, what did you do in the Great War?' At the time, the most popular poems were not the pained verses of Sassoon, Owen or even Brooke, but heavy-handed rhymes published in daily newspapers to bolster the war effort. For instance, Harold Begbie wrote:

> What will you lack, sonny, what will you lack,
> When the girls line up the street,
> Shouting their love to the lads come back
> From the foe they rushed to beat?
> Will you send a strangled cheer to the sky
> And grin till your cheeks are red?
> But what will you lack when your mate goes by
> With a girl who cuts you dead?

The high priestess of humiliation was the irrepressible Jessie Pope, as shown by her excruciatingly condescending poem 'The Call':

> Who's for the trench –
> Are you, my laddie?
> Who'll follow French –
> Will you, my laddie?
> Who's fretting to begin,
> Who's going out to win?
> And who wants to save his skin –
> Do you, my laddie?
>
> Who's for the khaki suit –
> Are you, my laddie?
> Who longs to charge and shoot –
> Do you, my laddie?
> Who's keen on getting fit,
> Who means to show his grit,
> And who'd rather wait a bit –
> Would you, my laddie?
>
> Who'll earn the Empire's thanks –
> Will you, my laddie?
> Who'll swell the victor's ranks –
> Will you, my laddie?
> When that procession comes,
> Banners and rolling drums –
> Who'll stand and bite his thumbs –
> Will you, my laddie?

The most infamous tactic of humiliation was the white feathers that women gave to men not in uniform. The practice began in September 1914, apparently on the instigation of Penrose Fitzgerald, a retired admiral. As one contemporary remarked, 'The bellicosity of these females was almost as terrible to the young man who had no stomach for fighting as an enemy with . . . guns.' After the war, one woman recalled the terrible day her father was given a white feather. 'He came home and cried his heart out. My father was no coward, but had been reluctant to leave his family. He was thirty-four and my mother, who had two young children, had been suffering from a serious illness. Soon after this incident my father joined the army.' The white feather ladies were cruel and insensitive but also brilliantly effective in the way they manipulated prevalent notions of masculinity – by attaching a badge of cowardice they cast doubt on the individual's manhood. Evidence nevertheless suggests that they were derided more than admired, in part because their scorn was often wrongly targeted. Essential workers, invalided soldiers and Tommies home on leave were frequently mistaken for shirkers. 'Would not the feather-brained Ladies,' *The Times* remarked, 'be better advised to learn to nurse the wounded, and thus become useful, instead of offending nuisances to the community?'[28]

The white feather ladies were merely the most blatant manifestation of using women to persuade men to volunteer. On 8 July 1915, the personal column in *The Times* contained the following: 'Jack F. G. If you are not in khaki by the 20th I shall cut you dead. Ethel M.' It was generally accepted that the most useful service women could perform was to cajole their men. 'We women ... recognise that, as women, we have no use for the man who will not fight for his King and country,' went one letter to *The Times*. Baroness Orczy formed the Active Service League, 'whose sole object will be that of influencing men to offer themselves at once to the nearest recruiting officer'. Women who joined had formally to swear that 'At this hour of England's grave peril and desperate need I do hereby pledge myself most solemnly in the name of my King and Country to persuade every man I know to offer his services to the country, and I also pledge myself never to be seen in public with any man who, being in every way fit and free for service, has refused to respond to his country's call.' An advertisement addressed to 'the Women of London' reminded the faint-hearted:

Is your 'Best Boy' wearing Khaki? If not don't YOU THINK he should be?

If he does not think that you and your country are worth fighting for – do you think he is worthy of you?

Don't pity the girl who is alone – her young man is probably a soldier fighting for her and her country – and for YOU.

If your young man neglects his duty to his King and Country, the time may come when he will NEGLECT YOU.

Think it over and then ask him to

JOIN THE ARMY – TODAY

A ubiquitous poster showed women at a window watching their men march away. The caption read: 'Women of Britain Say – GO!' Designed to influence women as much as men, the poster perfectly demonstrated how the threat of sexual emasculation proved a potent tool of recruitment.[29]

Whilst it was theoretically possible for the thick-skinned to carry on in a world of white feathers and Jessie Popes, more direct forms of coercion were sometimes impossible to ignore. Addressing both his workers and his fellow landowners, Lord Derby announced that 'When the war is over I intend, as far as I possibly can, to employ nobody except men who have taken their duty at the front . . . all things being equal, if two men come to me for a farm and one has been at the front there is no doubt who is going to get the farm.' One soldier recalls journeying to his depot in 1914 with eight servants of a peer who had told the younger members of his staff that they 'ought' to volunteer. On the third day of the war, the Nestlé company publicly announced that it expected all single male employees between the ages of 18 and 30 to sign up. It asked the public to 'excuse any unavoidable delay in despatch of goods ordered' arising from the shrinkage of its workforce. A firm of stockbrokers, ironically owned by Quakers, declared that it 'expects that all unmarried staff under 35 years of age will join Earl Kitchener's army at once, and also urges those who are married and eligible to take the same course'. Coercion of this sort caused *The Bystander* to remark: 'Men who put on uniform as a result of exhortation by squires, parsons, retired officers, employers, schoolmasters, leader-writers, politicians, cartoonists, poets, music-hall singers and women are not volunteers; they are conscripts. They have gone in because it would have been so infernally unpleasant to have stayed out.'[30]

Recruiting had a shady side, and also a distinctly sleazy one. The minimum age requirement was often ignored. George Coppard was sixteen when he presented himself at a recruiting office. 'The sergeant asked me my age, and when told, replied, "Clear off son. Come back tomorrow and see if you're nineteen, eh?" So I turned up again the next day and gave my age as nineteen.' During the first rush to volunteer, medical officers had to inspect up to 200 men per day, a situation that invited abuse. Men were often judged not according to their fitness at the time, but on an optimistic prediction of how their health would improve after three or four months of army training. Until May 1915, doctors were paid 2s. 6d for each man passed fit and recruiters a similar sum for each man enlisted, which meant that small fortunes could be made by the unscrupulous. When the payment to recruiters was reduced to 1s. in October 1914, that only encouraged greater dishonesty. Drunks in public houses were a favourite target. One Fulham recruiter would habitually roam the streets, aided by two chauffeurs and a boy scout, rounding up the 'unemployed and idlers'. Another was imprisoned for running an extortion racket which involved persuading men to enlist, take their King's shilling, and then desert. He would then sell their kit and split the profits. In October 1914, Londoner Ernest Adams was sentenced to two months' imprisonment for serial volunteering – he had signed up six times.[31]

This dark side of recruiting should not detract from what was, by any calculation, a massively impressive response to Kitchener's call. Between the outbreak of war and December 1915, nearly 2.5 million men joined the army without legal compulsion. This constituted almost half of the total enlisted during the war. Twenty-nine per cent of the volunteers joined in August and September 1914. Granted, a good many of these men, especially those who delayed, were bullied into volunteering. Cynicism, however, seems inappropriate; there is no denying what was an extraordinary willingness to serve. If there was a typical volunteer, it was perhaps Coppard, who described the irresistible pull:

> I was just an ordinary boy of elementary education and slender prospects. Rumours of war broke out and I began to be interested in the Territorials tramping the streets in their big strong boots. Although I seldom saw a newspaper, I knew about the assassination of the Archduke Ferdinand at Sarajevo. News placards screamed out at every corner, and military bands blared out their martial music in the main streets of Croydon. This was too much for me to resist, and as if drawn by a magnet, I knew I had to enlist straight away.

If one leaves aside the obvious indicators of Coppard's class and background, his testimony could have been expressed by so many of those who volunteered, be they wealthy, poor, educated or ignorant. This was an innocent, gullible generation which still believed in heroes, duty, service and glorious war.

For them, the war was not a disaster but an opportunity, a chance to prove oneself and do one's bit. When Britain needed men, they responded. 'We go into action in a day or two and I'm leaving this in case I don't come back,' wrote Ged Garvin to his father on 20 July 1916 from the Somme battle front. 'Try not to grieve too much for me. I hope my death will have been worthy of your trust and I couldn't die for a better cause.' He was killed the next day.[32]

The rhetoric of glorious sacrifice was a powerful magnet that pulled millions towards war. But at the moment of departure, that patriotic impetus melted away and an agonising uncertainty was exposed. Love of nation yielded to fear of loss. In *World Without End*, Helen Thomas told of her last night with her husband Edward. The children had fallen asleep. 'And we are left alone, unable to hide our agony, afraid to show it.' He undresses her and takes her to bed. 'All my strength gives away. I hide my face on his knee, and all my tears so long kept back come convulsively.' They try to talk of important things but occasionally take refuge in the mundane. 'You must not make my heart cold with sadness,' he pleads, 'but keep it warm, for no one else but you has ever found my heart, and for you it was a poor thing after all.' She protests: 'No, no, no, your heart's love is all my life. I was nothing before you came and would be nothing without your love.'

All night they talked, made love and cried. The next morning he rose early, made breakfast, said his goodbyes and walked away – over the hills, across the valleys, towards the train that would take him to France and war.

Panic seized me, and I ran through the mist and the snow to the top of the hill, and stood there a moment dumbly, with straining eyes and ears. There was nothing but the mist and the snow and the silence of death.

Then with leaden feet which stumbled in a sudden

darkness that overwhelmed me groped my way back to the empty house.

Helen never saw Edward again. He was killed at the Battle of Arras, on Easter Monday 1917.[33]

Chapter 4

Lions and Donkeys

In 1986, the drama series *The Monocled Mutineer*, loosely based on the 'mutiny' at the Etaples base in 1917, caused considerable anguish in Britain. Viewers objected to the portrayal of an army composed of cruel, sadistic officers and immoral, cowardly, conniving and unpatriotic men. The main character, Percy Topliss, undermined the myth of Tommy Atkins, the decent, honest, long-suffering working-class soldier who did his duty and survived by sheer pluck. Seventy years after the war, that myth remained sacred. The idea of a Tommy who cheated, lied, fornicated and mutinied seemed like blasphemy.

Prior to the war, the British did not have to like soldiers since it could easily ignore them. Kitchener's army, however, changed all that by building an army from the pedestrians on Civvy Street. Yet for the first two months of recruiting, most soldiers still came from the same groups as before the war: the dregs of society. According to Major General Sir George Younghusband, 'My early recollections of the British soldier are of a bluff, rather surly person, never the least jocose or light-hearted, except perhaps when he had too much beer. He was brave always, but with a sullen, stubborn bravery. No Tipperary . . . about it.' After war broke out, respect for this type of soldier increased even though his character remained unchanged. Since it was necessary for the public to love the army, the mythical Tommy

Atkins emerged as if by magic as an unconscious act of collective goodwill. The British looked at soldiers and saw the heroes they wanted. Arthur Graeme West, a young officer, remarked on how ironic it was that, quite suddenly, 'every man, woman and child is taught to regard [the soldier] as a hero'. On the march to barracks in St Albans during August, Rifleman Percy Jones of the 1/16th London Regiment noticed: 'The people along the line of the route showered things on us and refused to take any money. A gentleman in Watford bought out a whole fruit stall as it stood and told the lucky coster to give us the lot. When we halted people rushed out of their houses to distribute food and drink.' Private Harold Hunt of the 1/7th (City of London) Battalion found the change rather striking: 'Up to the war we youths had counted but little in the scheme of the things . . . but now we had become knights in shining armour.'[1]

Since the army did not have barracks to house a huge volunteer force, recruits were billeted with civilians, thus ending the segregation of army from society that had once suited Victorian sensibilities. Some prejudices remained. Rifleman Norman Ellison recalled being billeted with a woman who was suspicious and hostile until she summoned the courage to ask: 'Are you volunteers?' On being told they were, she replied with considerable relief, 'Oh, I thought you were common soldiers!' A retired army surgeon agreed to billet soldiers 'provided they are clean men who will not spit on the wallpaper'. A soldier in the Gordon Highlanders recalled that the community in which he was billeted 'had visions of all kind of savages armed with claymores descending upon them'. One girl asked 'if I didn't feel the cold at night, on the hills with only my plaid to cover me while sleeping'. Another person assumed that he had never seen, nor indeed used, a bathtub.[2]

Social problems prevalent in society were duplicated within the army. Lurking amidst the solid folk were thieves, villains, cowards and cheats. The Oxford-educated volunteer

J. Staniforth was distressed to find that his unit consisted mostly of 'tramps' who were 'drunk . . . seedy, lousy, unshaven' and given to 'smoking, spitting, quarrelling, making water all over the room . . . hiccuping and vomiting'. J. B. Priestley concluded that every random group of ten men included one who was 'twisted somewhere inside'. James Lovegrove spent his first night in the army in a tent on Woolwich Common.

> Mother had always told me to wear pyjamas or I'd get lumbago! Well, I was putting them on when the tent flap opened and a voice said 'Cor bloody blimey! Come and have a look at this bloke, he's a getting dressed to go to bed!' Well, they all had a good laugh at me. I don't think most of them had seen pyjamas before. They all seemed to sleep naked. And the foul language! I'd never heard such swearing before in my life.

The labouring classes, from which enlisted men were drawn, had health standards similar to those now associated with poorest Africa. The average life expectancy for English men was 51.5 years in 1912 and therefore lower still for the working-class. A recruiter in Anglesey estimated that the original height requirement of five feet six inches barred up to 70 per cent of the county's volunteers. Recruits were customarily given a medical examination that placed them into four categories: Grade I consisted of men in satisfactory health, Grade II those with a 'slight' disability. Both were eligible for combat. Grade III consisted of men with 'marked physical disability' that exempted them from combat but not from clerical duties. Grade IV were rejected outright. As a general rule, middle-class men fell into Grades I and II, skilled workers mainly into II and III and unskilled predominantly into III and IV.[3] This effectively meant that the higher one's social station, the greater the risk encountered. A pre-war sample of 1,000 Cambridge undergraduates yielded 700 in Grade I, 200 in II, 75 in III and 25 in IV. For the population as a whole, however, only 34 per cent made Grade I. During the war, this proportion varied according to manpower needs. In other words, shortages of troops led to health standards being applied less diligently. Nevertheless, even in the last year of the war, over one million men were judged unfit for front-line combat.[4]

For many men, army life brought a more wholesome diet, improved housing, better clothing (especially boots) and more regular medical care than previously experienced. Beer was weaker and access to alcohol considerably restricted. As a result, many recruits grew a couple of inches and gained considerable weight after taking the King's shilling. Army health standards improved during the course of the war, partly in response to the poor condition of its recruits, but also because of greater public awareness of health issues. The BEF, for example, took no dentists to France in 1914, but four years later 800 were serving with the forces – though they were mainly occupied pulling teeth. Men were made healthy in order to die for their country. 'If we had been more careful for the last fifty years to prevent the unheeded wastage of human life,' a *Daily Telegraph* leader argued with unintentional irony, 'we should have had at least half a million men available for the defence of the country.'[5]

Men used to a life of poverty, dirt and drudgery were a positive asset to the army. The average recruit came from a background of hard labour, few opportunities and low expectations, in which mere survival was a struggle and premature death relatively common. In this sense, army life was a continuation of ordinary life by other means. Enlisted men were drawn from the most class-conscious society in Europe, and placed in an army that reinforced civilian social hierarchies. These soldiers knew their place and fatalistically accepted what their 'betters' told them. Thus, their social background rendered them ideally suited to fight in this sort of war.

A persistent Great War myth holds that when these poor, downtrodden masses joined privileged middle-class officers in the trenches, the universality of experience encouraged an extraordinary sense of camaraderie and mutual respect. 'I love all the men,' wrote P. Jones, a subaltern, 'and simply rejoice to see them going day by day their own jolly selves, building up such a wall of jocundity around me.' An awakened sense of social responsibility is presumed to have developed among middle-class officers. The poet Wilfred Owen is often cited as one of the more prominent examples of this enlightenment:

I have made fellowships –
    Untold of happy lovers in old song.
    For love is not the binding of fair lips
    With the soft silk of eyes that look and long,
By Joy, whose ribbon slips, –
    But wound with war's hard wire whose stakes are
        strong;
    Bound with the bandage of the arm that drips;
    Knit in the webbing of the rifle-thong.
I have perceived much beauty
    In the hoarse oaths that kept our courage straight;
    Heard music in the silentness of duty;
    Found peace where shell-storms spouted reddest
        spate.
Nevertheless, except you share
    With them in hell the sorrowful dark of hell,
    Whose world is but the trembling of a flare
    And heaven but as the highway for a shell,
You shall not hear their mirth:
    You shall not come to think them well content
    By any jest of mine. These men are worth
    Your tears. You are not worth their merriment.

The sentiments were a touch hypocritical given that Owen had a very low opinion of the working-class. He treated the servants assigned to him like donkeys and once asserted that German losses were more tragic than British since the German army consisted of a better class of men. Some officers did have their eyes opened by the war, but one should not draw sweeping conclusions from particular (or indeed peculiar) cases. The myth of trench harmony has arisen because the sentiments expressed by a few war poets are assumed to be typical. Yet they were in fact hypersensitive, disillusioned, guilt-ridden and unique individuals who professed shame at the way their class treated ordinary soldiers. Few shared their sensitivity.[6]

According to the myth, class antagonism resulted from ignorance, which the trench experience eradicated. Yet it is nonsense to suggest that the middle classes were ignorant of workers or vice versa. The middle class supplied society's managers, owners, landlords, bosses. The workers were their drivers, servants, tenants and labourers – the men who cleaned the chimneys, delivered the coal, manned the assembly line and tended the fields. The nature of capitalism ensured that these two groups constantly interacted. True, the servile relationship of worker to boss was not conducive to real intimacy, but it requires a mammoth leap of reason to believe that barriers were broken down in the army – an even more rigid and hierarchical working relationship. Class distinctions, and the chain of authority that went with them, were essential to a smooth-functioning army. As Lord Wolseley said, the ordinary soldier was 'a daring and self-sacrificing fellow, [but] he must be well led, and as a general rule I believe that the leader must be a British gentleman'. Stated differently, army life was merely another form of the manager–worker relationship. This was particularly true in the trenches, in which the drudgery of life had much in common with the monotonous dehumanisation of the factory, except that the soldier had none of the rights enjoyed by unionised workers. Enlisted men's correspondence often referred to soldiering as a 'job'. 'We are absolutely fed up with this life although the job has got to be done,' one Tommy wrote. War was work, punctuated with bullets and shells.[7]

To most middle-class officers, ordinary soldiers were not only of a different class, they seemed a different species. The ability to lead was, after all, considered to be a product of good birth – in the genes. Edward Campion Vaughan wrote of his batman, Dunham: 'He has grown out of the stupidity which caused Hatwell to give him to me, and is now my most valuable possession.' Another officer, A. A. Hanbury-Sparrow, argued that ordinary soldiers were 'definitely inferior beings and you'd no illusions about them'; he considered the idea that officers should be worthy of their men 'claptrap'. Even Robert Graves, who sought to protect his men from the 'grosser indignities of the military system', often complained about their stupidity. Guy Chapman described his men as 'children moving in a haze of their own dreams, unconnected with practical things'. The reference to children was common; a 19-year-old subaltern would refer to a 32-year-old private as a 'lad'. The more enlightened middle-class officers, like Major Christopher Stone, may have been deeply affected by their trench experiences, but the effect was usually to encourage a heightened sense of paternalism. One of the characters in Stone's post-war novel, *The Valley of Indecision*, comments that the officer class learned 'To manage men. How? By example, partly. By setting themselves a higher standard than they expect of their subordinates. And by looking after their men: thinking of their men's comfort, mind you, before their own.' In other words, Stone's war experiences did not eradicate his sense of class superiority; he instead interpreted his responsibilities differently.[8]

The army fostered the officer's elite status, the better to underline his authority. Social barriers were buttressed with separate quarters, canteens, cinemas and even brothels. A father whose eight sons were all enlisted men complained bitterly about how officer casualty lists were published within a few days of an action, while those pertaining to the lower ranks 'are hardly ever available for many weeks, if at all'. In the trenches, the junior officer had a batman who looked after his kit. 'My servant,' Ged Garvin told his father, the editor of *The Observer*, 'is an awfully nice boy, a miner, but very clean and tidy.' Officers ate separately from their men, usually dining on better food, with freer access to alcohol and cigarettes. Upon reaching the front, Robert Graves was shocked to find

> Battalion Headquarters, a dug-out in the reserve line . . . happened to be unusually comfortable, with an ornamental lamp, a clean cloth, and polished silver on the table. The Colonel, Adjutant, doctor, second-in-command, and signalling officer had just finished dinner: it was civilised cooking – fresh meat and vegetables. Pictures pasted on the papered walls; beds spring-mattressed, a gramophone, easy chairs: we found it hard to reconcile these with the accounts we had read of troops waist-deep in mud, and gnawing a biscuit while shells burst all around.

The cruellest differentiation came in the treatment of shell shock. Officers were given specialist treatment in hospitals like Craiglockhart in Edinburgh, an extension of the idea that the mental health of society's elites was better (and therefore more responsive to treatment) than that of workers. 'Some of the men of course had it too,' wrote Captain Geoffrey Donaldson about the ailment. 'But I allowed none of these to go back. An officer is a different thing, because on him depends so largely the nerves of men.' The ordinary soldier who suffered a breakdown was usually accused of being a shirker and invariably disciplined. If the problem persisted, a trial for court martial might result; if found guilty, he was sometimes executed. Others were simply sent back to the front, on the assumption that the ailment could be driven from them by combat. A fortunate few received treatment.[9]

Charles Carrington complained that he 'did not want to belong to a distinct caste', but he was an enlightened exception. Most officers were keen to reinforce distinctions. Since 'good form' signified authority, officers worked diligently to look the part. At the beginning of the war, uniforms were carefully tailored, with rank badges large and conspicuous. Trench life (and the danger of snipers) necessitated greater simplicity, but where possible, standards were maintained. Graves recalled how he was sent to riding school after his first posting to the trenches – to ride well remained the mark of a gentleman and a potent symbol of authority. The introduction of tin helmets was stubbornly resisted because officers worried that they made them look too common and they also erased war's romance. Subtle distinctions became ever more important. Officers carried ornamental sticks instead of rifles; others favoured the implied status of a revolver.[10]

Before the war, the gentry frowned upon officers from the middle class. Manpower shortages during the war forced a lowering of standards; by 1917, officers from quite humble backgrounds were not uncommon. A great deal of snobbery was nevertheless expressed towards these 'temporary gentlemen'. They were temporary since real status was still connected to birth. They had jumped a class, but for reasons of expediency only – the transformation was not permanent, since class was supposed to be inflexible. The temporary gentlemen were nevertheless frequently criticised for failing to live up to their elevated station. In particular, they were accused of either being too familiar with their men or of failing to look after them properly. Thus, even if temporary gentlemen were closer in social status to their men than to the traditional officers, they were expected to make themselves a class apart.[11] They were twice cursed: held in contempt by the class to which they belonged and the class to which they aspired.

In order for a rigid class system to work harmoniously, those at the bottom must not perceive themselves as dispossessed or be unduly aroused by the iniquities of society. In other words, the workers must be not only servile, but docile. Those in the trenches were certainly that. The rising class-consciousness evident at home was not duplicated in the trenches – life was too cheap for soldiers to learn self-worth. Historians on the left have had enormous difficulty coming to terms with this image of willing cannon fodder, despite the fact that it accords with the submissive character of the British working-class and its traditional abhorrence of extremism. To those on the left, Tommy Atkins has been elevated into an icon of the working-class struggle, a man who stoically tolerated the injustices of a class society at war, while he deposited his suffering into a bank of consciousness to be drawn upon after the armistice. In truth, the account was virtually empty because few deposits were made.

While ordinary soldiers were more docile than the Tommy myth suggests, a few did rebel. An outlaw element (the Percy Topliss type) existed who resented being ordered about by officers whose authority stemmed from an accident of birth. Given the rigidly controlled army environment, it was difficult for these men to express their discontent without falling foul of the law. In the fog of combat, however, acts of retribution were sometimes possible. Unpopular officers were occasionally murdered or left to die in a shell hole when rescue might have been possible. The system nevertheless worked because this sort of rebellion was rare and deference the norm. The British Army experienced proportionately fewer problems of discipline than any other army in the war. In other words, contrary to myth, trench harmony was ensured not because class barriers broke down, but because they were maintained. An officer was respected and obeyed because he was considered superior. This was true be he subaltern or field marshal. There is, for instance, little evidence to support the assumption that senior commanders were deeply despised or that ordinary soldiers lacked confidence in their conduct of the war. One is again reminded of the dangers of using the war poets as evidence. Sassoon's 'Base Details', for instance, castigates the commander who 'speeds glum heroes up the line to death', while he sits 'guzzling and gulping in the best hotel'. The poem is an example of one man's middle-class guilt, not of widespread contempt for senior commanders. Granted, as the years passed, it became progressively easier to find old soldiers who described their commanders, and Haig in particular, as 'butchers'. That epithet is, however, a by-product of the post-1928 disillusionment with the war.

Serious criticism of the command would, admittedly, have been censored out of letters; therefore the evidence for contempt may have been destroyed. Nor can it be denied that some soldiers felt intense hatred. What is striking, however, is the countless examples of reverence expressed by soldiers towards senior officers during the war and immediately afterwards. Many examples exist of soldiers feeling extraordinarily fortunate to have caught a glimpse of Haig when his car passed while they were marching. Corporal H. Milward, given some food by Haig when they passed each other (Haig in a car, the soldier on foot), remarked:

I thought how extraordinary it was that a man with so much responsibility could find time to think of the wants of a humble soldier. To how many men in his position would the thought of my well-being have occurred?

What a contrast there must have been between us. He, handsome, well-groomed, spick and span, smart as a good soldier should be, I dirty, unwashed and wretched . . .

> I shall never forget that morning, for all question of
> rank was laid aside, and indeed he talked to me almost as
> though I had been his son.

In the army's social order, Haig was like royalty. Since a
member of the royal family was not expected to show humanity
or familiarity, the effect was all the greater when he did. So,
too, with Haig. Reverence arose from the mystery, pageantry
and pomp cultivated by senior commanders. Visual symbols
reinforced authority: the commander's dress and deportment
underlined his superiority, inspiring trust in his leadership.
Ordinary soldiers who saw Haig at all saw a handsome man
on a tall horse or in a huge car. His uniform was perfectly
appointed and his hat shielded his gaze – thus accentuating the
distance that went with authority. 'I remember being asked on
leave what the men thought of Haig,' one soldier recalled. 'You
might as well have asked the private soldier what he thinks of
God. He knows about the same amount on each.' 'He had none
of the lesser graces which make a general popular with troops,'
John Buchan admitted. Reverence was instead cultivated
through aloofness. When Haig died in 1928, the crowds lining
the streets of Edinburgh and London as the cortège passed were
nearly as large as those for a deceased monarch. Prominent in
the crowd were the soldiers who had served under him.[12]

Senior officers were under no illusion that this was a
democratic war that required them to share the suffering of
their men. Along with power went privilege. The fact that his
men slept in muddy holes was no reason for Haig to decline
a soft bed in a luxurious chateau. Along with a formidable
sense of entitlement went a gargantuan insensitivity towards
the iniquities that privilege cultivated. Grouse, salmon, fine
wines and the best brandy were sent by rich friends at home.
Nor did Haig perceive anything wrong with sending whole
lambs and butter from the army stores to his wife so that she

would not have to endure food shortages. Luxuries were the fringe benefits of high authority. In the same sense, extravagant rewards seemed perfectly justifiable after the war. Already in 1916, Haig assured his wife that 'a grateful nation will not allow me to have a smaller income than I am receiving now! So we will be well enough off to make ourselves comfortable.' There was, however, nothing extraordinary in any of this. Haig was simply acting to type. Few objections were raised about the luxuries he enjoyed during the war, or the rewards he received after it. Parsimony would have seemed peculiar.[13]

The British class system made things simple for Haig and for the officers below him. His was the most opulent existence, opulence proportionate to supreme power. Lower down the ladder, commanders enjoyed less luxurious food and more humble accommodation, but the principle – that of authority reinforced by the paraphernalia of power – remained the same. Ordinary soldiers were not supposed to understand the way battles were conducted – their duty was not to reason why but to do and die. For a commander to discuss the war with an ordinary soldier was about as logical to them as negotiating the size of a load with one's donkey. For the same reason, Haig did not feel it necessary to familiarise himself with conditions at the front – he had staff officers for that. After the war, when criticising the senior command became fashionable, it was frequently suggested that Haig should have visited front-line trenches in order to understand the real war. One former soldier replied in *The Scotsman* that the trenches were far too dangerous a place for a man so important. That was probably not an extraordinary sentiment.[14]

The soldier-poet Charles Hamilton Sorley commented in January 1915 that 'War in England only means putting all men of military age in England into a state of routinal coma, preparatory to getting them killed. You are . . . given six months to become conventional; your peace made with God, you will be sent out and killed.' The aim of military training is to destroy a man's individuality, so that he develops a herd mentality. As the highly respected commander Sir Ian Hamilton explained: 'men who are smart on parade are more alert, more readily controlled, more obedient, and move more rapidly and with less tendency to confusion and panic than troops which depend entirely on their individual qualities'.[15]

In the British Army, the group mentality was further developed through the regimental system. 'We all agreed,' wrote Graves, 'that regimental pride remained the strongest moral force that kept a battalion going as an effective fighting unit.' This might explain why the British soldier fought for four years without serious mutiny, but it does not sufficiently differentiate him from soldiers in the French, German or Russian armies, who felt similar group instincts but did mutiny. While it is impossible to provide a conclusive explanation for the British exception, there are some important differences between the various armies. British casualties, serious as they were, were significantly lower than those of any other major army that did experience mutinies. The British were also better fed and clothed, and the injured had a greater chance of survival. In a static war, these differences were enormously important. Furthermore, the continental armies were mainly conscript forces, while the British did not introduce conscription until 1916. Approximately one half of the total number of men who served during the war had originally volunteered. (In truth, many of those who reached military age after 1916 and were conscripted might have volunteered had compulsion not been introduced.) For the entire war, therefore, the proportion of volunteers, men who had essentially chosen their own fate, remained high. The most important factor contributing to the resilience of the British soldier was, however, the deference and fatalism of the working-class. Ordinary soldiers were characterised by a passive acceptance of authority: officers were officers because they deserved to be. Even when the war dragged on endlessly, the ordinary soldier, thought C. E. Montague, 'Instead of contracting a violent new sort of heat . . . simply went cold . . . a Lucifer cold as a moon prompted him listlessly not to passionate efforts of crime, but to self-regarding and indolent apathy.' The compliant character of the British soldier should be no surprise, given that the British working-class, in comparison to its European counterparts, has been the least militant, the least revolutionary and the least inclined to make political capital out of labour disputes. No wonder, then, that the experience of war failed to radicalise him.[16]

Haig gambled upon the loyalties of these men, but he did so with confidence. He had little doubt that his men could withstand the strains imposed. In the end, he was correct; while he did not fully understand the nature of British working-class loyalty, he correctly gauged its resilience. He did not fear an uprising like that which crippled the French army in 1917, nor did he worry about a Bolshevik revolution. What is ironic is that Haig, a man so aloof from his men, had a better understanding of their character than did Lloyd George, who considered himself their champion. Lloyd George feared that the slaughter of thousands of British soldiers would encourage a working-class rebellion – Bolshevism in Britain. For this reason, he desperately sought a less costly way to wage war, and also tried to bring Haig under control. He succeeded in neither aim. In contrast, Haig believed that his men could take it, and they did. His conception of the working-class as solid, simple and overwhelmingly obedient was fundamentally correct.

Occasional disturbances occurred, but they are the exceptions that prove the rule. There were 169,040 court-martials in the British Army during the war, but if one takes into account the extraordinary circumstances of war and an army obsessed with discipline, the figure does not suggest a crime rate significantly higher than would be expected in peacetime civilian society.

Court martials could arise from relatively minor offences like drunkenness. Those pertaining to mutiny, cowardice and self-inflicted wounds together account for less than 1 per cent of the total number of fighting men. The most notorious example of unrest was the Etaples 'mutiny', which, like other less famous episodes of insubordination, arose from specific grievances, not generalised discontent with the war. In this case, ill treatment by an insensitive officer, when combined with the temporary failure of food supplies to arrive (in particular jam), produced a brief expression of discontent, rather in the manner of a trade dispute. The incident was non-violent and was handled quite sensitively by senior officers. It is also significant that the Etaples incident took place behind the line; behaviour of this sort was virtually unknown in the forward trenches. While small disturbances occurred relatively often, they had no bearing upon the army's effectiveness. By their triviality, they demonstrate how cohesive, stable and smooth-functioning the army was.[17]

The German commander Erich Ludendorff is reputed (wrongly it seems) to have described the British Army as lions led by donkeys. The aphorism misses the mark. A lion is supposed to symbolise bravery, but is he really brave, or merely dominant? A donkey symbolises stupidity, but is he really stupid, or merely submissive, downtrodden and dominated? In other words, it is perhaps more appropriate to describe the British Army as donkeys led by lions. Officers and commanders were very lion-like: dominant, domineering, selfish and preoccupied with the preservation of their world. With no disrespect intended, the working-class soldier was a beast of burden, a man caged by a life of drudgery, squalor, powerlessness and social stasis. As such, he made the perfect soldier.

Part Two

Total War

Chapter 5

Business Not Quite as Usual

On Christmas Day 1914, British and German troops met in no-man's-land, played football and exchanged gifts. The Germans gave the British cigarettes which in all likelihood were British-made. This may seem odd, since belligerents are supposed to cease trading while at war. That was certainly the intention, but the evidence speaks for itself: the total weight of British tobacco exports to Holland increased from 367,680 lb in 1913 to 3,601,000 lb in 1915. Since it is impossible to believe that Dutch tobacco addiction increased tenfold in two years, it is safe to assume that the huge haul of cigarettes went to Germans.[1]

Perhaps it matters little, in the vast cataclysm of war, that harmless items like cocoa, tea, coffee and tobacco penetrated the trade embargo. Evidence, however, suggests that more essential commodities also made their way to Germany. One Great War veteran recalled seeing bags of Blue Circle cement in heavily fortified German trenches in 1916. Thus a British company helped to fortify the German line. In any case, in total war there should be no such thing as an insignificant commodity. Since total war means that every citizen becomes a combatant, it follows that every commodity is important. Unfortunately, because the British government was slow to understand the implications of total war, nefarious practices continued long after they should have been eradicated. The fault lay not with unscrupulous British businessmen (though corruption existed), but rather with the government itself: ministers were reluctant to provide centralised and coherent economic management. The nation paid dearly for the failure to prepare economically for war.

On 4 August, the Chancellor David Lloyd George, speaking to businessmen, promised that the government would 'enable the traders of this country to carry on business as usual'. This statement was in part an attempt to calm fears of unemployment, inflation and recession. It was also, however, part of a wider war strategy which had long gestation. The plan presumed that Britain's main contribution would be a naval blockade, which would eventually bring Germany to her knees. Behind this naval screen, the British economy would carry on as usual and, in fact, enjoy a trade boom from providing munitions, supplies and food to continental allies. The strategy of Business as Usual was an outgrowth of nineteenth-century liberal economics, the ideology which had made Britain powerful and produced a century of peace. Those who thought seriously about these matters took shelter in the illusion that the worldwide system of trade (what is today called globalism) could not tolerate a protracted war, which would bring economic ruin, massive unemployment and widespread starvation. They believed that wars would still arise but that economic dislocation would limit their duration. If carefully managed, a short war could still provide opportunities for economic advantage.[2]

Out of this thinking arose Business as Usual. The wish was the father of the thought: the British did not want to make a big military commitment to the war and therefore made up a strategy which made that desire feasible and logical. Britain planned, in the event of war, to do what she did best: British banks would loan money to allies to buy British goods, which would be carried in British merchant ships, protected by the

Royal Navy. According to Maurice Hankey (later Cabinet Secretary), the nation's task would be to

> continue our trade, and so to keep the economic conditions of life in this country tolerable, whilst they are becoming progressively more intolerable to the inhabitants of the enemy's country. By this means not only shall we enable ourselves to outlast the enemy, but we shall be in a position to render to our allies ... assistance of a material nature ... enabling them to sustain the burden of war while the enemy is rapidly consuming his resources.

Hankey understood that in order for Britain to maintain this role she had to avoid 'tremendous drains on our labour supply'. In other words, the country could not tolerate British workers dying in great numbers on the battlefield. The human cost would instead have to be shouldered by France and Russia.[3]

The strategy balanced precariously on dodgy assumptions. The war's impact upon the British economy would have to be minimised so that business could indeed carry on as usual. The blockade (of goods both leaving and entering Germany) would have to be sufficiently tight to cause the enemy economic and social ruin, but without annoying neutral nations, especially the United States. British manufacturers would have to capture German export markets disrupted by the blockade, especially the trade in commodities which Germany had previously dominated. As Hankey pointed out, such a scenario was possible only if Britain avoided the drain on her workforce which a large army implied. Finally, the strategy presumed that Britain's allies would be perfectly happy that their soldiers were dying in their thousands while the British grew rich by being the bank, the larder, the factory and the arsenal of the Entente. In fact, none of these conditions could be assured, which meant that Britain's strategy was quite simply a nonsense.

Behind the strategy lurked a fundamental faith in liberal economic principles, in particular the sanctity of the free market. The government assumed that businesses would make the decisions necessary to take advantage of the war and would not need much direction, management or coercion from Whitehall. Thus, free enterprise would be preserved and the government would intervene only on an ad hoc basis if it became apparent that the free market was not delivering the goods needed to win the war. No minister at this stage advocated far-reaching government intervention, which seemed not only unnecessary but dangerous.

The government nevertheless anticipated that some minor intervention might be necessary to facilitate Business as Usual: namely in the areas of food supply, transport, maritime insurance and the money market. As regards food, a large proportion of essential items like sugar and fats came from Germany and much wheat came from Russia – the latter would be threatened if the Dardanelles was closed to shipping. The war was not twenty-four hours old when *The Scotsman* reported widespread price increases and panic buying : 'A well-dressed lady was seen to leave a [Glasgow] provision warehouse wheeling a small barrow on which was a bag of flour.' 'People have lost their heads', Georgina Lee complained. 'All [are] seeking to hoard food . . . I hear of one woman who ordered £500 worth of groceries at Harrods, and another who actually bought over the counter £45 worth. Her chauffeur stood by, carrying parcels off in relays to her motor car.' The government understood that supplies of virtually all imported foods would be interrupted at least initially, with prices rising. Since the very poor could barely afford to feed themselves at the best of times, a sudden rise in prices had disastrous implications. Ministers feared that a starving population might force the government to make peace.[4]

As regards transport, the government anticipated that rail

disruption would be at its worst during the first two weeks of the war, when the system would be flooded with mobilised troops. Officials also predicted that naval action in the Channel might render east coast ports too dangerous for merchant traffic. For Business as Usual to work, seaborne trade could not be impeded. Maritime insurance companies, however, were reluctant to insure ships sailing in a war zone and crews were justifiably frightened. On 19 August, ten sailors of the cargo ship *Trevaylor* were jailed after refusing to sail in the North Sea unless they received risk compensation. Shipping rates threatened to rise to exorbitant levels, increasing the cost of British exports and making imports (like food) less affordable. The answer seemed to lie in the government taking a more active role to ensure that shipping was not disrupted.[5] Thus, against its better instincts, the government was forced to intervene.

Finally, Britain's position at the centre of the international financial market was frighteningly precarious. In 1914, German liabilities to London banks totalled about £1 million per day. If, in the event of war, repayment ceased, the effect upon the banking and finance systems would be catastrophic, causing an inevitable run on gold. An even worse situation would result if Britain declared an embargo on gold exports. Free trade in gold was essential to the international commerce upon which Business as Usual was built.

All of these problems were anticipated before 1914 and government commissions explored solutions. By the eve of war, however, no comprehensive plan for managing the economy had emerged. This lack of preparation should not come as a surprise, given the complacency described in earlier chapters. The small-war mentality encouraged the belief that the conduct of operations could be left to soldiers and sailors with little inconvenience suffered by civilians. The concept of total war was unknown and therefore unanticipated. The government saw its role as being to ease the disturbance to the domestic economy which war might cause rather than to mobilise the economy for war. There was little recognition of the need for civilian and military sectors to work in harmony.

Once war broke out, the government's efforts on the home front sought to make Business as Usual work. Of profound concern was how the working-class would react. Keir Hardie, the Independent Labour Party leader, and Ramsay MacDonald, the Labour Party leader, along with prominent trade unionists, had threatened that organised labour could stop a war in its tracks through a general strike. The threat seemed real, given the unprecedented levels of strike activity in the decade before the war. The government, while not underestimating labour's power, nevertheless felt confident that it could use the workers made redundant by war as strike-breakers. The prospect of high levels of unemployment nevertheless provoked widespread concern. Concrete plans for preserving public order were in place as early as January 1913. The Metropolitan Police, in cooperation with the War Office, drew up arrangements for protecting public buildings and utilities, food storage depots, abattoirs, flour mills and bakeries from rioters. These plans were implemented with reasonable efficiency at the end of July 1914, with armed guards mobilised on 2 August.

One of the first steps taken was to ensure a steady supply of food. A Cabinet Committee on Food Supplies was established, chaired by Reginald McKenna. Panic buying did not alarm ministers, since only the better-off had the necessary cash and transport. On 8 August, however, Parliament did pass the Unreasonable Withholding of Foodstuffs Act, which set strict punishments for anyone suspected of hoarding for the purposes of profiteering. From the 12th, McKenna's committee began purchasing large stocks of foodstuffs previously supplied by Germany, most notably sugar. A Royal Commission on Sugar Supplies was established. In addition, under the authority of the Admiralty, all British ships carrying food to enemy countries were directed to unload their cargoes in Britain, even if the commodities originated in a neutral country. Not surprisingly, this annoyed the Americans.

Significant steps were taken to avoid disruption of food transport. Control of the railways was assumed by the Railway Executive Committee, but the government, still expecting a short war and still determined to minimise economic consequences, limited its jurisdiction to one week only, with the effect that the requisition ritual had to be repeated every week for the next four years. An Admiralty committee provided daily bulletins on the safety of sea routes and the capacity of ports to handle goods. The Huth Jackson war risk insurance scheme, introduced on 3 August, addressed the concerns of shipowners by guaranteeing shipping. What is fascinating is the way pre-war objections to intervention of this nature simply melted away. McKenna, however, desperately maintained the charade that nothing very revolutionary was taking place. 'Our purpose,' he insisted, 'has been not to interfere with ordinary trade at all, but to leave the traders to conduct their own business.' In fact, the government was interfering on an unprecedented scale, but always with the purpose of creating an illusion of tranquillity amidst the chaos of war. Rather ironically, it quickly became apparent that Business as Usual implied an unusual level of government interference.[6]

Meanwhile, the government urged British traders, specifically those in markets hitherto dominated by Germans, to take advantage of the war. 'It will be long before [Germany] completely recovers from the troubles she has brought upon herself,' the economist and Liberal MP Leo Chiozza Money optimistically predicted. 'The British trader . . . who desires to take a hand in a most interesting and important game may confidently count upon several years freedom from German competition in which to prosecute fruitful experiment.' Georgina Lee was initially impressed:

Sir Edward Grey and Lewis Harcourt, the Colonial Secretary, are declaring a trade war against Germany. They have a scheme by which England is to regain the trade all over the world, that Germany has acquired during the last ten or fifteen years. The cheap wage for which a German artisan or labourer will work has enabled Germany to flood our markets with goods far cheaper than anything we can produce.

Trade fairs were organised to guide British manufacturers towards German goods that were ripe for picking. Walter Runciman, President of the Board of Trade, relaxed patent laws, thus allowing uninhibited copying of German products, including china, jewellery, clocks, glassware, haberdashery and especially toys. The Commercial Intelligence Branch of the Board of Trade reported in August 1914 that German toy exports to the United Kingdom totalled £1,147,400 in a year, with another £2,756,500 exported elsewhere. During the same year, British toy exports amounted to only £629,200. The consequences of the cessation of trade with Germany took Lee by surprise:

This theme was the cause of many lamentations [among the working-class] the first morning of the war. 'It's all very well, Mum, but I like them Germans. Where are we going to get our boots now, I want to know, we can't afford English boots – and look at my kitchen clock! I gave eighteen pence for it four years ago, and it's never cost me a farthing to keep going ... Hamley's, the fashionable toy dealers, admit that there'll be no toys for Christmas this year. They had just sold their last train and engine, German made, for 3/6, and had nothing cheaper than 25/– British made.

'There seems to be nothing attractive to the little ones,' Lee complained at Christmas 1914. 'So the great German toy invasion is one we mothers can only regret, until British manufacturers replace it.' As it turned out, opportunities which seemed promising on paper proved difficult to realise. In order to move into new areas, British manufacturers required huge amounts of investment capital, in addition to concrete assurances from the government that markets would be protected after the war. Since the government remained ideologically opposed to intervention on this scale, it was seldom able to assuage these concerns. Much to Lee's regret (and that of her young son), the toy shortage lasted the entire war.[7]

Few problems were more important than that of establishing stability in the money markets. Even before war had been declared, panic had begun to threaten the country's reserves and paralyse trade. On 29 July, a frenzied sale of securities began at stock exchanges in Europe and New York; two days later, the London Stock Exchange was forced to close. *The Times* on 30 July reported that seven brokerage firms had closed. Two more failed the following day. Lee witnessed the effects in a waiting room at Paddington: 'An elderly man sitting by me . . . told me in listless tones he had been on the Stock Exchange forty years, and had never known it close in a crisis, nor seen so many failures in a few hours.' Joint-stock bankers began calling in loans, rendering it impossible for accepting houses to finance international trade. Investors reacted predictably by demanding gold, prompting the Bank of England to raise the bank rate from 3 to 4 per cent on the 30th in an attempt to stem the drain on reserves. The rate doubled to 8 per cent on the following day. Over the three final days of July, the Bank lost £6 million, or 16 per cent of its reserves. The government faced a very real threat of being unable to finance the war – and to feed the population.[8]

On 31 July, a Cabinet Committee, chaired by Lloyd George,

was formed to deal with the crisis. Its objective was to create the financial conditions necessary to make Business as Usual work – in other words, to bring trade closer to pre-war levels. This explains Lloyd George's speech of 4 August, the first time the government actually used the words 'business as usual' to describe its policy. The Committee quickly introduced a one-month moratorium on all debts and extended the August bank holiday for three days to the 7th. Paper money in denominations of £1 and 10s., designed to relieve the pressure on gold, was issued. The notes carried a promise that they could be redeemed in gold, a promise the Bank hoped it would not have to keep.

By 7 August, some confidence had returned, but the banks were still not prepared to ease borrowing sufficiently to restore trade. Lloyd George threatened sanctions unless the banks took a more relaxed line. Bankers, however, knew that this was mere bluster, since the government's power to regulate was minimal. It instead opted to guarantee bankers against losses, through the Bank of England. This policy, along with the extension of the moratorium to 4 November, combined to revive trade. In the process, the government learned a compelling lesson: war had not changed the amorality of the financial world; patriotism and sentimentality were irrelevant in the counting houses. When one compares the government's actions towards the bankers with its willingness to use force to meet the threat of bread riots, one sees the first hint of what would become a consistent pattern.

The government failed to notice that a much more serious threat to Business as Usual came with the appointment of Lord Kitchener as Secretary of State for War on 5 August. That appointment seemed at first to make perfect sense. It was immensely popular, uniting the country behind the war while convincing doubters of the Liberal government's determination. 'We need hardly say with what profound satisfaction and relief we hear of Lord Kitchener's appointment,' commented

The Times. Asquith, perhaps sensing the difficulties ahead, nevertheless felt it was a 'hazardous experiment'. Kitchener, it should be noted, was extremely reluctant to take up the post.[9]

Kitchener was woefully unfamiliar with the economic consequences of modern war. Like a plough horse with blinkers, he forged straight ahead, oblivious to the crises piling up around him. He had waged a successful campaign in the Sudan on a tight budget and was confident that he could do the same in a massive European war. While he was prescient about the length of the conflict, his wisdom did not extend to predicting its consequences. Stated simply, Business as Usual was incompatible with a long war. The government's plans for the management of the war economy presumed a conflict lasting no more than nine months. An even more damaging blow to economic strategy came when Kitchener, on his second day in government, told Cabinet colleagues: 'We must be prepared to put armies of millions in the field, and to maintain them for several years.' He called for 500,000 men, then doubled that demand, then doubled it again. Conducting normal business would be impossible if 2,000,000 workers were withdrawn from the labour supply, nor could the export market withstand the diversion of resources which equipping such an army implied. Kitchener's appointment rendered Business as Usual dead on arrival, though the government, in a state of denial, pretended otherwise.[10]

One might question why the government tolerated such an immediate and drastic contradiction of its plans. The answer is simple: having created a Messiah, they were forced to follow him. Kitchener was, as Runciman lamented, 'the unattackable K'. In the immediate panic of August it would have been impossible to ignore the warnings of a great soldier and thus to carry on with plans for a small army and a minimal military commitment. Kitchener's prediction of a long war, Grey confessed, 'seemed to most of us unlikely, if not incredible . . . I believed the war would be over before a million new men could be trained and equipped, but that, if this expectation were wrong, the million men should of course be sent abroad to take part in the war. It was, therefore, clear that we should all agree to what Kitchener wanted.' The government was forced to play safe.[11]

Kitchener actually thought that his policy could coexist with, and enhance, Business as Usual. 'Our Army,' he explained, 'should reach its full strength at the beginning of the third year of the War, just when France is getting into rather low water and Germany is beginning to feel the pinch.' Stated differently, Britain would benefit from the exhaustion of both enemy and ally. She would put her force into the field at a time when it could dominate the contest and thus render Britain the prime shaper of the peace. In the meantime, Kitchener reminded the Commander-in-Chief of the BEF, Sir John French, that 'The numerical strength of the British Force, and its contingent reinforcement, is strictly limited, and with this consideration kept steadily in view, it will be obvious that the greatest care must be exercised towards a minimum of losses and wastage.' That advice, however, was about as relevant as a water pistol in a forest fire. France expected and was dependent upon immediate military aid from the British. In any case, in the first months of the war, the real issue facing British generals was not how to plan for the future, but how to avoid immediate annihilation.[12]

Just as Business as Usual hardly deserves to be called a strategy, the same can be said for Kitchener's policy which contradicted it. He shot from the hip, reacting impulsively to a seemingly catastrophic situation, without considering consequences. Rejecting the procedures for expansion set out in Haldane's army reforms, he instead, as his biographer Philip Magnus describes, 'with a wave of his baton ... started to conjure new "Kitchener Armies" out of the ground, formed in his image instead of that of Haldane'. 'The result', a bitter Haldane remarked, 'was the confusion which arises from a sudden departure from settled principles'. No infrastructure existed to support expansion on such a scale. The army had barracks sufficient for only 175,000 men. Munitions factories were equipped to supply a force of 100,000, not one twenty times that size. As Hankey reflected:

the government had no national plan for an expansion of the Army . . . None of the problems had been worked out or thought of at all – exemption from military service of skilled or unskilled labour, machine tools, raw materials, and national industrial mobilisation generally . . . there was no basis for programme making or for estimating future requirements and supplies, no warning was given to the armaments firms of what would be expected of them.

In other words, Kitchener's policy was as irrelevant to economic realities as Business as Usual had been to military ones. He failed to consider how such a vast army was to be housed, fed, clothed and armed, especially if those who would ordinarily supply the army were now soldiers. Among the volunteers who joined prior to January 1915 were 10,000 skilled engineers, 145,000 building trades workers and 160,000 miners – men whose skills would be wasted in the trenches. Some were sent back, but the army was not inclined to reject willing volunteers; it did not want to give the impression that its needs were less urgent than Kitchener claimed. The only way to regulate the flow of men and to minimise the damage to essential industries would have been to introduce conscription. Although the country might have accepted compulsion at this stage, the Liberal government would not. In any case, for those who liked their politics simple, the early flood of recruits seemed proof enough that conscription was unnecessary.[13]

'Today we are being urged to carry on our daily business, and return to our usual shopping, expenditure and employment of workers, in order to save the country from the risk of ruin,' wrote Lee on 17 August. 'People were so panic-stricken, at the outset of war, at the idea of losing all their income, that trade has suffered considerably.' The government's entreaties to carry on shopping had the desired effect, at least upon middle-class households like Lee's. Unfortunately, just when export trade was recovering and factories were returning to full production, Kitchener threw a spanner in the works by making huge demands upon the labour force. His New Army was like a python consuming itself: it made soldiers of the men needed to provide munitions, uniforms, fuel and food. Clearly, a mass volunteer army could not coexist with Business as Usual. Unfortunately, until at least May 1915, two incompatible strategies were forced to work in tandem. The result was anarchy.[14]

The problems with Business as Usual manifested themselves most profoundly in the shortage of labour. Kitchener's desire for a mass army depleted strategically important industries of valuable manpower. Skilled workers in these industries were often shamed into volunteering by a public ignorant of the contribution they were already making. Since Kitchener was reluctant to place restrictions upon the type of man allowed to volunteer, little was done to abate the flow of skilled men into the army. As a result, shortages of essential commodities and raw materials were evident from the first few months of the war. By December 1914, employment in mining was down by a net 11 per cent, but since those who had entered the industry since August 1914 were less productive than those who had left it, the problem was worse than the statistics suggested. The Treasury Agreement, negotiated with union leaders on 19 March 1915, was intended to alleviate the labour shortage by making it easier to introduce unskilled and semi-skilled workers into industry, but by early 1915, voluntary labour agreements were proving ineffective. More aggressive government direction seemed essential.[15]

Since the government remained wedded to liberal economics, only a fully fledged emergency would motivate it to act. That emergency came when troops at the front began to run low on ammunition. The fault lay not with industry but with government. The Boer War had revealed how Britain's armaments industry was incapable of responding to the demands of a protracted war. Yet the government, more interested in cutting the budget than in preparing for war, had refused to expand the industry. In fact, the Murray Committee of 1906–7 had decided to scale down the national ordnance factories. It was left to private armouries to respond to fluctuations in demand, a burden they could not possibly handle. When war came, armaments firms were suddenly expected to expand output of bullets and shells by a factor of fifty or more. From 25 August to 1 October, the War Office ordered as many artillery pieces as it had in the previous ten years. The demand for sandbags rose from 250,000 per month in December 1914 to 6,000,000 in May 1915. Sir Reginald Bacon of the Coventry Ordnance Works 'never ceased to marvel that Lord Kitchener tried to get my firm to supply more than we could'.[16]

The problems were exacerbated by the unexpected nature of this war. The army had anticipated a war of movement. In such a war, small-calibre mobile guns firing shrapnel shells would figure large and the need for heavy artillery would be minimal, since big guns do not move quickly. Once stalemate descended upon the Western Front, however, heavy guns became transcendent. Only high-calibre, high-explosive shells were even remotely effective against a heavily entrenched enemy. Not only did the army have very limited stocks of these shells (and the guns to fire them), munitions factories at home were ill-equipped to handle the demand. To make matters worse, the manufacture of high-explosive shells is extremely dangerous, requiring highly skilled workers, many of whom had already volunteered for the army.

On 11 February 1915, William Robertson, French's Chief of Staff, warned Haig, the First Army commander, that he would have to limit his use of shells in future actions. The shortage affected tactical planning for the battle of Neuve Chapelle, launched on 10 March, forcing Haig to implement a preliminary bombardment much shorter than he wanted. Haig subsequently insisted that with more shells he would have achieved a breakthrough. The situation worsened after the battle, when the artillery was cut to seven rounds per gun per day, from an optimum figure of at least thirty. Haig preferred a simple explanation for the shortage, blaming the workers' fondness for drink. 'The best thing, in my opinion, is to punish some of the chief offenders,' he told his friend Leo Rothschild. 'Take and shoot two or three of them, and the "Drink habit" would cease I feel sure. These sub-people don't care what the King or anyone else does – they mean to have their drink.' That letter was probably written in the evening, when Haig would customarily relax with brandy or vintage wine sent from Rothschild's superb cellars.[17]

Lloyd George seemed to agree with Haig. 'We are fighting Germans, Austrians and Drink, and so far as I can see the greatest of these deadly foes is Drink,' the Chancellor claimed on 29 March. Asquith – who liked his booze – felt that 'on the question of drink', Lloyd George had

> completely lost his head. His mind apparently oscillates from hour to hour between the two poles of absurdity: cutting off all drink from the working man, which wd. lead to something like a universal strike; and buying out . . . the whole liquor trade of the country, and replacing it by a huge State monopoly, which wd. ruin our finances and create a vast engine of possible corruption.

The tirade nevertheless seems to have proved convincing:

Britons joined enthusiastically in the demonisation of working-class drinkers who, according to popular perception, lived mainly in the north. Even the normally level-headed Georgina Lee swallowed the propaganda: 'The great trouble at present is that the workmen in the north get such high pay that they will only work two or three days out of the six and the rest of the time they drink.' Lloyd George admitted, in a candid moment, that 'The idea that slackness and drink, which some people talk so much about, are the chief causes of delays, is mostly a fudge.' He backed away from state purchase and instead pushed through piecemeal measures. 'Treating' – buying a drink for another individual – was banned, to the great annoyance of soldiers, who had been the chief beneficiaries. Opening hours of pubs and off-licences were drastically curtailed and, as we have seen, the King was persuaded to make an example by abstaining. While there is no doubt that alcohol was a problem, the shortage of shells had more to do with manpower management than with beer.[18]

The munitions problem painfully exposed the inadequacies of the government. On 20 April, Asquith, on information supplied by Kitchener, made the bizarre claim that no shortage existed. Kitchener's artifice is understandable given that he bore responsibility for munitions production. Yet there was, in truth, little he could do to evade blame for the worsening crisis. After six months on the job, he had become a liability. A massive ego prevented him from accepting that he was in over his head – managing a continental war was much more difficult than chasing Boers in South Africa. His recruiting policy, once an object of admiration, had rendered industry incapable of answering the demands of the massive army he had created. He often admitted that he knew nothing about civilian labour management, yet he still insisted on War Office control over munitions production. The Shells Committee, formed in mid October to provide advice on how to increase supply, folded in January because Kitchener was too busy to attend meetings.

Perhaps the burden he shouldered was too big for any man, in that it combined strategy, manpower and supply in a war larger than any previously encountered. Yet if that was the case, it suggests that the problem arose because he could not delegate authority. He ran the War Office like he conducted his earlier military campaigns: as an authoritarian surrounded by young sycophants whose primary purpose was to block outside interference. A government report later commented:

> There can . . . be no doubt that the principle of centralisation was pushed to an extreme point by Lord Kitchener. It proved eminently successful during the minor operations in the Soudan which he conducted with conspicuous skill. But it was unsuitable to . . . operations on so large a scale as those in which the country has recently been engaged. The result was to throw on the hands of one man an amount of work with which no individual, however capable, could hope to cope successfully.

Kitchener admitted that he found it repugnant to discuss military secrets with ministerial colleagues whom he barely knew. He preferred instead blind obedience, and, sadly, usually received it. 'The Members of the Cabinet were frankly intimidated by his presence because of his repute and his enormous influence amongst all classes of the people outside,' wrote Lloyd George. 'A word from him was decisive, and no one dared to challenge it at a Cabinet meeting.' He explained his tight-lipped attitude by claiming that he could not trust his colleagues because they repeated military secrets to their wives, with the exception of Asquith, who told them to other people's wives. Pillow talk, he felt, was endangering his army. 'If they will only divorce their wives I will tell them everything!'[19]

The munitions crisis revealed that a cooperative spirit, no matter how formidable, was not enough by itself to win a war. There was nothing wrong with Britain's commitment to the war; what was lacking was an organised approach. Business as Usual had militated against full mobilisation by encouraging an assumption that the war would not fundamentally disrupt the home front. As a result, the enormous surge of popular patriotism which followed the oubreak of war was not fully exploited. Even more seriously, a dangerous gulf developed between home front and fighting front, growing wider as the war progressed. Amidst the great fluster of activity there survived the traditional British assumption that wars were fought by soldiers who could be left alone while normal life went on undisturbed. In October 1916, Sergeant R. H. Tawney, who had already made a name for himself as a social campaigner, complained in *The Nation* about the 'dividing chasm' which separated those at home, with their 'reticence as to the obvious physical facts of the war', from those at the front – 'the people with whom I am really at home, the England that's not an island or an Empire, but a wet populous dyke stretching from Flanders to the Somme'. The chasm was to an extent unavoidable given that civilians, aside from the occasional bombing raid or shore bombardment, were not physically threatened. Nevertheless, the perceived gulf between citizen and soldier obscured the fact that, while experience was not shared, all were suffering in some way. Sassoon's bitterness might therefore be understandable, but his vitriol was still unfair:

> You smug-faced crowds with kindling eye
> Who cheer when soldier lads march by,
> Sneak home and pray you'll never know
> The hell where youth and laughter go.

Civilians might not have understood life in the trenches,

but they were fully aware of how destructive the war was. Ignorance, in any case, existed on both sides. Soldiers often derided the people at home, without appreciating the constant torment of worry.[20]

A more serious gulf existed between those for whom war meant loss and those for whom it meant profit. Returns submitted in 1916 showed that in the coal, shipbuilding, iron and engineering industries, average profits rose by 32 per cent over the pre-war level. The shipbuilding firm Cammel Laird saw its profits increase by 74 per cent. Farmers, benefiting from the scarcity of imported food, made vast profits. According to the economic historian E. M. H. Lloyd, opportunities were plentiful and lucrative: 'Anyone who could offer supplies could name his own price; and in order to get a contract, it was not always necessary even to possess the goods. An option was sufficient. The banks were quite willing to advance money on a War Office contract and thus enable the contractor to buy what he had already sold.' A complete novice in the yarn trade made £150,000 in six months, with hardly any capital outlay. 'The first interest of the taxpayer is that the supplies should be secured,' Lloyd George argued in January 1915. Thus the government turned a blind eye to profiteering as long as supplies remained dependable. In government-speak this meant that 'it may be to the public advantage to conclude contracts in the negotiations of which the prime necessity of securing expeditious and satisfactory delivery has been regarded as of more urgent importance than the actual terms of the bargain'.[21]

Profiteering was one thing, trading with the enemy another. In this area, the government failed to provide a lead. Producers were confronted with mountains of red tape but no workable guidelines for the new system of restricted trade. 'It is a curious comment on our old Free Trade system,' commented *The Times*, 'that when we come to the necessity of restrictions in trade we seem only able to improvise in this blundering manner.' Under the terms of the Trading with the Enemy Act of September 1914, it was, for instance, left to the exporter to determine whether goods shipped to a neutral country were destined for a belligerent one, a responsibility businessmen were reluctant to shoulder. Given the very high profits to be earned, it is not surprising that some occasionally failed to exercise vigilance. The Financial Secretary Edwin Montagu complained that trade with Germany, which was occurring 'on a very large scale', was 'done not so much by men who know that they are trading with the enemy but by men who take no trouble to make sure that they are not'. Nor did many traders understand that, in the entirely new circumstances of total war, every commodity was technically contraband, since every German was essentially a combatant. By failing to intervene, the government got the worst of all worlds: British profiteers grew obscenely rich supplying Germany with goods it desperately needed.[22]

Under the terms of the Treasury Agreement, profits of firms engaged in war work were supposed to be limited, but a clever accountant could easily find ways to sidestep the restriction. Generous allowances were made for depreciation, increased output, capital expenditure and reinvestment. Industrialists reduced their profits by purchasing defunct businesses or surplus machinery. In mid 1917, a government commission admitted that 'We have committed a serious mistake in making excess profits duty the cornerstone of our war taxation. This tax does not take the money out of the rich man's pocket in the same way that direct tax on his income would have done, and it has consequently failed in its moral effect on the working-classes as a symbol of sacrifice.' Since excess profits legislation applied only to war industries, there was no attempt to limit profiteering in basic commodities like food or coal. In most places, the price of household coal had risen by 20 per cent, exacerbating the workers' outrage. The General Federation of Trade Unions found in February 1915 that the price of grains had increased by between 34 and 72 per cent. This in turn caused a rise in meat prices. The poorer classes resorted to buying lower-quality food. 'Neck of mutton usually fetches from 2½d to 3d per lb; the poorest and dirtiest samples, colloquially known as scrag of mutton, are now fetching from 4½d to 6d.' Fish had become so expensive that virtually rotten samples were still commanding high prices, a state of affairs which prompted the Archbishop of Canterbury to encourage leniency regarding the Friday fast.[23]

Little was done about the problems of profiteering and trading with the enemy because they did not at first seem to affect the conduct of war. The government, however, failed to appreciate how these issues annoyed a population that was quickly developing a keen sense of justice. The word 'profiteer' attained common usage among workers as early as the spring of 1915. They could not fail to notice that their sacrifices were not being matched by those who employed them. Nor could they understand why a moratorium on profits, to match that upon strikes, could not be instituted. In this sense, the enormous outpouring of patriotism that was evident at the beginning of the war was squandered by a government reluctant to take a lead.

By the spring of 1915, the government was in serious disarray. 'Is there any sign,' Lord Milner asked Austen Chamberlain in mid May, 'that the Government have a clear idea what they want to be at, or by what definite procedure they hope to achieve victory or even to avert disastrous defeat?' The answer was no. The Dardanelles operation, Churchill's brainchild and the first of many attempts to find an easy route to victory, had settled into embarrassing stalemate. The resultant rows in Cabinet between Churchill and Fisher (who had opposed the plan, but not with sufficient energy) were rivalled only by those between Lloyd George and Kitchener, who fought bitterly over munitions. On 14 May, that problem reached a climax. *The Times*, acting on information French supplied to the military correspondent Charles à Court Repington, wrote of the Festubert operation that 'The need of an unlimited supply of high explosive was a fatal bar to our success ... It is certain that we can smash the German crust if we have the means. So the means we must have and as quickly as possible.' On the following day Fisher resigned. Asquith, worried that his government might not be able to survive the increasingly bitter attacks by the opposition and Fleet Street, sensibly chose to form an all-party coalition. There were posts for Tories and, significantly, a few for Labour. Churchill, as punishment for the Dardanelles fiasco, was demoted. The most significant change, however, came with the transfer of munitions production from Kitchener to Lloyd George, who now headed a new Ministry of Munitions.[24]

The government's action mirrored its response to every previous crisis in this war: the Ministry of Munitions was yet another ad hoc solution devised at the eleventh hour just before the meteor struck. True, Lloyd George was a dynamic believer in government intervention and, as such, the right person for the job. But the change was one of personnel, not ideology. The government still contained many powerful Liberals who would fight, ditch by ditch, any expansion of state control which might impede the freedom of the individual. In any case, the Conservatives, now partners in government, were by nature suspicious of state intervention, especially if directed towards the business community. There would be no 'Economic General Staff' equipped to mobilise the entire nation for war and to coordinate the needs of home and fighting fronts.

Worse still, the War Office, though shrunken in size, was still led by Kitchener, whose immense popularity rendered him unassailable. The episode revealed the dangers of hero worship. An ignorant public did not know what those in government knew too well. Angry crowds had burned copies of the *Daily*

Mail after the paper blamed Kitchener for the shell shortage. And then there was the problem of the Prime Minister, who paid the war less than wholehearted attention. 'Mr Asquith, do you take an interest in the war?' Lady Tree asked her friend during one of their frequent trysts in the countryside. Asquith, according to his biographer Roy Jenkins, was 'too eclectic to fill his mind with any single subject and too fastidious to pretend to an enthusiasm which he did not feel'. As long as he remained in power, muddle would masquerade as doctrine and virtue would be assigned to equivocation. 'The real criticism upon the Administration,' Walter Long told Asquith on 22 May 1915, 'is to be found in the phrase: "We want to be led; we want to be governed." In other words, it is time for an autocracy, not for constitutional government of the ordinary kind.' 'What distresses me,' wrote Georgina Lee in October 1915, 'is that the genius of our country is not such as to cope with the German in this respect. Our country is so unorganised, so hopelessly independent, that in a crisis like this, such as has never before happened in our history, one feels the lack of the mighty pull altogether which is our hope of survival.' The complaint was echoed by Mr Punch, who, in a cartoon, told Asquith: 'You'll get all the willing service you need, Sir, if you'll only organise it. Tell each one of us what is wanted of him, and he'll do it.' But, as *The Times* commented, 'the national life, if the Government would only realise it, is being thrown out of gear already to an infinitely greater extent for lack of direction than by any definite action of the State'. Britain was plagued by a government reluctant to govern.[25]

Chapter 6

Building a War Machine

When Kitchener called for an army of seventy Divisions on 7 July 1915, the Rubicon was crossed – the illusion of a limited commitment to the war was forever shattered. An army of that size meant but one thing: Britain was engaged in a long struggle of attrition that would require a significant and costly contribution on her part. Casualties would be massive, as would the disruption on the home front. While this might seem obvious in retrospect, the government at the time still refused to embrace the idea of total war, insisting instead that mobilising a large army need not imply mobilising the nation. For the rest of the war, Britain would simply improvise. Within her improvisation there were elements of Business as Usual and of Kitchener's ideas, and also, more impressively, of the sort of war Britain would fight from 1939–45. But consistency was absent. That was the legacy of the May coalition, a typically Asquithian balancing act between contradictory forces – a fudge, not a solution. Interventionists and free marketeers coexisted in a government which resembled a Pushmi-pullyu.

Wartime management adhered to the principle of the squeaky wheel. The free market was not interfered with unless production of a commodity fell below essential levels. When the government intervened, it first asked for voluntary compliance with stated goals, then gently cajoled, and only regulated as a last resort. This ad hoc approach meant that coordinated mobilisation became impossible. Wasteful practices easily slipped through the net: a factory produced fine gun-metal cigarette cases until late 1917 because the government failed to notice. Likewise, there were no restrictions (other than those of price and availability) upon the voluminous skirts women wore. Advertisers irresponsibly misled customers by claiming that the extra material would 'encourage our home industries'. More important than the waste of physical resources was the message implied: the people at home were given the impression that a half-hearted approach to the war was perfectly acceptable. In total war the mobilisation of the economy and of civilian morale needs to go hand in hand. Without comprehensive planning, it was impossible to achieve equality of sacrifice, to the further detriment of morale.[1]

Asquith has often been associated with ineffectual, laissez-faire war management; Lloyd George with dynamic intervention. In fact the difference between the two is not quite so distinct. Asquith had his successes, Lloyd George his failures. Asquith occasionally intervened, while Lloyd George was sometimes reluctant to do so. The progress from one war leader to the other was not a radical departure but a slow evolution. Failures evident under Asquith paved the way for remedies proposed by Lloyd George. The difference, at first, was mainly one of appearance. 'Whatever else he is,' J. L. Garvin, editor of *The Observer*, remarked to his son, '[Lloyd George] has the large imagination and the temperament of vigour and promptitude. We must get bigger things done, and all things done sooner.' The Welshman was certainly more dynamic, but dynamism masqueraded as method. Even though he might have believed in coordinated state control, he had colleagues who remained determined to resist state expansion.[2]

In total war, strategy is determined in large part by what the home front will bear. The size of a country's military force is strictly limited: too many soldiers means not enough workers to equip them. If the military grows disproportionately large, weaponry and supplies have to be purchased abroad. This, however, requires a huge transport burden and undue pressure on the navy. It also leads to a balance of payments deficit, which has to be financed either by borrowing or by depleting reserves. Thus it was dangerous for Britain to plan for Kitchener's seventy divisions since she lacked the infrastructure to feed and equip an army of that size. Yet this was exactly what transpired: strategic plans were devised not according to what the country could bear but rather by the generals' desire for an overwhelmingly powerful force capable of implementing a costly strategy.

By May 1915, the number one priority of British industry was to produce sufficient weapons to enable British forces to hold their own. Hopes of using the war to expand into export markets once dominated by Germany had long since faded. Henceforward, most of what British industry produced would be consumed by Britain or her allies. Responding to the needs of an ever-growing army was, however, not simply a matter of expanding output. As the army grew, the problems of equipping it grew exponentially. The original BEF of 120,000 men went to war with 334 lorries, 133 cars, 166 motorcycles, 300 guns and 63 aircraft. Such a force could easily be supplied without seriously disrupting regular industrial production. But by 1918 the BEF numbered nearly 2,500,000 men, who required 31,770 lorries, 7,694 cars, 3,532 ambulances, 14,464 motorcycles, 6,437 guns and 1,782 aircraft. Supplies were exhausted or destroyed at a prodigious rate, especially during gargantuan offensives. One mile of line required 900 miles of barbed wire, 6,000,000 sandbags, 1,000,000 cubic feet of timber, and 360,000 square feet of corrugated iron. 'A random selection of statistics,' writes the historian Denis Winter, 'shows 6,879 miles of railway specially built in France just for our army; 51,107 rubber stamps to have been issued; 137,224,141 pairs of socks to have been given out; 5,649,797 rabbit skins to have been cleaned and disposed of by the BEF; 30,009 miles of flannelette consumed in the cleaning of rifles'.[3]

The physical plant capable of supplying a massive army did not exist in 1914. New factories had to be built, supplies of raw materials had to be secured. The transport and energy industries had to be coordinated to new production priorities, while new sources of essential commodities previously imported from Germany had to be found. This expansion had to come at the expense of other industries, yet no central authority existed to prioritise demands. The war also revealed how British industry had failed to stay abreast of foreign competitors. Management was amateurish compared to America, and scientific expertise lagged far behind Germany. The free market was ill-equipped to provide the motivation for expansion and modernisation. Industrialists had to be confident that a secure market existed before they would invest, yet persistent rumours of a quick end to the war did not inspire the confidence to do so. For instance, a Wolverhampton firm complained in May 1915 that it was being asked to risk £150,000 against the slim security of a ten-week War Office contract. While still Chancellor, Lloyd George had begun to recognise the deficiencies of the free market in wartime. He tried to create a climate conducive to expansion by removing obstacles to investment, advancing necessary capital and guaranteeing firms against loss in the event of a short war.[4]

As has been discussed, the munitions crisis was exacerbated by the nature of this war. Static warfare requires much greater use of heavy artillery and high-explosive shells than mobile warfare, which in turn implied more complex production processes. The War Office responded to the munitions challenge by expanding orders with existing armaments firms, on the assumption that they would subcontract anything beyond their capacity. This approach had dangerous flaws. Control over operations dissipated as the supply train lengthened. Subcontractors did not always produce the desired quantity or quality of munitions on time. Hastily manufactured shells exploded in the barrels of hastily manufactured guns, or did not explode at all. The shell scandal was merely the most potent manifestation of a problem which, had it not been for Kitchener's secretive nature, would have surfaced much earlier. The problem was camouflaged by seemingly impressive production figures; during the first six months of the war the supply of munitions increased nineteen-fold. Unfortunately, this was still far short of requirements. In early 1915, there were enough 18-pounder guns (the workhorse of the army) to equip just 28 divisions, far short of the 70 Kitchener desired. Sufficient 4.5- and 5-inch howitzers existed for just 17 divisions and rifles for only 33. The army needed 70,000 hand grenades per day but received just 2,500. Over 26,000 machine guns were needed, but only 5,500 orders had been filled. Such was the challenge that Lloyd George faced when he formed his Ministry of Munitions.[5]

The Munitions of War Act, passed by the Commons in July, was a blank cheque: Lloyd George obtained the legal powers to do whatever was necessary to expand production. The Munitions Minister now had absolute priority over supplies of fuel, power and transport, and over the land on which new factories might be built. The de facto nationalisation of the coal and rail industries, begun before he took office, was given added impetus. In addition, he established procedures for commandeering stocks of raw materials and made vast forays into the import market, sending representatives far and wide to develop new supply sources. Lloyd George could now order factories to produce for the government and, where necessary, take them under government control. These 'controlled establishments' would eventually number in the hundreds. Four National Cartridge Factories, fifteen National Projectile Factories and an equal number of National Filling Factories were established. The largest of the latter, at Barnbow, near Leeds, was built on 400 acres of farmland which, when construction began in mid 1915, had no electricity, water, gas supply, sewage facilities or road and rail links. Yet within a year the factory was producing 6,000 shells per day. It eventually grew to 127,000 square feet, and by the end of the war 'over 36,000,000 breech loading cartridges had been charged and nearly 25,000,000 shells filled, apart from 19,250,000 shells completed with fuses and packed in boxes, making a grand total of 566,000 tons of finished ammunition'. At peak production, the factory employed 16,000 workers, 93 per cent of whom were women.[6]

The Ministry's impact had less to do with the Act's provisions than with the Minister's character. A marauder and empire-builder, Lloyd George started from the assumption that no industry could run better than one under his control. When the Ministry was torn from the War Office, the division of responsibilities was neither logical nor efficient. Unhappy with the way lines were drawn, he used the emergency and the hopes invested in him to expand his remit. First he insisted that the Royal Arsenals should come under his control, which seemed only logical. Then he annexed design, on the grounds that the War Office had been dangerously unimaginative in this area. Next he took over Kitchener's technical department and set up a Munitions Invention Department (MID) to rival a rather feeble effort at the War Office. As long as he delivered the goods, his piracy was tolerated. Kitchener grumbled, but remained at his post while it shrank beneath him.

Within one year of the Ministry's existence, its administrative staff numbered 12,000; by the end of the war it had grown to 25,000. A huge amount of energy was devoted to research and development, in order to find new solutions to this perplexing situation. For instance, at the Trench Warfare Department, boffins applied science to the unique problems of stalemate on the Western Front. Whilst fostering the development of new weapons, the department also adapted old ones, such as mortars and grenades, to new conditions. Both it and the MID were inundated with ideas from soldiers and private citizens. The preposterous (including plans for a 'death-ray' machine) grossly outnumbered the practical, but occasionally a weapon (like the Stokes mortar) was proposed which had enormous impact. Factories were encouraged to adopt modern technologies and management techniques, with the Ministry often providing the capital necessary to innovate. Plants which had resisted electrification were forced finally to embrace the twentieth century. Steel mills were likewise encouraged to install the latest Bessemer converters, which increased productivity and allowed much greater use of scrap steel and low grade iron ore than was considered possible before 1914.[7]

With the notable exception of the tank (which showed great promise by 1918 but remained unreliable), no scientific solution for breaking the trench deadlock was discovered. Science – under the patronage of the Ministry – made the British better at waging trench warfare but not good enough to escape the trenches. In fact, many of the developments to emerge were merely reactive – responses to or copies of German inventions. Such was the case with the gas mask, which had to be continually improved in order to provide protection against ever more deadly gases. Thus the Ministry enabled Britain to keep pace in a war which steadily escalated in size, complexity and ghastliness. Guns available to the BEF increased from 1,173 when Lloyd George entered the Ministry to 3,721 when he left, with a welcome improvement in the ratio of heavy to light. During that time, however, the length of the British line increased from 36 miles to 85, and the number of divisions from 14 to 42. Production expanded at a prodigious rate simply so that Britain could hold her own in this mammoth war.[8]

In June 1916, Kitchener drowned when the *Hampshire*, on which he was travelling to Russia, hit a mine off the coast of

Orkney. While the people mourned, politicians breathed a sigh of relief. Lloyd George took over at the War Ministry, and Edwin Montagu replaced him at Munitions. Lloyd George's effect upon arms production had been undeniably impressive. By the time he left in July 1916, manufacture of 18-pounder shells had increased seventeen-fold. The heavy howitzer ammunition which had previously been produced in a year now took just four days to manufacture. During the Ministry's first year, production of guns rose from 1,105 to 5,006, grenades from 68,000 to 27,000,000, machine guns from 1,486 to 17,679 and trench mortars from 312 to 4,279. While it is difficult to argue with these figures, it is essential to point out that many of the changes which facilitated this enormous expansion of output occurred before the Ministry was formed. Even the self-congratulatory official history concedes that 'by the time the Ministry was founded the principle of Government control of munitions materials was admitted, and the War Office had already introduced many of the methods which were later established as part of the ordinary machinery'. Nor was quantity the same thing as quality. The problem of dud shells was exacerbated in the rush to produce ever greater numbers. Long-term stability was sacrificed at the altar of short-term productivity. Lloyd George drove the munitions industry to the point of exhaustion; workers and machinery were strained to breaking point. Nor was his approach remotely systematic or coordinated. He reacted to perceived emergencies with appropriate alacrity, but plants which performed to his satisfaction were left alone. A seemingly efficient factory which avoided the Minister's attention operated in a very different world to one which he saw fit to control. This meant that labour relations lacked coordination, a problem that would become painfully apparent later in the war.[9]

The munitions crisis exacerbated but at the same time obscured an equally threatening problem of agricultural production. The calorific value of food produced on British farms slipped from 21.41 billion calories in 1914 to 19.39 billion in 1916. This has commonly been blamed on the fact that farmworkers were unable to resist either Kitchener's call or the high wages in munitions factories. In fact, the flight from the land was not as significant as is often assumed. When substitute workers are taken into account, farm labour supply declined by only 7 per cent from 1914 to 1916. Other factors explain the drop in production. At its peak, the army required over 400,000 horses, mules and donkeys, most of which were commandeered from British farms. In addition, the munitions industry had first call on nitrogen and phosphates, which previously went into fertilisers.[10]

In August 1916, a report by the Royal Society warned that average per capita food consumption was only 5 per cent above the nutritional minimum, thus underlining how threatening even a slight drop in supply or a problem of distribution might prove. Yet hard on the heels of the crisis in domestic production came the German resumption of unrestricted submarine warfare on 1 February 1917. It is as well to bear in mind that at the start of the war, domestic production was sufficient to feed the nation for only 125 days out of a year, with the rest bought abroad. Given this dependence upon imported food, the submarine campaign very nearly brought Britain to her knees. Her response to the submarine is, thanks to Lloyd George's capacity for self-promotion, widely misunderstood. According to the myth he encouraged, he applied the same creativity and dynamism to the U-boat problem as he did to the shell shortage, eventually convincing hidebound admirals to adopt a convoy system. In fact, Lloyd George was rather slow to recognise the urgency of the problem, much to the dismay of Maurice Hankey, the Cabinet Secretary. As late as 30 March, the latter was worried about 'the shipping outlook owing to submarines and the inability of the Adty. to deal with it and their general ineptitude . . . I have many ideas on the matter, but cannot get at Ll. George'. The following month brought disasters which could not be ignored. Enemy action sank 169 British and 204 Allied or neutral vessels – a total of 866,000 tons, or one quarter of the tonnage bound for British harbours. The effects upon the food supply were prodigious; from February to June 1917, 85,000 tons of sugar were lost, at one point reducing the nation to four days' supply. Huge stocks of meat also went to the bottom of the sea. On 30 April, Hankey noted that Lloyd George 'at last . . . has set himself to tackle the submarine question seriously, when it is almost too late'.[11]

The navy understood how to protect ships like dreadnoughts, namely by surrounding them with a cordon of destroyers to serve as a screen for torpedoes and to attack enemy submarines. Senior Admiralty officers did not, however, consider it practical to apply the same protection to merchant ships, given the scale and complexity of such an operation. Impending disaster forced them to reconsider, something they undoubtedly would have done with or without Lloyd George's intervention. On 10 May, the first convoy of 17 ships left Gibraltar. All arrived safely in Britain twelve days later. This small success presaged defeat for the U-boat campaign. Sinkings declined steadily for the rest of the year, as ever more ships were convoyed. Before the introduction of convoys, losses due to submarines averaged 10 per cent, rising to 25 per cent in April 1917. After convoys became the norm, this figure dropped to just 1 per cent. At the same time, destruction of U-boats increased steadily.[12]

A further response to the threat came with better coordination of shipping to ensure that cargo space was utilised effectively and that ships were loaded and unloaded as quickly as possible. The reforms were sometimes ridiculously simple: for instance, casting aside standard practice, the Ministry ruled that American wheat should be shipped as flour, rather than unmilled, thus reducing shipping space. These reforms could not, however, by themselves solve the food problem. Net food imports declined steadily, from 34.2 billion calories in 1914 to 31.1 in 1916 and 27.9 in 1918. This meant that the real solution to the food problem had to be found at home. Government intervention in agriculture was, however, no simple thing. This was partly due to the decentralised nature of farming, but more to the traditionally tense relationship between landowners and government. Farmers were by nature suspicious of change, especially when it came from politicians. The conservatism was reinforced by the fact that, in spite of shortages in manpower and raw materials, they were making a bundle from the war. As one farmer reflected: 'it was impossible to lose money at farming then'. Profits, which stood at £19.6 million in 1913, increased to £100.5 million in 1917. Since food shortages stopped short of causing actual starvation, the government proved reluctant to regulate agriculture. It instead resorted to incentives to encourage farmers.[13]

Underneath the surface, however, some progress was evident. Down on the farm, scarcity of labour and raw materials acted as a spur to modernisation. Pre-war agriculture was labour intensive, that of wartime increasingly mechanised. The government assumed its most active role after December 1916, when food shortages did reach a crisis point. The Corn Production Act, passed in 1917, guaranteed minimum prices for wheat and oats until at least 1922, thus reassuring farmers who were reluctant to invest in costly machinery. A wages board was established to administer a minimum wage for farm labourers, and the Board of Agriculture was empowered to see that land was properly cultivated. Substitute labour began to be made available, in the form of 84,000 soldiers, 30,000 prisoners of war, and 16,000 members of the Women's Land Army. Three million acres formerly devoted to pasture were ploughed up to provide staple crops, mainly grain and potatoes. A total of 7.5 million acres was added to cultivation by the end of the war.

This made it possible for the total output of wheat, barley, oats, rye, corn, peas, beans and potatoes to exceed 18 million tons by 1918, up from 14 million in 1914. Or, to put it differently, Britain could feed herself from her own produce an extra thirty days out of the year.[14]

The benefits of greater agricultural productivity were enhanced by changes in food processing designed to squeeze extra calories out of farm produce. Most notably, the composition of bread was altered by using a higher percentage of the raw wheat and by substituting other grains such as barley, maize and potatoes. The inspiration behind these changes came from the Food Production Department (FPD), a sub-department of the Board of Agriculture set up on 1 January 1917. The extraction rate of flour, which hovered at 70 per cent in peacetime, peaked at 91.9 per cent in April 1918. While these changes were encouraging, there were attendant costs. Bread production was more efficient, the bread itself more nutritious, but the loaves resembled a howitzer shell in weight and explosive power. At the same time, the shift from pasture to arable farming meant that the British diet was characterised by less meat and dairy products and more cereals and potatoes. Although the average calorie intake decreased by only 3 per cent from 1914 to 1918, the protein intake declined by about 6 per cent.[15]

Provision of food was a sore point throughout the war. Problems arose from distribution, more than supply. Because food followed money, the most strident complaints about rising prices and shortages came from the workers and the worst queues occurred in working-class areas. Workers were convinced that farmers, wholesalers and retailers were using the shortages to extract huge profits from them. Anger occasionally boiled over. In January 1918, for instance, troops were deployed to quell a food strike in Leytonstone. That riot was, however, the exception that proved the rule: the poor grumbled but weren't inclined to revolt. Since the problem was mainly one of bad temper rather than imminent starvation, the government was reluctant to step in to address shortages and profiteering. As in other areas, its first reaction was to appeal for voluntary restraint. The public was encouraged to cut consumption through economy drives and meatless days. Clearly affected by the government appeals, Georgina Lee remarked that she felt 'dishonest at going into the cake shops. We have no longer to think in pennies and shillings, but in ounces and pounds. Whatever I can save in terms of bread and flour . . . leaves the more for those who mainly live on these two essentials.' Great emphasis was given to symbolic gestures like the King's decision to convert the flower beds around the Queen Victoria memorial to vegetable cultivation and the dividing of some Royal Parks into allotments. The government also assumed powers to turn over unoccupied land to allotments, but its lacklustre enforcement of this power told volumes about where loyalties lay. The various government schemes were little more than propaganda designed to foster an illusion of action. The same could be said for the occasional prosecutions of merchants guilty of blatant profiteering and the regulations against wasting and hoarding food. While the Ministry of Food instituted meatless days, the registration of pickled herrings and rules concerning the size of bread rolls, civil servants like William Beveridge grew increasingly frustrated at the government's unwillingness to embrace meaningful regulation of consumption and supply. He was especially annoyed that the regulation of food was left to those who had private interests in the trade.[16]

In late 1917, the government reluctantly accepted that voluntarism would not by itself avert a food crisis. Working-class antagonism over supplies was escalating dangerously, in turn threatening industrial production. At the same time, a poor American harvest, a disappointing domestic potato and cereal crop and the depredations of submarines rendered supply precarious. These factors combined to drag the government to the threshold of rationing. Some local authorities in areas where supply problems were most severe had, in an effort to avert unrest, already introduced limited rationing. A more comprehensive scheme was adopted when Lord Rhondda took over the Ministry of Food in April 1917. Recognising that bread was the most important staple in the working-class diet, he immediately took action to ensure that supplies remained steady and prices did not escalate. Controls introduced in September in fact drove the price of a 4lb loaf down from 11½d to 9d.[17]

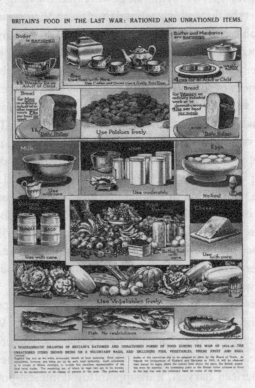

A government advice poster from 1918

By the end of 1917, the government had in place the machinery for comprehensive control of food distribution under guidelines suggested by Beveridge. Fifteen Divisional Food Committees were given powers to control prices, carry out inspections of processors and distributors and register retailers. But their main purpose was to provide the framework for rationing if and when it became necessary. By the end of the year, the first experiments in rationing had begun, with notable success. Controls continued apace in 1918. 'I am immensely pleased with the support which has been given by the public in very difficult circumstances,' Lord Rhondda told the *Observer* on 24 February 1918.

> I fully recognise the inconvenience and to some extent the
> privation to which the consumer is put; but in view of the
> conditions of war in which we are living, it is inevitable.
> And I am afraid it is no satisfaction to the man who has to
> go on a ration limited to half the meat he was getting in
> pre-war times to know that in Germany the average ration
> is less than half of what he will be getting in this country
> during the next few months.

The paper chipped in by advising readers that 'a little patience must be exercised with the butcher . . . It will take a little time to get this gigantic scheme into smooth working order.' By the end of the war, 85 per cent of all food consumed was bought and sold by firms under government control, and 94 per cent of all food was subject to price control. In the financial year ending March 1919, the Ministry had a turnover of £900 million. The rationing system was reinforced by 70,000 prosecutions and the levying of £400,000 in fines. The effects of all this activity were plainly apparent on the high street: by early March 1918, the number of people in food queues had fallen from 1,300,000 per week to 200,000. In addition, working-class diet improved, wastage was reduced and discontent alleviated. This success begs the question why controls were not introduced earlier. 'These measures should have been taken two years ago,' a disappointed Georgina Lee wrote in February 1917. Lloyd George, always keen to find a scapegoat, blamed working-class hostility. It was essential, he maintained, 'to approach [rationing] – as had previously been done with compulsory service – along the line of first exhausting the possibilities of voluntary control'. Yet just as there is no real evidence for working-class hostility to conscription, nor was there resistance to rationing. Workers undoubtedly preferred clipping coupons to standing in queues. The real reason for delay was that until the problem became an emergency, the government danced to the tune of producers, distributors and retailers, whose hostility to controls was severe and whose influence was profound.[18]

The management of manpower proved even more problematic than that of munitions and food. As the war progressed, the need for labour increased at the same time that supply decreased due to casualties on the Western Front. Blissfully ignorant or hopelessly irresponsible, the government gave its blessing to the army's unfettered expansion without recognising the need for comprehensive control. The provisions of the Treasury Agreement and the Munitions of War Act, by relaxing restrictive labour practices, created a false sense of security. Those measures, however, dealt with the management of labour rather than with the growing difficulty of actually finding workers.

As the war progressed and casualty lists lengthened, concern increased, especially at the War Office. The army secured 1,342,647 recruits by the end of January 1915, but during February volunteers numbered fewer than 22,000 per week, down from over 100,000 per week in September. The dwindling volume convinced those on the political right of the necessity for compulsion, perhaps extending to industrial conscription. Whether their enthusiasm was a genuine reaction to the crisis or a manifestation of a congenital desire to control the working-class is anyone's guess. There were certainly those who saw the war as an opportunity to erase fifty years of gains made by workers by forcing them under state control.[19]

The government, however, found itself pulled in opposite directions by two equally diehard groups: those demanding compulsion immediately and those (mainly liberals) who considered the choice of whether to die for one's country as the most important individual freedom. *The Times* warned on 6 May 1915 that 'The voluntary system has its limits and we are fast approaching them', while one Liberal countered that conscription would strangle civilisation 'in a garotte of steel'. Asquith, wary of the widening rift in his government, was determined that if conscription was to be introduced, its need had first to be demonstrated beyond a shadow of a doubt. Towards this end, a national register was introduced in September under which every British subject (male and female) between the ages of 16 and 65 was urged to make themselves known to the government. It revealed that 1,413,000 men in England and Wales (and another 150,000 in Scotland) were still theoretically available for military service, after taking into account those doing essential work at home. Those who compiled the register stressed that the figures were very rough and that the actual pool of labour was probably considerably smaller. No consideration was, for instance, given to the fact that as the army expanded so too would the labour force needed to supply it. Nevertheless, the difference between theoretical and actual manpower supply convinced many that compulsion was essential.[20]

The result was the Derby Scheme. On 5 October 1915, Lord Derby was appointed Director of Recruiting. 'Perhaps,' commented the *Manchester Guardian*, 'in the days to come when the history of the war is written, it will be said that Lord Derby saved the voluntary system.' In truth, that remark was based more on hope than logic. Derby did not share the paper's confidence, confessing that he felt like a 'receiver who was put in to wind up a bankrupt concern'. 'For my part,' he later wrote, 'though I had always been for compulsory service, I meant to do my very best to make the voluntary system a success up to the very end.' Under his scheme, men between the ages of 18 and 41 were encouraged to attest a willingness to volunteer, on the understanding that the youngest would be taken first and all single men would be taken before any married. It was widely understood that if an insufficient number of men attested, compulsion would be introduced. Speaking for the Prime Minister on 17 November 1915, the Conservative leader Andrew Bonar Law informed the Commons that the next step might be conscription. 'We do not mean compulsion if only a few refuse. What we mean is that if there is a general shirking of responsibility by single men, they will be called upon to go before those with wives and families to support.' Thus volunteering became less voluntary; men were encouraged to walk the plank in order to avoid being pushed later. Nevertheless, of the estimated 1,000,000 single men available for service, only 350,000 came forward, well short of Kitchener's demands. Though the scheme had failed, it had served its purpose by demonstrating that the well of volunteers was now essentially dry. Asquith conceded that conscription had to be introduced.[21]

The government therefore embarked on the road to conscription, but without any systematic accounting of the competing manpower needs of civilian industry, farming, the merchant marine and the Royal Navy. Kitchener blithely argued that since France (which had a smaller population than Britain) maintained an army of 108 divisions, Britain should be able to field 131. He clearly did not understand Britain's unique predicament: her naval role, her dependence upon imported food and her drastically different industrial structure. 'There has been no co-ordination of the different departments,' Robertson, the Chief of the Imperial General Staff, complained to Haig. 'I have been working up to 70 Divisions. L. George has ordered material for 100 Divisions. The Chancellor of the Exchequer did not till yesterday know either of these things.' Robertson was perturbed at the way the Chancellor, McKenna, backed by Runciman, President of the Board of Trade, had forced the Cabinet to consider the financial implications of a large army raised via conscription. McKenna argued that just 57 divisions would cost £5 million per day and cause a deficit of £2,000 million by March 1917. Runciman chipped in by arguing that the men could not be spared from industry. 'The attitude of some ministers,' Robertson subsequently complained, 'is ... to find out what is the smallest amount of money and the smallest amount of men with which we may hope, some day, to win the war, or rather not to lose it, whereas the proper attitude is to see what is the greatest number of men we can put into the field in the shortest possible period of time.' That comment merely revealed how senior military figures did not remotely understand the complexity of labour management. Nevertheless, Lloyd George, apparently agreeing with Robertson, was fully prepared to throw caution to the wind. 'We must win through even though we win in rags,' he told Austen Chamberlain. 'The notion of keeping up our trade as if there were no war is fatal. The single eye always triumphs in the end. Thus Germany fights – her trade gone and her people rationed on potatoes.' The Prime Minister failed to see that cautious management of the labour supply was still appropriate, if only to produce a more efficient fighting force. A solution might have been to introduce military and industrial conscription at the same time, thus enabling the needs of both sectors to be balanced. This was sensible, but far too revolutionary for the generation of 1914. In any case, Asquith understood that while opposition to military conscription was concentrated within Parliament and could be overcome, opposition to industrial compulsion was rooted within the trade union movement and therefore insurmountable.[22]

The Derby Scheme provided a safe bridge from voluntarist past to conscriptionist future. As such, it kept discontent to a minimum. This was recognised by the Labour leader Arthur Henderson, who remarked in a memo to the Cabinet:

> The unity of the nation is in danger. Our aim must be to handle the situation so that compulsion, if it comes, comes by the action of the people themselves. On the alternative of conscription or defeat they will be united again. But they cannot be brought to that alternative suddenly, or apart from the conviction that it is a military necessity. They must have time. And if the time is spent in a final endeavour, made after the most solemn appeal and on a full and reasoned statement of our obligations to our Allies, to meet those obligations voluntarily, I believe that one of two results will follow. Either conscription will be accepted without serious injury to the nation, or it will be proved to be unnecessary.

It is difficult to predict how the public would have reacted to the immediate introduction of conscription, without the proof provided by the failed Derby Scheme. One suspects, however, that opposition was never as powerful as some politicians feared. The group that mattered in the debate were the anti-conscriptionists, led by McKenna, Runciman and Sir John Simon, who, if they remained united, had the power to bring down the coalition. By failing, the Derby Scheme fractured that group and ensured that the Military Service Act of January 1916 passed without significant objection in the Commons. Only Simon followed his conscience to the back benches. McKenna and Runciman were mollified by Asquith's promise of a Military–Finance Committee to study the financial and manpower implications of conscription.[23]

The Act imposed conscription on single men aged 18 to

41, with exemptions for ministers of religion, the medically unfit, the Irish and conscientious objectors. In addition, men employed in work deemed essential could not be conscripted. Keeping to the decentralised approach, the government left it to local tribunals to decide which workers were essential. This led to great inconsistencies from region to region and hindered a coordinated approach to manpower. Worse still, the Act failed to provide sufficient men to satisfy the army. According to the War Office, too many single men were earning exemptions, without sufficient investigation into the possibility of finding substitute labour among married men or women. In late April, the government was forced to push through a second Military Service Act, which extended conscription to married men.

On the other side of the labour divide, conscription caused deep dismay at the Munitions Ministry and the Board of Trade, where it was felt that too many men were being taken from essential jobs. 'The matter is really most serious,' complained Montagu, the new Minister of Munitions, in August. 'I do wish the A[djutant] G[eneral]'s Department would indicate a more practical realisation of the state of affairs.' The army was oblivious to how its exorbitant demands affected the civilian workforce, so much so that the Adjutant General, Sir Nevil Macready, objected to the expansion of artillery production on the grounds that it deprived the army of potential soldiers. Senior officers shared the optimism of the new Commander-in-Chief, Sir Douglas Haig, who believed that the 1916 offensive on the Somme would break the back of the German army and quickly end the war. On that assumption, planning production for 1917 seemed pointless. Some attempts were made to balance the competing claims of the War Office, Munitions Ministry, Admiralty and Board of Trade, but despite the formation of a plethora of committees, workable solutions did not materialise.[24]

The Man-Power Distribution Board, established on 22 August 1916 and headed by Austen Chamberlain, was the first concerted effort by government to come to terms with competing labour demands. Originally designed to provide the government with objective advice about balancing manpower needs, the Board quickly fell prey to the rivalry it was intended to mitigate. The War Office and Munitions Ministry managed to pervert its aims by blocking reforms perceived as detrimental to their respective constituencies. A particularly acrimonious issue was that of badging, or the granting of exemptions to workers deemed essential. The War Office was certain that badges were granted indiscriminately, while the Munitions Ministry stubbornly resisted any attempt to review the system. In October 1916 about 1.4 million men were badged, rising to 2 million by April 1917 and to 2.3 million in October 1917. This indicates that the Munitions Ministry was actually quite successful in resisting the depredations of the conscription tribunals. A Cabinet Committee on Exemptions was formed to advise upon de-badging, but since it had no power to rescind exemptions, the Munitions Ministry freely rejected its advice.[25]

Meanwhile, food shortages and the expansion of the air war introduced new demands upon the labour supply. The Board recognised the emergency, but was incapable of suggesting workable solutions. Its last report proposed the formation of local manpower committees, but these were in truth little more than a replacement for the existing tribunals, which had already proved faulty. Reflecting its War Office bias, it also proposed the removal of all badges from men under the age of 26. An angry Montagu warned that the proposals would 'destroy Munitions output just as we are all coming to the conclusion that the war is a war of material'. The Board also failed to appreciate how its proposals would affect precarious labour relations. Threats to badging were, for instance, behind a decision by Sheffield engineers to down tools on 16 November 1916.[26]

Within the Cabinet, ministers seemed incapable of focusing on the big picture, preferring instead to promote their own departmental interests. Chamberlain was under the thumb of the army, yet to be successful he had to bring competing claims into harmony. Asquith's tendency to compartmentalise the war effort reinforced ministers' chauvinism. At times the arguments grew ridiculously petty; for instance, when the War Office accused the Munitions Ministry of poaching soldiers on furlough by offering them lucrative factory jobs. Munitions countered that the army was stealing precious workers with its sweeps upon pubs, betting offices and football grounds.

At the end of 1916, the Army Council calculated that there were still 2,500,000 men of military age in civilian life, and demanded 940,000 of them for the coming year's operations. Despite Haig's failure to break through on the Somme, the army still claimed first priority over manpower and grew increasingly annoyed with Asquith for failing to respect its prerogative. Lloyd George, having moved to the War Office and thus to the other side of the manpower debate, harried Asquith incessantly. Strange bedfellows came together to undermine the Prime Minister: Derby, Robertson and Lloyd George manipulated the manpower issue each to his own agenda.

Bowing to the pressure, Asquith agreed in principle to extend compulsory service to all men aged 60 and under. This temporarily quieted Derby and Robertson, but they seem not to have fully understood that extending compulsion did not necessarily mean more men for the army, but rather a more coordinated approach to manpower claims. Asquith, still rather lukewarm on full coordination, was probably trying to stifle criticism and play for time. A Civil Committee, headed by Lloyd George, which included Lord Robert Cecil, Austen Chamberlain, Runciman and Herbert Samuel, met to consider the possibilities for National Service, but since these men all approached the problem from very different angles, fundamental agreement proved impossible.

Before the Civil Committee could make any progress, a

political crisis toppled Asquith. Lloyd George, who had used the manpower problem to undermine the Prime Minister, was eventually able to form a new government because he had convinced a sufficient number of influential Tories that he would find a solution favourable to the army's interests. His promise to implement National Service proved just the trick for the army and its patrons. He was not, however, the man they imagined. His idea was a civilian-directed scheme designed to allow a flexible response to changing manpower demands, not a conveyor belt for transporting men into the army. Lloyd George was keenly aware that trade union support was essential to political stability and was not about to endanger that stability by introducing a scheme which alienated workers.

On the subject of manpower, Lloyd George proved hardly more dynamic than Asquith. Quickly backing away from a compulsory system, he suggested that just as military conscription had been preceded by voluntary enrolment (the Derby Scheme), 'so a similar procedure might be adopted in the present case'. This ran counter to the instincts of Neville Chamberlain, appointed to head the National Service Department. Chamberlain bravely spoke of an industrial army, working under conditions similar to the regular army, which would allow the government to direct labour where it was most needed. The idea, however, appalled the trade union movement and its new patron in the War Cabinet, Henderson. In truth, the National Service Department was little more than an illusion of action designed to quiet critics. Lloyd George asked it to conduct periodic assessments of manpower needs, but did not give Chamberlain the authority to make those studies meaningful. The army's recruiting branch was not absorbed by the Department, as logic would have dictated. Chamberlain, destined to plough the same hopeless furrow as his half-brother Austen (without even the consolation of a seat on the Cabinet), complained: 'I have never had even a scrap of paper appointing me or giving me any idea of where my duties begin and end. I don't know whether I have Ireland or Scotland as well as England. I don't know whether I have Munitions volunteers. I believe I am to have a salary but I don't know what. I suppose I can be dismissed by someone but I don't know who.' Lloyd George was reluctant to clarify Chamberlain's remit, since ambiguity allowed him to please two contradictory groups: those who demanded immediate action and those who feared such action. Thus, the War Office, Munitions, Board of Trade, Admiralty, Air Board and agricultural interests continued in fractious competition for the ever-dwindling supply of labour.[27]

The government did assume authority under the Defence of the Realm Act to forbid non-essential industries to hire men between the ages of 18 and 60, a seemingly impressive power, but then stopped short of compelling such industries to release men already working for them. For the moment, the government preferred that male workers should leave these industries voluntarily. Nor was any consideration given to moving children, women and old men from non-essential industries to essential ones. Throughout the war the government ironically had much more authority over the manpower policies of essential industries than it did over non-essential ones. This seems strange given that the non-essential industries were, by definition, not making a significant contribution to the war.

Ratcheting the pressure, the army demanded 100,000 men per month for the first four months of 1917, in order to launch a Somme-style offensive in the early summer. Senior commanders assumed the right to devise strategic plans without taking into consideration the manpower situation. The worsening food problem, however, meant that farms could no longer be depleted of men to provide new soldiers. The management of labour had come to resemble a complicated juggling act. In early 1917, for instance, Home Army soldiers were sent to the farms, in order to release agricultural labourers for the BEF. In addition, two divisions from the Home Army were sent directly to the Western Front, much to the disgust of its commander, who argued that 500,000 men were still needed to guard against invasion. The Germans, it was assumed, were prepared at any time to release an invasion force of 160,000 men, whose crossing neither the army nor, surprisingly, the Admiralty, were confident of preventing. In truth, alarmist talk of invasion had an ulterior purpose: it pressured the government to release more men from industry.

The National Service Scheme, a civilian variation of the Derby Scheme, was launched on 6 February 1917 at the Central Hall, Westminster. With suitable fanfare, the government called upon all males between 18 and 61 to enrol, regardless of whether they were already doing essential work. (Women were not to be enrolled until the scheme for men was up and running.) National Service Committees, formed by local authorities, were given the task of canvassing and publicity, with the actual direction of labour assigned to employment exchanges. Enrolled men who were not doing essential work could be moved to another job, perhaps in another area, with travel expenses paid. Wage rates were to reflect local conditions, with the minimum set at 25s. per week. 'What is less important must give way to what is more important,' Chamberlain emphasised. The scheme reveals how desperate the government was to keep alive the spirit of voluntarism, even this late in the war.[28]

The government hoped that at least 500,000 men would enrol by 31 March 1917. The actual response was hugely embarrassing, though not a surprise to Chamberlain, who was pessimistic about yet another voluntary scheme. Only 206,000 men enrolled by the target date, of whom half were already in protected trades. Eventually, 92,489 were processed by employment exchanges, but in the end only 388 men were directed into new employment. In many areas the scheme failed to materialise at all. Lloyd George subsequently confessed that he was 'disgusted' with Chamberlain, criticism that was partially justified. His repeated reference to the need for an 'industrial army' had alienated workers since it suggested that if voluntarism did not succeed, compulsion would follow hard on its heels. Lloyd George nevertheless deserves a share of criticism – his faith in voluntarism seems strange from a minister who made his reputation by promoting dynamic government intervention. It is difficult to avoid the conclusion that, like the Derby Scheme, the plan was never meant to succeed and Chamberlain was a convenient fall guy. Lloyd George's close associate Christopher Addison, scathingly critical of Chamberlain's performance, later admitted that the 'job . . . was impossible . . . He never really had a fair chance'.[29]

Chamberlain struggled on until midsummer. The scheme's huge advertising budget was a profound embarrassment, but the experience at least provided proof that the days when posters and rousing speeches could produce a flood of volunteers were long gone. On 19 July, the War Cabinet accepted a recommendation by a Parliamentary Select Committee that army recruitment be transferred to a civilian body. Lord Derby, the War Minister, agreed to the change, rather surprising from a man who was the poodle of Haig and Robertson. It is possible that he hoped to be able to shape the new scheme and thus limit its impact upon the army. If so, he was mistaken. On 8 August, Chamberlain, feeling thoroughly swindled, resigned. Three days later, Auckland Geddes took over a new Ministry of National Service, and was given much more authority than his hapless predecessor had ever enjoyed. The new ministry had nothing really to do with National Service, since Chamberlain's scheme had been abandoned, and no one intended putting a compulsory system in its place. Geddes instead assumed responsibility for army recruitment and for moving labour to vital war work – or at least for making suggestions as to where it should go. He eventually assumed power under the Defence of the Realm Act to close down non-essential industries and to direct labour from them to essential ones. (It is astonishing that it took so long for the government to assume this power.) A comprehensive list of reserve occupations was finally drawn up and Geddes eventually established a priority list for employment exchanges which weighed manpower demands against one another. By force of will he managed to establish some harmony between the various bodies competing for labour.

The rise of the National Service Ministry coincided with the decline of the army's power. Haig and Robertson, with their repeated promises of a breakthrough, had exhausted the trust of the government. The muddy disaster at Passchendaele, quickly followed by the cruel reverse at Cambrai, alienated even loyal friends like Bonar Law, Derby and Milner, who became much less supportive of demands for more soldiers. In a bitterly sarcastic statement to the Inter-Allied War Council on 12 November, Lloyd George remarked: 'We have won great victories. When I look at the appalling casualty lists I sometimes wish it had not been necessary to win so many.' The Prime Minister wanted the British henceforth to imitate the 'passive defence' conducted by the French during the latter part of 1917, which he assumed would reduce casualties. The Allies would then wait for the Americans to win the war in 1919 or perhaps 1920. What he failed to realise, however, was that the French had been able to rest their forces only because the British had constantly attacked. Misguided or not, the Prime Minister had settled upon a new strategy in dealing with the army: instead of trying to influence Haig's strategy directly, he would do so indirectly by limiting the supply of men.[30]

A new War Priorities Committee (of which Geddes was a member) was established, allowing the government at last to consider manpower needs in relation to action on the Western Front. Geddes calculated that of the 3.6 million men of military age in civilian life, only 100,000 could go to the army. To release more would result in a decline in munitions and food production or shipbuilding capacity. Around the same time, the army demanded 1,304,000 men for the coming year. The Cabinet Committee on Manpower, formed in December and advised by Geddes, decided in January that the Admiralty would have first call on manpower, followed by ship and tank construction, and only then by the army. The latter was ordered to make manpower savings by reducing the Home Army, reorganising into smaller divisions and redistributing redundant cavalry into infantry units. The latter was particularly painful to Haig, who still dreamt of horsemen galloping to victory. This full and frank assessment of manpower needs was a radical departure from previous practice. While the government was still a long way from a truly coordinated system, a comprehensive analysis had at least been undertaken. More importantly, the army tail no longer wagged the government dog.

Under the terms of the Military Service (No. 1) Act, passed on 6 February 1918, the government assumed the power to cancel certificates of exemption granted on occupational grounds, and also to streamline enlistment by removing its most aggravating delays. A Revised Schedule of Protected Occupations raised the minimum age of exemption to 23 in protected jobs, and set a series of age limits for non-protected occupations. For the moment these powers were not exercised, because of the priority given to ship, aeroplane and tank production. The new measures did, however, enable the government to respond quickly to the emergency of 21 March 1918, when the Germans broke through British lines to a depth of forty miles in some places.

Haig immediately blamed that disaster on Lloyd George, arguing that his army had been starved of troops, which was technically true. His protestations were nevertheless hollow. During 1916 and 1917 he had vehemently argued that the Germans were on their last legs. It was therefore difficult for him to sound convincing when, in 1918, he suddenly complained that his own army desperately needed reinforcement to meet a formidable German attack. Granted, Haig might have been able to foil the German offensive had he been provided with the men he demanded, but that presumes he would have used the troops wisely. Despite clear warnings that the attack would come on the 5th Army front, Haig had left that area poorly defended. Along the entire front the Germans had a six to four advantage, adequate enough for an effective British defence. But on the 5th Army sector the German advantage was five to one. Haig nevertheless claimed on 21 March that 'The enemy's attack seems to be coming exactly against the points on our front which we expected and where we are prepared to meet him.' So confident was he that the Germans would fail, he approved leave for 88,000 men on the eve of the offensive.[31]

The disaster was so profound that assessing blame seemed pointless. The army rightfully shot to the top of the manpower priority list. The Military Service (No. 2) Act, passed in April, raised the upper age limit to 50 years (55 in the case of doctors), provided closer regulation of appeals tribunals and empowered Geddes to enforce a minimum badging age of 23 years in all professions. The government backed away from conscripting ministers of religion, but did pass conscription for Ireland, a measure wisely never enforced. The Revised Schedule of Protected Occupations, passed in January but not implemented until April, released 9,000 recruits per week from munitions work. Since casualties from 21 March to 9 June averaged over 31,500 per week, however, these measures fell far short of alleviating the crisis.[32]

Despite the emergency, old manpower rivalries remained acute. Organised labour, especially engineers, reacted badly to the new measures, as did the Munitions Ministry. The Admiralty baulked at suggestions that more marines should be released for service in France, despite the fact that by no stretch of the imagination were they being profitably utilised. Geddes unfortunately lacked the authority to adjudicate between competing demands; the best he could do was to exhort colleagues to cooperate. Some significant sacrifices were nevertheless made, as evidenced by a 50 per cent fall in aeroplane and tank production in July.

Starting in April, 100,000 American troops per month began arriving at the front. When the German offensive petered out at the beginning of the summer, the government quickly decided to return priority to munitions, ship and aeroplane production. There matters remained until the end of the war. Haig was particularly perturbed at the government's refusal to increase the troops available to him, despite the stunning success of his offensive in early August. The government, however, no longer believed him, and was planning for 1919. The sudden victory of Allied forces in November rendered those plans irrelevant. Had victory not intervened, 1919 would have been a very lean year for the British. The size of the army would have been drastically reduced and, due to the fall in production during the spring 1918 offensive, a new munitions crisis would undoubtedly have developed.

In the absence of consolidated direction of labour, the government had limped from crisis to crisis. Mistaken assumptions about the public's tolerance for compulsion caused excessive caution, but in the main, government action was determined by an obsessive desire to preserve the liberal status quo. Ministers found it difficult to come to terms with total war. At no time did they exercise effective control over the civilian labour force, preferring voluntary appeals and benign exhortations to real management. Whilst the government occasionally invoked the rhetoric of an industrial army, it fled in fear from the actuality. No concerted attempt was made until the last year of the war to coordinate manpower needs, which meant that interdepartmental rivalries plagued those assigned the poisoned chalice of manpower management. During the Second World War, similar manpower problems were avoided by the creation of the Ministry of Labour under the all-powerful Ernest Bevin. Lloyd George did establish such a ministry, but mainly as a political gesture designed to win Labour Party support. It never even remotely enjoyed the power assigned to Bevin and was torn asunder by rivalries with other ministries and departments, especially the Ministry of National Service. There was no justifiable reason for two separate ministries to deal with manpower. 'You are not adding to the efficiency of your organisation of the state,' the former Labour leader Ramsay MacDonald warned Lloyd George. 'You are simply presenting new points of friction, misunderstanding and trouble.' In the end, Britain muddled through, somehow finding enough men to achieve victory.[33]

Wars cost money as well as lives. Given the emergency, financial questions seem unimportant during a war, but become crucial after it, when future generations bear the burden. As in other areas of government, measures for financing the British effort were shaped by the prevalent desire to limit the war's impact. Early on, the volunteer spirit prevailed: citizens exhibited an extraordinary willingness to donate money. In addition, investments in War Savings Certificates and war bonds continued with impressive constancy throughout the war, perhaps because patriotism of this sort was rewarded with compound interest. From October 1917 to September 1918 war bonds were still bringing in £1,000 million. Sale of war bonds was periodically encouraged through special appeals like Tank Week, War Weapons Week and a Feed the Guns Campaign. During the latter, a replica French village was constructed in Trafalgar Square, and £29 million in bonds was sold in just eight days. Many workers, particularly those who worked overtime in munitions factories, accumulated considerable savings for the first time in their lives by the purchase of bonds.[34]

Because manpower and production policies were chaotic, so too was budgetary policy. Ministers wielded taxes like a sledgehammer. Sudden and drastic increases caused considerable antagonism among a population already wearied by war and struggling to make ends meet. Three War Budgets raised income tax by nearly 150 per cent during the first year of the war. By late 1918, the standard rate stood at 6s., an eight-fold increase since August 1914. The tax threshold was also lowered, which, combined with the fact that incomes rose, meant that an extra six million people paid income tax. Aside from the need to raise revenue, lowering the threshold had the broad aim of widening political responsibility, a sentiment actually shared by organised labour. Herbert Smith of the Miners' Federation thought it would result in 'more active workers' who would 'know the[ir] position better'. By the end of the war the Treasury was collecting about £8 million from wage earners, or about 4 per cent of total tax revenue. At the same time, however, taxation exacerbated existing class antagonisms since the workers, convinced that they lived in an unfair world, believed that tax was yet another instrument of oppression. No wonder, then, that the refusal to pay tax became a new method of working-class protest. Most workers nevertheless agreed with the views expressed by a Scottish miner who, though objecting to the injustice of income tax, was prepared to pay it 'when the very existence of the country is at stake'. What few workers realised was that even though the poorer classes paid tax for the first time, taxation became more progressive during the war. Nor was it widely known that the supposedly ineffectual excess profits duties raised £200–300 million per year, a quarter of wartime revenue.[35]

The average worker paid a great deal more in indirect than direct taxes, but was less aware of doing so. That was the beauty of this form of taxation; the steelmaker Sir Hugh Bell argued that 'a tax on commodities is levied without the contributors being aware of its existence and so is levied without much grumbling ... it is possible in this way to get something towards the maintenance of the state out of the poor and indeed the poorest classes'. During the war, duties, imposts and licences were introduced or increased on beer, spirits, tobacco, matches, admission tickets, sugar, cocoa, coffee, automobiles, motorcycles and cheques. These taxes occasionally affected sales, much to the dismay of producers. Brewers, for instance, complained that beer taxes reduced consumption by up to 40 per cent, but there are too many factors involved to verify this claim. Taxes did produce a surge in home brewing. 'Don't stop smoking because tax on tobacco has increased,' a rather desperate message from Murray's Mellow Mixture read. 'It is your duty to the State to keep on smoking. The Chancellor increased the duty on tobacco to give smokers an opportunity of contributing towards the successful issue of the war.'[36]

When it came to budgetary policy, the need for victory outweighed fiscal prudence. By 1917, the war was costing £7 million per day. In 1918, costs exceeded £2,500 million, with tax revenues only £900 million. In addition, from mid 1916 Britain was financing French purchases abroad, while at the same time supporting the franc against the dollar. Financial support for Allies by April 1917 totalled £950 million, around £400 million of it disappearing down the Russian sinkhole. Britain's steadily increasing deficit was paid for by borrowing abroad, through war bonds or through the sale of overseas assets. The war resulted in the loss of 25 per cent of Britain's real wealth, most of it to the United States. Forty per cent of all British purchases relating to the war were made in North America. Taking into account all these debts, at war's end Britain owed the US about £1,000 million.[37]

It is easy to be critical of the government's management of the war. The reluctance to intervene resulted in great chaos, many avoidable emergencies and considerable injustice. But no master plan or great body of experience existed to guide politicians, who were pioneers in the realm of total war. If the British record in the Second World War seems more impressive, it is because later generations drew upon the experiences of 1914–18. Nevertheless, one cannot ignore the sometimes obsessive adherence to outdated values. Change was imposed with great reluctance. Because of the decentralised nature of government, departments competed and did not benefit from one another's experiences. Inconsistencies abounded. Voluntarism, for instance, remained sacred in some areas as late as 1918, while its utility elsewhere did not survive past 1915. Asquith was inclined to wait until the last minute before exercising government power, but so too did Lloyd George. The expansion of the state during the war resembled not a deluge (as some have argued) but a slow mountain stream which trickled past boulders of intransigence, its progress slowed by whirlpools of tradition.

Chapter 7

Shoulders to the Wheel

Historians too often allow what they wish had happened to affect their analysis of what did happen. Take, for instance, James Hinton, a man helpless to the romance of revolution. 'During the last weeks of January 1918,' he writes, 'it was touch and go whether or not the munitions workers would erupt into political strike, demanding immediate peace negotiations on the Bolshevik terms of no annexations, no indemnities.' And pigs might have flown. Granted, the workers made significant gains during the war: both the trade unions and the Labour Party were stronger in 1918 than they had been in 1914. But these gains were invariably used for pragmatic purposes. The workers wanted better pay and conditions, more secure jobs and steady rents. The unions and the Labour Party wanted a larger part within the political system, not the destruction of that system. Far from bringing Britain close to revolution, the Great War merely confirmed the unrevolutionary character of the British worker.[1]

The war's emergency profoundly altered the workers' relationship with employers and the government. Three factors worked in their favour: firstly, the war rendered certain key industries essential to the nation's survival. Secondly, manpower shortages made industrial harmony essential. Thirdly, workers were given the opportunity to demonstrate their patriotism and dependability, two attributes unappreciated before the war. Occasionally shabby treatment by bosses did not divert the workers from the necessity of winning the war. It was precisely because the workers did not attempt to stray down revolutionary paths that they made modest gains.

Early in the war, workers who did not volunteer still exhibited an impressive willingness to come to the aid of their country. Shortly after the declaration, the Trades Union Congress (TUC) announced an industrial truce, technically forgoing the right to strike. Thus, organised labour immediately surrendered its most effective weapon – the strike – without extracting anything significant in return. The effects of cooperation were immediately evident. At the beginning of August 1914, around 100 strikes were in progress, by month's end just 20. During the second quarter of 1914, 250,000 workers were on strike and 5,000,000 working days were lost. The fourth quarter of 1914 saw just 21,000 strikers and 160,000 days lost. Granted, the first few months of the war were exceptionally harmonious; unions even acted as unofficial recruiting agencies. Yet even in 1918, the worst year for industrial action, the number of days lost was 5.9 million, which compares favourably with 9.8 million in 1914, the same in 1913, and 40.9 million in 1912. During the war, the vast majority of strikes arose over pay and working conditions and were settled relatively quickly. Over 8,000 awards by arbitration tribunals were accepted without further protest.[2]

At the outbreak of war, many doubted the workers' loyalty. This was justified, since the previous four years had witnessed considerable industrial turmoil. Those strikes, however, tended to obscure an important fact: the trade union movement, despite containing left-wing elements, was predominantly reformist and pragmatic, not revolutionary. During the war, the most sensible course was to support the national effort. This eagerness to help was manifested in the willingness of trade unionists to surrender many of the hard-won rights secured during fifty years of confrontation with employers. For instance, in November 1914, the Crayford Agreement between the Engineering Employers' Federation (EEF) and the Amalgamated Society of Engineers (ASE) established that women could be employed as substitutes for men on machine work previously performed by unskilled or semi-skilled men, as long as the machine was serviced by a skilled mechanic.

The Shells and Fuses Agreement, signed in early March 1915 between the engineering unions and the EEF, confirmed this cooperative spirit. The unions accepted dilution, paving the way for skilled work to be performed by unskilled or semi-skilled labour. All they received in return were vague promises that the remaining skilled workers would not be materially affected; that semi-skilled and unskilled labour would be the first to be released when the war ended; that the unions would be consulted in the implementation of dilution; and that pre-war practices would be restored when peace came.

Dilution was contentious because it undermined the skill differentials upon which the worker's security was based. These prevented an employer from hiring less skilled workers prepared to accept lower wages. The social scientist and Labour activist Sidney Webb described how

the rules set forth what machines should be used for what particular jobs; how the machines should be placed in relation to each other, and the speed at which they should be worked; whether an operative should complete a whole job, or attend only to one machine, or form part of a team of specialised operatives each doing a different process; what wages, if any, should be paid in the intervals between jobs, or whilst waiting for material.

The rules were not always logical, since their purpose was to protect the worker, not to make production more efficient. The war provided employers with the perfect excuse to cast aside these barriers and introduce modern production processes. The dilutees were often women – doubly dangerous because they accepted lower wages and were not generally unionised. Male dilutees, however, aroused much more anger because they constituted a permanent threat to craft privilege, whereas women were considered an aberration that would not survive the war.[3]

The unions surrendered a great deal, but did so willingly. Theoretically, they were the dominant party in the negotiations. If ever a time existed when they held the highest cards, it was surely in early 1915, when labour was scarce and the BEF hungered for ammunition. Yet the workers (or at least their representatives) were reluctant to take advantage of that predicament. Responsible patriots that they were, they agreed to help their country, confident that their sacrifices would be rewarded at war's end. Granted, some shop floor workers judged the Treasury Agreement a sham, but most shared their leaders' sense of trust. The agreement was an outward manifestation of a deeply embedded truth: namely that among workers, loyalty to nation was always stronger than loyalty to class.

Behind the willingness of trade union leaders to cooperate lay an assumption that the war would be short. Sacrifices, it was thought, would be tolerable because they would be temporary, and because enormous rewards would follow. As the war dragged on, however, workers endured the costs of cooperation: the erosion of their status and the surrender of their only weapon, the strike. Wage negotiations that had been due to take place in August 1914 were postponed in the interest of industrial harmony. This meant that by the beginning of 1915, workers were paying dearly for their patriotism. Food prices were 20 per cent higher and general consumer prices 10 to 15 per cent higher than six months before. A wage rise was warranted, yet difficult to secure because the industrial truce prevented meaningful protest and employers were not inclined to be compassionate.[4]

The situation was most volatile in Glasgow, where a concentration of war-related industries rendered the area extraordinarily important to the war effort. A tradition of militancy ensured that Glaswegians were least likely to accept dilution with aplomb. In addition, the expansion of the munitions and shipbuilding industries had led to a massive migration of workers into the Clyde area, aggravating an already overstretched housing supply. The shortage of lodging led to overcrowding and meant that workers were forced into houses that were technically uninhabitable. Population density on the Clyde was the highest in Britain. Exploitative landlords, operating in a seller's market, imposed crushing rent increases. Responding to the crisis, the newly formed Glasgow Labour Party Housing Committee began in February 1915 to organise disgruntled tenants.[5]

The first unrest on the Clyde (and the first serious strike of the war) occurred in February 1915, when 5,000 engineers at Weir's of Cathcart downed tools because American workers had been brought in at higher rates of pay. The strike was only partially successful, but more important than its resolution was the fact that shop stewards, without the support of union leaders, were the initiators. The shop stewards' power was derived from the alienation of rank-and-file workers from official union leaders, combined with the recent involvement of shop stewards in crucial issues like the implementation of dilution. The movement has too often been judged by the conduct of those on the Clyde who used their new influence for political ends. Yet the vast majority of shop stewards were moderate, unrevolutionary individuals who provided valuable leadership during an unsettling and precarious time, thus easing the transformation to new industrial practices.

After the return to work, militant shop stewards formed the Clyde Workers' Committee (CWC). Alienation from the official unions became the CWC's rallying cry. 'We will support the officials just so long as they rightly represent the workers, but we will act independently immediately they misrepresent them,' a pamphlet pledged. 'We . . . represent the true feelings of the workers'. Behind the militant bravado there lurked an illusion – or perhaps delusion. The CWC was a classic example of militant desperadoes out of touch with the rank and file. The workers did not agree that the war was a capitalist intrigue; nor did they sympathise with CWC aims to 'maintain the class struggle until the overthrow of the wages system, the freedom of the workers, and the establishment of industrial democracy have been obtained'. Yet for the moment, a marriage of convenience prevailed: socialists obsessed with the class war joined forces with union members desiring job security and a decent wage. The government's big mistake was to assume that leaders and followers espoused the same agenda.[6]

Hard on the heels of the Clydeside unrest came a further concession by trade unions, namely the Treasury Agreement of 17–19 March 1915. Lloyd George was struck by the symbolism of 'those stalwart artisans . . . on equal terms negotiating conditions with the Government'. In truth, however, the agreement was hardly a radical departure in labour relations, given that the important sacrifices were made by the workers, not their employers. The unions agreed to suspend restrictive practices, reconfirmed the agreement not to strike, and agreed to compulsory arbitration in wage disputes. In return, the government vowed to confine dilution to war work, emphasised that pre-war practices would be restored when peace came, and promised to address excess profits. It was a bad bargain, but that was beside the point. More important than the details of the agreement was the fact that the government was negotiating directly with workers' representatives, leaving employers out of the equation. In other words, the latent power of the workers had been recognised.

The Treasury Agreement was essentially a treaty between unions and the government. It was not law but rather an endeavour on both sides to behave. Continuing unrest on the Clyde, which the government lacked the legal muscle to control, exposed the weaknesses of that accord. The passage of the Munitions of War Act in July addressed this problem by replacing flimsy agreements with the cold logic of law. While historians on the left contend that the Act was a declaration of war against the shop stewards' movement, this seems overblown. The government was worried about the problem of shop-floor militancy but in the main was more concerned about the manpower shortage. Rather than being cynical, the government was simply frightened.

For workers, the Act's most iniquitous provision was the hated 'leaving certificate', which required a worker to obtain permission from his employer before moving to another job. David Kirkwood, a CWC activist, argued with some justification that it had 'the taint of slavery about it'. Failure to comply meant the worker had to wait at least six weeks before taking up a new job, something few could afford. He might appeal to a Munitions Tribunal, but since better pay or conditions were not considered acceptable grounds for changing jobs, appeals were seldom likely to succeed. This meant that yet another power, the ability to barter their labour in a free market, had been surrendered without any significant protest by the official unions.[7]

Much had been surrendered, but the workers still possessed the power of their numbers. If thousands of strikers decided to ignore compulsory arbitration, the government was powerless – it could not arrest, prosecute and imprison them since it was desperately addicted to what they supplied. This was demonstrated on 15 July 1915 when 200,000 South Wales miners downed tools in protest over a national pay settlement. Since the miners' union had not signed the Treasury Agreement, it did not feel bound by its terms. Lloyd George confronted the miners head-on by declaring the South Wales coalfield a controlled establishment, but the government's legal adviser warned against a heavy-handed approach: 'It is of course impossible to summon and try 200,000 men, and only a few can at first be dealt with and the length of time before there can be any real enforcement of the sentence will, I fear, only lead the men generally to regard the Act as ineffective.' Meanwhile, Robert Smillie, the miners' leader, threatened a nationwide strike if his workers were arrested. Recognising a lost cause, Lloyd George promptly conceded the strikers' main demands.[8]

The official historian of wartime labour administration remarked that the South Wales strike 'demonstrated that if a sufficiently large body of men were determined to break the law, they could do so with impunity, as long as public opinion was not strongly against them'. The statement reveals two important limiting factors that acted in the government's favour. Firstly, a strike had to be sufficiently large to prevent effective action against it; secondly, it had to be popular in the wider community. If a strike was small or if it lacked local support, the government could afford to be aggressive. Fortunately for the government, most strikes were unpopular because they violated the people's moral code. Had this not been the case, there is no way that a ban on industrial action could have been remotely successful. Nevertheless, the South Wales strike demonstrated that workers could be pushed only so far. A government inquiry concluded that 'the men were driven to strike by the belief ... that the owners were "exploiting" the patriotism of the miners, believing it would inevitably prevent them from pressing home their claims by actually striking'.[9]

South Wales set a pattern for the settlement of wage disputes in key industries: the government realised that confrontation was usually counterproductive. Ministers nevertheless grew worried when wage claims seemed part of a wider political agenda, as was the case in Glasgow where shop-floor agitation was combined with discontent over high rents. By November 1915, around 20,000 tenants on the Clyde were participating in a rent strike, mostly in those areas housing shipyard workers. When eighteen of them were served summons for non-payment of rent, five shipyards went on strike. Since the strike was both popular and massive, there was little Lloyd George could do to combat it. He instead promptly pushed through a Rent Restrictions Bill, an important victory for people's politics in Glasgow, even though it did not completely solve the rent problem.

Clydeside engineers didn't overtly support the rent strike, since their beef with the government was over dilution. This subtlety escaped the notice of the government, which insisted on seeing a single militant monster rising on the Clyde. CWC activists took advantage of this confusion by describing their struggle against dilution in Marxist terms more suited to the rent strike. As a result, when Clydeside engineers grew increasingly militant, the government overreacted to what it perceived as a burgeoning workers' revolution. On Christmas Day, Lloyd George rushed to Glasgow, where he was shouted down by three thousand angry shop stewards in no mood for patriotic platitudes. The Independent Labour Party (ILP) journal *Forward* quipped: 'Last Tuesday Mr Lloyd George, the best paid munitions worker in Britain, came to Glasgow in search of adventure. He got it.' A man of smaller ego would have been suitably chastened, but he could not resist lashing out. In punishment for its temerity, *Forward* was suppressed, action that did little to cool tempers on the Clyde. 'D. says the men up there are ripe for revolution,' Frances Stevenson, his secretary and mistress, recorded. '[He] is convinced there is German money up there.'[10]

The CWC demanded what it called co-determination – joint consultation between employers and workers on all production matters, including dilution. This was essentially industrial unionism, under which workers would control the factories. The government was prepared to concede some control over the implementation of dilution, but stopped well short of shop stewards' demands. On this issue, the bulk of Clyde workers were closer to the government than to their representatives. Just as they had, in early 1915, felt misunderstood by their official unions, alienation that had inspired the formation of the CWC, so they now felt misunderstood by the CWC, whose political agenda failed to inspire.

After his initially febrile reaction to the engineers' dispute, Lloyd George came to his senses. The government's handling of the dispute from January to March 1916 was patient and clever. Once it realised that the CWC was merely a militant faction, it concentrated on reassuring skilled workers that their jobs were secure and that their power would be restored after the war. That was the carrot. The stick came in the form of a threat to conscript militants and tough action against CWC leaders. Literature was suppressed and agitators were charged with sedition and imprisoned or deported to Edinburgh – cruel punishment for a Glaswegian. The combination of carrot and stick isolated the CWC; it could not mobilise sufficient support to protest this treatment. The big difference between the Welsh dispute and the Scottish one was that the Welsh strikers were miners, salt of the earth, while the Glasgow militants were elite engineers for whom the rest of the working-class had little sympathy. Socialist romantics have made the CWC rebels into martyrs, but they do not wear that cloak well. This was not a case of workers cruelly crushed, but of a rank and file wisely rejecting misguided leaders who did not have their best interests in mind.

The Military Service Act of March 1916 spawned new tensions. The workers feared that the next step would be full industrial conscription. The CWC argued that the Act had been dictated not by military necessity, but rather by a desire to crush the unions. Activists anticipated that conscription would soon be used to curb strike activity. A more immediate threat was sensed by those men of military age who had so far resisted pressure to volunteer but had salved their consciences by performing work of national importance. Huge losses on the Somme from July to November 1916, together with improved munitions production (a result of greater efficiency and the flood of female labour), made it increasingly difficult for skilled workers to prove their indispensability. A war of attrition ensued between the government and the unions over the granting of exemptions.[11]

In 1917, industrial relations worsened, with 5.5 million days lost to strikes. The introduction of a new bill extending dilution to private factories, followed by the decision to abolish trade cards (which allowed unions to protect a proscribed number of members from conscription), prompted the ASE to order a strike in May. An anonymous poet responded rather appropriately:

> Don't take me in the Army, George,
> I'm in the ASE.
> Take all the bloody labourers,
> But for God's sake don't take me.
> You want me for a soldier?
> Well that can never be –
> A man of my ability,
> And in the ASE!

The ASE's stubborn elitism ensured that its action did not gain wide support. As the *Trade Union Worker*, journal of the Workers' Union, commented:

These people don't care how long the war goes on. They don't care who has got to go in the Army. They have no conscientious objection to manufacturing munitions of war for someone else to use. They are determined to push anyone into the Army; all may go, but not them. Nothing has been more discreditable to the labour movement than the attitude of this section of the alleged skilled men.

Conscription made a mockery of trade union solidarity, since every worker wanted his comrade to be called before him. When the government launched a comb-out of the pits in 1917, old-timers were quite ready to sacrifice new miners who had entered since 1914, because they were not 'bona fide'.[12]

Despite worsening industrial relations, the patriotism of the workers and their devotion to the war effort remained firm. Strikes increased in 1917 and 1918 not because the workers had become more militant but because their burdens – rents, food supply and escalating prices – had grown more acute. The cost of living was rising by about 27 per cent per year, without pay keeping pace. The issue became even more contentious because increasing numbers of workers were forced to pay income tax. They were convinced, with justification, that some citizens were growing very rich at their expense. Indeed, Lord Devonport, the ineffectual Food Controller, admitted to Lloyd George that 'profiteering is rife in every commodity – bread, meat, tea, butter, and the masses are being exploited right and left'.[13]

While discontent was rising, there were few overtly political strikes. The Ministry of Labour concluded that action in April and May 1917 had

> not arisen out of any desire to stop the war . . . On the one hand [the men] were reluctant to hold up the war to the detriment of their relatives in the trenches. On the other hand, it seemed important to them, in their own interests, to keep their trade privileges intact. One has an impression, in short, of unrest paralysed by patriotism – or, it may be, of patriotism paralysed by unrest.

At the Leeds Conference in early June 1917, the ILP and the British Socialist Party welcomed the Russian revolution and called for the formation of workers' and soldiers' councils in Britain. The reaction of rank-and-file workers, on the other hand, was decidedly lukewarm. In fact, pro-war militancy by workers caused arguably more problems for the government than did political agitation against the war. Working-class areas were prone to violent outbursts of anti-German feeling, physical harassment of pacifists and support for right-wing groups like the British Workers League. At one bullet factory in 1917, fifty workers downed tools when a conscientious objector was promoted to foreman. 'The man was dismissed and the matter settled,' a subsequent report concluded.[14]

In November 1917, 500,000 days were lost due to strikes, but only half that in December and January. The government noticed that whilst opposition to its new manpower proposals 'was in the first instance extreme, it is now reported that the Clyde Workers Committee have resolved not to strike in protest'. One might ask what had caused this quiescence. In truth, not much. A rudimentary rationing system, tax concessions for married men and a 12.5 per cent pay rise for munitions workers was enough to bring peace to factories, despite the introduction of the unpopular Manpower Bill. This suggests that during the worst months of 1917 the workers were perhaps annoyed and certainly exhausted, but they were not in the mood for revolution nor peace at any price. A government report accurately described their mood after three and a half years of war as 'loyal and temperamentally conservative'. This was apparent at the Labour Party Conference in January, where pacifists, revolutionaries and ILP members were pushed to the margin while the party raced headlong in the direction of mainstream respectability. Echoing a common sentiment, Beatrice Webb ridiculed Clydeside militants as 'rebels holding fast to the illusion of revolution'.[15]

The alarmingly successful German spring offensive of 1918 inspired a renewed commitment to the war and a temporary renunciation of industrial action. Only 15,000 days were lost in April. In other words, when it briefly appeared that the war might actually be lost, patriotism again surged and self-interest was set aside. Even miners and engineers, who had vehemently resisted comb-outs, were unusually cooperative in helping the government find extra recruits. Among those not called up, there was a corresponding determination to work harder. 'The response to the appeal to munitions workers to work over the Easter holiday was excellent, and indeed almost embarrassing,' remarked the Minister of Munitions. This peace lasted approximately four months, ending about the same time the German offensive stalled.[16]

During the final months of war, two new phenomena were apparent. The prospect of victory inspired a new and somewhat rabid surge of patriotism. Trade unions sent letters of congratulation to Haig and other commanders. This enthusiasm fuelled vociferous demands for a punitive peace. Coalition promises to 'Hang the Kaiser' were partly inspired by a desire to capitalise on the populist mood. The other noticeable phenomenon was organised labour's tendency to prepare for peace by seeking to consolidate power gained during the war. Both the mine and railway unions pressed for radical reorganisation of their industries, leading to nationalisation or at least a national wage system. These two phenomena encapsulate the predominant sentiments of workers throughout the war: steadfast (often jingoistic) support for the war existed alongside a desire to use the opportunities it presented to enhance labour's position within British politics.

War profoundly changed the relationship between government and the workers. Prior to 1914, the government legislated on labour issues and occasionally arbitrated disputes, but it was not, except in rare circumstances, an employer. During the war, this changed radically. The creation of the Ministry of Munitions resulted in the government owning, by March 1918, over 250 factories, mines and quarries, while it exercised authority over a further 20,000 controlled establishments. As one Labour Party activist commented in 1915, the government's definition of munitions was a wide one: 'Tents are munitions; boots are munitions; biscuits and jam are munitions; sacks and ropes are munitions; drugs and bandages are munitions; socks and shirts and uniforms are munitions; all the miscellaneous lists of contracts which fill up three or four pages of the Board of Trade Gazette, all, all are munitions.' This meant that by July 1918, nearly 5,000,000 workers were engaged on government contracts, less than half in heavy industry. R. H. Tawney estimated that 'not less than two-thirds of the gainfully employed workers in the country were by 1918 engaged in industries subject to one form or another of war-time regulation'.[17]

The state's involvement in production brought increased attention to the welfare of the worker. Over 1,000 canteens were established, 1,000 welfare supervisors were appointed to look after female munitions workers, and another 300 supervised boys in the factories. Lloyd George commented that it was a 'strange irony, but no small compensation, that the making of weapons of destruction should afford the occasion to humanise industry'. In truth, these developments were motivated by efficiency, not big-hearted paternalism. Britain could not afford a workforce prone to illness, discontent or bad timekeeping. The Health of Munitions Workers Committee, formed in September 1915, operated under the proviso that 'without health there is no energy, without energy there is no output'. The government had accepted that the labour force, like a machine, had to be kept in good working order. For the worker, however, the effect was the same regardless of motivation: in government-controlled factories, working conditions improved significantly. It is no surprise, then, that welfare supervisors sometimes tussled with shop stewards over who represented the true interests of the worker. The benefits that state control brought to the labour force can be measured by the eagerness of factory owners to abandon these controls after the war.[18]

The changed role of the state in industrial relations had other important ramifications. No longer could the government pretend to be an objective arbiter in labour disputes as it had before 1914. Because of the government's involvement, every labour dispute became political, even if the workers did not so intend. On the plus side, during the war, trade union representatives and ministers negotiated on a technically equal basis, significantly enhancing the former's status. The most profound manifestation of this was the inclusion of Labour members in the coalition governments. Finally, war experience convinced workers that government action could alleviate many of the problems afflicting industry. State control seemed to benefit all parties concerned. Workers assumed that, once having taken an active role in the economy, the government would not retreat. A short leap of reason likewise convinced them that the government's gratitude would result in rewards and better treatment after the war. The government did not discourage these assumptions, naive though they were.

Union membership doubled between 1906 and 1914, then doubled again by 1920, peaking at 8,348,000, or almost half of the working population. In other words, the increasing popularity of unions (and their consequent growth in power) was a trend not confined to the war. Similar developments occurred in Sweden, Germany, the United States and France, which all had different war experiences. The phenomenon has more to do with developments in industrialisation, education and urbanisation than with the relatively brief effects of war. Nevertheless, the war enhanced the power of trade unions by producing a period of labour scarcity that could be exploited. During the war, blackleg labour was not readily available and stoppages were not just inconvenient but disastrous. Wartime collective bargaining brought shop stewards into the negotiating process as never before, the effect being to enhance the political power of the ordinary worker. The rank and file attained an importance heretofore unimagined, as evidenced by the fact that the government could never ignore shop stewards completely and deal only with national union representatives.[19]

And what of women? It is appropriate to discuss their experiences working for the war separately, since that is how they were seen. Women were never fully incorporated into the workforce, and the problems they encountered were decidedly different from those of men. Because most were seen as temporary workers, the benefits they could derive from their wartime experience were limited.

At first, the war caused significant redundancies in industries dominated by women. Chief among these was the garment industry, where uncertainty led to a severe slump in the market for lace, fine needlework, dressmaking and millinery. Elsewhere, restrictions upon the fishing fleet meant redundancies among the predominantly female gutters, and the sugar shortage had a similar effect upon the confectionery industry. According to one estimate, 44.4 per cent of all working women were unemployed, for varying periods, in September 1914. As late as April 1915, 89,577 women and 20,815 girls were registered with the labour exchanges. In September 1914, *The Times* offered free advertisements to soldiers' and sailors' wives seeking positions in domestic service. The establishment of the Educated Woman's War Emergency Training Fund demonstrates that hardship was not confined to the lowest social scale; women working as governesses and journalists, for instance, often lost their jobs. The National Guild of Housecraft endeavoured to teach home-making skills to women from the 'luxury trades' (artists, actresses, musicians, models, milliners, confectioners) who had been made redundant, so that they might 'become good wives for the men who would return from the front'. So great was the hardship that charities like the Queen Mary's Work For Women Fund were established to find employment for redundant females. Work created through the fund paid below the sweated rate; 'it was felt undesirable', the administrators argued, 'to fix wages either so high as to attract from ordinary employment, or else so low as to fall below the barest subsistence level'. Sylvia Pankhurst rightly called the scheme 'Queen Mary's Sweat-shops' and railed against feminists and trade unionists who supported it. Yet such was the extent of hardship that the scheme never lacked for applicants.[20]

Since the turn of the century, women's suffrage campaigners had been a persistent nuisance for the government. That changed shortly after the declaration of war. The militant Women's Social and Political Union, led by Emmeline Pankhurst and her daughter Christabel, made an immediate pledge to support the war effort, while simultaneously demanding that the government make proper use of women's labour. 'The Militants,' Christabel announced, 'will fight for their country as they have fought for the Vote.' Millicent Fawcett, of the more moderate National Union of Women's Suffrage Societies (NUWSS), responded similarly. She had opposed the war up to its outbreak, but on 7 August wrote in *Common Cause* of her satisfaction that 'our large organisation, which has been completely built up during past years to promote women's suffrage, can be used now to help our country through this period of strain and sorrow'. A week later she urged followers: 'LET US SHOW OURSELVES TO BE WORTHY OF CITIZENSHIP WHETHER OUR CLAIM TO IT BE RECOGNISED OR NOT.' As the reaction of Fawcett and the Pankhursts suggests, supporting the war was both patriotic and opportunistic – war seemed to offer access to hitherto male preserves, which might in turn hasten emancipation.[21]

Not all feminists were keen to serve, nor were all those who came forward motivated by gender issues. The militant Annie Kenney objected to Emmeline's strategy: 'This autocratic move was not understood or appreciated by many of our members. They were quite prepared to receive instructions about the Vote, but they were not going to be told what they were to do in a world war.' Emmeline's other daughter, Sylvia, rejected her mother's move and instead opposed the war through her socialist Women's Suffrage Federation. 'I could not rest content that this jingo demonstration, with its demand for compulsory War service, would stand forth unchallenged as representing the womanhood of the nation.' 'My struggle,' she later wrote, 'was to prevent the exploitation of the people in the interests of the war.' Equally significant, half of the NUWSS committee resigned in protest against Fawcett's decision to commit her organisation to the cause. For the vast majority of women, however, war inspired an overwhelming desire to serve. 'Gradually it was borne to me,' wrote Florence Farmborough, a British nurse on the Russian front, 'that to be happy while the world was unhappy, to laugh while the world was in pain, was incongruous; in fact, impossible. I realised that my happiness lay with my duty, and . . . I had no need to be told where that was.'[22]

While it is dangerous to generalise, the most eager volunteers were often women of a certain type. Peter Englund describes that type rather beautifully in his account of Sarah Macnaughtan, a Scottish spinster who joined an ambulance service immediately on the outbreak of war.

For she is a serious woman. In terms of her age, Sarah Broom Macnaughtan is actually rather too old for this war . . . But she is in every sense a product of the Victorian age and there are few concepts that weigh heavier with her, that have a finer ring to them, than Duty. And Principles. Earnestness is integral to her lifestyle, her countenance and her attitudes. She is intelligent, religious, humourless, loyal, gruff, demanding, generous, moral and fearless. She lives alone, unmarried and childless, a woman who is economically and emotionally independent ... Hardly surprisingly, she is a committed suffragette, and nor is it surprising that she is prepared to throw herself wholeheartedly into this war, even though her initial reaction to its outbreak is one of surprise verging on shock. But now it is a matter of Duty. And Principles.

After working in Belgium, Macnaughtan took it upon herself to educate her fellow citizens about the realities of the war. 'Somehow I knew that I must speak, that I must arouse slackers, and tell the rotters what is going on.' She warned not only about the evil enemy, but also about the threats at home, namely strikes, class hatred, selfishness and greed. 'This was the time for every man to do his duty, and strain every nerve and muscle to bring the war to an end and get the boys home again.' Like many of her type, Macnaughtan believed that the war would bring purgation; the spirit of voluntarism would make Britain a better place, cleansing the nation of petty self-indulgence.[23]

Naomi Loughnan, another of the Macnaughtan type, confessed that she was 'sick of frivolling'; she 'wanted to do something big and hard, because of our boys and of England'. For many of these women, the war offered the attractive possibility of being able to imitate men, an understandable desire given the barriers to achievement that existed in that rigidly patriarchal society. Mairi Chisholm and Elsie Knocker, two thrill-seekers who could not only ride but repair motorcycles, used those indispensable skills to manoeuvre their way to the front. In their case, talent trumped prejudice, and middle-class confidence swept aside self-doubt. 'There is a splendid freedom about being in the midst of death,' Macnaughtan decided after her first day in a Belgian hospital, 'a certain glory in it, which one can't explain.' When the horror began to weigh on her, she fell back on her breeding. 'I have found that just to behave like a well-bred woman is what keeps me up best'.[24]

While interesting anomalies, these women did not become instant heroes; respectable society had no yearning for feminine standards to be trampled asunder. Therefore, despite the demands of the suffrage campaigners, the war did not immediately inspire opportunities for women to discover fulfilment through useful employment. Since the government did not anticipate labour shortages, it did not at first recognise the rich source of labour that women represented. Business as Usual was gender-specific: men and women would contribute to the war effort within established spheres. Even women with undeniably valuable skills were rejected by a hidebound establishment. When the pioneering Scottish doctor Elsie Inglis offered her services to the War Office (she wanted to form her own ambulance unit), the authorities reacted: 'My good lady, go home and sit still.'[25]

Women were instead encouraged to continue with their traditional pursuits, thus minimising war's disruption. Their value to the war effort, it was thought, would be manifested in womanly ways. They could knit socks, send parcels to soldiers and keep the home fires burning. The popular rhymer Jessie Pope offered advice about what should be sent to loved ones at the front:

> Some candles and a bar of soap,
>> Cakes, peppermints and matches,
> A pot of jam, some thread (like rope)
>> For sticking khaki patches
> These gifts, our soldier writes to say,
>> Have brought him untold riches
> To celebrate his natal day
> In hard-won Flanders' ditches.

Newspapers were full of patriotic advertisements for products to send to Tommies. Horlicks Malted Milk Tablets were 'invaluable to a soldier in the field and most efficient in relieving hunger and thirst and preventing fatigue'. Suppliers of yarn enjoyed an unanticipated boom as a 'needlework mania' gripped the country.

'People knit everywhere,' wrote Georgina Lee. 'We here ... never go into our meal without our knitting.' Theatre placards encouraged ladies to 'Bring Your Knitting'. The pastime, Pope suggested, was not only productive, but therapeutic:

> Shining pins that dart and click
>   In the fireside's sheltered peace
> Check the thoughts that cluster thick –
>   20 plain and then decrease.
>   . . .
> Wonder if he's fighting now,
>   What he's done an' where he's been;
> He'll come out on top, somehow –
>   Slip 1, knit 2, purl 14.

One correspondent to *The Times* complained that his wife and daughter, whose knitting abilities were strictly limited, had turned his parlour into 'a sort of factory'. 'My heart goes out to poor suffering Tommy Atkins if he is to be condemned to endure these miserably cut, uncomfortable and irritating garments.'[26]

Many women were, however, uncomfortable with the restricted roles allotted them. War, they sensed, would merely accentuate the rigid separation of the sexes. One woman told a recruiter: 'Take myself, an able-bodied woman, age 27, sound in health, and fond of a scrap.' The poet Nora Bomford regretted how the accident of birth had rendered her

> So dreadfully safe! O, damn the shibboleth
> Of sex! God knows we've equal personality.
> Why should men face the dark while women stay
> To live and laugh and meet the sun each day.

A large number of women, Vera Brittain notable among them, salved their frustration by becoming nurses in the Volunteer Aid Detachment (VAD). Their contribution was undoubtedly significant but hardly revolutionary, in that it reinforced the traditional female role of carer. In any case, strict rules determined where women were allowed to be nurses. With few exceptions, they were kept well away from the front.[27]

Some women rebelled against the restrictions imposed upon them, though there was little they could do to break down barriers to meaningful employment. A. B. Baker, daughter of a farmer, suffered profoundly as a result of that 'shibboleth of sex'.

> My father was too old to go. Also, he had the farm. My sister and I have no brother. Many relatives lived near us. All had men-folk who could go to fight – and did. Uncles, cousins, and cousins' sweethearts were all in the trenches or in training for the trenches.

Three or four times a week an aunt or a cousin would bring in her letter from the Front, and read it proudly. They were anxious of course. One cousin was killed. One uncle was wounded. But they were proud, above all. They said that Father and Mother were lucky, to have no one about whom they need be anxious. Yet even my young sister could see that they pitied us, too.

. . . I quickly discovered that Father did not count himself lucky. Their pity hurt his pride. With him, it was not only pride. The farm had been the family's for two hundred years. The country meant more to Father than flags waved and glib patriotic cant uttered. The old sorrow that he had no sons had become, I guessed, a new bitterness.

In 1917 came an opportunity for Baker to join the newly formed Women's Auxiliary Army Corps (WAAC). 'Father said little. Yet I knew that he was glad . . . He told me that he was proud of me.' Once mobilised, however, she found to her regret that it was the same old 'women's work'. 'I had got to France, but I had not got to the War. I was never very near the line. The devilish guns rumbled day and night. By day, the click-clacking of my typewriter keys drowned the rumbling of the guns. In that, I see now, lay a parable. I saw only unheroic monotony, then.' She did, in the end, discover one service only a woman could perform. A soldier who was morbidly afraid of death asked to go for a walk before he left for the front. 'He asked me if he could kiss me. I said, "Yes". He kissed me many times, and held me very tight. He held me so tight that he hurt me and frightened me. His whole body was shaking. I felt for him as I had never felt for any man before. I know now that it wasn't love. It was just the need to comfort him a little.'[28] The more things changed, the more they stayed the same.

As the experience of these women demonstrated, mere eagerness to serve was not enough to move a government and an industrial sector reluctant to employ women in war-related work. The Board of Trade in March 1915 did institute a Special War Register, designed to take note of women willing to serve, but two months later fewer than 1,816 of the nearly 78,946 who had registered had been given work. In the first year of the war, total female employment increased by just 400,000, while male employment increased by around one million. When, in early 1915, Kitchener's call for recruits caused labour shortages, the industrial sector did not immediately look to women. Employers instead called upon the unemployed (an estimated 480,000 men lost jobs at the outbreak of war), the retired, juveniles still in school, or men in non-essential industries. Employment of women was also hindered by the fact that it was more difficult for them to move around the country to take up jobs. Activists like Christabel and Emmeline Pankhurst, Millicent Fawcett, and Lady Londonderry drew attention to the untapped reservoir of female labour, but they initially opposed sending women into factories, feeling instead that more suitable employment existed in clerical and secretarial posts vacated by male volunteers. It is here that the earliest and most significant changes took place. In any case, for women to replace men in the factories required unions to agree to dilution. Thus, the Shells and Fuses Agreement, the Treasury Agreement, the Munitions of War Act and, indeed, the shell scandal were the essential prerequisites to widespread female factory employment. Aware that the ground was shifting, Pankhurst and Fawcett organised a massive demonstration on 17 July 1915, with banners declaring: 'We Demand the Right to Work', 'Shells Made by a Wife May Save a Husband's Life' and 'Women's Scissors Will Cut the Red Tape'. By that stage, however, they were pushing at an open door, since the shell scandal had finally exposed the need for labour – and the fallacy of Business as Usual.[29]

The female workforce increased by only 25.5 per cent during the war – from 4,934,000 in July 1914 to 6,193,000 four years later. This is significant, but hardly the flood of female workers often suggested. Before the war, the largest sector of women's employment was domestic service, with 1,658,000 employed. That fell by 400,000 during the war, but still remained the most popular employment for women. Georgina Lee employed twice as many servants in 1917 as in 1914, since she needed a nanny and an extra maid for her infant son. Textiles, the second most frequent employer, and notorious for its exploitation of women, slipped to third during the war but was still more common than munitions. The greatest numerical increase occurred in banking, finance and commerce, which took on an extra 429,000 women. Across the economy, approximately 962,000 women worked in white-collar or service employment during the war, while 697,000 worked in industry, farming or transport. While the distribution was largely determined by demand, female preference did play a part. Of 25,000 women who registered at labour exchanges by March 1915, only 3,600 expressed a wish to be employed in armaments. Thus, most women entered jobs that have since become synonymous with low-status female employment: bank tellers, secretaries and clerks. They were also more likely to hold on to those jobs after the war than they were the traditionally male occupations in industry that provided greater status. 'The development seems likely to be to a great extent permanent,' the economic analyst G. D. H. Cole correctly predicted in 1915, 'largely because it is doubtful whether the men will desire to return to their old jobs, but also because women's labour is cheaper.' In light of the attention given to the munitionette, it is ironic that the Great War actually provided better opportunities for women to become secretaries, and doubly so since the women concerned often preferred office work to the factory floor. It is interesting to note that there was no marked increase in female hairdressers or waitresses, since popular prejudice still held that these jobs were more suited to men.[30]

Before the war, a working-class woman stayed at a job until she found a man to marry and support her. Since almost all women took jobs out of necessity rather than for fulfilment, very few middle- and upper-class women worked – be they married or not. For a working-class woman to continue in employment after marriage was, except in the cotton towns of Lancashire, highly unusual, and in most cases occurred only when a husband was, through illness, redundancy or otherwise, unable to support his family. Only 10 per cent of married women worked outside the home. This changed during the war when, because of propaganda or necessity, married women were tempted back into the workforce. Thus the vast majority of the extra 1.25 million female workers during the war were women who had worked before or girls who entered the workforce earlier than normal. The expansion of female employment did not therefore mean a broadening of horizons, since it drew upon a pool of women for whom employment had been, or would soon be, entirely customary.[31]

Relatively few middle- and upper-class women took on factory work; if they worked at all they congregated in white collar and nursing professions. Employers in any case did not welcome women from the upper classes, since they demanded better facilities. Joan Williams, one of the rare exceptions, found that she had to deal with class *and* gender prejudice. 'I could quite understand,' she remarked, 'the foremen preferring to have real working girls under them to the "War Workers", who were apt to make much more fuss when displeased and complain to the higher authorities, without being able to be frightened by any threat of dismissal.' Middle- and upper-class women made up about 9 per cent of munitions workers, and were concentrated in skilled and supervisory positions. In other words, the rigid hierarchy of wider society was reproduced in the factory, with fillers at the lowest end of the social scale and inspectors at the top. Monica Cosens, who wrote of her experiences in *Lloyd*

George's Munitions Girls, commented that when a middle-class woman like her entered the workplace, 'there is a defiance in the air. She is not gently treated.' If the attitude of the welfare supervisor Naomi Loughnan was typical, that defiance is understandable:

> The ordinary factory hands . . . lack interest in their work because of the undeveloped state of their imaginations. They handle cartridges and shells, and though their eyes may be swollen with weeping for sweethearts and brothers whose names are among the killed and wounded, yet they do not definitely connect the work they are doing with the trenches. One girl, with a face growing sadder and paler as the days went by because no news came from France of her 'boy' who was missing, when gently urged to work harder and not to sleep so often, answered with angry indignation: 'Why should I work any harder? My mother is satisfied with what I takes home on a Saturday.'

For Loughnan, war work was an expression of patriotism. For those she managed, work was a necessity. Middle-class women sometimes had difficulty understanding the great difference between working for a living and working (temporarily) out of an excited desire to serve one's country.[32]

When a woman took on factory work, direct substitution was less common than dilution. Substitution meant that an unskilled or semi-skilled worker did a job previously performed by a skilled man. Dilution implied the reorganisation of the job, including the introduction of new machinery so that unskilled workers could perform component tasks. Barbara Drake, researching the munitions industry for the Fabian Society in 1917, concluded that 'Not one in a thousand of the scores of women introduced into shell and fuse factories proved a claim to take the whole place of a fully skilled tradesman.' Shell-filling, a common source of employment for women during the war, and one that inspired the image of a society in flux, was actually widely performed by women before the war, because it required little skill. According to one estimate, by the end of the war, five sixths of women in industry were doing work previously categorised as women's work or which had been restructured to cater to women.[33]

These statistics illustrate how women's contribution to the war was limited by workplace prejudice. In April 1915, a woman disguised as a man was discovered working in a Barrow shipyard. She explained that she needed money to support her family, and as a woman, access to good, well-paying jobs was blocked. Unions, male workers and employers fought a fierce rearguard action against the introduction of women or the expansion of their duties. Cole warned in 1915 that female workers would be deeply resented by the male wage-earner,

> who may well feel that his job is taken, or his standard of life threatened, by the competition of female labour. He is apt to regard women much as the Australian regards the Chinaman, or as the American regards the East European immigrant, as interlopers, whose different standard of life renders them not only dangerous, but also unfair competitors in the labour market. And the history of women in industry gives some warrant to this attitude.

Transport workers in Hull 'absolutely refused to work with women', threatening instead to strike. While their protests proved unsuccessful, Liverpool dockers did manage to block the employment of women for the entire war. Even the cotton unions, which had a long history of women members, fought the expansion of female roles in the mills. Prejudice played a part in this resistance, but more important were instincts of self-preservation. Male spinners feared that if females were employed 'we shall have the employers saying there is nothing in spinning if a girl can do it, and will pay accordingly'. The worries were real precisely because employers did resort to these arguments. They often justified low pay with spurious claims about lower female productivity. One railway employer actually argued that 'A woman ticket collector . . . can never be as successful as a man.'[34]

Government intervention was the best way to break down barriers to female employment. The number of women in controlled munitions establishments increased by 300 per cent up to October 1916, but by only 36 per cent in uncontrolled ones. Given proper training, the right conditions and support, women could perform almost any job previously handled by men, except those requiring considerable strength. They performed better than men in processes requiring great dexterity, and in repetitive work. Despite government coercion, persuasion and incentives, some employers stubbornly resisted the introduction of women. They followed a common logic, namely that female workers were by definition temporary. As one trade journal commented, 'The prospect to which a man looks forward is to earn enough money to keep a wife; the prospect to which a woman looks forward is that he may succeed.' That sentiment was widely accepted by both men and women. Employers therefore saw little sense in investing time, effort and money in training women who would shift their loyalties to husband and home after the war.[35]

Since women seldom directly replaced men, employers found it entirely logical to pay them significantly less. This placed male workers and their unions in a terrible quandary. As one woman worker remarked, 'they were torn between not wanting the women to undercut them, and yet hating them to earn as much'. In principle, unions opposed the introduction of women because of the threat to men's jobs and to long-established skill differentials. At the same time, however, they were inclined to argue that if a woman took on a man's job, she should be paid the same. This logic, it was hoped, would convince employers to stick with men. For some craft unions, the equal pay argument was a thinly veiled attempt to block the introduction of women and to protect men's jobs at the end of the war. Employers, on the other hand, had a ready arsenal of arguments (most of them spurious) to justify lower pay: women produced less, they were notoriously poor timekeepers, they required more supervision, they needed more costly facilities, etc. Feminists were divided on this subject: some saw equal pay as an important symbol of equality, while others feared that it would impede the entrance of women into previously male preserves.[36]

Lloyd George regarded equal pay as 'a social revolution which ... it is undesirable to attempt during war time'. In the government's list of priorities, fairness to women ranked well below satisfying employers, pacifying male workers and maintaining production. A cynical but effective compromise was reached. Aware that employers would be more inclined to take on women if they seemed a bargain, Lloyd George decided that women should be paid the same as men on piece rates, but not on time rates. (Piece rate meant pay was determined by productivity.) As it turned out, many women found this advantageous, since in jobs requiring dexterity, they were usually more productive than men, and could therefore earn more. Realising this, employers tried to keep women out of piece work. On time work they were paid between 50 and 66 per cent of the male rate. They were also subjected to unfair deductions (such as if air raids stopped production) which did not apply to men, and which often reduced the pay packet by as much as 25 per cent. Nevertheless, in the sorts of jobs women took up, rates of pay were higher than in those they left. Thus, though they were certainly discriminated against, they were often better off because of the war.[37]

The introduction of women into factories focused attention

on working conditions. Facilities that had seemed suitable for men were considered unsuitable for women. Washrooms, canteens and toilets had suddenly to be provided. With purpose-built factories this was not a problem, but at already established plants, managers were reluctant to provide for workers considered to be temporary. Various official committees monitored the welfare of female workers, but all of these bodies encountered a serious dilemma: they needed to ensure that factories were safe and the workers healthy (so as to improve efficiency) without seeming to promote the principle of female labour. This dilemma was most acute when it came to crèche provision. One doctor advised the Ministry of Munitions that free crèches would encourage mothers to take up factory work, yet it was widely held that no responsible mother would put her child in a crèche. Since it followed that irresponsible women made poor workers, it was feared that providing crèches would attract the wrong sort of woman and adversely affect productivity. The government eventually decided that since mothers would flock to the factories whether crèches were provided or not, in the interests of the children childcare should be available. The Ministry decided to sponsor crèches, but only up to 50 per cent of the cost. The number of available places always vastly exceeded demand.[38]

Welfare committees often discovered unsuitable or dangerous conditions that had existed for a long time, particularly in the textile industry, thus revealing another benefit of government intervention. Though much progress was made, the government was fully aware that excessively high standards limited production. For instance, not a great deal was done to regulate long hours, for obvious reasons. There was, on the other hand, concern about the poisonous effects of TNT, though this was motivated more by the threat to productivity than the risk to health. At Woolwich Arsenal, one study revealed that 37 per cent of female shell-fillers suffered from abdominal pain, nausea and constipation, 25 per cent had skin problems and 36 per cent suffered from depression and irritability. During the war there were 349 serious cases of TNT poisoning reported, with 109 deaths. In August 1916, a rather frank Ministry of Munitions official gave an indication of where priorities lay: 'unless measures are taken to meet this difficulty, serious interference with output may arise as if the operatives become frightened at the number of diseases and deaths of their colleagues, greater difficulty than ever will be experienced in procuring labour'. The government responded by providing sick pay of £1 per week, hospitalisation cover, and eventually a special diet allowance.[39]

Welfare supervisors were invariably middle-class women, who were assumed to possess a natural managerial ability. The job provided many women with their first opportunity to pursue a professional career, one in which, as personnel officers, women continued to be prevalent after the war. The maternal nature of the work, while suiting some women perfectly, sometimes conflicted with production priorities. In other words, the interests of the employer and those of the worker often came into conflict. On the other hand, some supervisors interpreted 'welfare' as those conditions calculated to make a woman work harder. This prompted the more assiduous to monitor conditions not only at work, but also at home: it was not unknown for supervisors to inspect workers' houses and offer advice on care of children, health, diet and hygiene. The worker's leisure interests also attracted attention. Since the war took women away from their home communities and thus, it was thought, cut them off from appropriate guardianship, supervisors saw themselves as surrogate parents. Extra vigilance was exercised against unwholesome entertainments: women workers were reprimanded for behaving improperly on the street, for consuming too much alcohol or for excessive cinema attendance. While the warden mentality was often taken to excess, one positive development was that supervisors did guard against sexual predators on the shop floor. Dark factories provided too many opportunities for unwelcome advances – according to the labour activist Beatrice Webb, 'Foremen ... have much power in their hands which is not always honourably used.' Nevertheless, while some supervisors felt genuine affection for their charges, most were despised for their intrusiveness and dictatorial nature. At its 1918 conference, the National Federation of Women Workers called for the abolition of welfare supervisors, on the grounds that they replaced organised labour relations with a rather patronising regime that undermined trade unions.[40]

In practice, the unions paid scant attention to the welfare of women workers, the exception being the exclusively female trade unions. Traditionally male unions took the view that any measures designed to make women's work more acceptable would act to the detriment of men. In any case, men held to the principle that female employment undermined a man's sacred claim to be paid a wage sufficient to support his family. Resentment also arose from the assumption that every female worker meant an additional male sent to the front. Despite these prejudices, many unions eased restrictions on female membership during the war, if only out of a selfish desire to swell their ranks. The National Union of Railwaymen, which had not accepted women before the war, changed its policy, and the General Union of Municipal Workers was positively welcoming. By the end of the war, 383 unions had female members, another 36 were women-only. Many unions, however, continued to ban women, including, of course, the ASE. Female membership of unions expanded significantly, from 437,000 members in 1914 to a peak of 1,342,000 in 1920, but when peace came, only one out of every six women workers were members. This indicates not only the unwelcoming attitude of the unions, but also that most women saw their work as temporary.[41]

In May 1915, Lord Selborne, the agriculture minister, called upon women to join the Women's Land Service Corps, which became the Women's Land Army (WLA) in January 1917. There was considerable romance attached to the idea.

> The men must take the swords,
>   And we must take the ploughs
> Our Front is where the wheat grows fair,
>   Our colours, orchard boughs.

The image of rosy-cheeked maidens in pretty bonnets looking after cows and sheep was great for propaganda, but in fact the response by women was quite small, as was their contribution. Only 16,000 WLA members assisted with the 1918 harvest, providing only 8,000 man-units to the production process. In contrast, the contribution of women from farming families rose steadily throughout the war, totalling 30,000 man-units by 1918.

Farming communities were extremely suspicious of female out-siders, with rumours of rampant licentiousness rife. No matter how hard they worked, WLA members struggled to convince farmers of their worth. Cognisant of the prejudice recruits would encounter, WLA organisers cautioned them as follows:

> You are doing a man's work and so you are dressed like a man; but remember that just because you wear a smock and breeches you should take care to behave like an English girl who expects chivalry and respect from every one she meets. Noisy or ugly behaviour brings discredit, not only upon yourself but upon the uniform, and the whole Women's Land Army. When people see you pass ... show them that an English girl who is working for her Country on the land is the best sort of girl.

The work was exhausting, dangerous and dirty, characterised by long hours, poor accommodation, strict regimentation and poor pay. Most working-class women had sufficient sense to realise that money could be made more easily in the cities. Lured by pastoral fantasies, middle-class women often joined the WLA, sometimes giving up well-paid jobs to do so. Reality bit hard, however, with many then escaping to the cities at the first opportunity.[42]

British society had an uneasy time coming to terms with changing trends in women's employment. The feminist campaigner Ray Strachey noted how the press 'began to say that "the nation is grateful to the women" – not realising even yet that the women were the nation just as much as the men were'. Government propaganda and newspaper reports praised women workers, but always with the hope that wartime changes would prove temporary. Jessie Pope conveyed both sentiments in her 'War Girls':

> There's the girl who clips your ticket for the train,
>> And the girl who speeds the lift from floor to floor,

There's the girl who does a milk-round in the rain,
   And the girl who calls for orders at your door.
      Strong, sensible and fit,
      They're out to show their grit,
And tackle jobs with energy and knack.
      No longer caged and penned up,
      They're going to keep their end up
Till the khaki soldier boys come marching back.

In February 1915, *The Times* argued optimistically: 'Even if many of the posts formerly held by men which women are now filling are for the duration of the war only, and will have to be yielded up should their original holder return safe and sound, they will have tested women's capacity in a way that may have a lasting effect on women work in future.'[43]

The increased visibility of women in pubs, cinemas, on the street and on the factory floor tested the tolerance of polite society. Gender and class prejudices fused into an obsession to condemn. The self-appointed guardians of virtue worried that working-class women with surplus income would inevitably get up to mischief. The young, single munitionette, strutting the streets in fancy clothes bought from inflated wages, was a popular wartime stereotype. Madeline Bedford's 'Munition Wages' reflected the mood of condescension and reproach:

      Earning high wages? Yus,
        Five quid a week.
      A woman, too, mind you,
        I calls it dim sweet.

      Ye'are asking some questions –
        But bless yer, here goes:
      I spends the whole racket
        On good times and clothes.

Female factory workers who appeared ostentatious in their dress or leisure pursuits were frequently suspected of earning money on the 'extra shift' – through prostitution. In fact, very few women earned more than they actually needed to support themselves.[44]

As one enlightened factory inspector commented in 1916, even the praise for women workers revealed prejudices: 'It is permissible to wonder whether some of the surprise and admiration freely expressed in many quarters over new proofs of women's physical capacity and endurance, is not in part attributable to lack of knowledge or appreciation of the very heavy and strenuous nature of much of normal pre-war work for women, domestic and industrial.' Such praise usually went hand in hand with references to femininity, suggesting an underlying hope that women would not be hardened by their work. 'Overalled, leather-aproned, capped and goggled – displaying nevertheless woman's genius for making herself attractive in whatsoever working guise' was how the *Daily Mail* referred to one group of factory workers. A famous wartime painting depicted a munitionette in pretty smock and bonnet cradling a shell as if it was a baby.[45]

Just as women's war work was presumed to be for the duration only, so too was the praise and gratitude they earned. The woman who tried to stay in 'man's work' a day past the Armistice was instantly transformed from war hero to selfish schemer. What few in authority understood was that most women, mothers especially, went into the factories not in search of fulfilment but out of necessity. Deprivation – caused either by paltry separation allowances or by the death of a husband at the front – proved an effective recruiter. In the factory where she worked, the writer Kathleen Dayus encountered a woman named Minnie who was the sole breadwinner in her family.

> She was a small, thin woman, very pale and came, she told
> me, from the Black Country. I asked her why she couldn't
> get a job nearer home but she said she had seven children
> and a husband to keep and this was the best paying job she
> could find . . . She looked as old as my Mum with her lined
> face but she told me she was not yet thirty.

A study of pre-war female employment by the Fabian
Women's Society found that 51 per cent of women workers
were supporting someone other than themselves and 80 per
cent were entirely self-supporting, leaving a small percentage
depending on others for partial support. 'This would seem to
prove,' concluded *The Times*, 'that in peacetime at least women
do not work unless they have to, and that the pocket-money
worker . . . is largely a myth.' If these women did not work in
industry after the war, they would have to work somewhere
else. The post-war problem of the 'surplus woman' was
recognised as early as February 1915, with possible solutions
like emigration to Australia and more extensive training in
domestic service discussed.

Dayus worked in a small shop making brass buttons for
soldiers' trousers. 'The workshop was dirty and reeked of oil.
In the centre of the room was a large, battered pipe stove filled
with glowing coke, the smoke from which went up the pipe
and out through a hole in the roof. Every now and then smoke
billowed into the room.' In other words, there was very little
glamour or glory on the shop floor. The assembly line was no
Yellow Brick Road. When myths are stripped away, the period
hardly seems a golden age of women's emancipation. Women
were seen as cheap and temporary substitutes for men. They
were easily exploitable labour, useful in a crisis or to break the
back of organised labour, but possessing very little value in
their own right. Then again, perhaps this was the road they had
to travel on the arduous journey towards equality. It does them

no credit, however, to pretend that the road was smooth or the progress swift.[46]

In March 1917, Georgina Lee was busy moving house from one neighbourhood of London to another. While waiting in a cold and empty parlour for the first vanload of furniture to arrive, she grew increasingly impatient with the 'extraordinary dilatoriness' of the typical British worker. 'But my anger was quickly disarmed at the sight of the 4 decrepit old fellows, knock-kneed and splay-footed. They could barely struggle under the chests and chairs they had to carry.' Those four men were a potent reminder of how completely mobilised the nation had become. A short time later, the government banned the use of outside labour for house removals and painting. Presumably the knock-kneed were given more important work to do.[47]

Chapter 8

Outlaws and Dissenters

In September 1915, the police court in Epping held its regular monthly meeting. For the first time ever, there were no cases to hear. According to the informal accounting of local magistrate Montagu Sharpe, crime had dropped by 90 per cent because of the war. 'The criminal is a patriot,' Mr Robert Wallace, KC, remarked in December 1914. 'Like the honest citizen, [he] is impressed by the war conditions, which make it every man's duty to give as little trouble as possible.'[1]

Attractive as that explanation might be, it seems too charitable to the criminal class. Crime fell mainly because poverty declined and alcohol sales were restricted. In addition, many of those on the fringes of society, who previously might have been drawn to lawlessness, wound up in the military. It is also the case that the British were much more regulated as a result of the war. An authoritarian fog swept across the country, smothering liberal values of tolerance and charity. Profound contempt was expressed towards those who strayed from strict definitions of propriety. Thus, even though crime declined, social order became an obsession. Since crimes were considered an offence not just against the immediate victim, but also against the war effort, courts took a stiff line with misdemeanours. Authority became intrusive, to the detriment of freedom and privacy. Britons displayed a remarkable willingness to police their fellow citizens, with factory inspectors and welfare supervisors monitoring not only the workplace, but also homes, cinemas and pubs. Over 1,000 female police volunteers patrolled the streets, partly in response to widespread fears that working-class women and girls were drifting into prostitution and preying on innocent soldiers. One volunteer recorded 383 cases of prostitution in polite Grantham in 1917, a number that suggests obsessive policing rather than an extraordinary level of vice. In 1914, Britain was a liberal, tolerant, freedom-loving society. By the end of the war, the nation resembled a police state.[2]

The first significant assault upon freedom came with the passage of the Defence of the Realm Act (DORA) just four days after the declaration of war. DORA, a wide-ranging law capable of being extended as necessity dictated, reveals how determined an otherwise liberal, anti-interventionist government was to secure the mechanisms of social control. The crucial part of the act gave government the power to 'authorise the trial by courts martial' of any person whose actions were deemed to 'jeopardise the success of the operations of His Majesty's forces or to assist the enemy'. While this might suggest a measure aimed at spies and traitors, in fact the government cast its net much wider. The act could be applied to any action deemed detrimental to the war effort, which, in truth, meant that the definition of jeopardy was limited only by the imagination of the courts and police. Thus, a woman who passed a venereal disease on to a soldier could be prosecuted under DORA, even if she was unaware of having the disease in the first place. A passenger on a London to Manchester evening train might be prosecuted for raising the window blinds, thus exposing said train to German aircraft. An extension of the law on 28 August 1914 created the offence of spreading reports 'likely to cause disaffection or alarm', which theoretically entitled the government to quash any dissent. A further extension added the authority to ban demonstrations that might make 'undue demands' upon local police forces. Wide powers of search were assumed, as was the right to hold suspects without charge. Naval or military authorities could deport from designated areas persons deemed hazardous to the war effort. Thus a militant trade unionist could be banned from the area around a factory or, as was the case with the Clyde Workers Committee, deported to another city.[3]

While ordinary crime declined, the war produced new types of offences that were obsessively policed. Uncertainty about the future made fortune-tellers popular, but since their trade was illegal, arrests multiplied. In time, DORA would be invoked against citizens who failed to observe the blackout, revellers who built bonfires on Guy Fawkes night, publicans who ignored early-closing regulations, brewers who made their beer too strong, shopkeepers who hoarded food and Londoners who whistled for cabs. In 1917, an Edinburgh baker was arrested for producing jam tarts on a designated 'sweet-free' day. A butcher from Kensington was fined £50 for selling bad meat to troops. A farmer near Wisbech was fined £140 for selling seed potatoes above the maximum price and a Worksop miller £23 for extracting only 48.5 per cent rather than the required 71.25 per cent flour from grain. In Bedfordshire, a farmer was fined £50 for allowing rats to invade his wheat store. A charge of conspiracy was brought against Ansell John Goudge, who had 'naturalised' his German pianos and sold them as British.[4]

Convictions under the Prevention of Corruption Act increased four-fold during the war, prompting the government in 1916 to increase the penalties for bribing public officials. As Christopher Addison recognised, the proliferation of munitions contracts brought forth 'a singular collection of sharks and adventurers from all parts of the earth'. In Dundee, a jute dealer was prosecuted for selling material for sandbags at three times the normal price. Two Glaswegians who roamed the Scottish countryside masquerading as government agents persuaded farmers to sell horses at patriotically reduced prices. Newspaper reports suggest that fraud increased (or became more unacceptable) as con artists preyed on the emotionally vulnerable. Trials for bigamy were frequently recounted in the crime columns. 'The professional writer of begging letters has now adapted his whine to a patriotic tune,' *The Times* commented. Impostors posing as wounded soldiers frequented railway stations asking for donations. Since charitable sentiments reached new heights, so too did the opportunities for trickery. 'The worst class of all' was the impostor who watched casualty lists and wrote to the relatives of a dead 'comrade' requesting the repayment of an alleged debt.[5]

Pacifism was seen as a particularly serious scourge. 'I consider the Pacifists a disease,' wrote Christabel Pankhurst in July 1917. 'They are a disease to which old nations seem to become subject. They are a disease which comes of over-prosperity, and of false security . . . a very deadly disease which you will find has afflicted every dead nation of the past.' Overblown though her comments may seem, one suspects that most of her fellow citizens agreed. Though political protest did not disappear, it did decline to the point of near insignificance. After 1914, fringe militants maintained a lonely and futile opposition to the government. Most of their pre-war followers took either a pragmatic or patriotic decision to support the war, leaving the pacifists, socialists and feminists who remained as leaders without followers. They came together in an anti-war movement of broad church: pacifists because they believed war wrong, socialists because it seemed a consequence of capitalism, and feminists because it underlined the scourge of patriarchy.[6]

The movement never lived up to pre-war expectations. On 2 August 1914, a huge peace rally took place in Trafalgar Square, addressed by the Labour politicians George Lansbury, Arthur Henderson and Keir Hardie, and the socialist H. M. Hyndman.

The consensus among the crowd was that Britain should remain aloof from the gathering crisis in Europe. Robert Smillie, the miners' leader, promised that his union would take part in any pan-European effort by trade unionists to bring the war to a halt. A short time later, however, Germany invaded Belgium and the British embarked upon a moral crusade. The Belgian issue pricked the pacifist balloon. Edward Pease, chairman of the Peace Society, was one of many pre-war pacifists who crossed over to belligerency. The TUC and the Labour Party also rallied behind the government, offering their services to the war effort. The novelist Arnold Bennett typified how pacifism dissolved: 'When one sees young men idling in the lanes on Sunday, one thinks: "Why are they not at war?" All one's pacific ideas have been disturbed. One is becoming militarist.'[7]

Alienated by the xenophobic nationalism which swept Britain, a small group of feminists, socialists, Christians, liberals and trade unionists remained true to the pacifist cause. The group most successful at uniting the disaffected was the Union of Democratic Control (UDC), formed by the Liberal MP Charles Trevelyan on 5 August 1914. Prominent members included the journalist E. D. Morel, the social activist Arthur Ponsonby and Norman Angell, author of *The Great Illusion*. Morel essentially admitted that there was little that could be done to stop the current war. 'The monster of militarism had mastered the diplomats . . . The people – dominated by fear and panic, neither informed nor consulted – had been whirled, after a few short weeks of confused and secret negotiations between their rulers, into a maelstrom of passions and mutual slaughter.' What, he wondered, was there left for pacifists to do?

> Should they confine themselves to the facile and popular task of denouncing the enemy and giving assistance to works of charity or relief for the victims of the war? Or should they attempt to evolve some constructive

programme; to provide some rallying centre for future
political action – national in its inception, international
in its ultimate aims – around which men and women
holding . . . diverse and even contradictory views as to the
origins of the war could, nevertheless, gather, restore their
shattered faiths, and strive to lay the foundations of a more
enduring edifice?

'We thought,' wrote the Labour MP Morgan Philips Price, 'that
the best way to expose the European anarchy that had caused
the War was to form a society of this kind to which people who
had not lost their heads could belong.' While theoretically non-
partisan, the group adhered to a form of 'bourgeois pacifism'
that undoubtedly rankled with socialists. An early pamphlet
by Morel argued that pre-war diplomacy had neglected 'the
business interests of the nation,' which essentially implied
that international harmony would come through a sincere
commitment to free trade.[8]

Given the belligerency that gripped Europe, Trevelyan felt
that direct action to end the war would be futile. The UDC
instead concentrated on educating the public on the war's
causes, the aim being eventually to establish mechanisms for
peaceful coexistence between nations. Thus it was not a case of
'Peace Now!' but peace at some vague point in the future when
nations came to their senses. The group's Four Points reveal its
modest aims:

1. There should be no annexation of territory without the
   consent of the population involved.
2. Parliament must exercise democratic control over the
   conduct of foreign policy. Secret diplomacy must be
   abolished.
3. International disputes should be resolved through the
   methods of conference and arbitration. A permanent

International Council, deliberating in public, should
replace balance-of-power diplomacy.
4. National armaments should be limited by mutual
agreement, and the pressures of the military-industrial
complex regulated by the nationalisation of armaments
firms and control over the arms trade.

Loose affiliation with the ILP provided the UDC with an
established network for communicating with those sympathetic
to its message. Labour's decision to join the coalition in May
1915 was a severe blow, though some party members did resign
and followed their consciences to the UDC. Annoyed by the
warmongering of the established churches, some Christians
also drifted in the UDC's direction. By the first anniversary of
its foundation, 50 local organisations had been established and
500,000 pamphlets sold. At its peak, the group had 100 branches
and some 10,000 members. Given the moderate nature of UDC
ideals, this does not seem very impressive. Since it aimed not
so much to stop the war but to build a peaceful post-war world,
it was entirely possible to support the war *and* be a loyal UDC
member. As Ellen Wilkinson of the ILP remarked: 'To the
ardent pacifist it is a tragedy that the advocacy of the cause of
peace should be largely represented in Britain by as cautious a
body as the UDC. Its "four points" are so admirably moderate
and remote that no intelligent person, not quite blinded by
party, could honestly disagree with them.' Bertrand Russell,
while sympathetic, found UDC members naively ambitious.
Their plottings on behalf of peace seemed to him 'like eight
fleas talking of building a pyramid'.[9]

In contrast to the UDC, the ILP insisted that only democratic
socialism, achieved through the international brotherhood of
the working-class, would bring lasting peace. Anyone looking
for a consistent line would, however, have fled in frustration
from the party. On 11 August 1914, it sent greetings 'across

the roar of the guns' to German comrades. Six months later, however, some ILP members (including Ramsay MacDonald) issued a joint statement with socialists from Belgium, France and Russia declaring themselves 'inflexibly resolved to fight until victory is achieved'. Lenin's view that the war would hasten the long-awaited revolution was both enthusiastically received and widely derided by ILP supporters. The party attracted both ardent socialists who supported the war and committed pacifists lukewarm about socialism.[10]

Ramsay Macdonald, who had resigned the leadership of the Labour Party when it decided to support the war, eventually admitted: 'Whatever our views may be on the origins of the war, we must go through with it.' His actions may have seemed perfectly logical to him, but they confused almost everyone else. Equally confusing was Hardie. He argued that the nation must be united behind the war, that soldiers 'must not be disheartened by any discordant note at home' and that 'German troops must be thrown back across their own frontier'. Yet what were potential followers to make of his calls for a compromise peace, his denunciation of Russian militarism and his argument that Britain was guilty of needlessly prolonging the war? When he died in September 1915, the subsequent by-election provided a revealing indicator of working-class opinion. The official Labour candidate, James Winstone, identified with the ILP and the heir to Hardie, was defeated by Charles Stanton, a miners' agent allied to the fiercely patriotic Socialist National Defence Committee. Stanton's tirades against the 'brutal butchers of Berlin' so impressed the voters that they gave him a majority of 4,000. A delighted Lloyd George called it a 'great triumph for the pro-War party'. Diehard socialists grumbled that politically naive workers were seriously in need of enlightenment.[11]

The feminist movement was equally fractured. As we have seen, some suffrage campaigners objected bitterly to the precipitous decision by Millicent Fawcett and Emmeline

Pankhurst to support the war. Their unease caused some to drift toward the UDC. The split widened when discontented NUWSS members and representatives of Sylvia Pankhurst's militant Women's Suffrage Federation announced plans to attend a Women's Congress in The Hague on 27 April 1915. The Congress was controversial because representatives from enemy nations would also attend. The prospect of British feminists conspiring with Germans caused a huge furore at home, the most vocal reaction coming from the suffrage establishment. Fawcett argued that attendance would be 'akin to treason', while Emmeline and Christabel Pankhurst maintained that, for suffragettes, the struggle against the Kaiser was 'a thousand times more important' than the fight for votes. Under that vitriol there lurked some logic. Critics of the Congress recalled how anti-suffragists had, before the war, argued that because women could not defend their country, they did not deserve to vote. Fawcett and the Pankhursts feared that attendance at The Hague would breathe life into that argument, thus negating the good impression women were making by working for the war. Many suffragettes who had earlier ditched Emmeline because of her militant warmongering now returned to the fold in disgust over Sylvia's clumsy peace campaigning. 'Subscribers are falling off like dead leaves at the end of a season,' she complained.[12]

Keen to stoke the outrage the controversy generated, the government played cat and mouse with the two hundred British feminists who wanted to go to Holland. McKenna, the Home Secretary, at first announced that no passports would be granted, then relented and approved passage for twenty 'women of discretion'. This had the effect (probably intentional) of causing a rift between those favoured and those rejected. Crystal MacMillan (who had been selected) lambasted Sylvia Pankhurst (who had not) for referring to the meeting as a peace congress: 'To call it a "Peace Congress" gives the impression that its object is to demand peace at any price.' That distinction was lost on all but the committed. In the end, last-minute obstacles prevented even the small group of twenty from sailing, much to the delight of the *Daily Express*. 'All Tilbury is laughing at the Peacettes, the misguided Englishwomen who, baggage in hand, are waiting at Tilbury for a boat to take them to Holland, where they are anxious to talk peace with German fraus over the teapot.' Only three British women eventually made it to The Hague, in contrast to twenty-eight from Germany. The Congress split over what to do, with a slight majority favouring the dispatch of envoys to belligerent governments to campaign for a negotiated peace. Most of the remainder assumed a position similar to the UDC, namely that energies should be devoted to avoiding future wars. The Congress did nevertheless inspire the formation of the British section of the Women's International League, which by the end of the war had 50 branches and 3,687 active members in Britain, most of them refugees from the NUWSS, and all very moderate pacifists. They linked pacifism to women's emancipation: 'only free women can build up the peace which is to be'. Fearful of public censure, the League banned British wives of resident aliens from membership, on the grounds that to admit them would attract 'a great deal of mud'. The struggles of feminist peace campaigners have received far more attention from historians than they deserve, especially when compared to the efforts of rabidly patriotic women, who were far more numerous and influential.[13]

Even more moderate than the UDC was the League of Nations Society, formed in May 1915 by the Cambridge classicist Lowes Dickinson, and numbering among its ranks the economist J. A. Hobson and the left-wing journalist H. N. Brailsford. Though they agreed with the UDC's concentration upon avoiding future war, they objected to its call for a negotiated peace, feeling certain that German militarism had to be defeated. Though Dickinson was president of the Cambridge branch of the UDC, he was not optimistic that democratic control over foreign policy would solve the problem of war. He favoured instead a system of mutual defence against aggression, what Hobson called 'collective security'. This group eventually gravitated towards the United States as the power most capable of leading the world away from belligerence, and were heartened when President Woodrow Wilson began to promote a League of Nations.

Maintaining an even moderately pacifist position in militantly pro-war Britain required considerable courage. The government, backed by the patriotic press, found pacifists useful for inciting public outrage. On the eve of a meeting in the Memorial Hall, the *Daily Express* printed pictures of Morel, Trevelyan and other prominent pacifists and asked: 'Londoners, what do you think of them? Is Germany to hear the wail of peace cranks from the City of the Empire?' Suitably provoked, an angry mob invaded the hall, seized the platform and threw stink bombs into the audience. Meanwhile, academics who campaigned for peace or opposed conscription were ostracised by colleagues, despite the profound admiration for all things German within academia before the war. In July 1916, following his conviction on a charge of making 'statements likely to prejudice the recruiting and discipline of His Majesty's forces', Russell was dismissed from his lectureship at Trinity College, Cambridge. Dickinson, who found that even his moderate pacifism rendered him a pariah in Cambridge ('I lived and ate alone . . . and saw almost nobody'), concluded after Russell's dismissal that universities were 'no place for genuine and independent minds . . . If you are honest and independent you must be a heretic and an outcast.'[14]

By the late summer of 1916, stalemate and a steadily mounting death toll on the Western Front convinced pacifists that the prospects for a negotiated peace had improved. They assumed that a growing sense of futility would render the British people more receptive to the UDC message. 'We should be inclined almost to despair of the future were it not that we still preserve our faith in the ultimate triumph of reason over the national and international dementia now prevailing,' wrote Morel, 'and . . . we believe there is a vast mass of opinion in this country not represented by the politicians nor by the Press, and considerably saner than either.' Morel envisaged an irresistible force sweeping the country and spilling over to France and Belgium. 'The effect ought to be very great,' he predicted, 'and combined with the steady operating force of economic factors, casualties [and] rising prices it might be decisive.' At rallies throughout the country, signatures were collected for a petition that urged the government to negotiate. The *Manchester Guardian* lent its weight, but the enormous effort proved futile – just 200,000 signatures were collected. Had they been more receptive to the evidence, pacifists might have noticed that, despite the setbacks, support for the war remained solid, as demonstrated by the enthusiasm that greeted the new Prime Minister's promise of a more dynamic conduct to the war. The Labour Party, surely the most promising source of pacifist converts, voted by a huge majority to support the parliamentary party's decision to join Lloyd George's government. In contrast, the British Socialist Party (BSP), which alone on the left called for an immediate peace, had only 6,435 members in 1917. Nor were the British very impressed when, in January 1917, President Wilson demanded peace without victory.[15]

The entry of the United States into the war in April 1917 provoked a variety of reactions among pacifists. Brailsford and Russell took the view that because America seemed untainted by the great power rivalries that had caused the war, it offered the best hope for peace. Wilson's pronouncements certainly supported that assumption. Ardent socialists, however, feared that the result would be a world made safe for American capitalism. They derived more hope from the Russian revolution, especially after the provisional government backed the Petrograd soviet's call for peace 'without annexations or indemnities'. Russell felt that the revolution 'has stirred men's imaginations everywhere and has made things possible which would have been quite impossible a week ago'. On 3 June 1917, over 1,000 representatives from trade unions, socialist organisations, feminist groups and peace societies met at the Leeds conference organised by the ILP and the BSP, under the banner 'Follow Russia'. One resolution called for the establishment of workers' and soldiers' councils. Mainstream labour, however, ignored the events in Leeds. Typical was the attitude of Ben Tillett, the dockers' leader, who argued that the conference 'did not represent working-class opinion and was rigged by a middle class element more mischievous than important'.[16]

The Labour Party and most trade unions nevertheless supported the revolution, while recognising its precariousness. They argued that a positive response from the allied nations was essential in order to give encouragement to the new Russian government and prevent it from signing a separate peace agreement. The upcoming international socialist conference scheduled in Stockholm seemed to offer an opportunity for conveying support for Russian revolutionaries. Henderson, the Labour leader, who was in Petrograd to try to persuade Russian socialists to renew their commitment to the war, was at first wary about the conference, but gradually became convinced that a failure to respond positively would encourage the Bolsheviks pressing for peace. That sentiment was prevalent at a special Labour Party conference on 10 August, where a large majority approved sending representatives to Stockholm. Lloyd George at first agreed, but by the time Henderson returned from Petrograd, he had decided that since Russia was already a lost cause, attendance would be inappropriate.

Underneath Labour's surface enthusiasm for the Stockholm conference lurked profound disquiet. The ILP saw it as an opportunity to end the war, while the Labour Party hoped it would help Russia renew the fight. At a second party conference on 22 August, support for attendance fell from 1,500,000 to just 3,000. Miners in particular were outspokenly opposed; they sent a delegation to Downing Street to 'proclaim their strong protest against the Stockholm Conference'. More significant was the reaction of Havelock Wilson's Sailors' and Firemen's Union, which refused to transport to Stockholm those whose 'sole object . . . is to secure a German peace'. The government's decision to deny passports to British delegates further isolated those members of the Labour Party who remained adamant about going. Henderson's embarrassment was exacerbated when he was told to wait outside the Cabinet Office while colleagues discussed how to discipline him. Called in like a naughty boy to the headmaster's office, he was sternly reprimanded by the Prime Minister. Certain that no Liberal or Conservative minister would have been treated so shabbily, Henderson resigned. He nevertheless insisted, at the party conference in January 1918, that Labour must remain in the government and tried to make out that the 'doormat incident' was a personal matter. Henderson understood that leaving the government would consign Labour to the wilderness and would squander all the progress that had been made. The party backed him by three to one.[17]

The resignation nevertheless enabled the Labour Party to develop a more independent line in British politics. Ardent socialists, banished when Labour joined the government, returned to the fold. Radical liberals alienated by Lloyd George were also impressed by Labour's promises of social welfare reform; if they happened to be pacifists, they took heart from the party's Memorandum of War Aims, a virtual carbon copy of the UDC's Four Points. By early 1918, pacifists were highly optimistic about the possibilities for a peace campaign under the auspices of the Labour Party.

That optimism again proved ill-founded. Pacifists assumed that the widespread public discontent evident in early 1918 would fuel enthusiasm for a negotiated peace. Granted, there was annoyance about the food situation, disappointment at the Cambrai and Passchendaele failures, dismay over new manpower proposals and general exhaustion. Discontent was not, however, the same thing as opposition to the war. Massive casualties, rather than convincing people of the futility of further offensives, tended instead to make them more determined to press for the victory that would make sacrifice worthwhile.

Committed pacifists – most of them middle class, all of them slightly deluded – had difficulty understanding working-class feelings about the war. Logic suggested that the workers would eventually tire of a capitalist war in which they had sacrificed so much. Yet anti-war activists did not comprehend that patriotism was hard-wired into the DNA of the average worker. Love of nation was as working-class as pigeons and pork pies. Typical of the deluded was John Maclean, prominent Glasgow Marxist and a subject of romantic adulation to this day. In late 1917, he concluded that the combination of stalemate at the front, turmoil at home and revolution in Russia presented a golden opportunity for both peace and socialism. 'There is a spirit of revolution developing in the workshops,' he argued. 'Our unified purpose should be to seize the chance when our enemy at home was weak, to sweep the capitalist class out of the way and bring about peace. We [are] in the rapids of revolution.'[18]

The rapids of revolution were in fact a Bolshevik backwater. Despite Lenin's triumph in Russia, few socialists in Britain considered the Russian example worthy of emulation. Even the ILP found Maclean's revolutionary fantasies too frightening to contemplate. Yet despite espousing a very lukewarm form of socialism, the ILP had only 35,000 members by the end of the war. Outside Scotland, its active branches actually declined between 1915 and 1917 from over 600 to fewer than 500. Socialist dreams of leading the country towards peace were smothered under a heavy blanket of working-class patriotism.[19]

Pacifism and left-wing dissent nevertheless convinced Lord Milner that Britain was riddled with revolutionaries bent on leading innocent workers astray. He sought to establish 'a purely working-class movement, which I hope will knock out the "Independent Labour Party"'. With money and support from Tories, the Socialist National Defence League (SNDL) was set up in April 1915, with Victor Fisher, one-time Fabian and member of the Social Democratic Federation, at its head. 'Governments most frequently do not realise that they are on the brink of a revolution,' Fisher warned around the time of the Leeds convention. He hoped the SNDL would act as a counterweight to the 'pernicious and pestilential piffle of Pacifist cranks'. In 1916 the group changed its name to the British Workers League. A favourite pastime of supporters was to heckle ILP and UDC meetings. Its newspaper, *The British Citizen*, had an average circulation of 30,000 per week.[20]

Lloyd George did not share the concern expressed by Fisher or Milner. When Emmeline Pankhurst urged him to 'counteract the pernicious influence of the UDC', he replied that no concerted action was necessary, since 'the evil effects are for the present confined to a minority'. Police occasionally harassed UDC speakers and some members were imprisoned for DORA violations, but in general the government preferred to show its contempt by ignoring pacifists. The Home Office briefly considered censoring peace publications, but wisely decided not to create an opportunity for martyrdom. The government was happy for the propaganda campaign against peace groups to be led by private citizens and newspapers, thus suggesting that the pacifists were out of touch with popular opinion. Basil Thomson, head of Scotland Yard, provided the National War Aims Committee, a government-sponsored organisation, with 'early intimation of any pacifist movement' so that it could 'arrange indoor and outdoor meetings as a counterblast'. The police were notoriously slow to respond to violence directed against peace campaigners. Helen Swanwick, a UDC activist, recalled that 'When mobs, assiduously worked up by a few papers or a few persons, broke up meetings or assaulted speakers, no protection was to be had, and the tone taken by the authorities was it "served them right".'[21]

Lloyd George understood the temper of the workers much better than did their self-proclaimed leaders in the ILP. He knew that their loyalty was resilient and only needed occasional buttressing. In June 1917, he reminded the people that they still had right on their side. 'It is a satisfaction for Britain in these terrible times that no share of the responsibility for these events rests on her' he remarked, with clear reference to those in the UDC who had suggested otherwise. 'She is not the Jonah in this storm. The part taken by our country in this conflict, in its origin, and in its conduct, has been as honourable and chivalrous as any part ever taken in any country in any operation.' When the war entered its darkest phase in late 1917, the government responded with limited food rationing and a pay rise for munitions workers. A declaration of war aims was, significantly, unveiled at a conference of trade unionists. That declaration sounded sufficiently of Wilsonian ideals to quiet those who worried about the prolongation of the war. The dark phase ended with the launch of the German spring offensive, when the war spirit was reinvigorated by the threat of defeat. While it might seem that deft manipulation of the workers destroyed the pacifist opportunity, in truth no opportunity ever existed.[22]

Running parallel to the pacifist campaign was the movement against conscription. Though many opposed compulsion, few actively resisted. In September 1915, the TUC openly voiced its aversion to the first Military Service Act, but did not press the matter further. Individual trade unions were too busy securing exemptions for their members to devote much energy to a wider campaign of opposition. Three Labour Party ministers tendered their resignations, but all returned to the fold when Asquith assured them that the Act pertained to the duration of the war only, that it would not be extended to industrial conscription, and that conscription tribunals would be composed of civilian, not military, representatives. At the party conference in January 1916, Labour's rank and file criticised the decision to remain in the government, but did not demand its reversal. Even the UDC took a fatalistic approach, concluding that conscription, however abhorrent, was inevitable and opposition futile.

Campaigning was therefore left to the No Conscription Fellowship (NCF), led by the ethical socialist Clifford Allen. In his view, conscription violated the most important liberal principle: 'There is one interference with individual judgement that no state in the world has any sanction to enforce – that is, to tamper with the unfettered free right of everyman to decide for himself the issue of life and death.' Founded in December 1914, the NCF campaigned hard against the introduction of conscription, but its main impact came later, in helping men who resisted the call. The group consisted mainly of young men vulnerable to conscription; half of the approximately 12,000 members served prison sentences during the war. Prominent pacifists also joined, including Fenner Brockway, C. H. Norman and Russell, who took over leadership when Allen was jailed. Female members included Sylvia Pankhurst, Lydia Smith (who edited the NCF journal *The Tribunal*) and the maternalist feminist Catherine Marshall, who reckoned that the crimes she committed in aiding conscientious objectors rendered her liable to 2,000 years' imprisonment. Less conspicuous but at least as important were the hundreds of ordinary women who kept the fight going when NCF ranks were depleted due to prison sentences. Among them was Alice Wheeldon, notorious for being tried and convicted (on suspect evidence) of plotting to kill Lloyd George and Henderson with poison darts. She was sentenced to ten years' penal servitude.[23]

Allen was optimistic that from the resistance to conscription would grow a wider movement to end the war, and eventually an invigorated socialism. 'In so far as we cause the Government to persecute those who believe in peace,' he argued, 'so we may ... stimulate the national consciousness in [the] direction [of peace].' That such a statement could have been made amidst all that militant patriotism is an indication either of Allen's commitment or of his delusion, or both. Unfortunately, he was wrong-footed by the government's flexibility once conscription was introduced. The Military Service Act effectively emasculated the NCF by enshrining the right of conscientious objection. It would henceforth prove difficult for the NCF to protest against a law that clearly recognised the principle of moral opposition to military service. Rather than accept this as a partial victory, the NCF objected: 'it is not fighting in particular which revolts us, it is war itself that we will not assist'.[24]

The government handled opposition to conscription rather adroitly. There was some clumsy harassment of the NCF, such as a June 1916 raid on its offices, but in general the authorities stopped well short of suppression. Members were jailed for resisting the call-up, not because of their affiliation. This rather lenient attitude forced the NCF into a role it never meant to assume: that of a watchdog against cruel treatment of conscientious objectors (COs). 'What had begun as a movement of resistance to the new apparatus of militarism, became itself a tolerated part of that apparatus,' wrote a disgruntled Allen. 'The political sting had been drawn from the pacifist witness.'[25]

After the passage of the Act, the NCF concentrated on helping the potential CO prove himself before local tribunals. Those tribunals have received a harsh verdict in history's court of justice, but in fact, 80 per cent of the men who came before them were granted some form of exemption. This suggests that tribunal members were considerably more open-minded than the general public, which tended to judge COs as traitors, cowards or shirkers. Those who passed the tribunals were enlisted in non-combatant corps: construction crews, grave details, etc. There remained, however, 'absolutists' who refused to undertake military service of any kind. In this area, tribunals showed neither understanding nor mercy, and instead felt obliged to break their will, in some cases by sending them forcibly to the front. Of those who maintained their refusal even to the battlefield, 34 were sentenced to death.[26]

THE CONSCIENTIOUS OBJECTOR AT THE FRONT!

OH, YOU NAUGHTY UNKIND GERMAN — REALLY, IF YOU DON'T DESIST I'LL FORGET I'VE GOT A CONSCIENCE AND I'LL SMACK YOU ON THE WRIST!

The death sentences were commuted to ten years' penal servitude, but the government still worried about creating martyrs. In May 1916, Army Order X ruled that court-martialled objectors would be turned over to the Home Office, to serve sentences in civilian prisons. Two months later, the government further defused the situation by setting up the Pelham Committee, which offered non-military alternatives to service. A Central Appeals Tribunal was established to review the cases of all individuals serving prison sentences to determine whether they qualified for this scheme. Again, rather than claim victory on this point, the NCF objected that the new measures merely freed other men to be sent to the front – what it called 'killing by proxy'.[27]

Of the approximately 16,100 conscientious objectors, 3,300 opted for the Non-Combatant Corps, 2,400 worked in ambulances or as stretcher-bearers at the front and 3,964 accepted work at home under Pelham Committee guidelines. Those who eventually took civilian work were usually employed on road-making and paid at soldier's rates but without separation allowances. The individual's family could apply for poor relief, but guardians were notoriously stingy towards a CO's dependents. Some 6,261 men took their objection with them to prison at least once, of whom approximately 1,350 absolutists refused all offers of compromise and faced a repeating pattern of arrest, trial and imprisonment, during the war and afterwards. Alfred Salter of the NCF recalled visiting a fellow member, Isaac Hall, in prison: 'I was horrified at the spectacle of a living skeleton – a gaunt, bent, starved, broken man, a coal-black man with ashen lips and sunken eyes. But he was broken only in body; his soul and spirit were as resolute as ever. One of the warders told me that Isaac Hall was the bravest man he had ever met.' Stories like this prompted the *Manchester Guardian* to conclude: 'The final test of sincerity is the willingness to face consequences, and the supreme test the perseverance to death. We hope that people will now be satisfied that the conscientious objector may at least be what he professes to be, and is not necessarily a mere coward masquerading under fine pretence.' In all, 71 conscientious objectors died in prison or as a result of injuries received while imprisoned. One inmate of Camberwell Prison, told he would be executed, was slowly taken through the motions of an actual execution, to the point of the gun being loaded and pointed at him. Inmates were force-fed, tied into straitjackets, beaten, kept in filthy cells, fed on bread and water and often tortured. Two told of being kept for 28 hours handcuffed to a bar high over their heads, with a 20 lb weight pulling them down. 'Only those prepared for death could face it,' wrote one CO of his ordeal.[28]

Stephen Hobhouse, a devout Quaker, took the absolutist line to the point of refusing even to subject himself to a medical examination. Since he probably would have failed the physical, he did not want to earn exemption from a system he refused to support. He chose instead to go to prison. This stubborn maintenance of principles eventually earned absolutists some grudging admiration from those who otherwise supported the war. *The Times*, for instance, expressed 'considerable sympathy'. Most people, however, saw 'conchies' as easy targets for abuse. Scorn also came from philosophical pacifists, who considered the NCF an unwelcome diversion from the campaign against war. Brailsford called the group 'a blind alley which won't bring us infinitesimally nearer to peace'. The NCF was widely criticised for settling into the role of advocate for COs, and thus becoming, in effect, a cog in the system. Some pacifists, like Lowes Dickinson, had trouble deciding who was more worthy of contempt, tribunal members who rejected all appeals or absolutists who rejected all offers of compromise. Even Allen, reflecting upon the NCF campaign in 1919, accepted that the absolutist argument had 'repelled' and 'muddled' public opinion. Antagonism towards absolutists mushroomed out of proportion to the actual size of the group, in the process creating a large obstacle to the communication of the pacifist message. 'We seemed,' Allen wrote, 'to wrap ourselves in coil after coil of finely spun logic, to raise our pedestal upon a mountain of phrases and formulas and to be unresponsive to the altered mood of those whose opinions we sought to change.' That was perhaps a bit too harsh, since the predilection for finely spun logic, and for ignoring the wider public's simple rationality of a just war, was common among all dissenters during this war.[29]

Pacifists and anti-conscriptionists were mainly ignored by

the government because they did not pose a serious threat to the conduct of the war. Their treatment contrasts sharply with that of enemy aliens, who were harassed out of all proportion to their actual danger. In addition, since they were unlikely to court public sympathy, the government felt free to take a harsh line. Liberal values were conspicuously absent.

The infrastructure for dealing with this 'problem' had been well established before the war, including the compilation of a secret register recording data on 28,380 aliens, fewer than half of whom were German or Austro-Hungarian. The day after the declaration of war, McKenna put the mechanism in gear by pushing through the Alien Restrictions Act. It gave the government the power to control where aliens congregated and, in particular, to remove them from prohibited areas around military installations and ports. All resident aliens were required to register with the police and to notify authorities if they moved. By 9 September 1914, 50,633 Germans and 16,141 Austrians and Hungarians had registered. Prosecutions for illegal movement came quickly, thus demonstrating the government's serious intent. On 24 August 1914, Karl Kley, a resident alien from London, was sentenced to three months' hard labour for travelling five miles from his place of residence.[30]

As the weeks passed, the legal matrix was extended and reinforced. New measures prohibited the posting of letters abroad and outlawed the ownership of carrier pigeons, wireless sets, firearms, cameras, military or naval maps and motor vehicles. Enemy aliens could not assume a new name without the permission of the Home Office. In October 1914, the rounding-up of all unnaturalised male Germans, Austrians and Hungarians of military age began. They were either interned or repatriated. This caused a crisis in the London clothing trade, since many tailors were German. By the end of November, new regulations stipulated that all persons moving into hotels or boarding houses, whether alien or not, had to register with the police. The government also assumed powers to close down premises, such as restaurants and bars, frequented by aliens. The distinction between friendly and enemy aliens became increasingly blurred; regulations were often applied regardless of origin. Yet no matter how harsh the action taken, the right-wing press remained unsatisfied, often accusing the government of protecting a German spy ring within Whitehall. Wild rumours of sabotage and espionage boosted newspaper circulation. By August 1918, the government, under enormous pressure from right-wing firebrands, assumed powers to revoke the citizenship of naturalised Germans and Austrians.

This was a bad time to be a pigeon in Britain. Leaving aside the fact that a good many were cooked into pies in order to alleviate meat shortages, overzealous patriots started shooting on sight any carrier pigeon, on the assumption that it was working for the Germans. *The Scotsman* reported on 16 Septermber 1914: 'Already all over the country numbers of birds, the property of innocent owners, have been shot. So serious has the menace become that the National Homing Union have issued a warning to the general public that the shooting of homing pigeons is illegal. A reward of £5 is offered to anyone giving information of such an offence.' Aliens seen in the vicinity of pigeons, or where pigeons congregated, were immediately suspect. Peter Duhn, a German living in London, was sentenced to six months' imprisonment after a witness testified seeing 'a pigeon on a level with his head about three yards in front of him flying away'. She admitted that although she 'did not actually see the pigeon leave his hand . . . it must have come from him'. In any case, 'it carried a little white paper under its wing'. A search of Duhn's residence found no evidence of pigeon-keeping.[31]

By late September 1914, there were 13,600 enemy aliens in internment camps – 10,500 civilians and the rest prisoners of war.[32] Since the facilities for holding them were stretched to breaking point, the government decided that henceforth only

Back in Blighty

those aliens who posed an immediate risk would be interned. That decision caused considerable outrage, leading to a wave of anti-German hysteria. Rudolf Rocker, a German living in London, sensed a 'poison in the air':

> In October mobs collected in the streets – in the Old Kent Road, in Deptford, Brixton, Poplar – and smashed and looted shops which they thought were occupied by Germans. There were real pogroms. Some houses were set on fire, and the people who lived there had to flee for their lives over the roofs. The police were helpless. The troops had to be brought in before the outbreaks were put down. About 40 people were arrested and punished, but they were not the worst offenders. The yellow press which incited them kept up its campaign to force the government to intern all enemy aliens.

Bowing to mob rule, the government reintroduced wholesale internment. Thereafter, the numbers interned fluctuated according to public tolerance. Women and men above military age were repatriated, though appeals against both internment and repatriation were allowed. In general, those interned did not suffer physically. Food supplies were maintained, though quality was poor. At the end of the war, internment camps were serving horsemeat five days a week and some internees supplemented their diets by eating cats, dogs and seagulls. Yet only 105 aliens died in camps up to April 1917, below the expected actuarial level. At the Knockaloe camp on the Isle of Man, the death rate was 2.5 per thousand, while it was 15.7 per thousand for the island generally. Since internment of aliens had little to do with the actual danger they posed, one has to marvel at the enormous energy wasted, especially given the manpower shortage.[33]

Every alien was assumed to be a potential spy. The security

services had prepared in advance a list of 22 German agents operating in Britain. On the outbreak of war, all but one were arrested. After questioning them, the authorities rounded up 14 more suspected agents. Not satisfied with this effort, Vernon Kell, the paranoid head of MO5(g), conducted an intensive campaign to root out 'conspiracies to commit outrage'. During the first month of the war, the Metropolitan Police investigated nearly 9,000 cases, but found no evidence 'indicating any combination amongst alien enemies . . . or any kind of military organisation among them'. The government's obsession with spies is indicated by the expansion of the security services. MO5(g) had a staff of 20 before the war. In January 1916 it was supplanted by MI5, which had 844 personnel when war ended. The other group dealing with aliens, MI9 (formerly MO9), expanded from 170 staff in 1914 to 4,861 at the armistice. In addition, at the outbreak of war a special constabulary for London was established; within three weeks it employed 20,000 amateur guards to patrol strategic points like bridges, tunnels, waterworks, gasworks and canals. The consequences were occasionally tragic. A man loitering near a railway bridge was shot and severely wounded when he failed to answer a challenge from a sentry. Subsequent investigation revealed that the man was stone deaf. Immense effort was mobilised against a German espionage network that was poorly organised, unprofessional and limited in scope. In truth, the Germans gave little attention to spying. By 1917, 201 people had been arrested for passing information to the enemy and 31 suspected agents were seized, of whom 24 were convicted and 12 executed. Few of those arrested were actually aliens resident in Britain. Most were commercial travellers of various nationalities who entered Britain perfectly legally. Not a single act of sabotage occurred during the war.[34]

Neither aliens nor dissenters posed any serious threat to Britain's conduct of the war. The general public's hostility toward both groups (occasionally spilling over into violence) indicates how solid was support for the war. Both inadvertently helped to sustain morale. The 'enemies in our midst' were a focus for hatred and a stimulus to hard work. They also provided easy scapegoats: ships were sunk because of spies; aliens sabotaged shell production; pacifists undermined recruiting efforts. The British people needed aliens and dissenters to keep their hatred stoked and their determination sharp. Bertrand Russell, Clifford Allen and their comrades probably did more for the cause of war than they ever achieved for the cause of peace.

Chapter 9

Thinking the Right Thoughts

In September 1915, the publicist, newspaper proprietor and former MP Horatio Bottomley addressed a rally at the Winter Gardens in Bournemouth. He told the crowd:

> Ladies and gentlemen, I want you to pull yourselves together and keep your peckers up. I want to assure you that within six weeks of to-day we shall have the Huns on the run. We shall drive them out of France, out of Flanders, out of Belgium, across the Rhine, and back into their own territory. There we shall give them a taste of their own medicine. Bear in mind, I speak of that which I know. Tomorrow it will be officially denied, but take it from me that if Bottomley says so, it is so!

At another meeting, Bottomley announced: 'Every hero of the war who has fallen in the field of battle has performed an Act of Greatest Love, so penetrating and intense in its purifying character that I do not hesitate to express my opinion that any and every past sin is automatically wiped out from the record of his life.' On both occasions, the crowd was mesmerised by Bottomley. He seemed a one-man propaganda machine – Britain's secret weapon. In fact, he was just another profiteer who saw an opportunity and exploited it.[1]

The British government, as has been seen, approached the problems that war produced by first appealing to the cooperative spirit of the people. That, however, meant that persuasion played a large part; citizens had frequently to be reminded of their duty to volunteer. Yet who was to do the persuading if the government instinctively abstained from interfering in the lives of citizens? Who would volunteer to encourage volunteers? A typically British solution was found. Mobilisation of public spirit was performed to the greatest extent by private individuals like Bottomley, John Buchan and Jessie Pope, who delighted in telling ordinary citizens what to do, especially if there was money to be made in doing so. Direct government intervention occurred only as a last resort, in a limited and surreptitious fashion.

This approach had distinct advantages. The British people had always been wary of a government that presumed to tell them how to think. The government was equally convinced that good causes should not require advertisement. Therefore persuasion originating from private sources seemed more acceptable to the body politic and more likely to be effective. Also, this method allowed the government to steer clear of propaganda's ugly side. Appeals to the people's base instincts were left to individuals, newspapers and fringe organisations.

The approach also had distinct disadvantages. With no coherent propaganda programme, there was considerable over-lap and contradiction among the private bodies working in this area. For instance, a patriotic newspaper might assure its readers that all was well at the front, in the process undermining a private recruiting committee's efforts to secure volunteers for the army. By failing to manage the news, the government allowed the newspapers to create a hero of Kitchener, thus rendering it impossible to get rid of 'Lord K of Chaos' when his deficiencies became apparent. Disorganisation was, however, a cost the government willingly paid in order to preserve the voluntarist principle. In the process, it fell prey to the spirit it refused to control. Emotions were given free rein, irrationality was often encouraged, and fraud sometimes occurred.[2]

On the home front, most of the morale-boosting was carried out unconsciously by ordinary citizens. Even at the worst of times, the vast majority of the population wanted to believe that the war was proceeding well, therefore they traded rumours which had precisely that effect. Optimism was bolstered by tales of an angel strengthening the British line at Mons, and of Russian soldiers in August 1914 (still with snow on their boots) travelling across Britain in the direction of the Western Front. One popular story concerned the alleged madness of the Kaiser, whose ear trouble 'seriously distempers and heats the brain'. A steady flow of German atrocity tales reinforced beliefs that the enemy was singularly heinous. Even the more frightening rumours, such as the arrest of five aliens for supposedly attempting to poison Chingford reservoir, acted as a spur to vigilance.[3]

Until late 1917, when war weariness grew, the government left propaganda to inspired amateurs in organisations like the Cobden Club, the United Workers, the Atlantic Union and the Victoria League. These groups mobilised well-known authors to write on behalf of the war effort. The Fight for Right Movement, for instance, included John Buchan, Sir Henry Newbolt, Thomas Hardy and Gilbert Murray. 'The spirit of the Movement is essentially the spirit of Faith,' its manifesto proclaimed. 'Faith in the good of man; Faith therefore in ourselves, Faith in the righteousness of our Cause, Faith in the ultimate triumph of Right; but with this Faith the understanding that Right will only win through the purification, the efforts and the sacrifices of men and women who mean to make it prevail.'[4]

The reference to faith, purification and sacrifice was common: the war was widely seen as a religious crusade offering spiritual purgation. Churches especially stressed this message, perhaps understandably given that the subject of moral regeneration was not the sort of message that usually came from the government. Some sermons were quite grotesque: P. M. Yearsley, a Wimbledon clergyman, cautioned parishioners that the Germans 'intended, in the event of a successful invasion of England, to destroy every male child'. Others, if not outright lies, were hardly appropriate to the pulpit: the Bishop of London's jingoistic recruiting efforts incurred the censure of many colleagues. Most clergymen were less blatant, preferring instead to make references to the beauty of Christ's sacrifice in the hope that parishioners would get the message.[5]

Private bodies produced nearly 2.5 million copies of 110 different posters on a multitude of themes in the first year of the war. Voluntary organisations stood poised to support, in a tangible way, every war-related government initiative. This pattern began early in the war with the large number of groups formed to persuade the faint-hearted to join Kitchener's army, most notorious among them the Order of the White Feather. Later, government agencies like the Ministry of National Service and the National War Savings Committee were aided by a plethora of voluntary groups that organised meetings and recruitment drives, and, in the case of the Ministry of Food, instituted campaigns to encourage food economy. Sarah Macnaughtan noticed a 'peculiar brutality' in supposedly well-meaning people prodding others to contribute to the war effort. 'I am reminded of birds on a small ledge pushing each other into the sea. The big bird that pushed another one over goes to sleep comfortably.'[6]

One of the biggest birds, literally and figuratively, was Bottomley. 'I am going to constitute myself the Unofficial Recruiting Agent to the British Empire,' he told his assistant in September 1914. 'These professional politicians don't understand the business.' He appealed directly to the population's coarser instincts, for instance by playing the role of prosecutor in a mock trial of the Kaiser in Bournemouth. As one observer described, these events were essentially 'music hall engagements disguised as recruiting meetings'. Bottomley's tactics were enormously successful in motivating the common people to contribute to the war effort, especially early in the war, when his recruitment drives produced undeniable results. After attending a meeting, George Bernard Shaw reflected: 'It's exactly what I expected: the man gets his popularity by telling people with sufficient bombast just what they think themselves and therefore want to hear.' No mainstream politician rivalled him in the crowds he attracted, nor in his ability and willingness to rouse working-class bigotry. At times, however, it was difficult to distinguish patriotism from self-promotion. 'I sell myself to the man with the most money,' he admitted. Recruitment speeches were given free, but at all other patriotic lectures (he delivered some 340 during the war) he claimed between 65 and 85 per cent of the money donated. A highly successful scheme for selling War Savings Certificates and Victory Bonds, advertised in Bottomley's *John Bull*, was eventually discovered to be fraudulent, resulting in his conviction and imprisonment in 1921.[7]

Early in the war, the most influential voluntary body was the Central Committee for National Patriotic Organisations (CCNPO), formed in August 1914. In theory an educational initiative, its purpose was in truth propagandistic. The presence of eminent government figures in senior, albeit titular, positions (Asquith was president, Balfour and Rosebery vice presidents) allowed groups like the CCNPO to claim political legitimacy without having to bear political responsibility. A similar pattern was followed by the Parliamentary Recruiting Committee (PRC), which became the model for quasi-governmental propaganda efforts. Though it had government backing, took advice from the War Office and cooperated with the Ministry of Munitions and the Home Office, it was not strictly speaking an official government body. Great efforts were made to maintain the illusion of voluntarism. Funding came from private sources and, though senior political figures headed the organisation, they did so as private citizens. The very nature of the PRC was a propaganda message: its non-partisan structure suggested a spirit of cooperation, while its private facade reinforced the voluntarist ethic.

Not until February 1917, with the establishment of the Department of Information, did the government openly acknowledge involvement in home-front propaganda. Lloyd George felt that after two and a half years of consistently gloomy news, a more dynamic, centralised approach was needed. The semblance of voluntarism was not, however, completely abandoned. The National War Aims Committee (NWAC), established by Buchan's Department of Information in May 1917, imitated the voluntary, non-partisan character of the PRC. The NWAC, which eventually absorbed the CCNPO, perpetuated the technique of shaping propaganda messages to local conditions. By early 1918 it was active in 345 parliamentary constituencies. During one fortnight in 1917, 899 meetings were organised.[8]

The MP Stanley Baldwin admitted that 'Propaganda is not a word that has a pleasant sound in English ears ... The Englishman dislikes talking about himself and dislikes advertising what he has done.' This in part explains the government's enthusiasm for volunteer efforts, since they seemed less vulgar. When government began to assume a more active role, some politicians did not react well. In a very hostile Commons debate in August 1918, one MP railed against 'the assumption that ... the influencing of thought and opinion amongst civilised nations, is a thing to be carried on in the spirit of a successful commercial traveller, and that the kind of thing that constitutes good advertising for business is the kind of thing that constitutes good advertising in the case of a great nation and a real war.' In order to appease its critics, the government had to promise that all propaganda bodies would be disbanded immediately after the armistice – a sop to those who feared that propaganda might be used to sustain an unpopular government in power. A strange contradiction arose: the government was assumed to be too righteous to require propaganda, but not righteous enough to use it honestly.[9]

The government's closer supervision of propaganda is demonstrated by the fact that from August 1917, the Department of Information and the NWAC were headed by the same man, Sir Edward Carson. Though the NWAC was at first dependent upon donations from party funds, this changed in November 1917, when £240,000 was allotted from the Treasury, the largest single sum the government spent on home-front propaganda. According to its charter, the NWAC was designed to 'counteract and render nugatory the insidious and specious propaganda of the pacifist publications' and to encourage the 'inflexible determination to continue to a victorious end the struggle in maintenance of those ideals of Liberty and Justice which are the common and sacred cause of the allies'. (The rather pompous, exaggerated prose brings to mind a sledgehammer and a nut.) Since women were assumed to be more susceptible to war-weariness than men, special attention was given to them. As with the government, NWAC volunteers had difficulty distinguishing between genuine pacifism and vague discontent arising from labour problems, inflation or food shortages. Efforts by middle-class volunteers to encourage renewed sacrifice from working-class audiences often annoyed the latter.[10]

As time wore on, the definition of war aims widened and the scope of NWAC activity broadened. By March 1918, the agency effectively controlled all home-front propaganda. Like the PRC, it concentrated on organising public meetings and producing pamphlets and posters, with distribution voluntarily managed by the newsagents W. H. Smith. From August to October 1917, some 3,192 meetings were held. At large public rallies a brass band would play and often a tank or other impressive weapon would be exhibited. The tactic of dropping leaflets from an aeroplane was occasionally employed, as during the Birmingham 'Win the War Day' on 21 September 1918. Great use was made of film, but since cinema space could not always be secured, the NWAC fitted out five motorised cinema vans that toured the country showing films outdoors on gable ends.[11]

The existence of a war aims committee does not mean that the government engaged in an open discussion of war aims with citizens. 'Once it was known we were discussing these questions,' a Cabinet document warned, 'the effective prosecution of the war might be rendered more difficult'. The problem was complicated by the fact that during 1917, a number of incidents dented public confidence in a noble cause. On 19 July, the Reichstag passed a resolution calling for a negotiated peace. Scorned by Lloyd George, it was nevertheless welcomed by a small but significant group of MPs. After the Russian revolution, the details of secret treaties were leaked to the press, raising embarrassing questions about the territorial claims of the Allies. Meanwhile, President Wilson had established a moral position calculated to separate the United States from its European partners. These developments rendered the NWAC's work much more difficult. In the absence of a clearly defined statement of aims, the NWAC instead tried to explain what was happening in the war, in a manner calculated to bolster support. This included peripheral information on all the belligerent countries and the nature of their governments – rather like a current-events seminar. Fearing that Bolshevism might be contagious, the NWAC prepared material and speeches directed specifically at the working-class. Pamphlets by prominent trade unionists like Ben Tillett explained why peace on German terms was unthinkable. Audiences and readers were told that Prussian militarism had still to be defeated and that peace short of full surrender would leave it ripe for resurgence. The incurable barbarism of the Teutonic race remained a common theme.[12]

Lloyd George finally issued a statement of war aims on 5 January 1918. In it, he claimed that Britain had no intention of destroying Germany nor of imposing democracy upon her. Instead, British aims were to defeat Germany's army uncon-ditionally and to use victory for positive ends. These included restoration of Belgium, the return of Alsace-Lorraine to France, self-determination for other conquered countries, reparations to the victims of German violence and the establishment of an international organisation to arbitrate disputes and control arms. While the statement answered demands for a declaration of war aims, one doubts it did much to bolster morale. By this stage, fatalism had set in: the war was there and it had to be won.

'To give up work seems to me a little like divorcing a husband,' Macnaughtan felt. 'So, however dull or tiresome a husband or work may be, one mustn't give up.' A similar fatalism was evident in the trenches. The British Army was built on duty, but it kept going by determination alone. Alfred Pollard went to war hating Germans and desperate to kill. He had craved the opportunities war seemed to offer. By early 1917, however, he was simply doing his job. 'Now I was a man with no hope of the War ending for years,' he reflected. 'I looked at a trench full of corpses without any sensation whatever. Neither pity nor fear that I might soon be one myself, nor anger against their killer. Nothing stirred me. I was just a machine carrying out my appointed work to the best of my ability.'[13]

Lord Lansdowne's letter to the *Daily Telegraph* in December 1917, warning that unless peace was negotiated all of Europe would soon lie in ruins, had impressed only those diehard pacifists who had argued just that since the beginning of the war. Given the feelings of those like Macnaughtan and Pollard, there was little that propaganda could achieve. In March, the government learned a lesson about the manipulation of morale. After four years of trying to convince the public that the Germans were on the brink of defeat, it had to admit that the enemy could still achieve a sizeable victory. The people responded magnificently: strikes stopped, recruiting offices were again crowded and production increased. Contrary to expectations, the public could handle bad news. Telling the people they were winning was not nearly as effective as warning them that they might lose.

The Germans, by conforming to popular stereotypes, inadvertently made the most valuable contribution to British support for the war. Their conception of total war was too aggressive for British tastes, their ambition too vulgar for a nation that pretends to be unambitious. The Germans were also very good at appearing evil, the execution of the nurse Edith Cavell being a case in point. In a strictly legal sense, her assistance to British soldiers stranded behind German lines was indeed espionage. 'It is undoubtedly a terrible thing that the woman has been executed,' the German Foreign Secretary Arthur Zimmerman admitted, 'but consider what would happen to a State, particularly in war, if it left crimes aimed at the safety of its armies to go unpunished because committed by women.' That was certainly logical, but in a rather cold-hearted (German) way. The Germans failed to understand that their cause would have been better served by showing mercy than by the strict application of law. Instead, a nurse was executed and a martyr created. The U-boat war, the shelling of Eastbourne and the bombing of London arose from Germany's acceptance that in modern war all civilians are combatants. Britain and the rest of the 'civilised' world were still a generation away from accepting that fact, even though it was a fact.[14]

The British have long been enthusiastic newspaper readers. During the war, they were offered a wide variety of papers; sixteen dailies served London alone. That seems a huge waste of journalistic effort, since the vast majority of them carried the same basic message. While some originally opposed the war, they shifted to pained acceptance after 4 August 1914, and to strident belligerence after news of the German invasion of Belgium filtered through. Newspapers were, in the main, voluntary propaganda agencies working on behalf of the British war effort. This was an important function, since journalists not only knew how to reach the ordinary citizen, they knew how to communicate with him in language calculated to fire his emotions. Witness, for instance, the massive circulation of the letter from 'A Little Mother', published in the *Morning Post* in 1916, with its exhortation to women to 'pass on the human ammunition of "only sons" to fill the gaps'. The letter, almost certainly a fabrication, was subsequently made into a pamphlet that sold 75,000 copies in less than a week, a far more impressive circulation than anything produced by the CCNPO, PRC or NWAC. It is ironic, then, that the government and the military remained so suspicious of the fourth estate, placing ridiculous obstacles in the way of reporters who were, on the whole, extremely loyal and unashamedly belligerent.[15]

Back in Blighty

An uneasy relationship existed between government and the press. On the one hand, most newspaper proprietors rose from the same stock and belonged to the same clubs as politicians. They were nevertheless a breed apart, rather like eccentric cousins who refused to conform to accepted codes of behaviour. The journalist's responsibility to question government was allowed in theory but caused conflict in practice, since criticism was easily confused with disloyalty. Ministers expected that they should be able to sit down with press lords and agree, over a few brandies, what the people should know. Most of the time this arrangement worked. C. P. Scott, editor of the *Manchester Guardian*, decided not to publish a letter received from a corporal who described how the British had accidentally shelled their own troops at Loos, because it would be 'too damaging' to morale. Occasionally, however, newspapers acted too independently, causing some politicians to demand stiffer controls. Because press lords felt that their loyalty was beyond repute, they resented talk of regulation. Needless to say, those who whistled the government's tune were given special favours, those who did not suffered unfairly. The relationship was usually symbiotic, but occasionally parasitic.[16]

The government's paranoid fear of spies had an impact upon the way newspapers went about their business. Some regulations were ridiculous: weather reports were banned on the grounds that the information was useful to the enemy, and the publication of chess problems (suspected of being a conduit for secret messages) ceased. More serious were the controls imposed by the Press Bureau, established on 6 August by the First Lord, Winston Churchill, in cooperation with Kitchener. According to Churchill, the Bureau was designed to ensure that 'a steady stream of trustworthy information supplied both by the War Office and the Admiralty can be given to the press'. In fact, the stream was seldom steady and the information rarely trustworthy. Journalists quickly discovered that the Press Bureau's function was not publicity but censorship – they dubbed it the Suppress Bureau. When F. E. Smith, the first head of the Bureau, resigned on 30 September 1914, in came the even more diligent Sir Stanley Buckmaster, who demanded sweeping powers to 'punish as well as threaten the press'. The government, however, wisely decided that further restrictions were unnecessary. Annoyed, Buckmaster subsequently complained that cosy relationships between ministers and certain press lords 'rendered the proper execution of my duties extremely difficult'. That was perhaps true, but only because Buckmaster was intoxicated by authority. The Bureau nevertheless continued to be dominated by the service departments, with the effect that secrecy remained an obsession. By November 1914, even the ever-cautious Bonar Law was questioning whether 'the Press is more muzzled than is necessary for military reasons'.[17]

Censorship came in two forms. Firstly, the information journalists received was strictly controlled; banned from close proximity to the fighting forces, they had to rely on official briefings. Kitchener wanted total secrecy, but found he could not be that restrictive. He instead started from the assumption that, since 'it is not always easy to decide what information may or may not be dangerous . . . whenever there is any doubt we do not hesitate to prevent publication'. The army's official correspondent, Colonel Sir Ernest Swinton, endeavoured to 'tell as much of the truth as was compatible with safety, to guard against depression and pessimism, and to check unjustified optimism which might lead to a relaxation of effort'. Swinton's colleague, Philip Gibbs, later explained that 'the principle which guided me in my work was above all to avoid helping the enemy. That appeared to me even more important than the purveyance of news to our own people.' Thus, censorship was intended both to prevent valuable information from getting to the enemy and to keep the public ignorant since bad news was thought to damage morale. *Punch* commented ironically on the fact that the best information on British forces came from American papers: 'Even their provincial organs often contain important and cheering news of the doings of the British Army many days before the Censor releases the information in England.' Buckmaster was determined to block any information which would 'unduly depress our people', a policy which prompted one irate citizen to remark: 'It seems incredible that an official in such a capacity could so entirely be a stranger to the sentiment and character of our British race as to think such a course advisable.' 'The papers are complaining, not without reason, that we keep them on a starvation diet,' Asquith noted in September 1914. Instead of relaxing press restrictions, he urged Churchill to add 'such a seasoning of condiments as your well-skilled hand can supply'.[18]

The second form of censorship involved the control exercised over what journalists actually wrote. The pre-war practice of voluntary censorship was continued; editors submitted to the Bureau any material felt to be sensitive, but were not required to do so. The Bureau regularly issued 'D' notices designed to warn editors about topics they should avoid. Self-censorship worked because editors understood that the government could impose heavy penalties under DORA if material deemed damaging to the war effort was published. The most notable example was the two-week suspension of the *Globe* after it published stories in November 1915 that Kitchener was being forced to resign. The story was essentially true, but that did not prevent prosecution under regulations that rendered it unlawful to 'spread false reports or make false statements'. No right of appeal was allowed. Editors could be prosecuted for publishing anything deemed valuable to the enemy even if the information originated from the Press Bureau. Furthermore, though the Bureau operated under the auspices of the Home Office, they were not one and the same. Thus, an article passed by the Bureau might still invite censure by the Home Office. Given all of these risks, cautious editors were sometimes more scrupulous than they needed to be.[19]

Since the press was overwhelmingly loyal, it would have made more sense for the Bureau to assume a public relations function rather than a regulatory one. Instead, for most of the war, but particularly in the first crucial year, the government failed abysmally in managing the news. 'No good is gained by keeping the country in a Fool's Paradise,' Georgina Lee complained. 'We believe in the ultimate result, for the nation is determined to go on fighting until victory is achieved. But what suspense there is from day-to-day, as to the fate and movement of our Army.' She regretted that the people were not being trusted with the truth. 'The meagreness of details given in the press is the subject of much criticism. We get most of our news from the French and Russian War Offices who are much less reticent. This misplaced reticence on the part of the War Office is having a bad effect on recruiting, for the nation is losing interest in a war of which they see and hear nothing.' The Bureau, for instance, did not confirm the embarkation of the BEF until three days after it arrived in France, thus annoying reporters who felt that not only did the public have a right to know, but that the efficiency of the mobilisation would have been a boon to morale. Rather strangely, no restrictions were imposed on reporting the retreat from Mons, a setback the government might have done well to keep under wraps. In contrast, the sinking of the battleship *Audacious* on 27 October 1914 was kept secret for the entire war, much to the annoyance of Rear Admiral Sir Douglas Brownrigg, the Royal Navy's Chief Censor, who felt that the decision 'cost us the confidence of the public both here and abroad'. Members of the public who strove to keep up with the news grew annoyed when important events revealed in foreign papers were completely ignored in British ones. Journalists found the lack of consistent guidelines governing what could and could not be reported deeply troubling. *The Times*, commenting on the *Globe* affair, remarked how the government had 'not for the first time . . . missed a golden opportunity of working with the press instead of attempting to mystify it, feed it with half-truths and finally to penalise it'. Obsessive secrecy convinced some journalists, in particular the *Times* military correspondent Charles à Court Repington, that censorship was 'a cloak to cover all political, naval and military mistakes' and that journalists consequently had a duty to expose them. Most reporters, however, patiently tolerated the restrictions.[20]

In the absence of real news, the press took to exaggerating relatively insignificant events, such as air raids. These provided exciting tales (unlike the Western Front) and conveniently underlined the barbarism of the Hun. The stories also escaped the jurisdiction of the censor, since they concerned information in the public domain. They nevertheless spread fear throughout Britain, even in places where German bombers could not possibly reach. The Press Bureau asked newspapers to 'refrain from publishing further articles which may add to the feeling of apprehension . . . already prevalent specially among the poorest and most ignorant classes', but the requests had little effect. Sensational reporting in turn reinforced the view that journalists could not be trusted. Yet the government had only itself to blame, since a more cooperative policy regarding the release of information would have made it easier to control news deemed inconvenient. The gulf between the home front and the fighting front, about which almost every soldier complained, was widened because of the obstacles put in place by the censors.[21]

In early 1915, the Press Bureau grew more accommodating towards journalists. Weekly ministerial press conferences organised by the Newspaper Proprietors Association began in February. In May, restrictions barring correspondents from the front were lifted. On Foreign Office instigation, senior army and naval officers began giving weekly briefings to journalists. The establishment of MI7 within the War Office in early 1916 further improved the handling of information, with better recognition of how censorship could serve propaganda. These changes did not, however, help the accuracy of reporting, since the high command, still deeply suspicious, imposed strict restrictions on where correspondents could go. Reporters were carefully provided with a 'headquarters view' that reflected official optimism. 'Our worst enemy for a time was Sir Douglas Haig,' Gibbs later confessed. 'He had the old cavalry officers' prejudice against war correspondents and "writing fellows", and made no secret of it. When he became Commander-in-Chief he sent for us and said things which rankled. One of them was that "after all you are only writing for Mary Ann in the kitchen".' Gibbs took exception to that and, to his credit, challenged Haig:

I . . . told him that it was not only for Mary Ann that we were writing, but for the whole nation and Empire, and that he could not conduct his war in secret, as though the people at home, whose sons and husbands were fighting and dying, had no concern in the matter. The spirit of the fighting men, and the driving power behind the armies, depended upon the support of the whole people and their continuing loyalties.

Haig responded in his usual manner, namely by grunting and then directing his attention elsewhere. At his GHQ, intelligence, censorship and propaganda were all handled by Brigadier General John Charteris who tended to confuse these various functions. On one occasion reporters were shown debilitated German prisoners as proof that attrition was working. In order to make the message more convincing, Charteris removed able-bodied prisoners before the inspection. Most reporters, being patriotically inclined, applied further embellishment to Charteris's already embroidered information.[22]

Arthur Ponsonby of the Union of Democratic Control felt that there was 'no more discreditable period in the history of journalism'. While he admittedly had an axe to grind, the criticism was justified. The press cooperated willingly in a collective effort to pull the wool over the public's eyes. Since the military provided few traditional tales of valour, desperate correspondents occasionally made them up. For instance, while Haig's horsemen dealt with obsolescence by playing polo, magazines and newspapers still reported impressive cavalry charges. Attacks that pushed the British line forward a few yards were reported as 'Dramatic Advances All Along the Front'. As Lord Rothermere admitted to J. L. Garvin, 'We're telling lies, we know we're telling lies, we daren't tell the truth.' Gibbs, one of the more honest war correspondents, commented candidly on the elusive nature of truth:

> My dispatches tell the truth. There is not a word, I vow, of conscious falsehood in them ... but they do not tell all the truth. I have had to spare the feelings of the men and women who have sons and husbands still fighting in France. I have not told all there is to tell about the agonies of this war, nor given in full realism the horrors that are inevitable in such fighting. It is perhaps better not to do so, here and now, although it is a moral cowardice which makes many people shut their eyes to the shambles, comforting their soul with fine phrases about the beauty of sacrifice.

What resulted was a fictional war that bore little resemblance to the one soldiers actually fought. C. E. Montague, who served as a press censor, felt that the journalists were rather too enthusiastic in producing propaganda:

The average war correspondent – there were golden exceptions – insensibly acquired a cheerfulness in the face of vicarious torment and danger. Through his despatches there ran a brisk implication that the regimental officers and men enjoyed nothing better than 'going over the top'; that a battle was just a rough jovial picnic, that a fight never went on long enough for the men, that their only fear was lest the war should end this side of the Rhine. This tone roused the fighting troops to fury against the writers. This, the men reflected, in helpless anger, was what people at home were offered as faithful accounts of what their friends in the field were thinking and suffering.

No wonder, then, that soldiers on leave often felt alienated from their families. Evidence suggests that in fact the British public responded well to adversity and could have been trusted with the truth. This issue caught the attention of the journalist Arthur Moore early in the war. Referring to the depressing news of September 1914, he remarked to his editor that 'it seemed incredible that a great people should be kept in ignorance of the situation which it had to face. It is important that the nation should know and realise certain things. Bitter truths, but we can face them.'[23]

Prosecution of newspapers was remarkably rare – evidence that self-censorship worked well. As Gibbs admitted, 'We identified ourselves absolutely with the Armies in the field. We wiped out of our minds all thought of personal scoops and all temptation to write one word which would make the task of officers and men more difficult or dangerous. There was no need of censorship of our despatches. We were our own censors.' The Press Bureau did admonish editors – sometimes as often as three times a week – but problems arose mainly from overenthusiastic reporting, not from wilful attempts to undermine or criticise the war effort. Granted, complaints about government were printed, most notably during the shell scandal, when Northcliffe used his power to challenge Asquith. Criticisms of the government were, however, designed to encourage a more dynamic prosecution of the war, not to protest Britain's involvement. Though relations between press and government gradually improved, change came on the latter's terms. Government gradually realised that journalists were willing propagandists. Emphasis then shifted from controlling the press to playing upon journalists' egos. Poachers were promoted to gamekeepers, as for instance in the appointment of George Riddell as a government adviser early in the war, and later with the drafting of the press barons Beaverbrook, Rothermere and Northcliffe into the Cabinet. Lower down the scale, journalists were kept sweet with minor posts in the Press Bureau, exclusive access to military sources or strategic use of the honours system. It was not a proud period for British journalism. 'I was thoroughly and deeply ashamed of what I had written, for the good reason that it was untrue,' wrote William Beach Thomas after the war. 'The vulgarity of enormous headlines and the enormity of one's own name did not lessen the shame.' The Harlot of Fleet Street sold herself cheaply. [24]

No restrictions applied when journalists wrote of German barbarity. Widespread circulation of atrocity stories immediately after the outbreak of the war has led conspiracy theorists to suspect a government plot, planned in advance. Yet it is impossible to believe that a government so amateur in other areas of propaganda could have been so adept in this one. It seems instead that the atrocity stories arose from a collective hysteria which made lies easy to tell and hard to discredit. Popular prejudice encouraged the public to believe the worst about the enemy and to pass on rumours that reinforced cultural stereotypes. For instance, severed hand stories, of which there were many variations, reflected prevalent cultural fears. The alleged victims were usually innocent children, young (virginal) women, members of the clergy or nuns – the latter suggesting religious martyrdom. Many atrocity stories had sexual/ sadomasochistic themes; Nurse Hume, it was alleged, had her breasts cut off by a German soldier. Without probing too deeply into psychological explanations for the public's fascination, one suspects that the stories allowed discussion of topics ordinarily considered taboo. 'A young woman ravished by the enemy,' wrote Harold Lasswell, historian of British propaganda in the war, 'yields secret satisfaction to a host of vicarious ravishers on the other side.'[25]

Myths and gossip aside, many atrocity stories had truth lurking within. During the advance through Belgium (the period from which most tales emerged) the enormous pressure upon the mainly conscript German army did cause a collapse of discipline. When Belgians resisted the invaders, sometimes viciously, German officers sanctioned a brutal response. Hostages were taken, human shields were used and rape was widespread. One study of the invasion has recorded in excess of a hundred incidents in which more than ten civilians were killed. An estimated 20–30,000 buildings were destroyed, not as a result of fighting between armies, but from malicious burning. The Germans did not deny their part in these reprisals, but were surprised when they were labelled atrocities by Entente authorities keen to exploit the propaganda value.

Real events combined with civilian imagination to produce powerful myths. The fear and excitement of autumn 1914 rendered the British susceptible to fantastic tales. Belgian refugees who escaped to Britain were only too happy to provide eyewitness accounts. Since the stories were by definition sensational, they made good newspaper copy, better than anything emanating from a stalemated front. German soldiers seemed believable as murderers, rapists, sadists and arsonists. In line with their propaganda function, newspapers occasionally fabricated stories that were felt to be true but lacked hard evidence. For instance, a pre-war photograph showing three German soldiers holding trophies won in an athletics contest was recaptioned by the *Daily Mirror* 'three German cavalrymen loaded with gold and silver loot'. A picture of a Russian pogrom against Jews in 1905 was reprinted in British papers as evidence of German atrocities in Belgium.[26]

While the public's appetite was limitless, so too was the German ability to provide raw material for British propagandists. Factual tales were almost as shocking as imagined ones. After the 'rape' of Belgium came the use of poison gas, Zeppelin raids and unrestricted submarine warfare. The shelling of Scarborough and Hartlepool in December 1914 resulted in over 700 casualties, with 137 people killed, for no apparent reason other than to spread terror. The fact that a party of schoolchildren was hit reinforced assumptions about German barbarity. The *Lusitania* medal likewise demonstrated the remarkable German ability to score own goals. That medal was actually designed to draw attention to British hypocrisy by pointing out that the *Lusitania* had indeed carried arms and that German warnings regarding such ships had been ignored. Yet it was too easily confused with a medal congratulating the successful U-boat crew on killing civilians, a misconception encouraged by British propagandists. Fed a steady diet of tales that had a firm factual basis, the public naturally tended to believe those stories that did not, such as rumours circulating in 1917 about German corpse-conversion factories.

The government encouraged the public to believe the worst. In October 1914, Asquith derided German 'hordes who leave behind them at every stage of their progress a dismal trail of savagery, of devastation and of desecration worthy of the blackest annals of the history of barbarism'. The NWAC published a 'German Crimes Calendar' with an illustration of a separate atrocity for each month, the specific date of the crime circled in red. The logic was that just when the citizen was growing blasé about one German transgression, a new month would bring a new outrage. A more sustained effort to make use of these atrocities came with the Bryce Report, formally titled the Report of the Committee on Alleged German Outrages. It was aimed at neutral countries, particularly the United States, but also at the British public. Its release one week after the *Lusitania* sinking was a lucky coincidence that magnified its impact. In the UK, where it sold for a penny, the price of a newspaper, demand was high. The 360-page report (with evidentiary appendix another 300 pages long) seemed by its very bulk to confirm German wrongdoing. It helped that Lord Bryce, formerly Ambassador to Washington, had impeccable credentials for honesty and was, rather conveniently, an admitted Germanophile who had initially opposed British involvement in the war. In the introduction he explained how his doubts had been overwhelmed by 'this concurrence of testimony, this convergence upon what were substantially the same broad facts ... the truth of those broad facts stood out beyond question ... If any further confirmation had been needed, we found it in the diaries in which German officers and private soldiers have recorded incidents just such as those to which the Belgian witnesses depose.' Bryce became convinced that Germany was guilty of 'murder, lust, and pillage ... on a scale unparalleled in any war between civilised nations during the last three centuries'. Crimes had been committed not because of poor discipline but as part of 'a system and in pursuance of a set purpose'.[27]

Appearances deceived: the Bryce Committee was not exactly a model of judicial rectitude. Depositions were not taken under oath and, as the Home Secretary Sir John Simon admitted, the committee passed judgement 'without themselves undertaking the work of interrogation'. Evidence that questioned the legitimacy of atrocity claims, such as that no actual victims of hand amputation could be found, was intentionally left out of the report. When one committee member, Harold Cox, expressed a desire to investigate the reliability of evidence, he was persuaded otherwise. One of the more malleable members of the committee, Sir Kenelm Digby, admitted that there was 'probably a good deal of exaggeration and inaccuracy' to the evidence, but retorted by proposing the concept of 'general truth', under which an allegation might be credible not because the specific events had actually occurred, but because they were in line with behaviour that had been observed. 'We ought as much as possible to avoid the appearance of relying on individual cases,' he wrote, 'and rest on the broader facts where you have concurrent testimony.' As Cox pointed out, however, the broader facts were all based on individual cases, therefore if the latter were suspect so too were the former. He nevertheless had difficulty influencing a committee determined to lie. This raises the question of how a man of such impecccable credentials as Bryce was led astray. Clearly, his loyalty to a greater truth convinced him of the necessity to tell smaller lies. In his mind Germany was evil and Britain's cause just. To question individual cases of atrocities threatened to bring the entire edifice tumbling down.[28]

Alleged German atrocities fired latent bigotry, the victims being those of German origin living in Britain. Cheap novels had prepared the ground for a surge of paranoia. The Hun invasion would be facilitated, so the stories went, by thousands of German bakers, barbers, butchers and waiters, members of sleeper cells quietly awaiting the call to assist the Fatherland. When war broke out, a gullible, frightened public assumed that every German shopkeeper or tradesman was an enemy agent. Stories circulated about waiters and butchers poisoning food, watchmakers constructing bombs, barbers cutting throats.

Newspapers warned against the 'enemy in our midst'. Early in the war the *Daily Mail* demanded a boycott of restaurants employing Germans: 'REFUSE TO BE SERVED BY A GERMAN WAITER. IF YOUR WAITER SAYS HE IS SWISS, ASK TO SEE HIS PASSPORT. THE NATURALISATION FORM IS JUST A SCRAP OF PAPER. ONCE A GERMAN ALWAYS A GERMAN.' 'I call for a vendetta,' wrote Bottomley from the pages of *John Bull*. 'A vendetta against every German in Britain – whether "naturalised" or not. As I have said before, you cannot naturalise an unnatural abortion, a hellish freak. But you can exterminate it. And now the time has come.' The paper conducted a vicious campaign against politicians with German-sounding names (like Sir Edgar Speyer) or those with pre-war business interests in Germany. The First Sea Lord, Prince Louis of Battenberg, born in Austria to a German prince, was a loyal and trustworthy public servant. But this was wartime, and public ire had been roused to fever pitch. He was hounded from office in October 1914 and later changed his name to Mountbatten. The politician who suffered most was Haldane, who had done much to prepare Britain for the conflict. Two days into the war, the *Daily Express* complained pointedly of the presence within the government of 'elderly doctrinaire lawyers with German sympathies'. *John Bull* made much of the fact that Haldane's dog was named Kaiser. 'Every kind of ridiculous legend about me was circulated,' Haldane recalled: 'I had a German wife; I was an illegitimate brother of the Kaiser; I had been in secret correspondence with the German government; I had been aware that they intended war and withheld this from my colleagues; I had delayed the dispatch and mobilisation of the expeditionary force.' It was no coincidence that, when the first coalition was formed in May 1915, a wary Asquith found no room for Haldane.[29]

The RAC and the stock exchange banned members of German origin for the duration of the war. Even the UDC decided that 'persons of enemy alien nationality should not be enrolled'. Bigotry proved lucrative for companies willing to tout their

Britishness. The C-B Corset Company called for an 'Invincible assault on corset trade which is not British'. Dunlop Tyres made much of its British origin, forcing its main competitor, Michelin, to insist that it had 'contributed more to the war than any other tyre company'. De Reszke cigarettes insisted that its products 'are British-made and all the shares in the company are held by British subjects. Mr Milhoff, the managing director, is a Russian by birth.' The drinks manufacturer Schweppes went to great pains to convince the public that it was originally a Swiss firm, now manufacturing exclusively in Great Britain. An advertisement by Onoto pens sought to inform potential customers that 'the Waterman Pen is sold in this country through the Austrian-controlled firm L. and C. Harmth ... Every Waterman pen sold therefore ... means profit to the King's enemies.' British flower bulb growers made much of the fact that Dutch growers were still trading with the enemy. 'Are you drinking German waters?' one advertisement ran: 'Apollinaris comes from Germany. Perrier comes from France. Perrier – the table water of the Allies.'[30]

When Manningham Mills in Bradford was discovered to be employing 27 Germans, its directors were informed that 'unless the people to whom objection was taken were dismissed there would be a general strike and the mills brought to a standstill'. They did as they were told. Aliens, driven to despair, resorted to every pathetic means to prove their loyalty. German commodities like liverwurst were given anglicised names, as were Turkish baths. Union Jacks were displayed prominently in shops. A Kentish Town barber displayed in his window a sign: 'THIS IS A INGELISCHE SCHOPP'. A baker adorned his van with signs that read: 'We beg to inform the public that we are Italian bakers, fighting side by side with the English.' He was apparently unaware that his home country had yet to decide its allegiance. Seldom, however, did these measures calm the baying crowds. Those of German origin suffered terribly. Despite the labour shortage, they found it difficult to get work. Graham Greene recalled dramatic incidents even in polite Beckhamstead, where he grew up. 'A German master was denounced to my father as a spy because he had been seen under the railway bridge without a hat, a dachshund was stoned in the High Street, and once my uncle Eppy was summoned at night to the police station and asked to lend his motor car to help block the Great North Road down which a German armoured car was said to be advancing towards London.'[31]

Aliens were accused not only of espionage but also of a concerted campaign of moral corruption. In the *Imperialist*, Captain Harold Spencer and the MP Pemberton Billing warned that

> There exists in the Cabinet Noir of a certain German Prince a book compiled by the Secret Service from reports of German agents who have infested this country for the past twenty years, agents so vile and spreading such debauchery and such lasciviousness as only German minds can conceive and only German bodies execute . . .
>
> It is a most catholic miscellany. The names of Privy Councillors, youths of the chorus, wives of Cabinet Ministers, dancing girls, even Cabinet Ministers themselves, while diplomats, poets, bankers, editors, newspaper proprietors, members of His Majesty's Household follow each other with no order of precedence . . . The thought that 47,000 English men and women are held in enemy bondage through fear calls all clean spirits to mortal combat.

These German agents were responsible for 'the propagation of evils which all decent men thought had perished in Sodom and Lesbia'. In a bizarre attempt to discredit Pemberton Billing, Lloyd George and his advisers persuaded Eileen Villiers-Stewart to seduce him and lure him into a brothel, where compromising photos could be taken. Unfortunately, after lunch with the MP, she fell under his spell, switched sides and later testified on his behalf, even to the extent of swearing to the existence of the Black Book. While few took the allegations seriously, fewer still, it seems, wanted them to cease, given their entertainment value. The Commissioner of the Metropolitan Police, Sir Edward Henry, began an investigation in 1916 of 28 coffee houses and cafés owned or frequented by Belgian refugees which were havens for 'prostitutes and other undesirables', including spies. The logic was clear: since perversion is foreign, most foreigners are perverts, or the perverted must be under foreign influence. Popular prejudice linked sexual deviancy with espionage: aliens used their lascivious ways to weaken Britain. Rooting out spies therefore helped to purify the nation. Paying attention to sex and spies was suddenly a patriotic act.[32]

The outpouring of hatred, sanctioned by government and press, erupted into mob violence whenever a highly visible German 'atrocity' occurred. Anti-German riots were the worst incidents of mob violence in twentieth-century Britain. The most serious of these took place in May 1915, prompted by the first German use of gas on the Western Front and by the *Lusitania* sinking, at least seven deaths were recorded. In Liverpool, an estimated £40,000 worth of damage was caused and 200 buildings were set alight. Of the 21 London Metropolitan Police districts, only two were free of disorder. Sylvia Pankhurst watched in horror as a crowd knocked a woman to the ground and kicked her until she was unconscious. No one came to her aid.[33]

Those on the political fringe benefited from the tide of hatred. Bizarre racialist creeds suddenly became acceptable. Disappointed by government inaction, Admiral Charles Beresford demanded full internment of enemy aliens and called for vigilante teams to search for spies. Dr Ellis Powell, editor of the *Financial News*, attracted huge crowds to his speeches about the 'Unseen Hand' – 'a magnetic and dexterous personality' of German origin 'at work permeating every department of our public life, rewarding subservience, and penalising independence'. The Anti-German League, which became the British Empire Union after 1915, counted among its ranks Beresford, Powell, the trade union leader Havelock Wilson and the future Home Secretary William Joynson-Hicks. It was dedicated to spreading hatred of all things German. The group produced the film *Once a Hun, Always a Hun* (1918), which advocated a ban on trading with Germany after the war. In August 1917, Brigadier General Henry Page Croft established the proto-fascist National Party. After the war he demanded that all Germans should be banned from living in Britain for ten years, and that 'no one not born a British subject and son of a British father' should be eligible for government service.[34]

The shock of the German spring offensive in 1918 prompted fresh outbreaks of anti-alien feeling, extending even to Belgian and French residents. Spy stories provided convenient explanations for the successful assault. The British Empire Union and the British Empire League sponsored rallies around the country calling for even more rigorous rooting-out of aliens. A rally on 13 July was, according to *The Times*, 'the biggest crowd seen in [Trafalgar] square since the outbreak of the war'. In August, an anti-alien petition bearing 1.25 million signatures was delivered to Downing Street, and the following month over a thousand demonstrators picketed the residence of the Foreign Office official Sir Eyre Crowe, whose misfortune it was to have been born in Germany to a German mother. His long, devoted service to his country was easily forgotten.[35]

D. H. Lawrence, himself a victim of irrational prejudice (his wife was a German), regretted the way that 'a wave of criminal lust rose and possessed England'. Pressure from 'indecent bullies like Bottomley of *John Bull* and other bottom-dog members of the House of Commons ... was steadily applied ... to break the independent soul in any man who would not hunt with the criminal mob'. Yet even he wrote, after the *Lusitania* sinking, that he was 'mad with rage ... I would like to kill a million Germans – two millions'. His reaction demonstrates how easy it was for those of sober mind to fall victim to xenophobia. Given the sturdy nature of British patriotism, it is difficult to see what the propagandists achieved, other than stirring up those who did not need to have their passions stoked. Even the cleverest manipulator of minds would have had difficulty putting a gloss on such a bleak war. For the best part of four years, the British people had little reason to feel cheerful, yet their morale held. The propagandists were probably most successful in encouraging an otherwise temperate people towards acts of hatred, bigotry and violence. As Sylvia Pankhurst remarked, 'Alas, poor Patriotism, what foolish cruelties are committed in thy Name!'[36]

Chapter Ten

Home Fires

'War is pre-eminently an outrage on motherhood and all that motherhood means', wrote the pacifist Catherine Marshall. 'The destruction of life and the breaking-up of homes is the undoing of women's work as life-givers and home-makers.' While that is partly true, it is important to stress that women's work in the home was enormously important to victory. Accounts of the war have tended to concentrate on what they did in the workplace, especially in jobs previously performed by men – thus perpetuating a male-orientated standard of contribution. Yet the most important achievement of women during the war came in holding homes and families together. Since many carried out that function in addition to full-time employment, their contribution is all the more impressive. British society survived intact because women, despite all the pressures upon them, kept home fires burning.[1]

In slum tenements before the Great War, conditions were atrocious – cramped, poorly heated, damp and vermin-infested. For the working-class housewife, maintaining the home meant cooking, cleaning and washing without the labour-saving devices taken for granted today. Homes were not only harder to clean, they easily became dirty, due to the general squalor and the scarcity of clean water. A 1901 Rowntree survey found that only 19 per cent of houses in

York had a separate water supply. Even fewer had baths or indoor toilets. Water had to be carried up flights of stairs, with waste water carried (or thrown) down. Local authorities were technically responsible for improving the housing stock, but slum clearance was stalled by lack of funds. Given the housing shortage, there was little incentive for private landlords to spend money on improvements.[2]

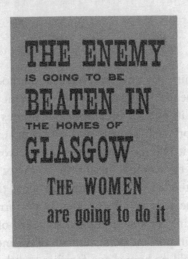

During the war, the Royal Commission on Housing in Scotland described 'dark, narrow and foul-smelling' tenements where the stairs are 'filthy and evil-smelling, and foul water run[s] down the stairs, sickly cats everywhere spread ... disease'. A similar study in Wales revealed that:

> The towns and villages are ugly and overcrowded; houses are scarce and rents increasing, and the surroundings unsanitary and depressing. The scenery is disfigured by unsightly refuse tips, the atmosphere polluted by coal dust and smoke and the rivers spoilt by liquid refuse from works and factories. Facilities for education and recreation are

inadequate and opportunities for the wise use of leisure are few.

Overcrowding was rife. The average pre-war family had 4.6 children; 71 per cent had four or more, 41 per cent seven or more. In 1911, more than 30 per cent of the population lived in conditions of more than three persons to two rooms. Yet between 1911 and 1915, more houses were demolished in London than were built. Across the nation, construction virtually ground to a halt once war began. As a result, the number of families sharing a dwelling increased from 15.7 per cent in 1914 to 20 per cent by war's end. The proportion of uninhabited to inhabited dwellings dropped significantly, which suggests that the desperate squatted in houses previously deemed uninhabitable. By the end of the war, the shortage of homes was estimated at 600,000. Meanwhile, large houses in the cities often stood vacant, temporarily abandoned by the wealthy who could no longer find servants to maintain them.[3]

The only significant housing construction during the war was government-funded schemes for armaments workers. The Ministry of Munitions built approximately 2,800 temporary cottages and 10,000 houses on 38 separate estates, at a cost of £4.3 million. In 1915 and 1916, over 12,000 rooms at Woolwich and Greenwich were provided, while in the same period only 30 private houses were built in all of London. Another 20,000 munitions workers lived in hostels, usually converted schools or church halls that offered a barracks-like existence, with unappetising food and poor heating.[4]

The housing shortage led to galloping rent inflation, a problem especially acute where war industries drew workers from around the country. Unscrupulous landlords raised rents of sitting tenants to intolerable levels in order to make way for more affluent migrant workers. Box and Cox arrangements were not unknown: lodgings were rented to one group of workers by day, another by night. Given its liberal inclinations, the government was inclined to stay out of the housing quagmire, but when landlords resorted to eviction orders, the police became involved and so too did the government. By autumn 1915, unrest over housing was occurring in Birmingham, Luton, Manchester, Glasgow and London. When over 5,000 people (mainly women) in Glasgow came out in support of an impoverished soldier's wife (and mother of seven) who faced eviction, the government was forced to act. The Increase of Rent and Mortgage Interest (Rent Restriction) Act, introduced in Parliament on 25 November 1915, pegged rents for working-class dwellings at pre-war levels and stipulated that mortgages were not to be foreclosed nor interest rates increased. The first rent restriction act passed in British history, it exceeded protesters' demands. Since rents were set at 1914 levels, with no account taken for wartime inflation, landlords were transformed overnight from profiteers to downtrodden. They reacted, perhaps understandably, by neglecting maintenance.

The housing problem was occasionally made worse by enemy action. In December 1914, German cruisers shelled east coast towns, causing minor damage and some 700 casualties. Far more frightening were the Zeppelin raids, which began in January 1915 and continued sporadically into 1916. Ordinary citizens were bewildered when war arrived on their doorstep:

> Who would think that vault benign
> God's last area free from vice,
> Initiates the aerial mine,
> With babes below as sacrifice.

After a raid on Hull, an angry crowd stoned a Royal Flying Corps vehicle, on the assumption that the airmen were to blame for failing to protect the population. The British did their best to adjust: lighting restrictions were instituted in London and along the east coast (later spread further afield), air raid shelters were constructed, a primitive early-warning system was developed, and crews of night fighters gradually perfected a defensive screen. *The Times* commented that the blackout at least meant that stars were now visible: 'London moves under a vaster and steadier horizon.' The makers of Hall's Wine, a nerve tonic, boasted that their product 'worked wonders when administered to the ladies, and prevented the nervous collapse of several when the bombs were dropping and the strain on the nerves was at its worst'. In fact, the tonic was not necessary, since most people greeted the Zeppelin with typical British aplomb. 'Nobody alters their plans for the chance of a raid,' wrote Georgina Lee. 'We all face it quite calmly and in a spirit of fatalists. What is to be, will be.'[5]

The Zeppelin was beaten by the end of 1916, but then came the even more fearsome Gotha bombers. Their first raid on London resulted in 162 deaths and 432 injuries, mainly around Liverpool Street station. In all, 51 Zeppelin raids and 57 aeroplane raids killed 1,413 during the war and injured 3,407. In terms of their actual effect, the air raids certainly never deserved the emphasis given them by newspapers at the time. Their propaganda value to the British heavily outweighed their strategic value to the Germans.[6]

The war, because it focused attention on the value of human life, increased awareness of living standards. The astonishing number of men deemed unfit for military service highlighted the squalid conditions from which they came. Critics protested that men prepared to sacrifice their lives for their country deserved better. 'To let them come home from horrible, waterlogged trenches to something little better than a pigsty here would be criminal,' the Conservative MP Walter Long argued. This sympathy inspired the 'Homes Fit for Heroes' slogan widely trumpeted during the 1918 election. Yet good intentions were one thing, action another. Since landlords were unlikely to invest in new housing, or repair the old, only the government was capable of constructing the homes required. Unfortunately, it was unprepared, ideologically and financially, to take on this burden.[7]

Housing worries affected only a fraction of the working-class. Concerns over the supply and cost of food were, on the other hand, universal. For the average working-class family, one-fifth of total food expenditure went on bread and flour. Yet six months into the war, the cost of wheat had risen by 72 per cent, barley by 40 per cent and oats by 34 per cent. A bumper harvest caused a fall in prices in spring 1915, but by the end of 1916 the standard 4 lb loaf cost 10d, up 4d from two years before. In autumn 1917, the government finally stepped in, pegging the price at the 1916 level. At various times, butter, margarine, sugar, bacon and cheese prices were also fixed. The cost of sugar rose most dramatically – 163 per cent in the first two years of the war. Potatoes, another working-class staple, stayed steady during the first eighteen months of the war, then doubled in price due to a bad harvest. The poorest cuts of meat, which workers had once found affordable, appeared on market stalls at double their pre-war price. Milk and butter also doubled during 1916, though they were not a normal part of the working-class diet. Producers tried to turn shortages into opportunities. 'Everyone has less money to spend on food', one advertisement lamented. 'The wise ones make nourishing Quaker Oats the stand-by . . . Your family won't miss expensive bacon and eggs if you serve delicious Quaker Oats.'[8]

Food shortages affected civilian morale more than price rises. A unity of spirit arose: everyone blamed the government or unscrupulous shopkeepers. The middle and upper classes were most vociferous in their complaints, since they were not accustomed to being denied commodities they could afford. Luxury items often disappeared completely, and uncertain supplies of meat made dinner parties precarious. The working-class, however, suffered the most, since they had less time to waste in queues and did not have the spare cash that could buy commodities from under the counter. 'Anyone who penetrated the poorer neighbourhoods became familiar with the queue,' commented Mrs C. S. Peel in her account of home life during the war. In December 1917, *The Times* reported food queues of more than a thousand people in some parts of London. The Society for the Prevention of Cruelty to Children drew attention to the problem of youngsters waiting in the early hours of winter mornings to buy bread. Tempers often flared, with violence against shopkeepers not unknown. In January 1918, the military was called out to restore order after munitions workers in Leytonstone looted shops because their wives had been unable to secure food. Much to the government's annoyance, workers increasingly took time off to queue. As has been seen, the government responded half-heartedly to popular demands for the regulation of supplies. Lord Devonport's voluntary rationing scheme of February 1917 urged each citizen to restrict himself to 4 lb of bread, 2½ lb of meat and 12 oz of sugar per week. This was a calculated attempt to shift consumption from grain, a mainly imported commodity, to meat, a mainly home-produced one. Yet it was irrelevant to the working-class diet since the poor could not afford that much meat.[9]

Creatures of habit, the British proved reluctant to change their eating patterns in order to find a way around shortages. Substitute commodities were treated with suspicion. Supplies of tinned fish were more dependable than those of fresh, but some consumers baulked at the price, others at the taste. Margarine consumption did quadruple during the war, but attempts to introduce horsemeat and eels into the regular diet were less successful. The poet Aelfrida Tillyard poked fun at measures adopted to stretch the limited supply of food:

> Here is a plate of cabbage soup,
>> With caterpillars in,
> How good they taste! (Avoid all waste
>> If you the war would win.)
> Now, will you have a minnow, love,
>> Or half an inch of eel?
> A stickleback, a slice of jack,
>> Shall grace our festive meal.
> We've no unpatriotic joint,
>> No sugar and no bread.
> Eat nothing sweet, no rolls, no meat,
>> The Food Controller said.
> But would you like some sparrow pie,
>> To counteract the eel?
> A slice of swede is what you need,
>> And please don't leave the peel.
> But there's dessert for you, my love,
>> Some glucose stewed with sloes.
> And now good-night – your dreams be bright!
>> (Perhaps they will – who knows?)

Since bread could not be substituted, it was doctored. The milling process was altered, transforming the loaf into what would today be called 'whole wheat'. Other grains and potato flour were added. The result was more nutritious, but it annoyed those who believed bread should be white. Despite the complaints, consumption was higher in 1917 than in pre-war years. In a lame attempt to reduce the desirability of bread, authorities forbade the sale of loaves not less than 12 hours old.[10]

In February 1918, the Ministry of Food, now led by Lord Rhondda, finally instituted a rationing system in London and the

Home Counties. Queues virtually disappeared. By mid-July a more comprehensive system was introduced throughout the country. Each household registered with a retailer, who was then supplied according to the needs of his customers. Weekly allowances stipulated 1½ lb of meat per person, 4 oz of butter or margarine and 8 oz of sugar. The bread allowance was 4 lb for women and 7 lb for men. Children under six were given half the meat ration, while adolescent males and men working on heavy jobs received supplemental allowances. Rationing provided an unanticipated lesson about what the poor actually ate. The Board of Trade was forced to admit that 'a certain part of the population, especially in Scotland and in some country districts . . . could not afford to purchase the full amount to which their ration entitled them'.[11]

With all the new regulations, the market became a den of crime. Shopkeepers were fined for hoarding food, and for selling it above prescribed prices. Consumers also fell foul of the law. According to William Beveridge:

> it became a crime for a workman to leave a loaf behind on the kitchen shelf of the cottage from which he was moving (£2 fine), for a maiden lady at Dover to keep fourteen dogs and give them bread and milk to eat (£5), for another lady in Wales to give meat to a St Bernard (£20), for a furnaceman dissatisfied with his dinner to throw chip potatoes on the fire (£10), and for a lady displeased with her husband to burn stale bread upon her lawn (£5).

In 1918, a Mitcham man was charged with shooting a deer at Morden Hall Park. He admitted the offence, but argued, 'It's a job to live on these meat rations, I must have something for my children.' In the same month, an inquest into the deaths of survivors of a shipwreck found that when the unlucky sailors were taken ashore, they were only served coffee, due to the 'too literal regard for food restrictions' among the local people.[12]

The *Win-the-War Cookery Book* advised housewives that 'The British fighting line shifts and extends and now you are in it. The struggle is not only on land and sea; it is in your larder, your kitchen, and your dining room. Every meal you serve is now literally a battle.'

During the war, there was no shortage of self-important busy-bodies ready to tell fellow citizens how to run their lives. The National Food Economy League, another gaggle of voluntary do-gooders, published guides on household management catering to the various classes. Titles included *Housekeeping on Twenty-Five Shillings a Week, or Under, for a Family of Five* (price 1d), *Patriotic Food Economy for the Well-to-Do* (6d) and *War-time Recipes for Households where Servants are Employed* (6d). A column in *The Times* advised the gentry to 'instruct your keeper to cease feeding your pheasants with maize and corn'. The birds would not suffer and might even 'afford better sport'. Another article advised 'the better class' to save tea leaves from the first brew, dry them and send them for distribution to the poor or to troops. Female readers were told that 'The woman who would feed her family well and yet reduce expenses must first of all learn to cook, so that she may instruct her cook in the best and cheapest methods of preparing food.' The cook, it was assumed, was too stupid to figure this out for herself. 'The great fault in English cookery,' argued the paper, 'has hitherto been the extraordinary wastefulness, and servants are the great barrier to all reform.' A leaflet was prepared advising servants how they could help their employers effect economies. 'Let us remember that the wealthy have much to do with their wealth,' it ran. 'War to-day is very costly, and if it should last long, it is the wealthies who rightly will have to part with the most – at all events in the way of money.' In other words, servants should prepare for wage cuts, which, given that they were for the good of the war, should be borne with equanimity.[13]

Government controls and food campaigns revealed a remarkable insensitivity to working-class privation. Recipes for 'patriotic' haricot bean fritters, barley rissoles and nut rolls were more relevant to those of the middle class who had the time and expertise to make them. Frequent 'thrift' campaigns (usually accompanied by fresh exhortations to buy war bonds) were likewise inappropriate to those who had never known extravagance. 'I must say I was surprised to read last month of women . . . being advised to lead the way in thrift,' one housewife remarked. 'Take the lead, Ye Gods! To advise us working women to be thrifty is about the limit!'[14]

Meanwhile, labour shortages during the first six months of the war combined with disruption on the rail network to wreak havoc upon the coal supply. Prices rose by about 20 per cent, and supplies remained precarious throughout 1915 and 1916, especially in large urban areas. In 1916, the need to conserve fuel led to a DORA regulation banning Guy Fawkes bonfires. Early the following year the problem reached crisis proportions, with police regulating crowds at coal distribution points. When winter came, coal rationing was introduced in London, with allocations determined according to the number of rooms in each house. Shortages hit the middle classes proportionately harder than the workers, since the affluent could no longer secure the supplies necessary to keep large homes heated properly. The poor, in contrast, had never had the luxury of warm homes. In fact, with many workers enjoying increased income, a warm hearth became one of the war's benefits. Thus rationing did not actually decrease consumption of coal, since workers bought up supplies denied to the middle class. Shortages also affected retailers: shops were forced to close earlier during winter to save on heating and lighting, thus making life even more difficult for harried housewives.

The food bill rose by 60 per cent during the war, to about £2 per week for the average working-class family. Rent and rates increased until restrictions came into force. Rising fuel costs added another 2s. to the household budget, clothing around 4s., though this is not an accurate indicator of the steep increase in costs since scarcity limited the amount spent. As for alcohol, a report released in 1917 revealed that consumption declined by 16 per cent from 1914 to 1916, but expenditure (due to taxes and inflation) rose by 24 per cent. Tobacco consumption increased, with expenditure rising even faster. New taxes also affected family income. McKenna's first budget of September 1915 rendered those earning over £130 a year liable to tax. By the end of the war, 32 per cent of workers earning over this threshold paid tax, the rest avoiding it because of various allowances. In addition, the average family paid 10 per cent of income in indirect taxes, up from 6 per cent in 1913. All this meant that weekly wages had to rise by about 22s. to compensate for inflation and tax rises during the war.[15]

Taking into account inflation, the real value of household incomes among the working-classes remained steady or improved slightly during the war. Since it was legal for a child to be employed at 14 (many took jobs even earlier), a family with older children could benefit significantly from the manpower shortage. Anecdotal evidence suggests that wage rises, abundant overtime and a competitive labour market often brought unaccustomed prosperity. Robert Roberts, whose family ran a shop in Salford, remembered how the clientele changed during the war: 'Some of the poorest in the land started to prosper as never before ... slum grocers managed to get hold of different and better varieties of foodstuffs of a kind sold before only in middle-class shops, and the once deprived began to savour strange delights.' Charities also noticed the change: by pre-war standards, there were few genuinely needy people. Tramps and beggars were much less common, and convictions for theft and vagrancy declined significantly. In December 1914, the Salvation Army reported that no more than 200 persons per night were using its shelters, less than a tenth of pre-war numbers. In January 1915, there were 70,596 people in London workhouses and 30,394 on the outdoor list. This represented a decrease of 4,045 on the previous year. Improvements were not, however, distributed equally, nor were they immediate. The first two years of the war brought considerable hardship, since wage rises did not keep pace with inflation. In June 1916, food prices were 61 per cent higher than in July 1914, while wages had risen by less than 20 per cent.[16]

Military service often entailed financial hardship. The government wisely realised that in order to maintain civilian morale, the wives and families of servicemen should not be forced on to the Poor Law. Separation allowances were therefore paid from the beginning, calculated according to the husband's rank. The wife of a private with one child received 15s. per week; inflation raised that to 23s. by the end of the war. Extra increments were paid for each additional child. By the end of the war, nearly £420 million had been doled out to 1.5 million wives and their children. In cases where the husband had, before the war, been in irregular or poorly paid employment, separation allowances could improve a family's circumstances. 'It seems too good to be true,' one wife quipped, 'a pound a week and my husband away'. More often than not, however, a family with father gone suffered terribly – for the average household, allowances covered only one half of expenditure.[17]

The scheme exposed a hidden aspect of twentieth-century life – living together out of wedlock was more common than presumed. After much agonising, the authorities decided that allowances would still be paid even if the claimant failed to produce a marriage certificate, a decision that angered religious leaders. In truth, the policy was hardly revolutionary, especially since other buttresses to conventional morality limited its effect. Allowances could, for instance, be terminated on grounds of infidelity, the government taking the view that since 'the woman by her infidelity has forfeited the right to be supported by her husband . . . there is no obligation on the State to continue this payment'. In addition, in October 1914, an Army Council memorandum on the 'Cessation of Separation Allowances and Allotments to the Unworthy' called upon police to monitor whether allowances were spent wisely. The furore was kindled by frequent allegations in the papers that soldiers' wives were 'drinking away their over-generous allowances'. According to an official investigation into the drinking habits of women and girls in Woolwich, women 'are the best customers at Plaisted's wine shop in the High Street. They also compose the queues outside Forster's shop for bottles of spirits on Fridays and Mondays. On these days we have seen such scrambles for the limited supply of bottles that, until the women tore off the wrappers from the bottles, they did not know whether they had paid 10/6 for gin, whisky or rum.' The chief commissioner of the Metropolitan Police took a more tolerant view, confessing that he could not 'understand why anybody should assume that the wife of a soldier is necessarily a person who required the police to look after her'. Popular prejudices, however, were immune to good sense. Before long, women discovered drunk or those who frequented pubs too regularly had their benefits terminated. In all, 16,000 women, 2 per cent of claimants, had their allowances withdrawn because of allegedly immoral behaviour. These rulings reflected a prevalent attitude that women on their own could not be trusted. 'No greater slander has ever been circulated,' judged the NSPCC, 'than the assertion that soldiers' wives as a class were lacking in the spirit of self-restraint.' The sister of Field Marshal Sir John French complained to the press that 'as the wife of a soldier', she deeply resented 'the insults to her class which were implied by the . . . instructions issued to the police to keep the wives and dependants of soldiers on active duty under police surveillance'.[18]

Some families suffered a marked decline in living standards as a result of the war. A government investigation in 1915 revealed that 'cotton operatives and certain classes of day-wage workers and labourers – are hard-pressed by the rise in prices, and actually have to curtail their consumption . . . Many people in receipt of small fixed incomes necessarily also feel the pressure; and it is obvious that . . . a family . . . in which the children are within school age may suffer exceptionally.' Sylvia Pankhurst, working among the distressed in London's East End, found that

> Even the women who had received the full separation allowances promised, were in sad case. The wife of a Territorial, with two young children and expecting a third, got 1s. 5d a day from the War Office. Having moved into London when her husband was called up, she got no London allowance. Her rent was 6s. a week. She wept with despair at finding herself with only 3s. 11d a week for food, fuel, light, and all the needs of her family!

In some cases, the hardship arose because of administrative negligence. The government was, for instance, notoriously slow in paying disability allowances to injured soldiers returning from the front. Both army pay and separation allowances ceased during the interminable period it took for disability to be assessed. Since so many soldiers came from very physical jobs in civilian life, even a relatively minor disability could prevent a return to pre-war occupations.[19]

Many professional families found that fixed incomes failed to keep pace with inflation. They felt aggrieved even if they did not actually suffer. When Vera Brittain's parents complained about the shortage of servants and good chocolate, they would not have been consoled by the fact that the poor had never enjoyed those luxuries. Nina Murdoch referred light-heartedly to middle-class privation in her 'Sing a Song of Wartime':

> Sing a song of War-time,
> Soldiers marching by,
> Crowds of people standing,
> Waving them 'Good-bye'.
> When the crowds are over,
> Home we go to tea,
> Bread and margarine to eat,
> War Economy!
>
> If I ask for a cake, or
> Jam of any sort,
> Nurse says, 'What! in War-time?
> Archie, certainly not!'
> Life's not very funny
> Now, for little boys,
> Haven't any money,
> Can't buy any toys.
>
> Mummie does the house-work,
> Can't get any maid

> Gone to make munitions,
> 'Cause they're better paid,
> Nurse is always busy,
> Never time to play,
> Sewing shirts for soldiers,
> Nearly ev'ry day.

Two charitable agencies, the Professional Classes War Relief Committee and the Professional Classes Special Aid Society, were formed to look after those forced, as one spokesman commented, 'to live the "simple life" with a vengeance'. This meant 'a smaller house, less food and clothing, fewer servants and cheaper education for our children'.[20]

The very wealthy managed for the most part to maintain pre-war standards. In December 1916, the first Public Meals Order limited day meals to two courses and those in the evening to three, but restaurateurs found clever ways round the ruling. Petrol rationing curbed motoring for pure pleasure, but other luxuries were hardly affected. Consumption of sparkling wine, champagne and port increased massively; the latter became the favourite tipple of white-collar workers. Readers of *The Times* were assured that stocks of champagne in France were safe and that 1914 would be a very good year, similar to 1870, the year of the Franco-Prussian War. 'Today the true patriot who can afford it will eat asparagus, not potatoes', the government advised. Potatoes, in other words, should be left for the poor. Adhering to the government's advice, Georgina Lee banned potatoes from her household, since they were 'a necessity to the poor'. There was no apparent fall in the wearing or buying of jewellery, and dress sales at fine shops actually increased between 1915 and 1917, much to the disgust of those who found the finery unpatriotic. A letter to *The Times* argued that 'wasteful changes of fashion are to be deprecated now at this, perhaps the greatest crisis in our country's history'. Another correspondent asked: 'Why should the women of England be in bondage to the dressmakers, who, even as things now are, engage the services of a vast number of persons who ought to be doing war work?' Siegfried Sassoon, home on leave, was shocked to see 'old men with their noses in their plates guzzling for all they're worth' at the Formby golf club. There were 'enormous cold joints and geese and turkeys and a suckling pig and God knows what'. If, as the historian Arthur Marwick suggests, the war created 'a strong breeze of egalitarianism', the wealthy managed to shelter from the wind.[21]

Wars are usually associated with poor health. The combination of bad diet and hard work, exacerbated by constant anxiety, loneliness and stress, normally exacts a physical toll. In Britain during the Great War, however, the opposite occurred. Health standards stayed steady or improved. Life expectancy for men in England and Wales rose from 49 to 56 years and for women from 53 to 60 years between 1911 and 1921. As the social historian Jay Winter has discovered, in almost every category of death, significant declines are apparent, suggesting that health problems associated with poverty and malnourishment were alleviated by the war. Improvement in health standards was most apparent at lower income levels. Infant mortality rates, the most sensitive gauge of changing social conditions, improved significantly in England and Wales (on average 8 per cent during the war years), while they remained constant in Germany and worsened dramatically in France, Italy and Austria. The rate declined fastest among the working-class in manufacturing cities like Manchester, Birmingham, Sheffield and Glasgow. In other words, the decline was more impressive in areas with high female employment than in areas unaffected by the rush of women into the factories.[22]

Granted, Winter's findings are open to dispute. He relies heavily on life insurance statistics as a basis for mortality rates. Since those statistics pertain mainly to skilled and semi-skilled workers, the 'underclass' is inadequately represented. Though female health generally improved, death rates for women aged 10–29 and 75–79 rose during the war. Female mortality rates from tuberculosis, pneumonia, bronchitis and influenza were higher in every war year than in the years immediately preceding 1914, even when the effects of the 1917–18 influenza epidemic are taken into account. This was probably due to the decline in housing standards and the movement of rural dwellers to urban areas where overcrowding and bad air exacerbated respiratory conditions. Using different statistics, including evidence on children's heights, Bernard Harris has challenged the assertion that infant mortality rates improved significantly and that the poorer classes experienced a significant improvement in health. 'The overall impression,' he believes, 'is one of continuity rather than discontinuity during the war years.'[23]

That said, continuity during a time of chaos, destruction and privation is still impressive. This is especially true since civilian access to medical care was severely restricted due to the army's demand for doctors. At the front, each doctor looked after around 376 soldiers, while at home each had 2,344 patients. The poor suffered the shortage most acutely because the military took proportionately more panel doctors and those from urban areas than private doctors or those from rural areas. Some districts in Glasgow had more than 5,000 patients for every doctor. (The present ratio varies between 500/1 and 800/1.) A Croydon doctor stopped for a traffic offence in 1918 told police he hoped they would send him to prison, as it was the only way he could get some rest. During the war, 20 per cent of the population was without adequate medical coverage – defined as more than 4,000 patients per doctor. Yet in areas like Shoreditch and Bethnal Green, where the doctor shortage was acute, health standards actually improved. This is perhaps understandable, since most of the population was not actually accustomed to regular medical attention. Furthermore, before the age of antibiotics, there was little a doctor could do to combat the major diseases that ravaged the poor. One study in fact reveals that women were more likely to die in childbirth if a doctor was present. This suggests that middle-class women were often more at risk, because they could afford a doctor.[24]

The significant fall in the number of deaths due to diarrhoeal disease and the fall (or at least stabilisation) in the mortality rate associated with pregnancy and childbirth would not have been possible had nutrition standards declined during the war. It is difficult to generalise about the wartime working-class diet, since wide variations existed between geographical areas and income groups. Nevertheless, some effects are obvious. As has been seen, increases in family income were most pronounced among the poorer classes. This meant that the poor spent more on food than they did before the war. Since the birth rate declined and families were smaller, that food did not have to stretch as far. In addition, over six million men were fed, for varying lengths of time, by the army instead of by their families. Since adult men previously received the lion's share at mealtimes, the rest of the family (especially the mother) now ate better. The establishment of industrial canteens, increased provision of school meals and the extension of health insurance and disability pensions also had positive effects. Factory welfare supervisors may have been motivated more by industrial efficiency than human kindness, but they did help to improve workers' health. For instance, they discouraged workers from bringing insubstantial or unhealthy dinners to work, urging them instead to use canteens. Looking further, the decline in sugar and alcohol consumption was beneficial. While sugar, butter and meat consumption declined significantly (the latter compensated somewhat by greater consumption of bacon), that of bread and potatoes rose. In other words, while mealtimes provided less pleasure, calorie levels were maintained and nutrition probably improved.[25]

As with income rises, so too with health, war's benefits were not equally shared. Young, single women who worked long hours in draughty factories and went home to damp, cold lodgings were particularly susceptible to tuberculosis. 'It is not only her health she is risking, but her youth as well,' one male worker observed. 'It makes me sad to see the young girls here; they come in fresh and rosy cheeked, and before a month has passed they are pale and careworn.' Smoking among women also increased. On 7 April 1918, the head of one of Britain's largest tobacco companies remarked with delight that 'There is no doubt whatever, that there is an increased consumption generally, both on the part of the army and on the part of the civilian population. Not only that but women and girls, having put on men's clothes, are adopting men's habits in the matter of smoking.' Medical statistics also provide little illumination of war's most common ailment, grief. A woman who lost a husband or son would have derived little consolation from the fact that her diet had improved.[26]

Ubiquitous death meant greater value was placed upon life. Babies, the chief beneficiaries of this wartime sentiment, became a symbol of hope for the future. This did not mean that more babies were born; the birth rate in fact declined from 23.9 per 1,000 population in 1914 to 19.4 in 1918. Each baby was, however, more highly valued. 'While nine soldiers died every hour in 1915, twelve babies died every hour, so that it was more dangerous to be a baby than a soldier,' argued the Bishop of London. 'The loss of life in this war has made every baby's life doubly precious.' Even the NUWSS grew concerned that wider employment opportunities for women posed problems for children. Fawcett reassured mothers who stayed at home that 'the care of infant life, saving the children, and protecting their welfare was as true a service to the country as that which men were rendering by going into the armies'.[27]

This 'cult of the child' inspired various pro-natalism

campaigns. 'The noble sacrifices in the battlefield, in the air and on the sea must not be made in vain,' argued the Babies of the Empire Society. 'Every effort must be directed to securing the future of the race.' National Baby Weeks of 1917 and 1918 sought to 'save every savable child'. Concern even extended to those who had once been seen as pariahs. The National Council for the Unmarried Mother drew attention to the high mortality rates among illegitimate children, and the Conservative MP Ronald McNeill urged that the unfortunate mothers 'both for the children's sake and for their own, should be saved from the degradation which too often follows a single lapse of virtue'.[28]

A report entitled 'The National Care of Maternity in Time of War' argued that it was 'increasingly incumbent upon the nation to assist mothers and to render the conditions of childbirth as favourable as possible'. The report demanded better medical provision, more and better-trained midwives, and greater attention to pre- and post-natal diet. A government investigation of factory conditions warned that 'the overstrain of industrial work immediately before or after childbirth involves the risk of grave injury to women and child alike . . . the strain of long-standing or continuous overwork in girlhood and later . . . may have far-reaching effects on the birth-rate and the degeneration of the race.' Needless to say, such profound attention to the welfare of children would have been no less appropriate in peacetime. In any case, while pro-natalists urgently demanded more babies, few paused to consider the consequences after they were born. George Newman, Chief Medical Officer to the Ministry of Health, was one of few to point out how 'we are sometimes apt to forget or ignore the heavy burden which a family of children near together in age places upon the working-class mother'. Birth control remained a sensitive subject, firstly because it supposedly threatened racial decline (since the middle class were more knowledgeable) and secondly because it implied that intercourse could have purpose beyond procreation. The National Birthrate Commission found that doctors advised patients to space out their births, but refused to tell them how. Doctors apparently hoarded their knowledge; according to census figures, they had the smallest families of all categories of occupations.[29]

The Women's Labour League and the War Emergency Workers' National Committee quickly jumped on the child welfare bandwagon. Feminists who had been notorious for their militancy before the war campaigned hard for measures to reduce the infant mortality rate, in the process emphasising maternalist ideals that they suddenly found empowering. For instance, Maude Royden argued: 'The State wants children, and to give them is a service both dangerous and honourable. Like the soldier, the mother takes a risk and gives a devotion for which no money can pay; but, like the soldier, she should not, therefore, be made "economically dependent".' Campaigns for family allowances, sometimes called 'the endowment of motherhood', gathered pace. Mary Stocks, editor of the *Woman's Leader*, defended the allowances as 'the conscious allocation to mothers qua mothers of resources adequate for the proper performance of their function'.[30]

Maternalist campaigns often had eugenicist overtones. *The Times*, for instance, managed to fuse two popular prejudices when it remarked that 'we do not all realise the increase in drinking there has been among the mothers of the coming race, though we may yet find it a circumstance darkly menacing to our civilisation'. Most advocates started from the assumption that more babies from 'respectable' families were needed to maintain the Empire. Some pointed out that better pre- and post-natal care was advantageous because it would allow more male children to survive. (The male infant mortality rate was higher than the female.) The fact that the middle-class birth rate had plummeted most markedly caused considerable distress. The 'particular and peculiar duty' of respectable women to bear children was frequently stressed, and some eugenicists (of the 'better dead' school) actually warned that better health provision worked against natural selection by allowing those of poorer stock to survive. The socialist Sidney Webb complained that the tax rates fell most heavily on the classes who should ideally be having the most babies. Meanwhile, 'the thriftless and irresponsible, the reckless and the short-sighted' paid no tax, with the effect that 'the community now breeds fastest from its socially least desirable stocks'. The solution, he felt, was tax incentives to encourage larger families. Other eugenicists regretted that men severely disfigured in the war were unlikely to find mates, yet genetically they still had the potential to produce excellent offspring. They suggested that these men should be awarded 'eugenic stripes' to be worn on their uniforms, in order to make them more attractive to women.[31]

Women were reminded (mainly by men) of their 'duty to the State to care for the babies that belong to the State as well as to themselves'. Authorities were confident that better training alone, rather than material improvements in living standards, could improve the lot of the child. 'Efficient housewives are more important than bricks and mortar to the making of healthy homes,' wrote one (male) authority. At this point, the maternalist argument spilled into the case for education reform. Demands were made for girls to be given a 'thorough training in cooking, housework, laundry work and needle work [which] leads up naturally to mothercraft'. A leaflet for the programme stated:

> A call comes again to the women of Britain, a call happily not to make shells or fill them so that a ruthless enemy can be destroyed but a call to help renew the homes of England, to sew and to mend, to cook and to clean and to rear babies in health and happiness, who shall in their turn

grow into men and women worthy of the Empire.

The novelist and feminist Rebecca West was not alone in suspecting that the training was actually designed to prepare young women for a return to domestic service.[32]

In the mothercraft debate, men argued with other men about how to manage the lives of women. Males occupied all the top posts on the National Baby Week Council. Captain Sir William Wiseman went so far as to advise mothers 'not to reprove, but to encourage' children who fought in the nursery. According to him, the rough and tumble of early childhood had rendered the British superior to the Germans at hand-to-hand combat. Female 'experts' could, however, be equally daft. *Labour Women*, a Labour Party sponsored journal, argued that the best mothers were those who strove to become 'thinking citizens'. Enlightenment would come through a system of 'co-operative housekeeping' under which cooking, cleaning, washing and mending would be done according to an efficient division of labour. 'Each woman ... set free from the incubus of home slavery, would be able to follow the work for which she is best fitted by temperament and training.' The writer, a woman, did not explain how these itinerant menders, cookers, cleaners and launderers would, at the same time, provide a stable home life for children.[33]

Pro-natalism did inspire concrete improvements in the provision of health visitors and clinics for women and children. Organisers of the Children's Jewel Fund, under the slogan 'a jewel for a baby's life', collected donations of money and jewellery to finance infant welfare centres. By the time the fund was wound up in 1920, £700,000 had been collected. (The Duchess of Marlborough gave a £5,000 pearl necklace.) The government was likewise persuaded to take action. Rather than simply leaving the matter to the vagaries of voluntarism, Parliament passed the Care of Mothers and Young Children Act of 1915, which empowered local authorities to set up facilities 'for the purpose of the care of expectant mothers, nursing mothers, and young children', with subsidies of up to 50 per cent provided by the Local Government Board. By 1917, 446 infant welfare centres were operated by voluntary bodies, with another 396 centres administered by local authorities. The number of full-time health visitors in England and Wales rose from 600 in 1914 to 1,355 in 1918. Some local authorities nevertheless resisted the move on the grounds that it undermined individual responsibility.[34]

Sylvia Pankhurst felt that 'in spite of all the purse-proud patronage and snobbery which has been displayed in connection with them, maternal and infant centres are proving a great boon to numbers of women'. The snobbery was nevertheless formidable. At the clinics, middle-class women dispensed advice formulated by middle-class men to working-class mothers. A clash of cultures inevitably developed, limiting the extent of improvement. Health visitors were prone to assume that the primary cause of infant illness was fecklessness or ignorance on the part of the mother, or, as one 'expert' explained, 'In searching for the cause of a polluted stream one naturally traces it backwards and towards its source.' Quite typical was the Middlesbrough Medical Officer of Health who blamed poor child health standards on the 'shiftless, careless, and dirty . . . habits' of mothers. Poverty was seldom acknowledged as a factor. That said, middle-class mothers also came in for criticism, in particular those who refused to breastfeed. The eugenicist C. W. Saleeby argued that such women should be 'ashamed to look a tabby cat in the face'. In the early days of these reforms, good intentions could be ruined by insensitive attitudes. All women, regardless of class, were suspicious of experts who tried to tell them how to raise children. Progress had undoubtedly been made, but great adjustments would be necessary before the real benefits would become apparent. As a result, the full potential of the clinics was not realised until well after the war. The significant fall in infant mortality rates cannot be attributed to them.[35]

Child welfare benefited indirectly from wartime regulations regarding the consumption of alcohol. The reduction of drunkenness inevitably makes the home a safer place. During the war, getting drunk was not only more difficult, it was also less socially acceptable. Intoxicated men or women were seen as unpatriotic – selfishly withholding labour from the state. In December 1914, *The Times* commented that early closing of pubs had resulted in fewer children on the streets after 10 p.m. 'The child's bedtime often synchronises with the public house closing hour. At last his poor, stunted body has the chance of getting an hour or two's "beauty sleep".' The most striking effect of the control of the drink trade was the fall in the number of infant deaths registered on weekends. A tragic scenario had previously been all too common: excessive Friday or Saturday night drinking led to 'overlaying' – babies sharing beds with parents were smothered by a drunken mother or father. After the introduction of drink controls, the weekend blip in the statistics disappeared.[36]

Concern for child welfare extended into education. Prior to the war, 75 per cent of children left school by age 14. Financing of education was precarious; since funds came from local rates, poorer areas had the worst schools. At first, the manpower problem militated against progress in this area. Thus, in the first year of the war, the number of children attending secondary school fell by 1,000. The autumn 1915 intake, however, rose by 3,000 and that of 1916 by 9,000. By 1921, there were twice as many working-class children in secondary school than in 1913. Working-class enthusiasm was further demonstrated at rallies held round the country by the Education Minister, H. A. L. Fisher. All this fervour, however, was held in check by a simultaneous rightward shift in British politics. As a result, action did not keep pace with progressive pronouncements. Fisher's maiden speech in the Commons called for improved pay for teachers, more nursery schools and better medical services at school, but left administration and financing in the hands of local authorities, thus perpetuating vast inequalities. Fisher expressed a hope that the school leaving age of 14 would henceforward be more strictly enforced, but stopped well short of advocating universal secondary education. With regards to the curriculum, the government seemed more concerned with preserving the civilising influences of classical studies than with closing the technology gap.[37]

Before the war, a hotchpotch of laws governed the employment of children, with wide variations from region to region. A child was technically supposed to stay in school until 14, but those with good attendance records could leave a year earlier. Factory work was technically not allowed until the required schooling was completed, but 'half-timers' could, from age 12, work up to 33 hours a week, as long as they still attended school part time. Street hawkers had to be at least 11, and boys could not work in mines until they were 14. During the war, the manpower shortage led to increased pressure upon local authorities to relax restrictions. In August 1915, the Headmistresses' Association approached the Home Secretary about the huge increase in girls as young as 12 employed in street-selling. Factory inspectors were supposed to prevent the exploitation of juvenile workers, but they could not possibly stop every abuse. Cases of children working over 100 hours a week or 35 hours continuously were not unknown. A firm that worked a girl for 30 hours at a stretch was prosecuted when a factory inspector intervened. The firm's solicitor, arguing that the Factory Acts were irrelevant in time of war, suggested that the Home Office 'ought to have struck a special medal' for the girl, instead of wasting its time in the 'fatuous folly' of prosecuting the employer. The firm escaped with a slap on the hand.[38]

In August 1917, Fisher claimed that 600,000 children had been put 'prematurely' to work during the first three years of the war. The pull of employment was difficult for children and their families to resist. By the end of the war, girls and boys were earning up to £2 per week in munitions factories. 'Parental control, so far as it formerly existed, has been relaxed through the absence of families from their homes,' a government committee complained in 1917. 'The withdrawal of influences making for the social improvement of boys and girls has in many districts been followed by a noticeable deterioration in behaviour and morality.' Granted, middle-class commentators make a hobby of criticising working-class habits and warning of delinquency. Nevertheless, some alarming changes in behaviour were evident. With fathers fighting abroad and mothers often working, children (especially boys) who earned undreamt-of levels of income were often tempted to misbehave. While the overall crime rate fell, offences committed by juveniles rose. Authorities in Bath noted a 284 per cent rise in juvenile crime between 1914 and 1918. A letter to *The Times* complained of a similar problem affecting middle-class households, where the children 'rarely see [their] "war mamma" who is involved in every worthy cause. They run wild, unobserved, for even nurse is war-working, and absorbed in knitting projects of a complicated kind.'[39]

The need for women's labour inevitably meant neglect of children, even by the most conscientious mothers. While most women workers were single and childless, the expansion of the female labour force was made possible by the willingness of mothers to work. The state was relatively quick to accept the necessity of female labour, but slow to recognise its consequences for childcare. Mothers made do as best they could: of 129 pre-school children of factory workers in Leeds in 1916, 83 were left with grandmothers or other family, 42 with neighbours, 1 with a landlady, 1 with a day nursery and

1 was boarded out. Some mothers went home at midday to feed children, though employers frowned upon this. State provision of childcare seemed to many a dangerous precedent, since mothers of young children were not under normal circumstances supposed to work. As *The Times* commented in 1916: 'It would be deplorable if the measures taken to preserve the health of girls and mothers in the war factories led married women definitely to abandon their homes for industrial work. If their incursion into skilled labour is to be permanent, then we have paid infinitely too high for any advantage to our arms.'[40]

Necessity forced the state to recognise responsibility. From 1917, the government agreed to pay 75 per cent of the cost of crèche facilities, to a maximum of 7d per child per day. Unfortunately, crèches were slow to materialise. Leeds had none until 1918, a not untypical case. At the large government-owned munitions factories, only 108 nurseries catering to just 4,000 children existed in 1917. As *The Times* quote above indicates, crèches were seen as a necessary evil. This explains why government provision was limited to munitions factories; other mothers, no matter how important their work, were left to their own devices. Even the supposedly enlightened *Labour Women* found it necessary to stress that 'No creches, etc. can ever make up to children for the mother's love. Whatever a childless woman may do for the community is nothing to the service rendered by her [*sic*] who gives it healthy and good children.' A note of reality was injected into the debate when a woman writing to *Reynolds Newspaper* challenged the president of the Local Government Board, an ardent opponent of working mothers: 'If the Rt Hon. John Burns will show me a way out of the difficulty [poverty] I shall be delighted, but it seems to me that until then I must work.' Absent from the debate was consideration whether working mothers might be a lesser evil than poverty-stricken children.[41]

Mothers bore the burden of blame for the erosion of family

stability. Official responses to war's disruption were often grossly insensitive. At large munitions factories welfare supervisors were given wide latitude to inspect workers' homes to check on cleanliness and care of children. For many supervisors, this would have been their first exposure to such places. Substandard conditions were carelessly blamed on slovenliness rather than on poverty. It was a no-win situation for working mothers. If they neglected their homes in order to be good workers, they were cursed by society for being poor mothers. Yet if they took time off work to look after their family, they were criticised for being unreliable and unpatriotic. As one factory manager remarked, 'A day's washing may be a very serious thing for a woman, but to stay away and leave her machine idle for a day's wash does not appear to be anything but trivial to her employer.'[42]

British women of the Great War generation have been consistently misunderstood. The dominant images peddled in school textbooks and television dramas have been those of young female factory workers discovering themselves through meaningful work and afterwards finding a freer life of short skirts, cigarettes and less inhibited love. Icons like Vera Brittain commemorate female success in a man's world. Yet if the stereotyped munitionette or VAD had been typical, it is difficult to see how British society could have held together. There were undoubtedly liberating forces at work, but most women did not recognise them as such, seeing the changes instead as but a brief interruption of the status quo. The vast majority of women during the war did what women always do: they raised children, fed families and maintained the home. Home fires were kept burning.

The housewife's tasks were performed under enormous strain. Improvements in living standards and health did not necessarily mean an easier life. Food queues and price rises caused endless aggravation. The quality of housing stock declined, if not through bombs then due to neglectful landlords. It was a thankless task trying to balance the roles of mother and factory worker. Misplaced patriotism and social do-goodery shed light on the ideals of mothercraft, which in truth meant that mothers were judged according to ever more rigorous standards. Children had to be looked after, often without the help of a father, at a time when they were more easily led into temptation. The war gave with one hand and took with the other: a steady income often meant family disruption. A woman with a husband in France might have found that, with her wages and his separation allowance (not to mention one less mouth to feed), household income was steadier and more substantial than before the war. But she would still have to balance family demands with those of her employer, amidst the pain of separation and the hollow ache of loss.

Regardless of her class, a woman in 1914 was defined in terms of a man. She was someone's wife, sister, daughter, mother or sweetheart. The war did not alter this arrangement other than to make it more precarious. The young soldier Charles Hudson recalls a late-night conversation with a sergeant in his unit:

> 'It's all very well for you, you are unmarried and haven't a wife and children to worry about, but if I am killed what, I wonder, will happen to my family? My wife is not the managing sort, she has always depended entirely on me, and she has never been strong. Her people are dead and my mother is an invalid herself.'

After a century of bewildering change, it might be difficult to understand how vulnerable these women must have felt when their men went off to war and they were left to cope alone in what remained a man's world. For some, the experience was undoubtedly enervating. Many found that patriarchy was built on a foundation of sand, that they could do nearly everything that men once did. Some even enjoyed being freed from boorish or bullying husbands. 'The war's been a 'appy time for us,' one mother told Mrs Peel. 'It's the only time since I've been married as I and the children's 'ad peace.' Yet no matter how unequal marital relations may have been back then, it is difficult to believe that this comment was typical. Most women found that the absence of a man, especially if he was in danger, acted like acid on the soul.[43]

Because mourning is by nature an individual act in Western societies, we know little of how British women coped with separation and loss. Each persevered in her own unique way. Some were bewildered, some stunned. Some grieved loudly and uncontrollably, others in stoical silence. Those who seemed on the surface unaffected hid a soul that would remain forever hollow. Some went blatantly mad. A survey conducted after the war found that 12 per cent of widows died within a year, 14 per cent reported seeing the ghost of a deceased loved one and 39 per cent felt his presence. Vera Brittain's feelings after the loss of her fiancé Roland Bainton were shared by many:

> But, though kind Time may many joys renew,
>   There is one greatest joy I shall not know
> Again, because my heart for loss of You
>   Was broken, long ago.

Out of disruption and death arose a desire to rebuild. During and immediately after the war, 'experts' reminded women, a bit too condescendingly, of their value to society: 'Home and motherhood remain woman's great and unique work,' stressed *The Times*. By 1917, the feminist Catherine Gasquoine, who had once dreamed of a 'golden age which was to come with the self-assertion of women', took a more realistic view: 'with the outbreak of war we women were brought back to the primitive conception of the relative position of the two sexes . . . Again man was the fighter, the protector of woman and the home. And at once his power became a reality.' The Countess of Warwick wrote that 'my own dream and my own vision are of woman as the saviour of the race. I see her fruitful womb replenish the wasted ranks, I hear her wise counsels making irresistibly attractive the flower-strewn ways of peace.' Most women would not have expressed this sentiment quite so floridly, but they would have agreed nonetheless. Moralising propaganda for mothercraft and pro-natalism reflected a popular will, it did not create that will. After four years of destruction, a child offered an opportunity to create. The war was the past, families the future. Rather than encouraging women out of the home, the war's greatest effect was to draw them back.[44]

Chapter 11

Having Fun

The Bloomsbury Group, much admired for its erudition but seldom ridiculed for its silliness, had a rather enjoyable war. Champagne was still plentiful and the war itself provided endless opportunities for pompous judgement. 'Ottoline [Morrell] . . . took it upon herself to keep us all merry & gave a party every week,' wrote Vanessa Bell of her friends. She did her bit to pull 'all the celebrities of the day' out of the gloom by providing a steady regime of good food, clever jests and witty conversation. Every once in a while, when the war weighed heavily, they escaped to a 'funny little house by the sea . . . [where] we live without newspapers . . . & no horrors of any kinds'.[1]

Since leisure is by nature an extravagance, of time or money, those both idle and rich had the most opportunity for fun. The greater one's wealth, the easier it was to keep war's privations at bay. Diaries and letters indicate that life was no less lavish after August 1914; in fact, opportunities for excitement increased. Every week brought an occasion for celebration: dear Tristan's departure for the front was marked at the Ritz or Peregrine's return at the Savoy. News of the war or of politics brought spice to dinner conversation, with gossip trading at inflated prices. 'Some of these women,' complained the Cabinet Secretary Maurice Hankey after lunch at Ciro's (the 'latest fashion freak restaurant'), 'talk too much and know too much.' When two Serb diplomats visited London to raise awareness about their starving people, they were given a lavish dinner at the Carlton. 'It was . . . rather terrible to those Servians to see hundreds of people eating oysters and drinking champagne', wrote Lady Scott. While quick to criticise such ostentatious displays, she never could quite resist them. On 6 May 1916, she dined 'at the Piccadilly of all awful places. I was shocked to death to see the extravagance of the women's dress – & we eat foie gras, I eat it too with a feeling of disgust at the gaudy brilliantly lighted place.' The military correspondent Colonel Charles à Court Repington admitted a similar vice: 'Lady Ridley and I discussed what posterity would think of us in England. We agreed that we should be considered rather callous to go on with our usual life when we were reading of 3,000 to 4,000 casualties a day . . . she supposed that things around us explained the French Revolution and the behaviour of the French nobility.'[2]

Everyone deserved an escape from war's cruelty, but among the rich moderation was rare and hypocrisy ran deep. While they indulged, they expected others to maintain a spartan approach to war. Government ministers enjoyed the luxuries of high office while lecturing the public on the need for austerity. Sir Edwin Montagu, Financial Secretary to the Treasury, apparently saw no contradiction between his pleas to the public to cut consumption and his own lavish parties, nor did Asquith feel that wartime decorum necessitated a modest wedding for his daughter. The King forswore alcohol, but few of his upper-class friends followed suit. They were, however, quick to criticise the drinking habits of the workers. At times, the hypocrisy grew so blatant that even *The Times* was motivated to express democratic disgust: 'there are whole circles of society in which the spirit of sacrifice is unknown', it remarked in 1917. 'There should be no exceptions to the rigorous rule of self-denial which has been willingly undertaken by the great mass of our people.' The editor probably thought up that leader over lunch at the Savoy.[3]

One of the most blatant examples of hypocrisy came in reaction to football, the working man's game. Middle-class critics condemned the way professional matches continued as if peace still reigned. 'We ... had a shock ... on our way to Wimbledon, as we passed the grounds of the football club, to see young men swarming in thousands to watch a match', wrote Georgina Lee on 22 August 1914. 'Those are the men we want so badly now in our army.' Complaining loudly about the 'scandal of professional football ... with the huge "gates" of loafing lads', Sir George Young concluded that 'among the poor and ignorant, the uprising of the proper spirit is slow work'. *The Times* expressed its scorn through verse:

> Come, leave the lure of the football field
> With its fame so lightly won,
> And take your place in a greater game
> Where worthier deeds are done.
> No game is this where thousands watch
> The play of a chosen few;
> But rally all! if you're men at all,
> There's room in the team for you.
> . . .
> Then leave for a while the football field
> And the lure of the flying ball
> Lest it dull your ear to the voice you hear
> When your King and country call.
> Come join the ranks of our hero sons
> In the wider field of fame,
> Where the God of Right will watch the fight
> And referee the game.

To a great extent, the outcry was a revival of the old 'gentlemen vs players' debate; because the football enjoyed by the workers was professional, it aroused the scorn of the middle class, who insisted that games should remain amateur. Likewise, it was argued, they should be played, not watched.

Devotees of less plebeian games delighted in showing off their patriotism. The cricketer W. G. Grace made snide remarks about the disreputable behaviour of football fans, while a smug Marylebone Cricket Club secretary boasted that cricketers 'now look for their heroes on the great field of battle'. Philip Collins of the Hockey Association claimed that abandonment of all football matches would release 40,000 men for the armed services, a figure he neglected to explain. A St Andrews University rugby player turned soldier wrote in *College Echoes*:

> There's not much good in grousing,
> Work lies here to be done;
> 'Varsity days are sweetest,
> Though soldiering's just A1.
> So we'll have a good go at the Germans,
> An', by conch, won't we make 'em run!

Rugby clubs in Kent made great publicity of the fact that they had cancelled fixtures, and the Rugby Football Union formed a Pals battalion of player volunteers.[4]

On 2 December 1914, the *Stratford Express* reported on a speech by the Bishop of Chelmsford in which he argued 'that the cry against professional football at the present time was right. He could not understand men who had any feeling, any respect for their country, men in the prime of life, taking large salaries at a time like this for kicking a ball about. It seemed to him something incongruous and unworthy.' The Football Association (FA), keen to improve its image, allowed recruiting campaigns at league grounds. Supporters were bombarded by messages like 'Are You Forgetting There's a War On?' and the ubiquitous 'Your Country Needs You'. Posters sought to turn team loyalty into battalion solidarity.

MEN OF MILLWALL

Hundreds of Football enthusiasts are joining the Army daily.

Don't be left behind.

Let the Enemy hear the "LION'S ROAR."

Join and be in at

THE FINAL

and give them a

KICK OFF THE EARTH

Apply:
West Africa House, opposite National Theatre, Kingsway.

The FA, however, stubbornly maintained that 'in the interests of the people of this country, football ought to be continued'. Meanwhile, the numbers volunteering at matches dwindled as the year ended, which critics took as further evidence that football fans were unpatriotic. Of the 16,450 attestation cards distributed by Lord Derby at a Liverpool–Everton match in January 1915, only 1,034 were returned, and of those only 206 expressed a willingness to enlist. When another effort at Arsenal proved equally unsuccessful, the editor of *The Times* remarked that the tepid response 'contrasts strongly with the wholesale volunteering which has distinguished the performers and devotees of other forms of sport. Rugby Union clubs, cricket elevens, and rowing clubs throughout the kingdom have poured men into the ranks.' In truth, by this stage the volunteer spirit was in decline everywhere. Critics ignored the fact that, of the nearly 1.2 million men who had volunteered by the end of 1914, some 500,000 had connections to football clubs.[5]

Greatest scorn was reserved for the footballers themselves. 'From the very nature of their trade they are in the prime of manhood, more qualified to pass any test of age and health, and physically the flower of our potential recruits,' *The Times* argued. Managers, it was alleged, were 'bribing [the players] away from their country's service'. The FA responded by pointing out that of the 5,000 professional players on teams in 1914, some 2,000 had already volunteered and another 2,400 were married. That left only 600 men who could remotely be considered 'shirkers', yet many of them in fact had jobs in industry. The *Athletic News* poured scorn on what it rightly saw as blatant class hypocrisy:

> The whole agitation is nothing less than an attempt by the ruling classes to stop the recreation on one day in the week of the masses . . . What do they care for the poor man's sport? The poor are giving their lives for this country in thousands. In many cases they have nothing else . . . There are those who could bear arms, but who have to stay at home and work for the army's requirements, and the country's needs. These should, according to a small clique of virulent snobs, be deprived of the one distraction that they have had for over thirty years.

The masses, unfortunately, were fighting a losing battle. Heavyweight newspapers heaped scorn on players and fans. Bowing to the pressure, the FA formally suspended League football after the spring of 1915.[6]

Angry football fans retaliated by pointing out that 'Amongst the most vigorous critics of football are numberless racecourse frequenters, fox hunters, and golfers.' A witch hunt ensued;

sport, once worshipped, was now deemed frivolous and unpatriotic. *The Times* summarised the mood:

> It would not be easy to imagine a more infuriating sight, in the present state of the public temper, than that of a young man in flannels carrying a racket. A year ago, if he attracted notice at all, he suggested one blamelessly bent on healthful exercise tempered by flirtation. Now he would be regarded as a double-dyed traitor. It would be said of him that not only was he not at the front, but that he was wanting in the sense of right conduct at home.

The Boat Race was abandoned for the first time since it became an annual event in 1856. Turf enthusiasts maintained a rearguard action, claiming that their sport 'employs many people unfitted for other work' (short jockeys), while it promoted English bloodstock. In time, however, pressure grew intolerable and, with the exception of Newmarket, all meetings ceased after May 1915. Golf was still played, though courses grew increasingly shabby for want of greenkeepers. In March 1918, golfers in Eastbourne were fined for illegally using petrol to get to their course. Boxing somehow remained unaffected, perhaps because its aggression seemed appropriate. 'Here are something of the ingredients of war – blood and sweat and struggle, the cunning manoeuvring for blows and the taking of them cheerfully,' wrote *The Times*. 'We are filled with admiration for sheer courage above all qualities and here is the courage of the battle in miniature.'[7]

Britons argued incessantly about the proper way to behave during wartime. Many a newspaper editorial urged citizens to 'do their part by setting an example of seriousness and self-denial'. Temperance campaigns increased in popularity, in part because the brewing of beer now seemed wasteful of resources, but also because the enjoyment associated with alcohol seemed inappropriate. On the other hand, some people felt, with good reason, that an occasional escape from the war was good for morale. Thus, despite the difficulties of train travel and the ravages of German artillery, seaside holidays remained popular. Resorts marketed themselves as suitable substitutes for German and French spas. 'Visit St Andrews,' went one newspaper advertisement. 'The picturesque old city. Beautiful Scenery, Sea bathing, &c. Specially Excellent Golf. Everything Quite Normal.'[8]

Those who allowed themselves a week amidst the charms of the Old Course often still criticised workers who spent an hour at the pub. If the worker happened to be a woman, animosity ran deeper. Men resented these strange invaders on their hallowed ground. Annoyance encouraged cruel judgement – the women were condemned as unpatriotic, immoral or, worse, on the game. Polite society indulged in a proper panic over the ruin of young women. Welfare supervisors became surrogate parents, without the love. It was confidently assumed that mothers would appreciate 'that someone will support her daughter in her effort not to succumb to evil talk and foul insinuation, to the temptation to join in drinking parties or in pleasures that look harmless to the high-spirited girl and are full of peril'. In October 1914, *The Times* warned of a serious threat to propriety:

> Little imagination is needed to picture the evils which may arise when a young girl in a state of mental restlessness produced by the war finds herself at once unemployed, with such free time on her hands, with a sudden and absorbing interest thrust upon her through the presence of a large number of troops stationed in her town, and with a desire to help with no ability to do so.

The enthusiasm many young women felt towards men in uniform caused considerable alarm. One commentator reported seeing 'some young Colonials running for their very lives to escape a little company of girls. One might have thought, to see them, that they had tigresses at their heels.' Whether this constituted an actual threat to society was debatable. Fawcett felt that the desire of girls to visit the camps was 'quite natural and wholesome', but she still felt that 'in the absence of proper control it certainly leads in very many cases to deplorable consequences'.[9]

'Plenty of girls', a private noted with delight after enlistment. 'They love the boys in khaki. They detest walking with civilians.' Mr E. B. Turner, chairman of the National Council for Combating Venereal Diseases, wrote in 1919 of an epidemic of licentiousness, fired by patriotic motive. 'I believe a great deal of the going wrong among girls lately is due to what I describe as a wave of patriotic immorality going over the country. They think the soldiers have been prepared to give so much for them, that they would give anything, even their best treasure.' Khaki fever, if it existed at all, did not last much longer than the rush to the colours. The fallout, however, continued for the rest of the war. According to Sylvia Pankhurst:

War-time hysterics gave currency to fabulous rumour. From press and pulpit stories ran rampant of drunkenness and depravity amongst the women of the masses. Alarmist morality mongers conceived most monstrous visions of girls and women, freed from the control of fathers and husbands who had hitherto compelled them to industry, chastity and sobriety, now neglecting their homes, plunging into excesses, and burdening the country with swarms of illegitimate children.

Moralists warned that a large army would encourage an 'amateur drift' of otherwise decent women into prostitution. In Cardiff, women were banned from pubs between 7 p.m. and

6 a.m. and from the streets between 7 p.m. and 8 a.m. According to a member of the Women's Police Service, a similar measure in Grantham forced genuine prostitutes to entertain men 'in their houses instead of . . . on the streets', which did 'more harm than if the women had actually been in the public houses and in the streets where people could see them'. What the controversy over khaki fever revealed was that the British love to talk about sex, expecially if they can, at the same time, indulge in a spot of moralising. Envy from watching young women having fun was easily converted into disdain.[10]

Fears of an epidemic of immorality prompted the formation of the Women Patrols Committee (WPC) and the Women Police Service. These were voluntary groups, inspired in part by middle-class feminists who worried that the 'foolish, giddy, irresponsible conduct . . . of the young girls might . . . [lead] them into grave moral danger'. By patrolling cinemas, ports, camps, parks and any areas where soldiers congregated, the women police aimed to save girls 'from their own folly'. 'A special duty from the very first was to turn girls and lads out of the deep doorways and shop entrances,' one member explained. 'This is a job the police constable did not care to do, owing to the amount of abuse he got. But we never have any difficulty.' The Home Office, fully supportive of the scheme, made it clear that 'the women patrols . . . are being organised primarily with a view to the care of girls and women who are not prostitutes and would not ordinarily come under the notice of the police . . . their object is mainly preventive'. Stated differently, one WPC pamphlet warned that 'Often girls sink so low in their sin that they can never rise again, but sink lower and lower until they die a lonely and terrible death.' Some concern was also shown towards the men who were the objects of their attention:

> there is a great danger of the men being damaged and made unfit for the hard and awful work in front of them unless

parents and employers try to prevent the girls from getting excited, running wild in the evenings and forgetting their honour, their purity, their self-respect ... It is terrible to think that the folly and sin of any of the women and girls should make these men less fit to die and send them away with a guilty conscience.

When American troops began to flood into Britain in 1918, they brought along their own female police. Observers wondered whether they had come to protect British women from American soldiers, or vice versa. The female police and the women they watched were both, in their own way, enjoying the freedoms that war produced. Both groups found pleasure in walking the streets in search of excitement. The differences between the two groups are, however, more important than the similarities. The women police were almost without exception middle-aged and middle class, whereas those they monitored were predominantly young and working-class. The former looked backward to an imagined past of impeccable virtue, while the latter gazed longingly towards a future overflowing with freedom. A clash of moral codes led inevitably to conflict. Perfectly innocent behaviour, such as a married couple fondling in a park, could attract the officious attention of prudish policewomen. 'It is about time something was done about ancient spinsters following soldiers about with their flash lights,' wrote one angry correspondent to the *East Grinstead Observer*. 'I have seen a great deal of the soldiers who have been here and I consider that they have have been unfairly treated. Walking in the roads and fields accompanied by friends is no crime. What would these spinsters think if soldiers flashed a light upon them in their gardens or darkened drawing rooms?' The patrols occasionally performed a valuable function when they rescued girls from unwelcome advances, but there is also no doubt that the uniform of the WPC gave voyeurs and busybodies undeserved legitimacy.[11]

War is erotic. Its effect upon the libido has been grossly exaggerated, but as with any myth, this one has a basis in fact. Take a man in a crisp uniform and leather boots, throw in the machismo of combat and guns, add a woman susceptible to romance and excitement, bring them together in the urgency of a 48-hour leave, and the result can be volatile. Casual sex increased during the war mainly because there was more opportunity: greater mixing of the sexes, more of a tendency to throw caution to the wind, less of the censure and control that tightly knit communities once exercised. According to the popular novelist Stephen McKenna, 'Anyone who lived in London during those feverish months had forced upon his notice a spectacle of debauchery which would have swelled the record of scandal if it had been made public but which is mercifully forgotten because it is incredible.' The sexologists H. C. Fischer and E. X. Dubois described a similar scene, albeit more luridly:

> the primitive, bestial instincts that lie dormant in civilised man exploded in an almost universal orgy of sexual license and debauchery . . . the war enthusiasm of the first weeks suddenly broke down the established concepts of sexual morality . . . as the war proceeded . . . women on the 'home front' were driven by sex hunger to adultery and worse . . . sexual perversions, from homosexuality and Lesbian love to the most horrible manifestations of sadism developed and spread through the length and breadth of Europe . . . while the guns thundered and the screams of mutilated and dying men filled the air at the various warfronts, men and women in the big cities of Europe, maddened by the strain of war and sex starvation, indulged in degrading sexual orgies under the influence of drink and drugs; and

... finally, venereal disease increased a hundredfold in all the belligerent countries, to avenge the sins of a mad world on a generation yet unborn.

While that was undoubtedly fun to read, it was far from the truth. Mary Agnes Hamilton was more understanding:

Life was less than cheap; it was thrown away ... All moral standards were held for a short moment and irretrievably lost. Little wonder that the old ideals of chastity and self-control in sex were, for many, also lost ... How and why refuse appeals, backed up by the hot beating of your own heart, or what at the moment you thought to be your heart, which were put with passion and even pathos by a hero here today and gone tomorrow?

Sarah Macnaughtan found it all rather puzzling and sordid. Civilisation seemed to be crumbling before her eyes. 'Beautiful women and fast women should be chained up,' she argued, taking the side of poor, innocent Tommy Atkins. 'Let men meet their God with their conscience clear. Most of them will be killed before the war is over. Surely the least we can do is not to offer them temptation. Death and destruction, and horror and wonderful heroism, seems so near and so transcendent, and then, quite close at hand, one finds evil doings.' Taking a decidedly more practical view, the feminist journalist Helena Swanwick went so far as to argue that 'Sex before marriage was the natural female complement to the male frenzy of killing. If millions of men were to be killed in early manhood, or even boyhood, it behooved every young woman to secure a mate and replenish the population while there was yet time.'[12]

The loosening of inhibitions was not necessarily good for women; a moment's weakness often meant years of woe. The pressure upon 'decent' women to do their bit for a soldier was often intense and the desire for intercourse not always mutual. A. B. Baker, a WAAC stationed in France, found most of the soldiers well behaved, but on one occasion 'a Tommy who wasn't a hero, and not much of a man, tried to make love to me ... I had respected myself, and this man wanted not to respect me. I got away from him, and ran. He ran after me. I could run better than he.' Charles Cain was shocked at the behaviour of his fellow soldiers, who 'were rough with women, boasted of their conquests, many of whom were actually raped, but there were no prosecutions to my knowledge. Suffice it to say that ten soldiers were billeted on one woman who had three teenage daughters, and the mother and all the daughters finished up in the family way.' When pregnancy or disease resulted, the weight of scorn fell on the women, not the soldiers. The old double standard still applied: a woman who surrendered to male pressure or to her own desires was automatically deemed 'not the right sort'. Quite typical was the reaction of an officer to news that his occasional sexual partner was pregnant: 'I met her in the latter end of January and kept company with her for about six weeks ... she is not the class of girl for me ... I am shortly leaving for the Front, and am putting the affair in my mother's hands. She is in possession of all the dates, and should they tally with the birth of the child, I have instructed her to make a small allowance for the maintenance of the child.'[13]

In April 1915, the Tory MP Ronald McNeill spread fears of a population explosion of 'war babies' around military camps. Two values collided: an old one that abhorred illegitimacy and a new one that treasured every newborn baby. 'No one wants to mete out and apportion blame in this matter,' complained *The Times*, 'but it is an even worse mistake to begin to glorify human frailty as though it were praiseworthy.' The newspapers delighted in moralising about a problem that did not in fact exist. In time, an official inquiry discovered that 'the rumours which have circulated have been proved beyond doubt to have no foundation in fact'. The proportion of illegitimate births did rise by 30 per cent during the war, but since the overall birth rate fell, the actual number declined.[14]

Venereal disease, on the other hand, was a serious problem, with 32 out of every 1,000 soldiers afflicted by 1917. Though medical checks at brothels near the front were frequent, frenetic activity rendered the problem difficult to control. The implications were serious, firstly for manpower and secondly for the spread of the disease at home. The Royal Commission on Venereal Diseases, reporting in 1916, estimated that in working-class areas of London, 8 to 12 per cent of men and 3 to 7 per cent of women suffered from syphilis, with the figures higher for gonorrhoea. The Commission recommended 'a franker attitude toward these diseases', but feminists criticised its failure to provide guidance on prevention. The 1916 Public Health (Venereal Diseases) Regulation Act did establish a network of clinics offering free confidential diagnosis and treatment. Less progressive, however, was the double standard that applied. Whereas the Edwardians had viewed VD as something that men gave to helpless women, during the war the disease was seen as a scourge inflicted by lascivious women upon innocent Tommies. The temperance advocate Marr Murray argued that 'it is . . . an undoubted fact that as a result of the swarms of loose women . . . which have flocked to the garrison towns, numbers of men have contracted venereal disease'. Regulation 40D of DORA, passed in March 1918, made it illegal for a woman afflicted with VD to have intercourse with a serviceman. This meant, in effect, that a woman suffering from VD could be arrested for having sex with her husband, even if he infected her in the first place.[15]

On 29 May 1918, the 'trial of the century' began when the dancer and actress Maud Allan launched a libel suit against the notorious homophobe Pemberton Billing. Allan was at the time acting in Oscar Wilde's *Salome,* which Billing described as a degenerate play by a 'known pervert' that glorified unbridled lust and deviancy. In his journal *Vigilante,* he published an article entitled 'The Cult of the Clitoris' in which he suggested, by roundabout means, that Allan was a lesbian. He was acquitted, largely because, during cross-examination, she was forced to admit that her real name was Beulah Maud Durrant, but that she had changed it in order to escape association with her brother Theo, who had been executed in the United States after committing a series of sex crimes. Billing suggested that deviancy ran in the family and also argued that Allan had studied in Germany, a nation known for perversion. On hearing of the acquittal, Cynthia Asquith wrote:

> It is monstrous that these maniacs should be vindicated in the eyes of the public . . . Papa came in and announced that the monster maniac Billing had won his case. Damn him! It is such an awful triumph for the unreasonable, such a tonic to the microbe of suspicion which is spreading through the country, and such a stab in the back to people unprotected from such attacks owing to their best and not their worst points.

The acquittal probably reflected the temper of the times, not to the extent that people believed Billing's wild accusations, but rather that they enjoyed hearing them. Debauchery was less common than gossip suggested, but the gossip, for a generation that lacked easy access to pornography, provided a handy source of titillation. Decent people who despised licentiousness delighted in hearing about it. The Assistant Commissioner of Police, on hearing of plans by the London Public Morality Council to investigate sexual activity in parks like Hampstead Heath and Clapham Common, pointedly remarked that the Council might 'bear in mind that the conduct of which they complain only constitutes an offence when committed within the view of the public'.[16]

Marwick claims that the war 'spread promiscuity upwards and birth control downwards'. That seems too simplistic and, in any case, reinforces stereotypes of a lusty working-class while overstating the dissemination of contraceptives. Condoms were widely available by the end of the war, but they were seen mainly as a measure to control VD, not as an aid to uninhibited sex. Despite the near epidemic of VD, there was still considerable anxiety that condom usage encouraged immorality. The increased use of contraceptives amongst middle-class married couples does nevertheless suggest wider acceptance of the idea of sex for enjoyment. *Married Love*, published by the birth control pioneer Marie Stopes in March 1918, sold 2,000 copies in its first fortnight and by 1924 had undergone 22 reprints. As the title of her book suggests, however, Stopes was an advocate of sex within marriage; the promotion of contraceptives for premarital sex was at least another generation away. As for the working-class, drawing conclusions about something as private as sex is difficult. Leaving aside the gossip, one imagines that the war stimulated the heart more than it activated the libido; there was more romance than intercourse. Much gossip surrounded the supposedly immoral behaviour of WAACs, who disposed of their scruples when they donned their uniforms. A suggestive cartoon in the *Sporting Times* asked: 'Would you rather have a slap on the eye or a WAAC on the knee?' A 1918 Commission of Inquiry investigating fears of licentious WAACs could nevertheless 'find no justification of any kind for the vague accusations of immoral conduct on a large scale which have been circulated'. If intercourse outside marriage did increase, that does not mean it was always consensual. Women on the shop floor were often seen as prey by male supervisors. Likewise, one WAAC complained that 'once we are in uniform any Tommy thinks he can make advances'.[17]

Fears about women overcome by carnality were only slightly more hysterical than those about women intoxicated by alcohol. On the basis of prejudice rather than evidence, *The Times* confidently concluded that 'Unhappily there is no reason to doubt that drinking among the poorest classes of women has increased considerably since the outbreak of the war.' Social workers wrote to the paper in October 1914 complaining that women who insisted their children were starving were 'all the time puffing into our faces fumes of whisky, gin and the like'. The Women's Advisory Committee of the Liquor Control Board cited excessive drinking among soldiers' wives as the cause of a rise in crime, 'reckless procreation', infidelity, 'feeble-mindedness' and improvidence, all leading to 'race suicide'. Yet the NSPCC found that female drunkenness actually declined during the war. Women interviewed by the historian Gail Braybon confirmed these findings, claiming that they seldom went to pubs during the war, and almost never alone.[18]

The country did have a drink problem, though it was never confined to the working-class or to women. Rubber-legged workers spilling out of pubs at all hours were more visible than soused gentlemen in clubland. There was nothing particularly new about the nation's taste for drink. Prior to the war, most pubs in London opened at 5 a.m. and closed at 12.30 a.m. Factory hands drank before and during work. This sort of behaviour was, however, inappropriate to wartime. The Intoxicating Liquor (Temporary Restriction) Act, passed on 31 August 1914, addressed the problem by granting licensing authorities the power to restrict opening hours. The new regulations (imposing a closing as early as 9 p.m.) were first applied to munitions areas, but gradually spread across the country. A government report released on 29 April 1915 linked poor production at factories in Barrow with workplace intoxication. Scotsmen who had migrated to the area for war work were blamed – a cheap shot, one suspects. In response, the government, under the authority of DORA, established on 10 June a Central Control Board to regulate liquor sales in areas important to the war effort. Fourteen areas were initially named, in which the sale of alcohol (both on premises and off-sales) was restricted to as little as 4½ hours per day. As the war progressed, the number of areas increased, so much so that by 1917 the Board held jurisdiction over the drinking habits of 93 per cent of the population. The government, through the Board, also encouraged the establishment of model pubs designed to make the drink trade more respectable while controlling consumption. Cheap restaurants and canteens were established as an alternative to disreputable drinking dens.

Other regulations included the banning of spirit bottles smaller than quarts (less easy to consume quickly and less transportable), restrictions upon the purchase of spirits with a beer chaser, and the prohibition of bottle sales on Saturday and Sunday. One of the more ingenious measures (or iniquitous, depending upon one's point of view) was the banning of 'treating' – buying a drink for another individual. The measure was partly designed to cut down on drunkenness among soldiers, who found that wearing a uniform in a pub virtually guaranteed a night of free drinking. Alfred Pollard discovered in 1917 that the rule did not apply to those honoured with the Victoria Cross – he never again had to open his wallet. (He also found that the woman who had previously spurned his offer of marriage was suddenly interested.) The government progressively lowered the permitted alcohol content of beers and pegged the potency of spirits at 70 per cent proof. Weaker beer, universally derided, not only curbed drunkenness, but also helped to conserve food supplies and farm labour. Liquor duties further reduced consumption and raised revenue. The price of a pint rose from 3d in 1914 to as high as 10d by the end of the war, due mostly to taxation.

State action did reduce consumption. Convictions for

drunkenness and assault, which stood at 62,882 in 1908, were down to 1,670 by 1918, although other factors also influenced the decline. A study released in 1917 revealed that arrests for drunkenness among women decreased from 40,815 in 1914 to 24,206 in 1916. 'There has never been so great a reduction spread over so large a population in the same space of time,' remarked an editor in *The Times*, one of the leading contributors to the myth of rampant female drunkenness. The *New Survey of London Life and Labour* commented favourably on the

decrease in the amount of drinking per head . . . and the decreased extent to which actual excess, and the economic effects of excess are found. The social status of drunkenness has steadily fallen in the eyes of the working-class population. Where once frequent drunkenness was half admired as a sign of virility, it is now regarded as, on the whole, rather squalid and ridiculous.

The *Brewer's Gazette* remarked on how 'great traffic centres, like the Elephant and Castle, at which immense crowds usually lounge about until 1 o'clock in the morning, have suddenly become peaceful and respectable'. With the acceptability of drinking on the decline, the middle class turned to a less visible drug to deaden the pain of war. Cocaine usage increased to such an extent that the government eventually had to prohibit its importation, except under licence. Possession and consumption, however, remained legal. 'The apostle of the cocaine cult finds many disciples,' wrote *The Times*, 'for he offers a new release from time and circumstance.' In the pomposity stakes, the paper had few rivals.[19]

While the popularity of pubs declined, other forms of entertainment boomed. The nightclub, a harbinger of the roaring twenties, thrived. It was almost exclusively the preserve of the wealthy, especially since drinks were exorbitantly priced and gambling required spare cash. Ranging in quality from swanky to downright seedy, the clubs demonstrated that, despite the war, the appetite for hedonism remained healthy. With scantily clad dancing girls, bawdy songs and tarty waitresses, they provided wonderful opportunities for the moralistic middle-class to parade their hypocrisy. Dance halls displayed a cleaner image, but, perhaps because they were popular among the workers, self-appointed moral guardians campaigned vigorously against them. Dancing itself, other than the folk variety, was initially a middle-class entertainment, but grew more common during the war. American ragtime and jazz, and the dancing styles they inspired (such as the foxtrot and Charleston), raised fears of cultural pollution, especially given their identification with blacks.

Lovelorn couples who wanted a few private hours together often migrated towards the cinema. Before the war, most cinemas had staff specifically employed to reprimand and remove viewers more interested in fondling than the film. They carried long sticks to poke the excessively amorous. The manpower shortage rendered these monitors a luxury, much to the dismay of the National Council of Public Morals, which warned of widespread depravity. A representative of the London Cinema Exhibitors thought the fuss rather overblown: 'When investigation is made, it is usually found that the alleged misconduct is nothing more than the privileged manifestation of affection between the sexes.' Since cinemas were enormously popular among the working-class, the moral censure was probably yet another manifestation of class prejudice: just as workers could not be trusted with drink, so too they could not be trusted to behave properly in the dark. No amount of moral censure could, however, stop the cinema's enormous growth in popularity; audiences of around 20 million per week attended 3,000 cinemas in 1914.[20]

Perhaps because of its image as a cheap imitation of the

theatre (anything so popular must be of low quality), the cinema was at first scorned by the better off. Its popularity widened during the war, partly because newsreels offered 'authentic' scenes from the front. Going to the cinema thus became an act of participation in the war effort. An advertisement for a film depicting the battle of the Ancre maintained that 'It is your duty and your privilege to see it.' Quite by accident, and somewhat late in the day, the government discovered that it was actually a good thing for the public to be given controlled doses of the war's horror. After viewing *Battle of the Somme*, Frances Stevenson, Lloyd George's secretary, confessed that the film allowed her 'to understand what [my brother] Paul's last hours were: I have often tried to imagine to myself what he went through, but now I know: and I shall never forget'. A correspondent to *The Times* wrote: 'I have already lost two near relatives, yet I never understood their sacrifice until I had seen this film.' Geoffrey Malins, the official director of newsreels, nevertheless insisted that war scenes had to be handled with great care:

> You must not leave the public with a bitter taste in their mouth at the end. The film takes you to the grave, but it must not leave you there; it shows you death in all its grim nakedness, but after that it is essential that you should be restored to a sense of cheerfulness and joy. That joy comes out of the knowledge that in all this whirlpool of horrors our Lads continue to smile the smile of victory.

Battle of the Somme apparently achieved this effect. Though the film was unusual in its depiction of British soldiers being killed, viewers still, according to the *St Andrews Citizen*, felt 'a thrill of pride in the British race as [they saw] the long column of Tommies bravely marching to the attack. There is no air of despondency about them; they look like heroes going to conquer.' The *Times* reviewer was 'more convinced than ever of the invincible spirit of his fellow countrymen in France'. Grim reality of this sort nevertheless bothered the Dean of Durham, who expressed dismay with viewers who felt 'no scruple at feasting their eyes on pictures which present the passion and death of British soldiers'.[21]

Since the war was such an integral part of everyone's life, almost any representation of it was automatically popular. *Battle of the Somme* had 2,000 bookings in its first two months, with profits reaching £30,000. A deadly boring film about the war could still attract large audiences, and huge ticket sales. The stodgy and humdrum *Britain Prepared*, a three-hour epic that one American critic judged 'as uninspired as a hardware catalogue', provoked drools of delight from an English critic: 'To say that [it] is marvellous, wonderful, stupendous, magnificent and so on would fall very short of the real truth.' Cinema audiences, eager to watch almost anything, were sitting targets for propaganda. To the credit of the government, however, newsreels were primarily conveyors of news. Most of the 700 war films produced were realistic portrayals of a nation at war. Inappropriate material may have been edited out but fictitious scenes were not generally inserted. Trench footage in *Battle of the Somme* was staged, but the aim was not to lie but to recreate the truth when the limitations of technology prevented the reality from being filmed. 'I have tried to make my pictures actual and reliable', Malins wrote. 'Above all I have striven to catch the atmosphere of the battlefield.'[22]

Commercial producers, on the other hand, had fewer scruples. They understood that the war provided wonderful opportunities for profit under the guise of public service. The public wanted the drama that war fostered and did not mind at all if the film had a heavy-handed patriotic message. D. W. Griffith came to understand this new market. His *Intolerance* (1916), though a recognised classic, was a box office flop because of its pacifist theme. Brought to Britain in 1917 to make war films, he learned to pander to popular belligerence. *The Great Love* and *Heart of the World*, generally seen as lesser achievements, were massively popular, much to the delight of the government. The latter, which includes a scene in which Lillian Gish is nearly raped by a vile German officer, combined everything calculated to please a wartime audience: action, romance, a hated villain, a bit of sex and a happy ending. 'The tried and popular elements of drama have not been swept away by a wave of militarism, but have been ingeniously adapted to a new state of things,' one critic gushed. Some filmmakers, however, avoided the war in an effort to provide an escape. Charlie Chaplin's ability to provide a restorative tonic for the soul eventually smothered carping criticism that he was 'not doing his bit'. Even the most frivolous films, by distracting attention from the war, had a positive effect. The cinema drew people out of their homes where they might otherwise have been mired in gloom. It was also a shared experience that reinforced national solidarity. When fire broke out in the Lanark Picture House, the pianist had the presence of mind to strike up 'It's a Long Way to Tipperary'. The audience joined in, nerves were cooled and an orderly exit followed.[23]

An opportunity to escape was also provided at the music halls. Largely populated by the better-off working-class, they were perfectly suited to wartime, since they catered to the peculiar British tendency to confront adversity by breaking out in song. The acts were essentially crude political cartoons put to music, with fat German soldiers, sausages hanging from their pockets, providing a rich vein of ridicule. Responding to wartime demand, London County Council granted full music licences to picture palace managers so that they could include patriotic singing on their programmes. An astute piano supplier recognised an opportunity to recreate the music hall atmosphere at home: 'The "Pianola" piano enables you to celebrate good news fittingly,' went one ad. It was 'always ready to play the music that expresses your present mood'.[24]

Previously middle-class theatres were democratised during the war. In cities across Britain, drama companies enjoyed packed houses and extended runs. The London Palladium, for instance, put on 1,043 performances in 1916, which drew three million people. The audience was composed of 61 per cent women, 8 per cent children and 31 per cent men, nearly half of the latter in uniform. London theatres switched mainly to matinee performances, so that audiences would not have to worry about air raids. The theatre's popularity was achieved in part by diluting previously highbrow content, much to the annoyance of traditionalists. Managers, like film producers, understood the marketability of war. A steady fare of crudely patriotic dramas (often, again, providing opportunities for singing) was offered. At the same time, managers recognised a popular need, especially among soldiers, to escape the war. 'The great charm of Peter Pan is that it enables the onlooker to forget for a few hours the worries of everyday life,' wrote *The Times* critic. 'It was a real joy at the Duke of York's theatre to leave the thoughts of European war outside.' Another critic explained the theatre's immense popularity: 'between the desire to learn about the war and the desire to forget about the war, we have the crowded houses which puzzle our foreign friends'.[25]

High culture survived the war intact. An increased sensitivity to the preciousness of life inspired a thirst for the sublime. 'In wartime the temper of a section of the people for a while becomes graver, simpler, and more concentrated,' remarked the conductor Sir Thomas Beecham. 'The opportunities for recreation and amusement are more restricted, transport is limited, and the thoughtful intelligence craves and seeks these antidotes to a troubled conscience of which great music is perhaps the most potent.' Tastes in classical music nevertheless harmonised with the wartime mood. Audiences became familiar as never before with Russian music, at the expense of German or Austrian. Overtly martial music, like the '1812 Overture', became popular.[26]

Paintings and sculpture also provided a welcome escape. At first, attendances at the National Gallery declined, which convinced an economy-minded government that it could close galleries. An angry protest in the press brought a reversal of the decision, though hours were restricted. By war's end, eager art lovers were flooding in as never before. Museums also provided popular diversion, with exhibits often taking on a war theme. Perhaps the most bizarre was the fly exhibition at the Scottish Zoological Park, which included an exhibit of the 'body louse which has been a source of great pain and annoyance to the troops at the front'.[27]

One might be inclined to explain the enormous and profound poetic output during the Great War as symptomatic of Beecham's thirst for the sublime, but some qualifications are necessary. The modernist literature and painting for which the war was famous were not invented in the trenches. Both existed before the war. In other words, Rupert Brooke's romantic poetry about the glory of dying for England was already old-fashioned at the time it was written. Modernism's stark realism was, however, particularly appropriate for conveying the horrors of industrialised war, particularly a war that lacked the overt heroics upon which romanticism depended. Nevertheless, though modernists found a rich vein to tap, their work was not popular at the time. The poems of Wilfred Owen and Siegfried Sassoon (or the paintings of Paul Nash and Muirhead Bone) have been admired by subsequent generations because they conform to and reinforce retrospective judgements of the war. Though the Great War generation was a poetic one, the vast majority of what was read and written was characterised by tortured rhyme, sugar-sweet romanticism and patriotism driven home with a drumbeat. This sort of poetry could even be written after the carnage of the Somme:

> So when you went to play another game
>> You could not but be brave:
> An Empire's team, a rougher football field
>> The end – perhaps your grave.

In other words, the war inspired a popular hunger for romantic pap. An excessively confident St Andrews student gave the following advice to mothers who had lost sons:

> Why would ye mourn and be of heavy heart
> Ye who have lost your children in the fight?
> Rather rejoice that they should play their part
> And fall so nobly in the cause of right.

While subsequent generations have elevated Owen to sainthood, during the war the British preferred Jessie Pope. As for the visual arts, the populist sketches of Bruce Bairnsfather were more widely treasured than the shattered landscapes of Nash. Poetry and painting were seen as a way to escape the war, or at least to give it a gloss that obscured its terrible cruelty. In this sense, the favoured poets had much in common with the music hall artistes: the popular culture of 1914–18 suggests that the public wanted to be amused, diverted, uplifted, and persuaded that the war was noble and right.[28]

Vera Brittain felt that the war erected a 'barrier of indescribable experience between men and the women they loved'. No matter how real some of the newsreels and films were, they could never be real enough. The longer the war lasted, the wider this gulf became and the more alienated the soldiers felt. 'I was thoroughly "fed up" with the attitude of most of the people I met on leave,' wrote the poet Herbert Read in 1917. 'They simply have no conception whatever of what war really is like and don't seem concerned about it at all.' When asked whether he had told his wife about conditions at the front while on leave, an English soldier replied, 'I didn't get a chance, she was so busy tellin' me all the news about Mrs Bally's cat killin' Mrs Smith's bird, Mrs Cramp's sister's new dress, and how Jimmy Murphy's dog chewed up Annie Allen's doll.' The stubbornly mundane nature of home-front life fuelled the bitterness of war poets like Sassoon and shame-ridden civilians like Edith Sitwell. Her poem 'The Dancers' is a strident attack upon wartime merriment:

> The music has grown numb with death –
> But we will suck their dying breath,
> The whispered name they breathed to chance,
> To swell our music, make it loud
> That we may dance, – may dance.
>
> We are the dull blind carrion-fly
> That dance and batten. Though God die
> Mad from the horror of the light –
> The light is mad, too, flecked with blood, –
> We dance, we dance, each night.

The condemnation heaped upon the home front, though understandable, is not entirely fair. Georgina Lee demonstrated that it was not all that difficult to be well informed about the nature of the war and yet still find cause for happiness. The assumption that a gulf in understanding existed is just another element of the manufactured guilt inspired by Brittain, Owen and Sassoon and subsequently set in stone by generations bent on melancholy. There was insensitivity and hypocrisy in this war, but the army did not have a monopoly on virtue. The Great War revealed that, in the interests of morale, leisure pursuits should carry on as closely as possible to normal. It took a while for the government to realise this fact, but in the end it did. Enjoyment during wartime is not evil. A collapse of morale on

the home front would have ended the war much more quickly
than a German breakthrough on the Western Front. Dancing
and drinking, watching Chaplin or going to the seaside made
it possible to cope. Laughing in boisterous company was much
better than grieving in silent solitude.[29]

Chapter 12

And Then, Suddenly, It Was Over

'All the lights are out,' Sarah Macnaughtan remarked on returning home from her work in a military hospital in Belgium. 'So many of the guests have left, and the fires are going out, and I am tired.' For her, the illusions of noble war died quickly because she was exposed so directly to its carnage. Worn down by the war's refusal to conform to her ideals, she died of exhaustion on 24 July 1916. It was probably best that she passed away before the war turned *really* dreadful. Her experience was not unique. Others took longer to fall victim to the germ of disenchantment, but fall they did. One by one the British forgot the heroic war and sank into a swamp of despond. C. W. Mason recalls a telling moment while waiting to board a troop ship in Southampton. 'A huge hospital ship came in filled with wounded. From the upper deck a voice shouted, "Are you downhearted?" to which we replied to a man, "No!" Back came the voice, "Then you bloody soon will be!"'

On 31 December 1917, New Year celebrations were muted. The past year had been hell. Passchendaele had repeated the Somme's ghastliness. Action at Cambrai in late November seemed to promise a bright future when British tanks eviscerated the German line. Church bells celebrated the stunning advance, but then came a massive German counterattack. The British, weakened by months of slaughter, were pushed back, past their original line. While gravediggers buried the legions of dead, politicians and generals indulged in an ugly orgy of blame. Elsewhere, the news was equally bleak. In late October, the Italians were routed at Caporetto. An armistice on 17 December between the Central Powers and Russia cleared the way for the transfer of German troops to the West. Why, ordinary people wondered, was an enemy supposedly tottering on the brink of defeat capable of such success? The year had provided only two causes for optimism. The first, the declaration of war by the United States, lost much of its lustre when the Americans proved slow to arrive. The second, Allenby's capture of Jerusalem, merely indicated how desperate the British were for something, anything, to lift their spirits. As everyone realised, the real war was on the Western Front. From that vantage point, only a fool would have predicted victory in 1918.

At home, the war intruded in ways never imagined. A more dynamic government imposed greater limitations on individual freedom, be they in the ability to travel, the access to basic commodities, or the choice of whether to serve. Gotha bombers – a horror infinitely more ghastly than the Zeppelins – attacked in earnest. The rail system finally reached breaking point: services were cancelled at short notice and trains were stuffed with tired, harassed, sweaty passengers. There were shortages of coal, paper, food and soap. Hygiene suffered; bodies stank. Queues outside shops grew, as did resentment towards profiteers who capitalised on the public's misery. On the streets, the ubiquitous presence of severely disabled ex-soldiers provided a constant reminder of war's cruelty. Georgina Lee found that the weight of tragedy threatened to smother her otherwise buoyant spirit. 'The consciousness of it all is never absent,' she wrote. 'It makes us extraordinarily lacking in vivacity or spontaneity and curiously silent. I am conscious now of not wanting to go out to see friends, or to have them here. I have suddenly nothing to say to them, and I find myself uncomfortable, realising that I am being dull and uncompanionable.' To the miseries of war were added the scourge of disease. An influenza epidemic, which began in the latter half of the year, was surprisingly democratic: it attacked young and old, rich and poor. It eventually claimed more than 200,000 lives.[2]

Against this backdrop, 1918 seemed to promise something worse. Yet neither disease nor countless casualties, shortages, taxes and harsh regulations broke the British spirit. The frenzied belligerence of 1914 was long gone, replaced by a grim determination to carry on. The stunning success of the German offensive in March made the British more resolute, not less. *The Times* advised its readers: 'Be cheerful, face facts and work; attend volunteer drills regularly; cultivate your allotment; don't exceed your rations; don't repeat foolish gossip; don't listen to idle rumours and don't think you know better than Haig.' The flurry of recriminations that followed the March setback revealed that the political and military establishment was far less united than its citizenry. While Haig grumbled about being starved of troops, Lloyd George went public with claims that the British Army was numerically stronger in January 1918 than it had been in January 1917. Whilst technically correct, this was in fact an attempt to hoodwink Parliament and the public, a fact pointed out by General Frederick Maurice in an accusatory letter to the press on 7 May. That letter provoked an acrimonious Commons debate – one of the few times during the war when Parliament provided real drama. Lloyd George tore Asquith to shreds, eventually emerging with his power enhanced. In truth, however, the Maurice debate was a sideshow, a bit of sound and fury that is important now because it was not important then. As with the March offensive itself, it did not dent the British public's determination to carry on with the war; it reveals instead how stable was the status quo.[3]

Not long after the political storm quieted, the German offensive did likewise. Fortunes shifted decisively towards the Allies. Spirits lifted, but no one expected an early victory. The British felt confident that they had absorbed the worst the Germans could deliver, but still foresaw a long and costly effort to dislodge them from France and Belgium. The heavily fortified Hindenburg Line seemed impregnable. The Germans, it was assumed, would rest out the winter, replenish their forces with a new call-up in 1919 and resume the fight. The British Cabinet made war plans for 1919 and 1920. Since factories had been depleted of manpower in the aftermath of the March offensive, supplies of munitions were dangerously low. A new shell crisis seemed imminent.

The Cabinet, however, had reckoned without Haig. His optimism, which had once seemed ridiculous, was suddenly appropriate. Victory piled upon victory. The French army, inspired by the turn of events, discovered an untapped reserve of strength and resumed the attack. And then the Americans began to pull their weight. September and October brought fresh cause for optimism: an Austrian peace effort, the signing of an armistice by Bulgaria and Turkey, a German peace note.

Quite suddenly, it was all over. On 8 November, the *Manchester Guardian* reported that Germany was seeking an armistice. At the front, happiness was mixed with incredulity. A soldier near Valenciennes shouted: 'It must mean the end of the war . . . Surely it is the end at last! Who would ever have believed it?' Amazement echoed down the line. Three days later, it was indeed over. On the morning of Monday, 11 November, engineers were hastened to the Tower of Parliament to reactivate the striking mechanism of Big Ben. The bells of the big clock would ring at 11 a.m., the first time since August 1914. At 10.55 Lloyd George made a short statement outside Downing Street: 'At eleven o'clock this war will be over. We have won a great victory and we are entitled to a bit of shouting.'⁴

Shout they did. When Big Ben tolled, echoed by church bells round the country, a massive release of emotion took place. Victory had 'rushed on us with the speed and impact of a comet', the socialite and author Osbert Sitwell remarked.

> that night it was impossible to drive through Trafalgar Square: because the crowd danced under lights turned up for the first time for four years – danced so thickly that the heads, the faces, were like a field of golden corn moving in a dark wind. The last occasion I had seen the London crowd was when it had cheered for its own death outside Buckingham Palace on the evening of 4th of August 1914; most of the men who had composed it were now dead. Their heirs were dancing because life had been given back to them. They revolved and whirled their partners round with rapture, almost with abandon, yet, too, with solemnity, with a kind of religious fervour, as if it were a duty.

A reporter for the *Manchester Guardian* jotted down random impressions:

> Singing. No fares on buses, crowded with sailors, WAACs, soldiers, munitionettes on bonnet and overdeck. Vans and waggons commandeered by girls marching in from East End. Joy-riding everywhere. Smart motors with officers – even a major – and service girls with flags all over and horns honking. Worthington ale waggons rushed. Man puts up his hands and opens cases. Crowds gather round and drink the bottles.

Revellers at Buckingham Palace chanted 'We want the King!, We want the King!', just as they had on 4 August 1914. He reluctantly appeared, waved to the vast crowd then quickly disappeared inside. A short time later, he ended his wartime abstinence by breaking open a bottle of brandy originally laid down by the Prince Regent to celebrate victory at Waterloo. It tasted 'very musty'.[5]

At the front, the end seemed distinctly bizarre. On the morning of the 11th, an official announcement went round the units informing them that the war would end at 11 a.m. precisely. One soldier recalled:

> At about 10.45 we were in action against the Germans, east of Mons, and one of our troops had just charged some German machine-guns. A private soldier came galloping towards us; he was much excited, had lost his cap, and could not stop his horse. As he passed us he shouted: 'The war's over! The war's over!' We thought, undoubtedly, the poor fellow was suffering from shell-shock.

Artillery fired right up to eleven o'clock. Men died in the last seconds. Then all went quiet. Action ceased as if a referee had blown a whistle. 'The match was over and it had been a damned bad game,' recalled one officer. Some soldiers joined in a frenzy of celebration, some could only manage a tired smile, others still were overcome with sadness. For most, celebration marked survival, not victory. One soldier, overcome by the weight of conflicting emotions, wrote of his 'worst ever depression'. 'We were very old, very tired, and now very wise,' thought Guy Chapman. 'What a victory it might have been – the real, the Winged Victory, chivalric, whole and unstained!' a rather jaded C. E. Montague remarked. 'The bride that our feckless wooing had sought and not won in the generous youth of the war had come to us now: an old woman, or dead, she no longer refused us.'[6]

In cities and towns, massive street parties erupted. They lasted for hours, in places for days. The end of the war was excuse enough to kiss (a) any soldier and (b) any young woman. 'The most noticeable thing about the crowds,' wrote Lee, 'is the expression on their faces – the transfiguration – smiles and gladness, shining through the sorrow and unutterable regrets which are the lot of the bereaved.' By the end of the day, everyone was kissing everyone else in decidedly un-British fashion. 'Custom and convention melted away as if a new world had indeed dawned,' recalled Caroline Playne. High spirits inevitably gave way to low behaviour: excessive drinking, vandalism, violence, thievery, recrimination. Oswald Mosley recalled seeing his future wife Cimmie Curzon draped in a Union Jack singing patriotic songs at the Ritz. Later, she 'tore around Trafalgar Square with the great crowd setting fire to old cars and trucks'. A throng of Sandhurst cadets emerged from the gates of the college and jumped on an old horse-drawn coach waiting for customers. 'The ancient vehicle collapsed under the weight and the old cabbie was left, clay pipe in hand, surveying the wreck whilst cadets rushed along the Great Southwest Road.' That was perhaps a metaphor for how little had changed in Britain: it remained perfectly acceptable for toffs to treat plebs with contempt.[7]

Those unable to forget the war's immense tragedy found it impossible to share in celebration. Florence Younghusband, wife of General George Younghusband, was on a bus edging through the celebrating crowds. In the seat in front of her sat two soldiers, one with a badly scarred face. He sat silent while his mate cried uncontrollably. The bus conductress collapsed on to the seat next to Florence, leant her head on her shoulder and also cried. 'I lost my man two months ago,' she spluttered. 'I *can't* be happy today.' The young Victoria Smith remembered her school being let out at the sound of the bells. As the children rushed into the streets, she saw 'amidst the empty desks . . . the geography mistress, head in hands, quietly but copiously crying. She had been widowed by the war.' Vera Brittain, who had lost her brother, her fiancé and two close friends, felt that peace had 'come too late for me ... All those with whom I had really been intimate were gone: not one remained to share with me the heights and depths of my memories.' 'I keep seeing all these horrors, bathing in them again and again,' the writer Katherine Mansfield reflected, 'and then my mind fills with the wretched little picture I have of my brother's grave. What is the meaning of it all?'[8]

'The war is over,' the *Manchester Guardian* remarked, 'and in a million households fathers and mothers, wives and sisters, will breathe freely, relieved at length of all dread of that curt message which has shattered the hope and joy of so many. The war is over. The drama is played out.' That wasn't quite true. The war had been officially over for an hour when a War Office messenger delivered a telegram informing Wilfred Owen's mother of her son's death a week earlier, during action on the Sambre.

> 'Strange friend,' I said, 'here is no cause to mourn.'
> 'None,' said the other, 'save the undone years,
> The hopelessness. Whatever hope is yours,
> Was my life also; I went hunting wild
> After the wildest beauty in the world,
> Which lies not calm in eyes, or braided hair,
> But mocks the steady running of the hour,
> And if it grieves, grieves richlier than here.
> For by my glee might many men have laughed,
> And of my weeping something had been left,
> Which must die now. I mean the truth untold,
> The pity of war, the pity war distilled.'[9]

Part Three

The Reckoning

Chapter 13

Back to Blighty

The war was a separator of sexes. Yet the feelings of A. B. Baker, WAAC, on coming home were remarkably similar to those of the male soldiers she once served. 'The day of Armistice came, and the War stopped,' she recalled.

> I remember that I drank four glasses of champagne, and afterwards had a very bad headache. Later I felt ashamed. Demobbed, I went home. There they wanted to treat me as a sort of heroine. Their talk hurt me . . .
> They praised me for all the wrong things. When I tried to tell them what the War had taught me, they were hurt in their turn.[1]

When the bell of Big Ben struck, there were 3,750,000 British soldiers, sailors and airmen in uniform around the world. In addressing the problem of what to do with them, the government had two basic concerns: the first was to avoid mass unemployment when a flood of veterans with no secure promise of a job was released; the second was to guard against runaway inflation caused by industry's inability to convert to peacetime production quickly enough to meet pent-up demand. The solution seemed to lie in controlled demobilisation based upon the needs of industry. In other words, economic stability would take precedence over social justice.

Under demobilisation plans prepared well before the armistice, military personnel were to be divided into five groups. The first and smallest was the 'demobilisers', those men (mainly civil servants) who would administer the process. 'Pivotal men', the second group, consisted of those considered job creators, men whose return to civilian life would expand opportunities for those who followed. They might, for instance, be highly skilled engineers essential to the transition of an industry to peacetime production. An expert within each industry was appointed to dole out the strictly limited number of pivotal places.

'Slip men', the third group, were those guaranteed jobs at home. The 'slip' referred to the section torn off from the civil employment form that the individual presented to his commanding officer, confirming that he had been promised employment. These men were to be released in a controlled fashion after the beginning of general mobilisation, according to a scale of priority that assessed their importance to reconstruction. Thus a man guaranteed a job in a coal mine would take priority over one promised work as an insurance clerk. The remaining 'non-slip men', those without guaranteed employment, were divided into two groups: those with skills likely to land them quick employment in industries vital to recovery, and those with no real prospects.[2]

According to the plans, the lucky possessor of a slip would be sent to a camp behind the lines and then to one of 26 dispersal stations, where he would be processed within 24 hours and released on a 28-day furlough, after which he would be formally demobilised. At the dispersal station he would be given a railway warrant, ration book, pay for the period of the furlough and either an allowance of 52s. 6d for the purchase of civilian clothes, or a demob suit. The government stockpiled huge quantities of grade-three standard cloth for suits. He would be allowed to keep his uniform and his helmet. Greatcoats could be retained or sold back to the government for £1 at any railway station. He would also receive unemployment insurance, worth 29s. per week for himself, 6s. for his first child and 3s. for each additional child, up to a limit of twenty weeks.[3]

Within each category, further priority would be calculated on the basis of marital status, length of service and time spent in the front line. Men already at home were to be treated the same as those stationed abroad, thus ruling out the possibility of unfair advantage being given to those already on leave. Fairness, however, stopped there. The system was the child of cold bureaucracy; it was logical but remarkably unjust. Those with short service records had automatic advantage, since they were more likely to have retained close ties with employers. Thus, a single man conscripted in 1917 who never saw active service but had been promised a job could be given priority over a volunteer of 1914 with wound stripes, a wife and children but no promise of employment. Somewhat accidentally, the government had created a system of 'last in, first out'.

Ministers, preoccupied with an election campaign and peace negotiations, failed to anticipate the fallout from a system so iniquitous. *The Herald* commented sarcastically:

> We leave the matter of finding him employment to the owners and we present him with cash and promises, which work out to an average of about 9s. a week for fifty-two weeks, provided he is unemployed for twenty of them. It is superb, immense. None but an imperial people, victorious against its enemies, but overcome with emotion and thankfulness before its returning heroes, could have done it.

Because of the rather ambiguous end to the war (an armistice, not a surrender), release of demobilisers and pivotal men did not begin until 9 December. Industrialists, keen to begin the transformation to peacetime production, but prevented from doing so by the labour shortage, grew increasingly impatient. By 7 December, *The Herald* had given up on irony:

> Send the boys home. Why in the world the delay? The war is not officially 'over', but everyone knows that in fact it is over. Munition-making has stopped; motorists can joy ride; the King has had a drink; society has had its victory ball and is settling down ... Danger of too rapid demobilisation? Bunkum! There are thousands of men for whom jobs are waiting, but the Army won't let them go. And – even if a man hasn't a job – why not let him go home at once?

Wounded by the criticism, the government began tinkering. On 13 December, it unveiled a 'contract system' whereby a serviceman on leave could be demobilised if he was able to secure an offer from a pre-war employer. Six days later, Lloyd George, under increasing pressure, appointed Eric Geddes to coordinate the fourteen separate departments concerned with demobilisation. On the same day, the government began paying out gratuities according to a scale agreed by the Commons on 20 November. At the top of the list, Field Marshal Haig and Admiral Beatty were granted £100,000. Lower down the scale, lieutenants were allotted as much as £226; corporals £28 and privates £20. The gross inequality of the rewards seems striking today, but at the time most veterans were impressed by the government's generosity.[4]

The gratuities did not, however, stifle discontent. On 3 January, 10,000 soldiers protested at Folkestone by refusing to board ships back to France. Another 2,000 demonstrated at Dover and 8,000 at Brighton. For the government, the most embarrassing incident of rebellion was a relatively small one that took place in Whitehall. Arriving in lorries, soldiers picketed government offices with signs like 'WE WON THE WAR, GIVE US OUR TICKETS'; 'GET A MOVE ON, GEDDES'; 'NO MORE RED TAPE'; 'WE WANT CIVVIE SUITS' and 'PROMISES ARE NOT PIE CRUST'. Behaviour of this sort was all the more shocking given that nothing remotely similar had occurred during the worst periods of trench warfare. The combativeness of the protesters arose in part from fears that they would be dispatched to Russia to fight the Bolsheviks (20,000 had already been sent), but more specifically from a desire to extend leaves so as to take advantage of the contract system. Realising its mistake, the government on 7 January suspended the contract system and wisely decided not to take action against the rebels. Lloyd George meanwhile reminded the country that the war was not yet officially over and that 300,000 men had already been demobilised, arguments that contradicted one another.[5]

The election took place on 14 December, but the new government was not in place until the end of the month. Churchill took over the War Ministry with a remit to sort out demobilisation. After consulting Haig and Geddes, he devised Army Orders 54 and 55, which, despite claims to the contrary, signalled a complete abandonment of the old system in favour of one based on age, length of service and combat experience – essentially 'first in, first out'. Under the new regime, any soldier who had enlisted before 31 December 1915, or was over 37, or had three wound stripes, would be released immediately. Some 1,300,000 men satisfied none of these criteria. From that number, 400,000 were to be released as pivotal men or on hardship grounds, leaving 900,000 to guard the Rhine bridgeheads or to serve as a home defence force. They were pacified with a doubling of pay, bringing them closer to comparable civilian wages.

The new system was a vast improvement, but it depended

upon quick implementation. The need for haste was underlined when soldiers returning to Calais from leave refused to rejoin their units – the largest protest to date. Haig, certain that the rioters were 'led astray by Bolshevist agitators', ordered that 'the disturbances are to be quelled at all costs, and as soon as possible. Discipline must be maintained, and rioters if they cannot be arrested must be shot.' That frightened Churchill, who feared that intemperate action might plunge the army into full-scale revolution. Fortunately, order was restored without soldiers being shot. Haig, a man insensitive to political subtleties, nevertheless insisted that the ringleaders should be executed in order to maintain discipline. Churchill demanded leniency, much to Haig's chagrin. He insisted upon his sovereign right to shoot the mutineers, but grudgingly obeyed Churchill's wishes.[6]

Quick implementation of the Churchill scheme prevented further serious revolt. Men were released, according to Churchill, 'at the enormous rate of 13,000 or 14,000 daily'. Within ten weeks, 56 per cent of eligible officers and 78 per cent of eligible men had been demobilised. The process was applied equally smoothly to sailors and airmen. After one year, only 125,000 eligible men still awaited release. By that stage, the army had shrunk to 381,056 men, mainly volunteers. (The requirement of 900,000 was abandoned after the Versailles settlement was signed in June 1919.) This was, by any reckoning, an enormously impressive achievement. The government's initial concern that demobilisation had to be slow and controlled in order to avoid unemployment and economic disruption seems to have been unwarranted. In 1919 and 1920, the average annual rate of unemployment was 2.7 per cent, virtually the same as in 1913. By 1921, however, the jobless total rose above 1 million, and did not dip below that level again until 1940. Yet even if this rise was due in part to hasty demobilisation, there was no other alternative. Given the disturbances which had taken place, it would have been impossible to retain men in the services for any longer in order to manipulate the labour supply more effectively.[7]

Of those who returned from war, roughly one quarter suffered some form of disability. The government began to study this problem in May 1916, when the War Injury Pensions Committee was formed. The full disablement pension was eventually set at 25s. per week, with an extra 2s. 6d for each child. This was pitifully small, about what an unskilled labourer earned. The pension was then reduced according to scales of disability: for instance, a man missing an entire arm would get 16s.; if the loss was above the elbow: 14s.; below the elbow: 11s. 6d. The left arm was valued less generously, unless the veteran was left-handed. Rates were also determined according to the rank of the person concerned. That distinction had no logic, however, since a private was more likely than a lieutenant to be a manual labourer, and therefore less able to cope with a disability.[8]

Ministers believed that, as in the past, the disabled should rely in part upon charity. Their scheme inspired nearly universal scorn. Haig, to his credit, delayed acceptance of a peerage in order to embarrass the government into reconsideration. He insisted that 'Officers and their wives . . . will not, and ought not to be asked to, accept Charity.' (That suggests that he considered it acceptable for ordinary soldiers to do so.) The pressure forced the government to pass a somewhat more generous scheme in 1921 which increased the full pension rate to £2 per week and 26s. 8d for a widow. In March of that year, 1,187,450 pensions were granted in nine categories of disability. Nearly 40,000 received the full amount, and 192,678 widows' pensions (covering, in addition, 344,606 children) were granted. Another 10,605 pensions were awarded to orphans. Despite the fact that the amount paid was still miserly, officials worried that amputees would attract 'an undesirable class of women . . .

seek[ing] to entrap the soldiers for the sake of their monetary value'.[9]

Article 5 of the Pensions Act stipulated that claims had to be made within seven years of the date of discharge, thus excluding those who developed complications from wounds (both physical and psychological) long after the war. The Act also specified that rates could be revised downwards if the cost of living fell. Government parsimony roused the ire of John Galsworthy, who edited a Ministry of Pensions journal for disabled ex-servicemen:

> The State, like the humblest citizen, cannot have it both ways. If it talks – as talk it does, with the mouth of every public man who speaks on this subject – of heroes, and of doing all it can for them, then it must not cheese-pare as well, for that makes it ridiculous. Britain has climbed the high moral horse – as usual – over the great question of our disabled; she cannot stay in that saddle if she rides like a slippery lawyer.

In fact rates were never reduced, but the cost-of-living clause continued to annoy. In 1929, a final award was made to all veterans with disability no greater than 20 per cent. This left 229,034 still in receipt of pensions. Again iniquities arose, since there was nothing to protect the unfortunate ex-serviceman removed from the pension rolls in 1929 who subsequently found that his disability worsened.[10]

Pension boards put budgetary prudence over humanity. A particularly heartless case of officiousness arose when a woman was denied a widow's pension because she had married her husband after he had received his eventually fatal war injuries. Apparently she had knowingly bought damaged goods. Cases involving respiratory diseases or mental disability were open to wide, and often unfair, interpretation. Instances abound of men who had been perfectly healthy before 1914 contracting respiratory diseases that Pensions Boards refused to accept were war-related. According to Ministry records, approximately 80,000 men died of war-related illnesses or injury after the war. A more sensitive interpretation of 'war-related' would obviously have yielded a much higher figure. Cases of what would now be called post-traumatic stress disorder (some leading to suicide) were denied compensation on the grounds that the malady had not been apparent during the war. Under pressure from the British Legion, the government in 1938 investigated whether war service caused a generally higher propensity towards illness, premature ageing and early death. Though there is considerable evidence that it did, the official actuary advised that conclusive judgements were impossible, which allowed the government to escape responsibility. Coroners thought differently – fifty years after the war, they were still listing war service (in particular the effects of gas) as a contributory cause of death.[11]

The disabled received little in the way of rehabilitation or retraining. The British Legion demanded a law obliging employers to hire a small percentage of disabled veterans, but the government preferred a purely voluntary arrangement. The King's National Roll scheme encouraged employers to take on disabled ex-servicemen to a minimum of 5 per cent of their workforce. By 1926, 28,000 firms were participating, with 365,000 disabled men employed. The figure seems large because 'disabled' could mean something as minor as a missing finger. The seriously affected benefited little from the scheme. In any case, when unemployment became widespread, the disabled were often the first to lose their jobs and had the hardest time finding new ones. 'They have the greatest claim on the country, and yet many able to do a day's work are not able to get it,' one sympathetic critic wrote. 'Who can blame them if, instead of being honoured and contented, they become broken wanderers with curses on their lips?'[12]

Hardly any attention was paid to the problem of preparing the able-bodied for peacetime. George Coppard, who lied about his age in order to enlist in 1914, expressed a common bitterness at his treatment after demobilisation:

> Although an expert machine gunner, I was a numbskull so far as any trade or craft was concerned. Lloyd George and company had been full of big talk about making the country fit for heroes to live in, but it was just so much hot air. No practical steps were taken to rehabilitate the broad mass of demobbed men, and I joined the queues for jobs as messengers, window cleaners and scullions. It was a complete let-down for thousands like me . . . there were no jobs for the 'heroes' who haunted the billiard halls as I did.

The short post-war boom actually worked to the detriment of ex-servicemen, since it convinced the government that re-employment of veterans could be safely left to market forces. When boom turned to bust, however, they were often the first to lose their jobs, since they had the least seniority and the fewest skills. Between 1921 and 1939, the number of unemployed ex-servicemen averaged around 500,000, with peaks over 700,000. Veterans grew annoyed by the way their war service often rendered them less employable than those who had not served. Positions on apprenticeships or courses went to younger men, old jobs had disappeared or were already filled, and business opportunities had evaporated. The problem was toughest for those who had joined up at 18 (or younger), before starting an apprenticeship. In 1922, there were 300,000 ex-servicemen under the age of 30 without formal skills. Nor had they much prospect, once the recession began, of receiving the training they desperately needed. The government concluded that it did not have the resources to help. Some concession was granted in

1922 when it was stipulated that 75 per cent of men employed on public works projects had to be ex-servicemen, but since these projects were rare, the effect was minimal.[13]

The 'temporary gentlemen' also suffered. Coppard recalled that 'It was a common sight in London to see ex-officers with barrel-organs, endeavouring to earn a living as beggars.' The ones who suffered the most were perhaps those who had been promoted from the ranks. They had to go back to being working-class but, officially, were still treated like officers. The government assumed that because officers traditionally had private means, it was not necessary to make provision for them, even if they might have come from humble stock. They were not entitled to free unemployment compensation, nor were they allowed to use the labour exchange. 'When it is borne in mind that in a very large number of cases this class of officer did not ask for a commission but was nominated by his Commanding Officer', one critic complained, 'the fact that he should be worse treated on discharge than if he had remained in the ranks seems almost impossible to defend.'[14]

Demobilisation also meant releasing women from war service. Stated simply, thousands of ex-soldiers quickly found jobs because women were pushed out of them. By the end of 1918, an estimated 750,000 female war workers had been made redundant. Within a few months of the armistice, only 200,000 remained in engineering, just 30,000 more than pre-war figures. Within the Ministry of Reconstruction, there was little sympathy for women; the priority was to return quickly to the pre-war status quo. Women who had been told that it was their patriotic duty to join the workforce were now told that it was unpatriotic to hang on to a job that rightfully belonged to an ex-serviceman. The ASE, in a spirit of vindictiveness, found that it could use the legal mechanisms of the Restoration of Pre-War Practices Act to force the pace of female redundancies. Unions representing women benignly accepted a moral obligation to give way to men.[15]

Female workers on government contracts received two weeks' pay in lieu of notice and a free rail pass home. They were also covered by an 'out of work donation' of 20s. per week for the first 13 weeks, 15s. for the next 13 weeks, and then nothing. Those in receipt of benefit were subject to virulent scorn; newspapers derided the 'dodgers' and 'loafers' now 'taking a holiday at the public expense'. The *Daily Telegraph* joined the chorus of scorn: 'a little investigation (at the labour exchange) showed that since they have "been in munitions" women have acquired to a remarkable extent a taste for factory life. Many of them of course, might return at once to the domestic service from which they came, but, for the moment at any rate, they literally scoff at the idea.' The government eventually decided to deny benefit to any woman who refused to take a job offered her, which often had the effect of forcing her into domestic service. (A man was only denied benefit if he refused an offer in his specific trade.) At one employment exchange, an official entered a room in which forty women were waiting for offers of employment and asked, 'Who is for domestic service?' When no one replied, each was handed an official notice terminating benefit.[16]

Unscrupulous employers took advantage of the system by offering women work which paid well below the benefit rate and then threatening to report them to the labour exchange if they refused the offer. Meanwhile, an informal public relations campaign sought to improve the image of domestic service. These tactics were remarkably effective. In March 1919, 494,000 women were registered unemployed. Eight months later, the figure had fallen to 29,000, the result of women being forced back into service or being removed from the unemployment register for failing to take a job.[17]

Women went from being heroes to pariahs in a matter of

months. They were cursed if they accepted unemployment benefit and and also if they refused to give up jobs rightfully belonging to men. The latter complaint was especially common in 1920, when unemployment began to rise. 'The girls were clinging to their jobs, would not let go of the pocket-money which they had spent on frocks,' complained the war correspondent Philip Gibbs. A typical attitude was expressed in the *Southampton Times*:

> While it would be a shame to turn women out of their jobs at short notice in cases where such a procedure would mean absolute hardship, and, perhaps, starvation, there is no reason to feel sympathetic towards the young person who has been earning 'pin money' while the men have been fighting, nor the girls who left women's work, to which they could return without difficulty.

A headline in the *Daily Sketch* on 28 June 1919 told of the 'Scandal of the Proposed Retention of Flappers while Ex-Soldiers Cannot Find Jobs'. Ironically, quite often females who had served their country were forced to give way to men who had carefully avoided military service. Before long, critics began to discredit the contribution women had made. A *Leeds Mercury* journalist welcomed the dismissal of female bus conductors: 'Their record of duty well done is seriously blemished by their habitual and aggressive incivility, and a callous disregard for the welfare of passengers. Their shrewish behaviour will remain one of the unpleasant memories of the war's vicissitudes.' So successful was the effort to force women out of employment that in July 1921 just 30.8 per cent of women were employed, down from 32.3 per cent ten years earlier.[18]

Married women workers were treated especially harshly. The *Edinburgh Evening News* demanded that 'this class of social scrounger' should be sacked immediately. It was commonly assumed that, since a husband must be supporting them, they were simply greedy. Yet few critics paused to consider whether a woman calling herself 'Mrs' might be widowed, and therefore in need of work. Once the out-of-work donation ceased, unemployed married women often found themselves ineligible for benefit as they had not paid the requisite stamps prior to 1914. In 1922, the government, keen to reduce welfare costs, ruled that married women were ineligible for the dole unless total family income was less than 10s. per week. When unemployment began to rise, employers came under increasing pressure to lay off the few remaining married women so as to free jobs for men. In 1921, London County Council made all married female staff (excluding doctors and teachers) redundant. They were also excluded from government-sponsored training schemes for women, the one exception being a course in 'home arts', which offered wives 'an opportunity to perfect themselves in household accomplishment which will make the home fit for the ideal family life'.[19]

Women who remained in work did so largely by returning to their pre-war employment. Labour exchanges reported that placements in domestic occupations increased by 40 per cent during the first year of peace. Those who remained in industry had to accept menial jobs at lower pay. Almost all women bus conductors and railway guards lost their jobs; those who stayed usually became booking clerks. The only areas in which women were conspicuously successful at retaining jobs were office and shop work – the one significant change in the pattern of employment. Since these had always been low-status jobs for men, the change hardly seems significant.[20]

Women workers in traditionally male industries were in essence 'temporary men', useful only for the duration of the war. When peace came, a return to normality was widely welcomed (even by women) because it implied that society had not been fundamentally altered by the need to employ women in men's jobs. Some women did protest – 6,000 marched on Parliament in 1919 – but more typical were the 1,500 women who left Woolwich Arsenal every week during the demobilisation without a murmur of complaint. Women were, above all, obedient. During the war they had been told to go to work, and they did. Now they were told to go home. And they did.[21]

Even if the government had been more sympathetic to women workers, it could not ignore the demands of returning soldiers. Fears of angry mobs of ex-servicemen had preoccupied Whitehall from the moment the Military Service Act was passed. Conscription implied a contract: men taken against their will expected something in return. The relationship between the soldier and the state had been altered, but so too had the nature of the soldier himself. Concerns expressed by Haig were quite widespread:

under the Military Service Act a leaven of men whose desire to serve their country is negligible has permeated the ranks. The influence of these men and their antecedents generally are not such as to foster any spirit but that of unrest and discontent, they come forward under compulsion and they will depart from the Army with relief. Men of this stamp are not satisfied with remaining quiet, they come from a class which like to air real or fancied grievances.

Memories of pre-war strikes and fears of Bolshevism combined to produce rampant alarm. The image of loyal, patriotic Tommy Atkins quickly faded, replaced by that of a greedy, ruthless, violent worker-revolutionary bent on claiming exorbitant reward for his service. Fears were exacerbated by the uncomfortable knowledge that for the past four years these workers had been agents of violence. A worried Home Office agent noted that 'in the event of rioting, for the first time in history, the rioters will be better trained than the troops'.[22]

The government was especially worried by the proliferation of ex-servicemen's associations that agitated on issues like pensions and employment. The National Association of Discharged Soldiers and Sailors was established in September 1916, followed in 1917 by the Comrades of the Great War and the National Federation of Discharged and Demobilised Soldiers and Sailors. The Association had Liberal sympathies, while the Federation had links with the Labour Party. Both were keen to work within the political system and were in no sense revolutionary. The conservative Comrades, formed by Lord Derby, was intentionally designed to provide a counterweight to these groups. It attracted right-wing thugs malevolently inclined towards labourist politics.[23]

Despite the tame nature of the Association and the Federation, the government suspected that wolves lurked in sheep's clothing. Peaceful agitation was easily confused with revolutionary activity, so much so that Basil Thomson, head of Special Branch, was ordered to infiltrate the groups. Beginning in spring 1918, agents filed weekly reports on their activities. Try as he might, Thomson failed to discover any remotely threatening behaviour. A report submitted in October depended on desperate conjecture: 'there is a determined attempt among extremists to capture the Discharged Soldiers' Federation, and the demand for better allowances should be carefully watched for if they succeed in getting the soldiers and their wives to back them, they will be a very numerous and dangerous body'. Since Special Branch infiltrators had to justify their existence, they needed to find a threat of revolution. Yet the predominant characteristic of ex-servicemen's groups was the willingness to work within the political system. This tendency was reiterated when veterans voted at the 1918 election.[24]

A potentially more serious threat arose in February 1919. The Soldiers', Sailors' and Airmen's Union (SSAU) aimed specifically to stir up discontent among servicemen awaiting demobilisation and actively opposed intervention in Russia. In March the SSAU attracted a prominent recruit in the form of Lieutenant Commander J. M. Kenworthy, RN. After infiltrating a meeting, the Special Branch at first concluded that the threat was minimal:

> Plans for a coup d'etat of a very childish description were discussed, and Kenworthy is asserted to have declared that the navy was ripe for mutiny. Other speakers talked of arms and bombs being secretly stored and of soldiers who were ready to join them in establishing a republic. There is no cause for alarm in this, for such talk is the stock in trade of these extremists when they get together.

According to the terms of the Derby Scheme, men who enlisted could be retained by the services no more than six months after the termination of hostilities. The SSAU, deciding that the government had no legal jurisdiction over these men after 11 May 1919, advised them to leave of their own accord. At the same time, sailors were urged to take control of ports and join in a general strike. Since this was tantamount to inciting mutiny, Special Branch now took the threat seriously and on 8 May raided SSAU headquarters. In truth, however, mutiny was avoided because of working-class complacency, not alert policing. The British soldier was simply not the raw material of which revolutions are made.[25]

The fortunes of two avowedly radical ex-servicemen's associations – the National Union of Ex-Servicemen (NUX) and the International Union of Ex-Servicemen (IUX) – provide further proof of this fact. Both campaigned for a profound transformation of society, with the IUX slightly more extremist than the NUX. Like the SSAU, they provoked considerable alarm within government but eventually demonstrated, by their ignominious failure, the predominantly moderate nature of ex-servicemen. At its height the IUX attracted only 7,000 members. The NUX, more mainstream, was slightly larger.

The demise of the IUX and the NUX coincided with the rise of the British Legion, an amalgamation of the Comrades, Federation, Association and the more recently formed Officers' Association. Haig, by insisting that one united ex-servicemen's association would have greater impact upon government policy, was instrumental in bringing the groups together. He was also, of course, interested in using his influence to steer ex-servicemen away from left-wing politics. Immediately after the armistice, he warned that his men 'are still soldiers though without arms, and no doubt will go in for fresh groupings for new objectives, hitherto unthought of by the present race of politicians! Above all, they will take vigorous action to right any real or supposed wrong! All this seems to me to make for trouble unless our Government is alert and tactful.' Haig hoped that the British Legion, by reproducing the camaraderie of the trenches, could provide a calming influence during a time of political uncertainty. As he explained in 1922:

> Subversive tendencies are still at work, short cuts to anarchy are still the fool's talk of unstable intellectuals. There is all the greater need for men of all ranks who are determined . . . to stand stoutly together. A rallying ground for such men is offered by the Legion. It appeals to all who have worn the King's uniform, and who, therefore, realise the nobility of service, to enrol themselves to win the peace, even as they won the war.

Though Haig claimed to have in mind an entirely democratic organisation, without privilege of rank, he confessed privately that he was against a separate officers' group because it would 'withdraw the real leaders from the ex-servicemen'. In other words, the social order that had worked well in the trenches would be perpetuated. The potentially disruptive tendencies of ex-servicemen would be further harnessed by directing their attention outward: the Legion would 'foster the spirit of self-sacrifice which inspired servicemen to subordinate their individual welfare to the interests of the Commonwealth'. This meant steering clear of domestic politics: 'I think our politics should be Imperial and in no sense partisan.'[26]

Haig was successful in creating one ex-servicemen's association, but less successful in making it popular. The Legion's membership never exceeded 500,000, rather small when one considers the total number of veterans. (Over 3,000,000 men joined a similar organisation in France.) This lack of appeal is difficult to explain, but may have been due to the characteristics Haig deemed essential: namely the abhorrence of politics and the tendency of ex-officers to dominate. The Legion eventually became, as Haig intended, a bastion of traditional values. As for its record in campaigning for ex-servicemen's interests, it failed to have significant impact. Its campaign against the seven-year rule governing disability claims was not conspicuously successful, nor did it do much to draw attention towards the problems of unemployed ex-servicemen. This was precisely because it was Legion policy to remain aloof from politics. Its most conspicuous success was the poppy appeals, which coincided with Remembrance Day and did raise significant sums. Yet this is ironic given Haig's insistence that veterans should not have to rely on charity. Honorary presidents of the Legion, like Haig and Jellicoe, were establishment figures reluctant to confront Conservative-dominated governments. By divorcing itself from politics, the Legion ended up being easily manipulated by politicians.

By 1921, ex-servicemen had effectively been tamed. They were never likely to threaten the government's power. Left-wing historians, susceptible to romance, look back at the period 1918–20 and marvel at possibilities. Walter Kendall, for instance, claims that the prospects for revolution 'were probably the most serious since the time of the Chartists'. That, however, is hardly cause for a sharp intake of breath. Historians are supposed to analyse, not fantasise:

> if socialist influence had existed within any of the services, if there had been, for example, a common front between soldiers and sailors in 1918–19, if the soldiers had launched a co-ordinated movement, or established links with any of the trade union struggles pending, then the whole future of the state might well have been called into question.

If pigs had wings, they might have flown. The above seems as ludicrous as the pipe dreams of Kenworthy and the SSAU. There was very little revolutionary spirit within the services. Given their passivity during the war, their willingness to accept an iniquitous system of pensions, their tolerance of an unfair distribution of gratuities and their acquiescence in the placid British Legion, it should not be remotely surprising that they showed little interest in radical politics.[27]

The government never quite understood that the vast majority of ex-servicemen simply wanted a quiet life. They wanted to return to their homes, find a job and raise a family. The popularity of domesticity can be seen as further proof of the widespread desire to return to normality. In 1917, a wedding ring maker applied for exemption from conscription on the grounds that his firm was doing an enormous trade and the work was of national importance. He had a point, even if the tribunal did not agree. The family provided a safe harbour after years of turbulence. Political grievances were aired only when this haven seemed threatened, in particular by poverty. It is a pity that the government saw every ex-serviceman as a potential Bolshevist and thus failed to understand just how moderate were his desires and how cheap was the price of the harmony he craved.[28]

Chapter 14

The Dead, the Living and the Living Dead

The village of Upper Slaughter in Gloucestershire has an ironic distinction. It sent 24 men to the battlefields of the Great War, and all 24 returned. (During the Second World War, 36 villagers left to fight, and again, all returned alive.) Upper Slaughter is one of 52 so-called 'Thankful Villages' in England and Wales in which tragedy did not strike. (There are none in Scotland or Northern Ireland.) It therefore has no war memorial per se; it has instead a simple wooden board listing the names of the 24 who served. Given that there are over 16,000 parishes in the country, the Thankful Villages are significant because they are rare; they illustrate, in an indirect way, how universal was sacrifice in this war. Incidentally, the least fortunate village was probably Wadhurst, in East Sussex. On a single day in 1915 at the battle of Aubers, 25 men from that village were killed – nearly 80 per cent of those who had volunteered.

For a long time, the tendency of old women to outnumber old men on the streets of Britain was commonly blamed on the Great War: husbands or potential husbands, it was assumed, were killed on the battlefields of France and Flanders. The disparity still exists, yet the explanation is no longer credible since the war was too long ago. (The old women are not *that* old.) The real reason for the maldistribution of the sexes on the streets of Britain resides within gender relations among the elderly; husbands tend to wait at home while wives do the shopping. If there is indeed a surplus of widows, it is because women live longer than men.

The image of the war as a demographic disaster stubbornly persisted throughout the twentieth century. Popular myth held that the war produced a lost generation – a group notable because they were absent. The Lost Generation is defined either as all of the dead or, specifically, as those elites who would otherwise have become post-war leaders of politics, business and industry. The decline of Britain after 1918 has been blamed on the absence of these men of promise. The country was henceforth ruled by 'pygmies', as the eminent historian Charles Loch Mowat once maintained. As will be seen, there is little evidence to support a demographic disaster. Many very promising men died in the war, but to blame the dull decades of the twenties and thirties on their disappearance is to engage in futile counterfactual reasoning. The Lost Generation remains important nevertheless as a myth – a popular explanation for the course taken by history and a handy excuse for unfulfilled expectations.[1]

No one knows how many Britons died in the Great War. Estimates range from around 550,000 to over twice that number. Figures vary according to the purposes of those who cite them: there was, for instance, a tendency to underestimate the dead in official reports released immediately after the war. On the other hand, historian Denis Winter, keen to exaggerate the war's destruction, put the number at precisely 1,104,890, a figure he refused to explain. Given his exhaustive investigations, the data supplied by Jay Winter in various studies are probably the most reliable. He claims the total dead from the army, Royal Navy and Royal Flying Corps numbered 722,785. This does not, however, include 15,000 fatalities in the merchant navy and fishing fleets as a result of enemy action, nor 1,266 civilian deaths caused by bombing or bombardment, nor the victims of munitions factory explosions, nor the suicides brought on by grief and despair.[2]

Jay Winter's figure seems sufficiently large to justify assertions of a lost generation. Over 514,000 men under the age of 30 died in the war, a loss one might think would take decades to replace. In strictly demographic terms, however, there was no *net* loss. In the period 1911–14, migration to and from Britain resulted in a net population decline of over a million people. During the war, emigration virtually stopped. In fact, expatriates rushing back to defend the mother country resulted in a net gain of 100,000 people in 1914 alone. Presuming that pre-war migration trends would have continued had war not intervened, Britain would have lost a further million people. Instead, as a result of the war, 725,000 were killed, a difference on the credit side of over a quarter of a million. Those who left Britain before the war were predominantly single males between 18 and 30, the same group from which soldiers were predominantly drawn. Thus, neither the size nor the social structure nor the gender distribution of the British population was fundamentally altered. After the war, a sharp rise in the birth rate and better civilian health caused the population to increase further. In demographic terms, the Lost Generation myth has no foundation.[3]

What, then, of a lost generation of elites? Examining the numbers of officer casualties relative to other ranks reveals that the middle class suffered proportionately higher casualties than the working-class. (Though not all middle-class men became officers, the vast majority of officers were middle or upper class.)

Distribution Between Officers and Men of War Losses

	Officers			Other Ranks		
	Served	Killed	%	Served	Killed	%
Army	247,061	37,484	15.2	4,968,101	635,891	12.9
Navy	55,377	2,937	5.3	584,860	43,244	6.8
RFC/RAF	27,333	4,579	16.8	326,842	1,587	0.7
Total	329,771	45,000	13.6	5,789,803	677,785	11.7

Though senior officers and their staff encountered very little danger, junior officers in the trenches (because they led assaults) suffered the highest risks of any military personnel. The disproportionate death rate among junior officers is revealed in fatality rates for members of Oxford and Cambridge universities. Since Oxbridge students were thought to have high leadership potential, they had the greatest chance of becoming officers and therefore the greatest likelihood of dying. (Only 3 per cent of the nearly 1,000 Balliol men who enlisted, for instance, served in the ranks.) Bearing in mind that the fatality rate for all troops was 11.7 per cent, that for Oxford was 19.2 per cent and for Cambridge 18 per cent. For those who matriculated between 1910 and 1914 (those most likely to become junior officers), the figures climb to 29.3 per cent for Oxford and 26.1 per cent for Cambridge. Similarly high figures can be derived from the rolls of honour of elite public schools. The fact that approximately 19 per cent of peers under the age of 50 who served were killed provides further evidence of the risks faced by those of elevated class.[4]

None of this is intended to discount the sacrifices of the working-class. After all, fully 96 per cent of infantry casualties came from the ranks. The above figures do nevertheless suggest a statistical justification for the belief in a lost generation of elites. The middle-class male was more likely to volunteer, partly for cultural reasons, but more importantly because he would not have been troubled by the financial implications of doing so. He was also more likely to be passed fit and less likely to be engaged in a reserved occupation. Finally, given the strong possibility that he would be made an officer, he was more likely to be killed. The knowledge (or intuition) that the middle and upper classes experienced a disproportionately high mortality rate prompted the Bishop of Malvern to contend that the loss of public school boys in the war 'can only be described as the wiping out of a generation'. Many similar claims have been made, but seldom so vehemently than by J. B. Priestley: 'nobody, nothing will shift me from the belief which I shall take to the grave that the generation to which I belonged, destroyed between 1914 and 1918, was a great generation, marvellous in its promise'.[5]

Priestley's sentiment is understandable, but his assertion is impossible to prove. How does one measure the potential promise of a group of casualties against the actual contribution of a group of survivors? Those who believe in the idea of a lost generation of elites cite noteworthy individual deaths like that of Raymond Asquith, described by his contemporaries as a genius, or the promising poets killed in the war, among them Wilfred Owen. Yet Owen, it has to be said, was a by-product of the war, so in that sense the war merely destroyed what it created. In any case, tragic as the losses were, in order to thrive, Britain needed not poets and classical scholars, but scientists, technicians and engineers – ironically, the very sort held in contempt by that gloriously aesthete Edwardian generation. Granted, some promising scientists were killed, among them H. G. J. Moseley, the gifted disciple of Ernest Rutherford, but since the interwar period was a golden age for British science, it is difficult to imagine that scientific output would have been even greater if not for the war.[6]

Since previous generations of politicians arose from the crop of classical scholars produced at the good public schools, it could be argued that the war deprived Britain of promising political leaders. Yet that elite was based upon social standing, not necessarily merit. Had they lived, this lost generation of elites would have grabbed the baton passed by their fathers, the same fathers who had presided over a society in which talent was abominably wasted and the economy was in persistent decline. It requires an impressive act of faith to presume that the 1914 generation, had they survived, would have taken Britain on a fundamentally different course. In other words, the leadership potential of those lost is dubious.

Vera Brittain, egotist, elitist, mistress of self-pity and principal spokeswoman for the Lost Generation, described male survivors of the war as 'fussy, futile, avid, ineffectual'. They 'wallowed in nauseating sentimentality and hadn't the brains of an earwig – simply provided one proof after another that the best of their sex had disappeared from a whole generation'. On the question of sentimentality, one can only reply that this is a fine example of a pot calling a kettle black. The Lost Generation myth is traditional, prescriptive, misogynist and anti-democratic. It ties the destiny of Britain to a 'few good men', ignoring the potential contribution of men from outside the elite and from all women.[7]

A better way of looking at the Lost Generation is brought to mind by a few lines of a Charles Hamilton Sorley sonnet, written in 1915:

> Such, such is Death: no triumph: no defeat:
> Only an empty pail, a slate rubbed clean,
> A merciful putting away of what has been.

The myth customarily refers to those who died. Yet 'it is easy to be dead', wrote Sorley. Perhaps instead the Lost Generation was those condemned to go on living, those who had to shoulder the burden of loss that the Great War caused, those who had to continue in horror, grief and guilt. Margaret Postgate Cole described this fate:

But we are young, and our friends are dead
Suddenly, and our quick love is torn in two;
So our memories are only hopes that came to nothing.
We are left alone like old men; we should be dead
– But there are years and years in which we shall still
    be young.

'I had great ambitions,' wrote the novelist Storm Jameson at war's end. 'I have none now ... very little in me is real except the absolute need, intellectual and spiritual, for withdrawal.' Florence Farmborough, who did her best to escape the constraints imposed by gender, did not, in the end, find the fulfilment she sought. 'I had always hoped that my war experiences would, despite their misery and bitterness, act as a stimulus to my spiritual life, would heighten my compassion, would "strengthen my soul in all goodness". But now I wanted to find a quiet spot where the world was at peace.' For her, the end brought profound emptiness. A similar sense of futility plagued C. E. Montague:

So we had failed – had won the fight and lost the prize; the garland of war was withered before it was gained. The lost years, the broken youth, the dead friends, the women's overshadowed lives at home, the agony and bloody sweat – all had gone to darken the stains which most of us had thought to scour out of the world that our children would live in. Many men felt, and said to each other, that they had been fooled.

After the armistice, each survivor – civilian and combatant, male and female – had to shoulder an individual anguish. Some adjusted, others never did.[8]

Soldiers often felt emotions more intense than most men would ever experience in peacetime. They experienced greater fear, grief, disgust, but also greater love and camaraderie.

'How,' asks the protagonist in *Last Men in London*, 'can things be so wrong, so meaningless, so filthy; and yet also so right, so overwhelmingly significant, so exquisite?' As Guy Chapman described, the love he felt for comrades was more intense than that he felt for anyone: 'I found that this body of men had become so much a part of me that its disintegration would tear away something I cared for more dearly than I could have believed. I was it, and it was I.'

> My love is of a birth as rare
> As 'tis for object strange and high:
> It was begotten by Despair
> Upon Impossibility.

To have the object of such love destroyed was more than some could handle. Witness Ivor Gurney's grief in 'To His Love':

> He's gone, and all our plans
> Are useless indeed.
> We'll walk no more on Cotswold
> Where the sheep feed
> Quietly and take no heed.
>
> His body that was so quick
> Is not as you
> Knew it, on Severn river
> Under the blue
> Driving our small boat through.
>
> You would not know him now . . .
> But still he died
> Nobly, so cover him over
> With violets of pride
> Purple from Severn side.

> Cover him, cover him soon!
> And with thick-set
> Masses of memoried flowers –
> Hide that red wet
> Thing I must somehow forget.

Those who suffered this profound and unique grief often considered themselves a race apart, and felt more affinity with one-time enemies than with those at home. 'The man who really endured the war at its worst was everlastingly differentiated from everyone except his fellow soldiers,' argued Sassoon. In 1968, Charles Carrington wrote:

> We are still an initiate generation, possessing a secret that can never be communicated . . . Twenty million of us . . . shared the experience with one another but with no one else, and are what we are because, in that war, we were soldiers. There are many such dedicated societies in the world, but no other, so far as I know, which comprises a whole age-group of the able-bodied men, while excluding other age-groups and the other sex.

Ford Madox Ford, poet, novelist and ex-soldier, complained of the 'slight nausea that in those days you felt at contact with the civilian who knew none of your thoughts, phrases or preoccupations'. The war experience was a fully laden pack that the ex-soldier could not discard, even had he so desired. The archaeologist and ex-soldier Stanley Casson thought that he had 'put the war into the category of forgotten things', but eventually found that 'The war's baneful influence controlled still all our thoughts and acts, directly or indirectly.' 'The rank stench of those bodies haunts me still,/And I remember things I'd best forget,' wrote Sassoon.[9]

Chapman felt that 'England had vanished over the horizon of

the mind. I did not want to see it.' He instead volunteered for the Allied Army of Occupation. Captain Frederick Osborne could not bear to leave dead comrades and chose instead to spend the rest of his life tending their graves in Belgium. Another veteran quickly returned to France to live the life of a peasant: 'I realised that this was what I needed. Silence. Isolation. Now that I could let go, I broke down, avoided strangers, cried easily and had terrible nightmares.' These, however, were extraordinary reactions; the great majority returned with their heavy burden of memories to a now alien home, strangers in a strange land. Some were driven mad remembering. Others wrote memoirs or poetry in an ambitious, but usually futile, effort at purgation. Many simply reminisced with other old soldiers, in pubs or British Legion clubs. Coppard was delighted to find a member of his old division living close by: 'my heart leaps when I spot him walking up the road. We never miss a natter, and his eyes shine as we go over the umpteenth episode of our war experiences. We catch vivid memories of the past and are glad that we were young in 1914.' For some, the war was the best years of their life and demobilisation a painful divorce. In stark contrast to Vera Brittain, Dorothy McCann, another VAD, felt that 'I was very privileged to be given the opportunity of doing what I did . . . I wouldn't have swapped those years for the gayest in the world'. Others despised the war, but hated the staid complacency at home even more. For many, therefore, peace brought terrible loneliness, an emotional vacuum stretching indefinitely into the future.[10]

Some men could not excise the horror of war; it consumed them like a relentless cancer. Forty-eight special hospitals were established to handle emotional casualties. In 1922, 65,000 shell-shock victims were receiving disability pensions and 9,000 were still hospitalised. Not all had received treatment before the armistice; instead, they tried for a time to hold back terror, finally succumbing to its overwhelming power. In the first ten years of peace, 114,600 men applied for pensions for mental disorders. As Owen wrote:

– These are men whose minds the Dead have ravished.
Memory fingers in their hair of murders,
Multitudinous murders they once witnessed.
Wading sloughs of flesh these helpless wander,
Treading blood from lungs that had loved laughter.
Always they must see these things and hear them,
Batter of guns and shatter of flying muscles,
Carnage incomparable, and human squander
Rucked too thick for these men's extrication.

Many existed in a limbo between madness and sanity, suffering from what would today be called post-traumatic stress, but suffering alone, unaware, befuddled and without professional help. Around three million men had witnessed at first hand the horror of trench warfare, and rare was the soldier who had not seen men brutally killed. Some could shrug off the horror, others pretended to do so, others still were torn apart by it. 'All was not right with the spirit of the men who came back,' wrote Gibbs. 'They were subject to queer moods, queer tempers, fits of profound depression alternating with a restless desire for pleasure. Many of them were easily moved to passion when they lost control of themselves. Many were bitter in their speech, violent in opinion, frightening . . . Something seemed to have snapped in them.' 'When I was demobbed,' one veteran recalled, 'I used to have bad nightmares. I used to wake up in the middle of the night bathed in perspiration.' Haunted by the vivid memory of killing a wounded and unarmed German who had dragged himself into a pillbox, a British ex-soldier found, twelve years after the war, 'still at night comes a sweat that wakes me by its deadly chill to hear again that creeping, creeping'. Some soldiers were plagued by ghosts for the rest of their lives. Smells, sounds, faces would suddenly bring to the surface long-forgotten agonies.[11]

Time was not always a healer when the mind was wounded. 'I have seen sights which no man should ever see,' Private Charles Holman remarked, 82 years after the armistice. 'Sights which stay firmly in your mind for the rest of your life. Vivid images of my mates and comrades-in-arms, lying face down in the trenches with scores of rats scavenging their exposed flesh. I can see it as if it were yesterday, men clambering over the bodies to get out of the line of fire, limbs and torso entwined. Shell-shocked men wallowing in the blood-soaked mire they called home.' The Reverend George Duncan, Haig's personal padre at GHQ, had a relatively easy war. He was nevertheless plagued for the rest of his life by the memory of a pile of bodies at a casualty clearing station. Prominent among the jumble of torsos and limbs were two dead soldiers entwined in a loving embrace who had provided one another a final moment of comfort from the pain and horror of approaching death.[12]

Writing in 1917, Caroline Playne confessed to her 'sickness and horror' at the 'sights of hundreds of men on crutches going about in groups'. During the war, more than 41,000 men had limbs amputated; 272,000 suffered leg or arm injuries that did not require amputation; 60,500 were wounded in the head or eyes; and 89,000 sustained other serious wounds to their bodies.

> Some cheered him home,
> but not as crowds cheer Goal.
> Only a solemn man who brought him fruits
> Thanked him; and then inquired about his soul.
> Now, he will spend a few sick years in institutes,
> And do what things the rules consider wise,
> And take whatever pity they may dole.

Tonight he noticed how the women's eyes
Passed from him to the strong men that were whole.
How cold and late it is!
Why don't they come
And put him into bed?
Why don't they come?

The horror of war was mapped out on the bodies of the broken men who returned. Imaginative inventors of weapons were the progenitors of previously unimaginable wounds. Trooper Samuel Rolfe had nearly all his skin removed by mustard gas. Contact with air was excruciatingly painful. Dressing him in clothes saturated with Vaseline provided little relief. Doctors eventually immersed him in a perpetual bath until 1925, when death finally allowed escape from the torture. A new network of hospitals had to be created in order to deal with the human detritus of war:

By 1920 there were 113 special hospitals, with 18,603 beds, dealing with the most severely disabled and supplemented by 319 separate surgical clinics, thirty-six ear clinics, twenty-four eye clinics, nineteen heart centres . . . One hospital specialising in the removal of steel between April 1919 and March 1925 treated 771 officers and 22,641 men surgically. Queen Mary's hospital, Sidcup, which touched only facial injuries, in the same period operated on 2,944 men.

As with mental cases, many physical injuries were slow to materialise. In 1928, 5,205 artificial legs, 1,106 arms and 4,574 eyes were issued for the first time. Eye ulceration resulted in 33 new cases of blindness in 1933. Those who survived their wounds did not always feel fortunate:

> Crippled for life at seventeen,
>   His great eyes seem to question why:
> With both legs smashed it might have been
>   Better in that grim trench to die
>   Than drag maimed years out helplessly.

Fellow soldiers sometimes knew best how to react to disabled comrades:

At one of our patriotic teas, a young soldier beckoned me with his head and eyes to come to him. I went to speak to him and he whispered to me, 'Would one of your young ladies feed me please? I have no arms.' I went up to one of our young waitresses and asked her if she would. But we both cried so we had to hide ourselves for a few minutes. The soldier who sat next to him was so tender and held up the cup for him to drink from and put bits of cake into his mouth.

Twenty years after the war, there were still 442,000 men whose war injuries rendered them unable to work at all or only with diminished efficiency. Over 8,000 had one or both legs missing, 3,600 had one or both arms missing and over 90,000 had severely damaged limbs. Some 10,000 were still suffering the effects of gas, 15,000 had metal plates in their head and a similar number were deaf from the result of explosions. Around 14,000 had wounds that were still unhealed due to 'latent sepsis'. A fair number of these cases would eventually result in amputation.[13]

The Times insisted that the disabled 'bear the heritage of all our endeavours since we became a people. The qualities they incarnate are those that have upheld our name in strength and honour ... They must be won back from despondency and incapacity, restored to independence and usefulness.' They were fine words, but where was the commitment? Where was the money? An agency was established to find wives for them; to father children would, it was felt, restore their manhood and make them vicariously whole. 'Does it matter? – losing your legs,' a bitter Sassoon wrote. 'For people will always be kind.' The line between kindness and condescension proved exceedingly fine. In time came contempt or neglect, born of the guilt and embarrassment the disabled innocently inspired.[14]

Many survivors were plagued with guilt at being singled out for good fortune. During the war, death had been bizarre, mysterious, inexplicable; to go on living sometimes seemed capricious injustice. In Richard Aldington's *Death of a Hero*, the protagonist admits to a vendetta against the living:

> What right have I to live? . . . When I meet an unmaimed man of my generation, I want to shout at him: 'How did you escape? How did you dodge it? What dirty trick did you play? Why are you not dead, trickster?' It is dreadful to have outlived your life, shirked your fate, overspent your welcome . . . You, the war dead, I think you died in vain, I think you died for nothing, for a blast of wind, a blather, a humbug, a politician's ramp. But at least you died. You did not reject the sharp, sweet shock of bullets, the sudden smash of a shell-burst, the insinuating agony of poison gas. You got rid of it all. You chose the better part . . . But why weren't we one of them! What right have we to live?

No wonder, then, that men like Aldington, Sassoon and Carrington felt that those who had not served (men or women) could never properly remember those who had. They could not possibly understand 'the hell where youth and laughter go'. Sorley touched upon the inadequacy of remembrance:

> When you see millions of the mouthless dead
> Across your dreams in pale battalions go,

Say not soft things as other men have said,
That you'll remember. For you need not so.
Give them not praise. For, deaf, how should they know
It is not curses heaped on each gashed head?
Nor tears. Their blind eyes see not your tears flow.
Nor honour. It is easy to be dead.
Say only this, 'They are dead.' Then add thereto,
'Yet many a better one has died before.'
Then, scanning all the o'ercrowded mass, should you
Perceive one face that you loved heretofore,
It is a spook. None wears the face you knew.
Great death has made all his for evermore.

'I have an old platoon roll before me', Chapman wrote a
generation after the war.

three pages of names, numbers, trades, next-of-kin,
religions, rifle numbers, and so forth. Faces come back out
of the past to answer to these barren details, the face of
this man dead, of that vanished forever. Here and there
rise memories of their habits, their nicknames, the look of
one as he spoke to you, the attitude of another shivering in
the night air, as he leaned over the parapet, watching with
tired bloodshot eyes. Some of the faces have disappeared.
Did I know you? I censored your letters, casually, hurriedly
avoiding your personal messages, your poignant hopes.

Some veterans were tortured by the futility of memory; others
were consumed by the need to remember that 'one face'. Coming
to terms with the war often meant honouring the lost loved one
as a hero whose cause was worthy and whose sacrifice noble.
Death had to have justification, for futility combined with loss
would be too much to bear. Sarah Macnaughtan, writes Peter
Englund, 'was struggling to find a solution to the conundrum

of whether sacrifice can be magnificent even if it is meaningless – indeed, whether the very fact that it is meaningless can make it even more magnificent'. Macnaughtan strove desperately to find a war that matched her ideals. She developed for herself a mantra that usually kept the zombies of doubt at bay: 'I do know that by these simple, glorious, uncomplaining deaths, some higher, purer, more splendid place is reached, some release is found from the heavy weight of foolish, sticky, burdensome, contemptible things. These heroes do "rise" and we "rise" with them.' It remained important to believe in heroism and heroes. And in the beauty of sacrifice. After 1918, many felt the need to see the war in the same way they had seen it in August 1914, in other words as a great crusade. It was a 'great triumph and a great deliverance', the *Daily Mail* assured its readers on Armistice Day 1919; 'how great will only be realised in days to come . . . though our hearts may swell with the legitimate pride of victory, our minds should dwell on the sacrifices of success and on the burdens it has laid upon our shoulders'. 'Sacrifice' was a handy word, used often, as armour against pain.[15]

Around three million Britons lost a close relative in the war. 'I am beginning to rub my eyes at the prospect of peace,' wrote Cynthia Asquith in October 1918. 'I think it will require more courage than anything that has gone before . . . one will at last fully recognise that the dead are not only dead for the duration of the war.' Whereas the literature of those who fought evokes the memories of the 'pale battalions' who forged a brotherhood of suffering, that of civilians is more particular, focusing on a single individual. Those at home might have been unable to comprehend the millions of mouthless dead, but they had no difficulty comprehending an empty chair at dinner. Civilians who grieved grieved alone over a very personal loss. The loneliness of bereavement was described by Harry Lauder, who lost his son John:

My only son. The only child that God had given us . . .
For a time I was quite numb. Then came a great pain and
I whispered to myself over and over again the one terrible
word 'dead'. It seemed that for me the board of life was
blank and black. For me there was no past and there would
be no future. Everything had been swept away by one
sweep of the hand of fate . . . I was beyond the power of
human words to comfort.

On the death of his own son, Asquith wrote: 'Whatever pride
I had in the past, and whatever hope I had for the far future,
by much the largest part of both was invested in him. Now all
that is gone.' The war was over, but it left behind a profound
emptiness:

> They mingle not with laughing comrades again;
> They sit no more at familiar tables of home;
> They have no lot in our labour of the day-time;
> They sleep beyond England's foam.

One of the most poignant examples of emotional desolation
is Rudyard Kipling, whose patriotic writings inspired the
generation of 1914. 'Who stands if Freedom fall?' he wrote
before the war. 'Who dies if England live?' Fired by his father's
stirring words, John Kipling cajoled his way into the army at
the age of 17. After John's death at Loos in September 1915,
Kipling was never the same. On the one hand he felt a most
intense grief:

> My son was killed while laughing at some jest. I would
>   I knew
> What it was, and it might serve me in a time when jests
>   are few.

On the other he was extremely bitter towards those deemed responsible:

> If any question why we died
> Tell them, because our fathers lied.

To Kipling, the lying fathers were British politicians, the Pope, the German enemy, et al. But who is to say if, in his darkest moments, he did not include himself among the guilty.[16]

Because of the taboo against female soldiers, women did not experience the strain of battle, the sight of comrades being blown apart or the savagery of killing. The lack of understanding, however, cuts both ways; for just as women had not killed, men had not given birth. No soldier, no matter how seasoned, could have understood the grief of Mrs Shaw and Mrs Fraser, each of whom lost five sons in the war, or of Mrs Coster who lost four of her five, the last a few days before the armistice. These were ordinary housewives made extraordinary by their gargantuan loss. A mother (signing herself 'Hope') who lost two sons, one at sea, made a desperate plea to the government in 1919 to conduct a search of islands in the Mediterranean and the Indian Ocean for survivors of torpedoed ships who might 'have no possible chance of sending home news of their escape'. The historian Jeremy Seabrook recalls how, when he was growing up in Leicester, a woman in his neighbourhood would every night call her three sons in from play. All three had died on the Somme. Vera Brittain told of a terrible moment when she opened a box containing Roland Leighton's kit that he was wearing on the day he was killed. His mother was also present. The clothes were covered in blood. The worst part, however, was the odour.

> The charnel-house smell seemed to grow stronger and stronger till it pervaded the room and obliterated

everything else. Finally Mrs Leighton said, 'Robert, take those clothes away into the kitchen, and don't let me see them again; I must either burn or bury them. They smell of death; they are not Roland, they seem to detract from his memory and spoil his glamour. I won't have any more to do with them.'

'No, they were not him,' Brittain concluded. Love and memory could not sit side by side with such direct evidence of carnage.[17]

After the battle fronts and weapons factories went quiet, the war continued to produce an endless supply of sorrow. The historian attempting to convey that grief is spoiled for choice – the well of sadness is so deep. 'How should you leave me, having loved me so?' asked a bereft Marian Allen in 'The Wind on the Downs':

> I think of you the same and always shall.
> We thought of many things and spoke of few,
> And life lay all uncertainly before,
> And now I walk alone and think of you,
> And wonder what new kingdoms you explore.
> Over the railway line, across the grass,
> While up above the golden wings are spread,
> Flying, ever flying overhead,
> Here still I see your khaki figure pass,
> And when I leave the meadow, almost wait
> That you should open first the wooden gate.

Allen was unique only in her eloquence; the desolation she felt was shared by many women. The historian Trevor Wilson encountered a woman who remarked as late as 1975 how she had lost her sweetheart at Loos. Never subsequently married, she would undoubtedly have sympathised with Olive Lindsay:

The best of me died at Bapaume
  When the world went up in fire,
And the soul that was mine deserted
  And left me, a thing in the mire,
With a madden'd and dim remembrance
  Of a time when my life was whole.

'She lies with Raymond's two last letters in her hand, doesn't care to see the children [and is] utterly distraught,' remarked Asquith of his daughter-in-law. It is no wonder that in the years following the war, the popularity of spiritualism and seances grew, as mourners attempted by whatever means to communicate with those gone. One woman, rendered rudderless by the war, put an ad in the 'personals' section of *The Times*: 'Lady, fiancé killed, will gladly marry officer totally blinded or otherwise incapacitated by the War.'[18]

Chapter 15

'Daddy, What Did You Do in the Class War?'

On 29 November 1917, Lord Lansdowne openly called in the *Daily Telegraph* for a negotiated peace. To push on to victory would, he maintained, 'spell ruin to the civilised world'. All that had made Britain great would be destroyed; 'we are slowly killing off the best of the male population of these islands'. Lansdowne was not a pacifist, but an elitist who feared that, with the best men slaughtered, England would drift aimlessly into republicanism, socialism and decline. He was scorned during the war, but afterwards his ideas were incorporated into the culture of pity. Continued fascination for the Great War derives in part from its imagined status as a catastrophic event which swept away all that was noble and great and replaced it with something drab, common and coarse.[1]

That myth is very English – the Scots, Welsh and Irish seek pity in other ways. The myth implies a pre-war England reminiscent of a Turner landscape – a pastoral idyll devoid of social discord, industrial unrest, poverty or class conflict. Lansdowne and his disciples ignored the extraordinary capacity of British society to accommodate social change behind a facade of cricket, Pimm's and cucumber sandwiches. The mighty British Empire was built on Sheffield steel, Newcastle coal and Clydeside engineering, yet the prevalent images remain those of stately homes, cottage gardens, hollyhocks and strawberries. Social strife did not suddenly arise during the Great War. That men like Lansdowne could convince themselves it had demonstrates how well progress had been contained, conflict hidden and values preserved since the Industrial Revolution. Nor was this process of containment an elitist conspiracy; some of the greatest admirers of 'Merrie England' were the workers denied its luxuries.

The war was insufficiently cataclysmic to destroy this fundamentally stable social system. Granted, social change did result. The workers' experiences altered their world view and their position within society. The same could be said for the middle and upper classes. Likewise, the relationship between men and women and the role of the latter within society evolved. But nearly a century later, what is striking is how much of pre-war society has survived. The war was not a deluge that swept all before it; it was more like a winter storm that briefly swelled the rivers of change. Though it provided opportunities for social reform, it also stimulated conservatism and counter-reaction, rendering progress erratic.

On the plus side, a noticeable redistribution of income did occur. Tax increases, death duties and rent controls rendered the very wealthy worse off in 1925 than they had been ten years earlier. Inflation plagued those who derived their income from investments. Landowners who made their money from produce did well, but those (the majority) who lived off rents suffered. In contrast, workers, because of the manpower shortage, commanded higher wages as the war progressed, allowing most to keep ahead of inflation. This redistribution should not, however, be confused with an erosion of class barriers or a widening of opportunity. The gains and losses of various groups instead led to heightened consciousness among all classes. The conflict this engendered inhibited progress for society as a whole.[2]

369

The social impact of the war is best examined by starting at the top. The monarchy, that great anchor of stability, had a good war. Frequent opportunities arose to increase prestige and impress the citizenry. Great attention was given to the fact that the royal family had to endure rationing and that it forswore alcohol. The anglicisation of names harmonised nicely with anti-German prejudices. The mass outpouring of nationalistic sentiment throughout the war allowed the royal family to become a focus for patriotic affection. If society appeared to be disintegrating, the monarchy provided a reassuring affirmation of stability and tradition.

The gentry, depending on one's point of view, either declined drastically or expanded during the war. Since identification with the upper class is theoretically defined by birth, one can appreciate that its ranks were depleted by a disproportionately high casualty rate. In addition, war taxes forced the sale of many estates and left others financially precarious. Fiscal measures introduced during the war remained in force after it, as governments quickly found new uses for the revenue. The economic historian F. M. L. Thompson, studying two representative estates, found that whereas tax claimed 4 per cent of gross rental income in 1914, it took 25 per cent in 1919. These taxes, though mildly redistributive, did not lessen class distinctions. The wealthy felt greater animosity towards those, namely the working-class, assumed to be the winners in this redistribution.[3]

Old estates were thrice cursed: firstly by additional financial burdens; secondly by the deaths of young men capable of managing them in the future; and thirdly by the post-war agricultural depression. Hard times should not, however, be confused with real penury. Archibald Sinclair, Baronet of Ulbster, warned his new wife in 1918 that 'Large theatre and dinner parties, a big London house, quantities of dresses and jewels, shooting parties . . . on the pre-war scale, these things we cannot aspire to and must dismiss altogether from our minds.' A much more modest life was nevertheless defined as a medium-sized London house (in addition to his Caithness estate) with full retinue of servants, including butler, cook and parlourmaid, nurse for the children, chauffeur and a groom for four polo ponies. Parties were slightly less opulent than before the war, but still grand enough to attract glamorous guests. Sinclair's experience was probably pretty typical. In hard times, the fittest survived: the more dynamic members of the upper class diversified their portfolios, selling land to finance more lucrative investments.[4]

A rung lower stood those men of entrepreneurial talent with the means to mimic the gentry. Their number increased, since the war offered plentiful opportunity to amass huge fortunes. Lloyd George's tendency to draft business leaders into politics gave them the added cachet of service to the state. After the war, their new status was symbolically confirmed by the Prime Minister's corrupt distribution of honours and peerages. This illustrates the fundamental flexibility of British society, even in its most traditional enclaves. The composition of the upper class changed, but its essential nature, its position in society and its power remained intact.

The middle class changed significantly during the war era. White-collar workers increased by over a million between 1911 and 1921, rising from 12 to 22 per cent of the working population. Some sections of the middle class did well; others suffered. The law profession was healthier in 1918 than in 1914, if only for the fact that German guns reduced the supply of lawyers. Shopkeepers also prospered, especially those catering to groups who enjoyed a rise in income. For instance, women's clothiers had a good war, since war work gave some women spare income. In January 1917, the Forestreet Warehouse Co., drapers, announced that 1916 profits had increased by 58 per cent over 1914. According to the coalition minister Auckland

Geddes, 'quite small persons' who amassed huge profits in the haberdashery trade purchased 'estates of several hundred acres in the country'. On the other hand, inflation was hard on landlords, on those with fixed incomes, and on those whose occupations were not sufficiently important to earn them salary rises. Small businessmen in non-essential industries found it difficult to keep skilled (or any) labour, with disastrous effects upon production and profits. The highest-paid industrial workers often earned more than the lowest-paid white-collar workers. In 1917, a middle-class Yorkshireman complained bitterly about how the workers had unlimited access to food, coal, beer and entertainment. 'The war instead of being a terror has almost come to be regarded as a blessing in disguise, and our people continue to live in a fool's paradise regardless of the future.' Fearing the social disintegration that would result from this condition of plenty, he warned that 'our . . . rulers will only have themselves to blame for the results which must inevitably follow'.[5]

War hit small families hard. Before 1914, birth control had allowed the middle class to stretch limited incomes by restricting the number of dependants. These families paid dearly. 'The "only child" or "only son" which was before the war the sole luxury permitted to so many,' wrote the Liberal politician and journalist Charles Masterman, 'has perished in the ultimate and fierce demands of war. He went out – in the great majority of cases – a volunteer. Every spare farthing had been spent on his upbringing from babyhood. He was to be the pride and assistance of his parents when they attained old age.' Alarmed by this misfortune, the eugenicist Dean Inge warned of imminent racial deterioration. Somewhat less apocalyptic, Masterman complained that 'the Middle Class . . . is being harassed out of existence by the financial after consequences of the war'. In truth, the middle class was being harassed *into* existence. Charities and special interest groups like the

Professional Classes War Relief Committee and the Professional Classes Special Aid Society, formed in response to war's distress, fostered a class solidarity that had not existed before. Newspaper editorials moaned about the 'New Poor', who suffered a peculiar martyrdom in which servants were unavailable or unaffordable, laundry was no longer sent out and worn clothes were mended, then mended again. 'Doing without' became the shibboleth of a group previously unaccustomed to frugality. Georgina Lee thought that some good might come of the privation. 'We shall all have to alter our mode of living,' she predicted, 'but one great boon to mankind will be the disappearance of the terrible amount of luxury and pleasure and frivolity which has been growing steadily for some years now. We shall have to return to more simple tastes and modes of living.' A sense of adversity fostered a middle-class consciousness even among those who did not suffer. This bunker mentality was both anti-labour and anti-capitalist; the enemies were overpaid, lazy workers and unscrupulous profiteers, both of whom cheated honest taxpayers. These antagonisms inspired the formation of the Middle Class Union, the anti-waste campaigns of the 1920s, the aggressive response to the 1926 General Strike and the post-war protests against high taxation. When circumstances eventually improved, most middle-class families found themselves better off than they had been in 1913. Lee's expectations proved ill-founded. Deflation was a welcome boon, inexpensive housing was readily available, new consumer goods flooded the markets, female unemployment provided cheap servants and jobless rates were consistently below those of the working-class. Scruples were discarded as profligacy rose again, triumphant. As a bonus, class solidarity, formed in adversity, survived the return of good fortune.[6]

The working-class changed most significantly during the war. Again, a process of homogenisation occurred. On the factory floor, once-distinct status, skill and income differentials were blurred in the quest for productivity, with the result that the entire class became more cohesive. 'The skilled worker can no longer think of the less skilled workers as he was apt to think of them before the War,' G. D. H. Cole observed, 'and the less skilled worker will no longer be conscious of the same subordination to the skilled worker . . . the fundamental effect is to draw the two groups more closely together.' Wartime industrial relations could, however, both unite and divide workers, as the issue of badging demonstrated. Workers united to resist removal of badges, but the less skilled resented the way skilled workers were protected from conscription. Wage rates also fostered antagonism. On the one hand, wage demands were often expressed in class terms, for instance in response to profiteering or rising rents. This encouraged the working-class to think and act as a unit, a development reinforced by compulsory collective bargaining and national pay awards. On the other hand, competition for wage increases caused rivalries within the working-class. For instance, automated machinery and other efficiency improvements sometimes meant that the less skilled workers on piece rates – where pay was determined by the volume produced – earned more than skilled workers on time rates. Addressing this anomaly, the Minister of Labour decided in October 1917 to give skilled workers a 12.5 per cent war bonus. That generosity backfired when unskilled and semi-skilled workers protested. Since their objections could not be ignored, the bonus was extended to all munitions workers, much to the disdain of the skilled. In other words, the fact that the unskilled did proportionately better than their skilled comrades brought some homogenisation of the working-class, but not necessarily harmony. Bizarrely, but perhaps understandably, a crafts union spokesman asked Lloyd George to 'devise ways and means of eliminating the skilled knowledge which the semi-skilled men will have acquired'. Many feared that the decline of skilled trades would weaken trade unionism.

In fact, in 1920, a Ministry of Labour spokesman discovered that something else was happening: '"class consciousness" is obliterating the distinctions between those who follow different occupations in the same works'. This contributed to an 'increasing tendency for the trade unionists of one shop, works or small district, to act together, irrespective of their divisions into crafts or occupations'.[7]

Pride in being working class – in struggling through a precarious life whilst maintaining respectability – was undoubtedly strengthened by the war. This was not antagonistic to patriotism; in fact, since the demands of war gave the worker new importance, class-consciousness and patriotism reinforced one another. Divisions did not, however, completely disappear. Before the war, workers were rigidly arranged into a social hierarchy of immense complexity. The war erased some of the myriad distinctions, but skill differentials – real or imagined – were still cherished and never willingly surrendered. The war also added new points of tension. Under dilution, skilled workers were increasingly placed in supervisory positions, overseeing unskilled dilutees. The friction that inevitably arose was exacerbated by resentment among skilled workers who did not feel that their pay sufficiently reflected their new status. Furthermore, the widening of the tax base created antagonism between those who paid and those who did not. Finally, considerable friction existed between those workers who fought in the trenches and those who avoided service. Antagonism arose not just because of the great danger combat implied. As one contemporary journalist remarked: 'Whilst Mrs Jack Tar or Mrs Tommy Atkins have found it a tight squeeze to stretch the money far enough to cover ordinary necessities, Mrs Nouveau-Riche of munition fame, and Mrs Dockyard Matey have been able to indulge in finery that never came their way before 1914.'[8]

While internal divisions certainly existed, the working-class presented a more united front at the end of the war. Class identity was reinforced by pride in their contribution to the war and by growing antagonism towards other classes. During the war, social inequalities were made apparent in previously unaccustomed ways. Workers could not help but notice that their contribution to the war effort often involved considerable sacrifice – either financial or corporeal. In contrast, businessmen managed to get rich *and* stay safe, while still appearing patriotic. 'Put bluntly it does not matter a damn to us selfishly how deep in the soup [the country] gets as it will be all the more profitable to pull it out,' the shipbuilder James Lithgow candidly admitted to his brother. 'But both of us can lay definite claim to having been guided by better motives in all we have done since this trouble arose.' That sort of cynicism rankled with the worker. A Cabinet paper regretted the fact that 'The popular adoption of the word "profiteering" and the application of it to particular abuses of profit-making has ... contributed to bring profit into wider disrepute.' Profiteering did more to encourage the growth of consciousness than did specific industrial disputes. Arguments over pay or dilution often divided the working-class, but worries over the price and supply of food were shared. An official report admitted that profiteering did 'a great deal ... to destroy the spirit of unity which permeated the country in the early stages of the war'. The lawyer George Askwith, a veteran of many a labour tribunal who understood industrial unrest as well as anyone, remarked that 'A shipowner who stated that he made profits, was going to make profits, and had a right to make profits, did more harm than a great naval defeat would have done ... The profiteer's statement would rouse class against class.' Workers felt that the sacrifices they had made had allowed employers to amass huge profits. It seemed only fair, then, to restrict these profits so that sacrifices might be more evenly distributed. Though they won this concession, it was mainly a symbolic victory, since excess profits duties never really solved the moral problem of excess profits, though they did raise a great deal of revenue.[9]

Numerous other flashpoints served to intensify class consciousness. Food queues were worst in working-class areas. Scheming landlords preyed upon the poor. Finally, the government seemed more inclined to regulate and control the worker's life (leaving certificates, conscription, prohibitions on strikes, pub opening hours, etc.) than that of the capitalist. Though this was hardly the worker's first encounter with injustice, the iniquities seemed to contradict the rhetoric about a nation united in struggle. Workers in consequence became more assertive. A railway clerk confessed how, before the war, going on strike produced 'a sense of personal degradation' because he and his fellow workers 'had a childlike belief in the good intentions of the companies'. As a result of the war, however, 'this state of confidence has given way to an attitude of deep distrust and in many instances of grave suspicion'.[10]

On concrete issues of working conditions, income, and job stability, gains and losses for the working-class probably cancelled each other out. Conditions and job stability improved, but wage increases did not always keep pace with price rises, especially early in the war. The workers gained power as a group, but patriotism impeded the exercise of that power. Militant trade unionists remained optimistic that the workers would soon wake up to their exploitation. 'Daily I see signs amongst the working-class of a mighty awakening,' the miners' leader A. J. Cook remarked in April 1916. 'The chloroforming pill of patriotism is failing in its power to drug the mind and consciousness of the worker. He is beginning to shudder at his stupidity in allowing himself to become a party to such a catastrophe as we see today.' That statement, however, was inspired more by hope than reality. Patriotism remained a potent sedative. 'Even the running up of a Union Jack outside the factory was known to have a very salutary effect on morale,' writes the social historian Bernard Waites. Many men preferred to work in controlled establishments because they seemed an overt manifestation of their contribution to the war. The workers sacrificed much for the war effort, but did so willingly. Their cooperation was motivated by patriotism, morality and by a naive confidence that virtue would be rewarded.[11]

Arthur Gleason, an American observer of British post-war society, wrote: 'An old Oxford friend said sadly to me: "Ten years ago, when I came into a crowded bus, a working-man would rise and touch his cap and give me his seat. I am sorry to see that spirit dying out."' The anecdote indicates that workers had become less reverential, but it does not necessarily follow that society became more equal. Gleason's middle-class friend still perceived class distinctions and felt them worthy of preservation. Likewise, the worker's refusal to touch his cap and surrender his seat is as significant an indicator of class barriers as was his willingness to do so before the war. His actions should not be confused with an assumption of equality; they were instead an assertion of hostility towards someone once respected, now scorned, but still distinctly different.[12]

And what of Tommy Atkins? The highly traditional, heavily authoritarian military quarantined soldiers from the social changes that were occurring on the home front. Thus the men did not experience the same awakening of awareness that took place at home. Granted, some junior officers felt a resurgence of the *noblesse oblige* that had declined during the previous generation of industrial strife. That paternalism was, however, dependent upon rigid class barriers. 'What have the officer class learned?' an officer in Christopher Stone's *The Valley of Indecision*, asks. 'To manage men. How? By example, partly. By setting themselves a higher example than they expect of their subordinates. And by looking after their men: thinking of their men's comfort, mark you, before their own.' Paternalism should not, however, be confused with intimacy, or with equality.

A similar sentiment was evident in the factories, where 'lady superintendents' looked after the welfare of the working-class women they supervised. In both instances, the assumption of care arose from a sense of superiority. As Ernest Bevin remarked in 1919: 'my experience with all this good feeling . . . is that the leopard has not changed his spots. It is as big an effort now to get a bob or two a week for your work-people as ever it was.' The national emergency may have camouflaged class divisions, but it did not wipe them out. Class antagonism quickly resurfaced when peace returned. Noble Tommy Atkins, shorn of his uniform and rifle, became a lazy, selfish, grasping proto-Bolshevik, derided and feared by the middle class.[13]

The survival of old norms is evident in the experiences of the 'temporary gentlemen' – men from humble backgrounds who became officers, much to the disgust of those who considered themselves the 'real thing'. Wilfred Owen derided the 'privates and sergeants in masquerade' in his unit. 'Two at least of the officers are quite temporary gentlemen,' he sneered. 'I'd prefer to be among honest privates than these snobs.' 'I felt the bottom of the barrel had been scraped for officer material,' judged the novelist Stuart Cloete. The popular writer Alfred Burrage was alarmed to find his favourite West End haunt full of interlopers. 'Judging by the manners and accents,' he remarked, 'they were nearly all Smiffs, late of Little Buggington Grammar School, who had been "clurks" in civil life.' These attitudes contradict the optimism of those who heralded the temporary gentlemen as the death knell of class distinctions. Those favoured with promotion had few such illusions. A former salesman remarked: 'I try hard to remind myself that the three stars which I now wear are only the temporary marks of proficiency that the war will, in ending, wipe out, and that I will step back into that drab old life.' Wartime status provided little advantage after 1918, as one ersatz captain found: 'We have got to wipe this "war record" clear off our minds, drop the "captain" and "lieutenant" off the

advertisements, and regard ourselves as fit young civilians who
have had a "jolly fine holiday for four years".' R. H. Mottram
referred to a process of being 'de-officered', which for him meant
the added indignity of 'finding our earning capacity lower in
the peacetime jobs to which we thankfully returned'. Since
the temporary gentlemen had attained their status because of
genuine merit (intelligence, initiative, integrity), it must have
rankled when the arbitrary standards of birth were restored.[14]

In *Military Organization and Society*, the sociologist Stefan
Andreski proposed that the greater society's participation in
a war, the more comprehensive the social change that results.
That idea was taken up by Arthur Marwick and turned into
a gospel during the 1960s, the decade when progress seemed
everywhere apparent. From a more distant perspective,
a number of problems with the notion reveal themselves.
Participation meant improved income for many, but income
levels and social status are not intrinsically linked. Class
differences are based on deep-seated cultural distinctions that
cannot be erased by better employment opportunities alone –
as the temporary gentleman learned. The biggest problem with
the participation mantra, however, is that it fails to acknowledge
the precariousness of the workers' wartime gains. However
well they may have done during the war, they were ill-equipped
to weather the economic storms of the 1920s and 1930s. The
manufacturing work taken on during the war was harder to
find in peacetime and, with manpower suddenly plentiful, did
not pay as well.[15]

Before the war, working-class assertiveness was constrained
by low self-esteem, by deep divisions within the class, by
precarious employment and by limited outlets for discontent.
The war rendered the working-class more homogenised
and more inclined to interpret problems in class terms. Thus
society as a whole became less harmonious and the working-
class stronger. The growth of working-class solidarity did not,

however, destroy the social order, as Lansdowne feared. A more assertive working-class was matched by more assertive middle and upper classes, each prepared to defend interests more aggressively. Thus class awareness was never enough on its own to achieve for the workers greater status or mobility. Their power is derived from real or manipulated scarcity of labour. After the war, labour surpluses rendered that power impotent. Class solidarity survived and was even enhanced by mass unemployment. Solidarity by itself was not, however, enough; workers were powerless when jobs were scarce.

An awakening of working-class identity should not be confused with radical politics. The miners, for instance, were slow to embrace the Labour Party and were suspicious of socialism, yet they had a highly developed sense of identity. In the 1918 election, a rise in working-class awareness coexisted with resounding support for the Tories. This is not difficult to understand. During the war, the workers were among the most patriotic in society. In the 1918 election, the Tories presented the image of toughness and resolution that harmonised best with heightened patriotism. Belligerent Tory promises of revenge upon Germany dovetailed well with working-class xenophobia. The Tories also presented a nationalist image which neither the divided Liberals nor sectionalist Labour could mimic. For all these reasons, the Conservative-dominated coalition seemed the best prospect for achieving the land fit for heroes that workers coveted. Thus, Tory-voting workers were neither misguided nor unaware; they simply saw their interests as best represented by the Conservatives.

The condition of the poor improved significantly during the war. Most of these improvements survived the armistice. There were fewer in poverty, the result partly of wartime redistribution of income, but also of a fall in family size. Food was more affordable, health care more accessible and health standards consequently better. Government spending on social services, which stood at 4 per cent in 1914, hovered around 8 per cent between the wars. Unemployment benefit was available to 2.25 million workers before the war and 12 million after the passage of the Unemployment Insurance Act of 1920. The increased attention to social services can be explained by two factors connected with the war. Firstly, the conflict broke down resistance to higher taxation. Secondly, it revealed the extent of deprivation and encouraged a desire to alleviate it. This sense of goodwill was not, however, universally felt, nor did altruism survive long past the armistice. Many agreed that social welfare was desirable, but there was little consensus on how to pay for it.[16]

Peace revealed that there were strict limits on social progress. The 8-hour day and 48 hour week became standard, with few exceptions, after the war. This brought increased opportunities for leisure and relaxation, but poverty prevented their exploitation. Unemployment benefit covered short-term emergencies, but it was inadequate during long-term joblessness – a depressing feature of the interwar period. Union assertiveness and working-class confidence diminished when dole queues lengthened. The redistribution of income apparent between 1913 and 1924 did not continue into the next decade. Despite the general improvement in the lot of the poor, in rural areas, malnutrition actually increased during the 1920s.

Modest welfare reforms ironically strengthened the class system. Because life became more tolerable for those on society's lowest rungs, they grew more accepting of its iniquities. As the old adage goes, the revolt of the hungry ends at the baker's shop. Pacified by a better diet and slightly warmer homes, the poor had no truck with revolution. Rich and poor, privileged and downtrodden, shared a fundamental conservatism. The extreme patriotism of workers during the war, and their consistent antagonism towards socialist politics after it, suggest that most linked the continuation of British greatness with a preservation of the social system. Even in the lowest trough of the slump, few workers wanted anything more radical than an amelioration of their plight.

After the war, Britain returned quickly to normal. Those for whom 'normal' was never nice did not protest. For example, concern about poor working-class housing had inspired Christopher Addison's Housing and Town Planning Act of 1919, with its schemes for 500,000 new homes in three years. *The Times* commented in April 1919 that there was 'no doubt that the country regards this as far and away the most important Bill in the government's programme of social reconstruction'. Houses, it was hoped, would wean the poor from radical politics. 'One of the great difficulties of the future will be unrest,' commented the opposition leader Donald Maclean, 'and one of the best ways of mitigating it is to let people see that we are in earnest on this question.' Yet real commitment, financial and emotional, was lacking. Within two years Addison was out, the victim of Conservative-inspired parsimony and a growing abhorrence of anything that smacked of egalitarianism. Tories took shelter behind the principle that housing construction was not a justified area for state intervention. Welcoming the government's change of heart, *The Times* commented in June 1921 that the Addison plans had been 'ill-advised . . . at a time when the whole reaction of men's minds was against over-government and towards individualism and freedom of personal enterprise'. It seems, then, that 'homes fit for heroes' was never anything more than cheap electioneering, punctuated by post-war sentimentality.[17]

Education reforms proved even more disappointing. Progress here would have provided the best opportunities for social mobility. The Fisher Education Act of 1918 raised the school leaving age from 12 to 14, with 'continuation classes' of eight hours per week provided for those leaving early to take up employment. Local authorities were encouraged (not required) to provide more nursery places and better medical care in schools. The Act was, however, rather superficial; it did not attack the traditionalism and elitism of the old system. There was no acknowledgement of the need for universal secondary education and no fundamental reform of the curriculum. In any case, rather like Addison's housing measures, Fisher's modest proposals were never fully implemented. A penny-pinching government killed continuation classes. The best education at secondary school and university remained private. Fisher's reforms, he predicted, would in time provide Britain with 'all the types of schools which are required to give every section of the children of the people that education which is best adapted to provide them with a good start in life'. (Despite the tortured syntax, the class bias is plainly evident.) From 1910 to 1929, 39 per cent of middle-class boys went to secondary school, and 8.5 per cent to university. The figures for working-class boys are 10 per cent and 1.5 per cent, respectively. Those for girls in both categories were, needless to say, even lower. Leaving aside the fact that this made social mobility (and gender equality) extremely difficult to achieve, the figures also demonstrate that the country was wasting huge resources of talent. Middle-class commentators who moaned about the Lost Generation failed to notice the ability that lurked around them, in factories, mines, dole queues and on the street. According to one study, in the period before the Second World War, 73 per cent of able children never made it to secondary school, while nearly half of those who did make it did not, on the basis of their intelligence, belong there.[18]

The war revealed many problems worthy of attention, but their solutions were often incompatible with tradition or fiscal prudence. Social improvement seemed a luxury only a prosperous society could afford, and throughout the inter-war period Britain did not feel prosperous. The cul de sac of working-class existence became a little less drab, and a bit more secure, but it remained difficult to escape. The privileged classes were intent upon preserving their own way of life, which in effect meant keeping the working-class in their place. The workers, better off than they had been before the war, did not for the most part complain. Rudimentary social welfare, cheap entertainment, better working conditions and improved health were effective opiates for the people.

And what of women? Elsie Inglis, the doctor whose offer of help to the war effort was rebuffed early in the war, later concluded that 'ordinary male disbelief in our capacity cannot be argued away. *It can only be worked away.*' The overly optimistic Millicent Fawcett reassured herself that this was indeed what occurred. Writing in 1920, she argued that 'The war revolutionised the industrial position of women. It found them serfs and left them free. It not only opened opportunities of employment in a number of skilled trades, but, more important even than this, it revolutionised men's minds and their conception of the sort of work of which the ordinary everyday woman was capable.' Fawcett needed to believe in progress, since she spent her lifetime fighting for it. She was, unfortunately, wrong. While women undoubtedly made some progress, at the same time the war reinforced masculine values, reinvigorating the notion of separate spheres. Wars are by nature misogynistic: men fight and women tend the home fires. In the process, women are forced back into the feminine roles that men imagine themselves to be defending. Brave warriors fight for the motherland – a politically loaded word. The conflict produced endless opportunities for men to act strong, virile and heroic and for women to be sensitive, caring, motherly or feeble. It is no wonder, then, that many women allowed a helpless victim mentality to engulf them. While they sat knitting socks by the fire, fantasies of chivalric heroes provided a substitute for sex. The novelist Storm Jameson recognised the futility of those like Pankhurst and Fawcett who hoped that the war might bridge the gap between the sexes: 'Why do not women know that in any war, the enemy is not on the other side? Their enemy is war itself – which robs them of their identity: and they cease to be clever, competent, intelligent, beautiful, in their own right and become the nurses, the pretty joys and at last the mourners of their men.' Granted, during the war, many women broke the chains of femininity, but the culture quickly absorbed those escapees. Female munitions workers were idealised in soft-toned propaganda posters so as to disguise the dirt and drudgery of the factory. The reality of what they were doing – creating weapons of destruction – was also obscured. Two wartime heroines, Mairi Chisholm and Elsie Knocker, drove motorcycles and ambulances close to the British line. They did this because they were attracted to the opportunity of doing what women were not supposed to do. Yet to the public they became the Angels of Pervyse – the masculinity of their work subsumed by the femininity of that imagery. Likewise, Inglis, in every sense a professional, tended to be praised for her female, nurturing characteristics, not her skill as a doctor.[19]

Women in paid employment increased from 4.93 million to 6.19 million during the war. This seems significant, but the vast majority who took up new jobs were working-class women who had worked previously or, being teenagers, had expected to enter employment shortly. Wartime work was different in that it was generally better paid, more stable and was crucially important to the nation's survival, thus providing women with a sense of pride. These differences and the experiences they engendered were, however, fleeting. Working-class women were changed by the war, but few could enjoy those changes after it.[20]

Wartime employment was a double-edged sword. Some women cherished the opportunity to serve their country. In February 1916, Marylebone magistrates investigated the case of Elsie Mary Davey, a 17-year-old girl who had been missing from her home for a month. She was eventually found working at a munitions factory. Her mother admitted that she was 'mad on munitions'. Alec Holmes captured this same sentiment in *The Munitions Worker*, a one-act play produced during the war. In it, Tina, a munitionette who is dying of consumption, is urged by her doctor to rest:

> TINA [eager again] No, ah, no, I couldn't! I loves my shells. Like children they are to me. And when they go, flying away . . . over there . . . I says to myself p'raps that's your shell . . . p'raps it's going now . . . so . . . away from the big gun . . . Boom, and it's gone . . . and they're dead . . . heaps of them are dead . . . they that kill our lads . . . an' p'raps . . . I've killed them. [Breathlessly] That's what I says to myself.
> DOCTOR [laughing] This will never do. Tina, you'll be dreaming of your shells next, all night.
> TINA I do dream of them. That's just what I do. Nights and days I dream of them. I see them flying . . . always flying away there . . . to the enemy . . . to our enemy . . . going over to them, and [softly] I see the lads going over too, and the shells make a way for them and save them, some of them. That's why I love the shells.

While the play was written by a man and for propaganda purposes, it captured a common sentiment amongst women. Not all women liked what war work implied, however. Making munitions meant edging closer to killing, something that had previously been the preserve of men. 'The fact that I am using my life's energy to destroy human souls gets on my nerves,' one woman wrote in a factory magazine. She was proud that she was 'doing what I can to bring this horrible affair to an end. But once the war is over, never in creation will I do the same thing again.' Mary Gabrielle Collins felt that war work threatened the ruin of women:

Their hands, their fingers
Are coarsened in munition factories.
Their thoughts, which should fly
Like bees among the sweetest mind flowers
Gaining nourishment for the thoughts to be,
Are bruised against the law,
'Kill, kill.'
They must take part in defacing and destroying the
     natural body
Which, certainly during this dispensation
Is the shrine of the spirit.
O God!
Throughout the ages we have seen,
Again and again
Men by Thee created
Cancelling each other.
And we have marvelled at the seeming annihilation
Of Thy work.
But this goes further,
Taints the fountain head,
Mounts like a poison to the Creator's very heart.
O God!
Must It anew be sacrificed on earth?[21]

Not surprisingly, excessive attention has been paid to the war experiences of middle-class women. The VADs, popularised by Vera Brittain, did make a significant contribution, but few of the women who joined (one third of VADs, incidentally, were men) saw the experience as anything other than a brief interruption of an otherwise conventional life. The service was not significantly different from the voluntary and charitable activities in which women of similar social status had long engaged. Katherine Furse, who took the first VAD detachment to France, gave each member of her unit a poem before their departure:

And only the Master shall praise us, and only the Master
   shall blame.
And no one shall work for money, and no one shall work
   for fame,
But each for the joy of working, and each in his separate
   star,
Shall draw the thing as he sees it for the God of things as
   they are.[22]

'Of course I made awful mistakes,' the Scottish novelist Naomi
Mitchison wrote of her time as a VAD. 'I had never done real
manual household work; I had never used mops and polishes
and disinfectants. I was very willing but clumsy. I was told to
make tea but hadn't realised that tea must be made with boiling
water. All that had been left to the servants.' Quite unwittingly,
some of these women, being unaccustomed to employment,
underwent a metamorphosis. By their actions they contradicted
Victorian notions of female frailty. Some found fulfilment by
escaping the stifling predictability of middle-class existence.
Few were feminists; some had even opposed the extension of
suffrage, but they inadvertently contributed to the advancement
of women. They progressed along the road to emancipation,
largely because they had the means to realise their new-found
sense of freedom after the war. They could, after all, pay
working-class women to look after their homes and children
while they went out and conquered the world.[23]

The Great War has customarily been seen as a time of
progress for women because it broke down gender-based
barriers to employment. This undoubtedly happened. Yet
while women were striding forward, a conservative counter-
reaction was under way. Pay scales symbolically confirmed
women's inferiority. Separation allowances, as we have seen,
underlined their status as dependents of their husbands. Since
the allowances could be withdrawn on evidence of moral

delinquency, they confirmed the husband's ownership of his wife's body, with the state as trustee. This counter-revolution intensified after the armistice, when women came under intense pressure to leave wartime jobs. 'The idea that because the State called for women to help the nation, the State must continue to employ them is too absurd for sensible women to entertain,' argued the *Daily Graphic*. 'As for women formerly in domestic service, they at least should have no difficulty in finding vacancies.' Most women willingly surrendered their jobs to returning soldiers. As for those who refused to do so, the government used legislation, in particular the 1919 Restoration of Pre-War Practices Act, to force a return to the status quo. Various official studies proposed bans upon married women working, limits upon hours women could work, and prohibitions on women in trades deemed 'unsuitable'. While not all these ideas were implemented, what is striking is the revulsion against the changes war had wrought. 'The attitude of the public towards women,' commented the *Daily News* in March 1921, 'is more full of contempt and bitterness than has been the case since the suffragette outbreaks.' According to Ray Strachey, author of the 1928 study *The Cause*, 'public opinion assumed that all women could still be supported by men, and that if they went on working it was from some sort of deliberate wickedness'. Before the war a woman doing a man's job was considered an interesting anomaly. After the war she seemed a threat. Women became dangerous when they proved that they could do men's work.[24]

The Hills Committee, which reported on the issue of female employment, took the view that women 'must be safeguarded as home-maker for the nation'. For women, then, 'reconstruction' often meant a return to traditional family life, which militated against emancipation. Yet those most enthusiastic for a return to normality were often women. 'Why,' complained Winifred Holtby after the war, 'are women themselves often the first to repudiate the movements of the past hundred and fifty years, which have gained for them at least the foundations of political, economic, educational and moral equality?' Holtby (like many radical feminists) simply could not understand that women might actually enjoy the prosaic pleasures of motherhood. Employment outside the home has become a symbol of emancipation, but at the time it was seen as a necessary evil caused by the husband's inability to support his family – or the lack of a husband entirely. 'No decent man would allow his wife to work,' Isobel Pazzey, a former munitions worker at Woolwich, wrote to the *Daily Herald* in October 1919. 'And no decent woman would do it if she knew the harm she was doing to the widows and single girls who are looking for work. Put the married women out, send them home to clean their houses and look after the man they married and give a mother's care to their children. Give the single women and widows the work.' War work, monotonous, dangerous and often badly paid, hardly seemed liberating, especially if it made childcare more complicated. Thus for some women, freedom meant being able to stay home and look after the kids. This explains why the National Federation of Women Workers, the largest women's union, argued that married women should ideally not have to work. Behind the land-fit-for-heroes rhetoric lurked a rigidly patriarchal ideal: men would get jobs and women would retreat to their separate sphere and do what they did well. In fact, since that ideal was not fully achieved, quite a few married women were forced, out of necessity, into ill-paid, low-status jobs after the war.[25]

'Let us glorify, dignify and purify motherhood by every means in our power,' proclaimed John Burns, President of the Board of Trade. The TUC pushed for mothers' pensions, arguing that 'if we have got to have an A1 nation we must protect the mothers . . . the institution of pensions for mothers would go a long way towards checking the race suicide that is going on'. This sort of argument irked Holtby. 'Throughout

391

history,' she remarked, 'whenever society has tried to curtail the opportunities, interests and powers of women, it has done so in the sacred names of marriage and maternity'. That is undoubtedly true, but the maternalist ethic was not merely a male conspiracy to keep women shackled to the burdens of motherhood. Women, even more than men, wanted better provisions for their children. In any case, even though the motivations behind the reforms might have been suspect, there is no doubting the beneficial results. The provision of health visitors was dramatically improved and the benefits of breastfeeding were widely publicised. Some of the most enthusiastic supporters of these campaigns were feminists like Fawcett, Eleanor Rathbone, Selina Cooper and even Sylvia Pankhurst. During the war, the *Woman's Journal* published a cartoon showing a woman holding a baby and shouting 'Votes for Women'. A soldier nearby utters the common anti-suffrage argument that women don't deserve the vote because they 'can't bear arms'. The suffragist replies: 'No! Women bear armies.' In other words, women deserved the vote not because they could be like men, but because they were uniquely good at being women. Unfortunately, by raising motherhood to a level equivalent to soldiering, these women inadvertently played into the hands of those keen to restore Victorian notions of separate spheres.[26]

While maternalists promoted motherhood, sexologists promoted intercourse. The post-war sex reformer Magnus Hirschfield argued that the war had provided 'an opportunity for throwing off, for a while, all the irksome repressions which culture imposes and for satisfying temporarily all the repressed desires'. Walter Gallichan, in *The Poison of Prudery*, warned that 'many daughters of cold mothers die spinsters' – a rather insensitive remark at a time when war had killed off potential husbands. In a direct attack upon feminists and spinsters, Janet Chance advocated the banning of 'non-orgasmic' women from politics, fearing that they would spread their repressive ways throughout society. (One has to wonder how a test might have been administered.) In truth, advice to wives to set free their libidos was thinly disguised pressure upon them to serve the needs of their husbands. The campaigners wanted women to lie back and think of England. Contrary to the fantasies of Marwick, women did not win 'sexual liberty' during the war, nor did 'official opinion [come] very near to condoning any consolation which might be offered to war heroes briefly returned from the trenches'. Society still scorned women who sought satisfaction outside the bounds of propriety. According to the *Manchester Guardian*, there existed an 'unwritten law' that a man was 'held to be justified in killing his wife on obtaining proof, as to the sufficiency of which he is himself the judge, of her infidelity'. In mid 1915, the Newcastle Assizes heard the case of William Simpson, a soldier who cut the throat of his young son. His defence was provocation – his wife had 'not behaved properly during his absence at the front'. The jury found him guilty but recommended mercy.[27]

After fulfilling her duties as mother and sexual plaything, it is a wonder how women were expected to have any time for housework. Yet after the war, housekeeping was elevated to the status of a science or profession, albeit one that did not carry a salary. For the working-class woman, domestic service was promoted as useful training for home management. One (obviously male) 'expert' blamed industrial unrest on bad digestion brought on by poor cooking. 'Girls [leave] school knowing all about William the Conqueror in 1066, but very little about the method of preparing a first-class steak and kidney pudding.' Meanwhile, magazines like *Good Housekeeping* encouraged greater professionalism and creativity in the housewife, in so doing curbing the pursuit of interests outside the home and setting standards that many women could not possibly meet. Appliances that made cleaning easier could not keep pace with increasing standards of cleanliness. The germ was a cruel tyrant.[28]

Much can be learned from studying the heroes who emerge from an era of change. Vera Brittain has been elevated to sainthood; feminists and pacifists alike admire her *Testament of Youth* because it supposedly evokes both the futility of the war and the opportunities for women's emancipation that occurred during it. Yet a close reading of that book reveals a very different Brittain who subordinated her identity to that of the men around her, mainly her brother and Roland Leighton. As for recognising the futility of war, Brittain was closer to Brooke than to Sassoon, as her poem 'To My Brother' reveals:

Your battle-wounds are scars upon my heart,
    Received when in that grand and tragic 'show'
You played your part
    Two years ago,

And silver in the summer morning sun
    I see the symbol of your courage glow –
That Cross you won
    Two years ago.

Though now again you watch the shrapnel fly,
    And hear the guns that daily louder grow,
As in July
    Two years ago,

May you endure to lead the Last Advance
    And with your men pursue the flying foe
As once in France
    Two years ago.

Brittain's diaries reveal that she was an enthusiastic supporter of the war who, in contrast to her father (treated rather unfairly in the book), felt that her brother must do his duty and enlist.

Nor is her sense of sisterhood all that striking. Hers was an individual quest; her writings reveal little cognisance of the plight of women, especially working-class women. She was one of the foremost marketers of the Lost Generation myth, yet she apparently failed to understand its implications for women. The myth reinforces women's inferiority and helplessness by attributing catastrophic consequences to the loss of a small group of men. In 'This Generation of Men' (1934), Brittain warned that society was becoming increasingly matriarchal because men who survived the war were poor physical specimens with weak wills who lacked vitality and dynamism. The consecration of Brittain has meant that we have willingly accepted her misguided conception of the world in which she lived, a world where naive idealism, chivalric war, the end of innocence and romantic masculine heroes figure prominently.[29]

Monica Cosens, author of *Lloyd George's Munitions Girls*, ended her book by unconsciously demonstrating how little the war had done to change attitudes to class and gender.

And last of all the Nation – what will it think of Miss Tommy Atkins when the War is over, and it has the time to stand still, to look back and think how these light-hearted, gay, simple-minded children – for that is what they are – have borne the heat of battle, how they fought smiling all the time, no matter if the day was hard and long?

Then it will be the turn of the country to shake them by the hand and echo the words spoken by Mr Tommy Atkins:

'It's great what you have done!'

In fact, feelings of gratitude quickly diminished, though condescending attitudes did not. Anecdotal as the Cosens quotation might be, it is nevertheless a great deal more appropriate than Brittain's retrospective impressions of a world changed beyond recognition. Subsequent generations have admired Brittain because she seems to represent a metaphoric bridge across the deluge. Both a victim and a survivor of the war, she provides a link between the age of innocence and the modern age, in so doing confirming that the Great War was a watershed of the twentieth century. Yet both the age of innocence and the concept of modernism are arbitrary constructs, relevant to high culture but meaningless to real life. Brittain's turbulent world existed only in her mind and in the minds of those unrepresentative elites to whom far too much attention has been given when judging this war. The real world was much more prosaic and boringly stable. War was tragic, in some cases catastrophic. But for most people it was an extraordinary event of limited duration which, as much as it brought change, also inspired a desire to reconstruct along traditional lines. If war is the locomotive of history, the rolling stock in this case was typically British: slow, outmoded, and prone to delay and cancellation.[30]

Chapter 16

The Triumph of the Hard-Faced Men

'And now what?' all of Britain asked. On the day after the armistice, the *Manchester Guardian* remarked:

> By the hundred thousand, young men have died for the hope of a better world. They have opened for us the way. If, as a people, we can be wise and tolerant and just in peace as we have been resolute in war, we shall build them the memorial that they have earned in the form of a world set free from military force, national tyrannies and class oppressions, for the pursuit of a wider justice in the spirit of a deeper and more human religion.

Almost everyone in Britain agreed. There was, however, little consensus on how to realise this New Jerusalem.[1]

After the election of December 1918, Stanley Baldwin candidly described the new House of Commons as 'a lot of hard-faced men who look as if they had done very well out of the war'. That was an accurate description of the new political order, particularly of the Conservative Party Baldwin would eventually lead. Yet that new order was 'new' only in the sense that it contained a significant number of men who had entered

397

the Commons for the first time in 1918. The political instincts of the hard-faced men were decidedly traditional. They were determined to limit the changes war had brought and were remarkably successful at doing so. By their success, they rendered Britain ill-equipped to thrive in a decidedly different post-war world.[2]

The strength of conservatism in British politics can be measured by the fact that the political complexion hardly changed after the 1918 Representation of the People Act expanded the electorate from 8 million to 21 million. That Act will forever be synonymous with votes for women. Yet female enfranchisement was just a clause in an act dealing primarily with male suffrage. Existing residency requirements (at least one year in the same dwelling) had disenfranchised many soldiers and industrial workers. For obvious reasons this injustice had to be addressed. The residency requirement was therefore reduced to six months, with the prospective voter no longer required to stay in one dwelling, rather only in the same general area. The Act also enfranchised a group that made a special contribution to the war, namely men aged 19 or 20 on active service. Otherwise, the voting age for men remained 21. Displaying conspicuous pique, Parliament withheld the vote from all conscientious objectors for five years, unless they could prove that they had performed work of national importance. Men on poor relief were no longer disenfranchised. Plural voting, by which an elector could vote in the constituencies of his residence, his university and his place of business, was reduced to two constituencies only.

The Tories enthusiastically supported the Act on the grounds that, since some reform was inevitable, it made sense to be associated with it. They did not want enfranchisement to become an electoral issue, exploited by a demagogue like Lloyd George. In any case, the party no longer had reason to fear mass democracy. The big change had come in 1884, the last time suffrage was determined strictly along class lines. Relaxing registration requirements would first give the vote to a layer of middle-class natural Liberal supporters; relaxing them further would bring in a large contingent of workers, many of whom would actually be inclined to vote Conservative.

In February 1918, by a majority of 385 to 55, the Commons extended the franchise to women over 30 who were ratepayers or were married to a ratepayer. At first glance this seems an enthusiastic recognition of the wartime contribution of women. That is certainly the way subsequent generations have judged it. In fact, the war had little to do with hastening women's suffrage. The argument for female enfranchisement had essentially been won before 1914; all that was required were terms acceptable to the Commons. Of the 194 MPs who voted in both the 1911 and 1917 divisions on the issue, 18 had moved in favour and 4 against, a net shift of a mere 14. Success came not as a consequence of war-inspired good feelings towards women, but because the terms of the reform were more acceptable than those proposed in 1911. The 1918 reform was tolerable precisely because it was limited. The age, property and marriage restrictions addressed fears that women would become a majority of the electorate, fears made more acute because of the carnage on the Western Front. (A total of 8,479,156 women were enfranchised, as against 12,913,166 men; or almost exactly four women for every six men.) The women who had made a significant contribution to the war effort were, for the most part, barred by the age requirement. It would take another ten years before women were given the vote on equal terms with men. Those enfranchised in 1918 were acceptable essentially because they seemed stable and unaffected by war's disruption. In other words, the typical female voter would be a mature wife and mother primarily concerned with the preservation of her home life. She would not, it was presumed, be interested in a career, nor in feminist causes. Tories were further mollified by the fact that women tended to be more conservative than their male counterparts, since they were less likely to be influenced by trade unionism. In this sense, the enfranchised women would act as a conservative counterweight to the potentially more radical men who had been given the vote.[3]

Most suffrage campaigners welcomed the measure despite its limitations. Realising that antagonism between the sexes would increase with the post-war competition for jobs, Fawcett concluded that women were lucky to get what they did. She in fact supported the householder stipulation:

> There was some outcry against this on the part of ardent suffragists as being derogatory to the independence of women. While understanding this objection, I did not share it; I felt, on the contrary, that it marked an important advance in that it recognised in a practical political form a universally accepted and most valuable social fact – namely the partnership of the wife and mother in the home.

Thus the hour of woman's emancipation was something of an anticlimax. Had women been granted the vote before August 1914, militant campaigners could have claimed a monumental victory. Direct action would have been vindicated. Instead, the franchise was extended in a limited fashion during the war, at a time when suffragists were quiet, and as part of a bill primarily concerned with male enfranchisement. Women had been rewarded for behaving.[4]

Granting votes to women did not highlight women's issues in politics. In subsequent elections, women voted rather like men; gender had little influence upon political allegiance. The absence of a women's party (an attempt by Christabel Pankhurst to form one failed miserably) demonstrates that agreement on 'women's issues' was impossible. During the interwar period those women who were interested in politics tended to join the women's sections of established parties, such as the Women's Labour League and the Primrose League. This tended to limit their influence upon the greater party. Female enfranchisement thus reinforced the party machines after 1918, without fundamentally altering the nature of politics and the issues considered important.

The expanded electorate first exercised its muscle at the general election on 14 December 1918 – a rather schizophrenic contest. At first, politicians stressed reconstruction and magnanimous victory. 'We must not allow any sense of revenge, any spirit of greed, any grasping desire, to over-ride the fundamental principles of righteousness,' argued Lloyd George on 12 November. The ideal of 'a fit land for heroes to live in' harmonised with these noble aims. On the other hand, the nation had for four years been whipped into a state of apoplectic fury. Those passions would not cool quickly. The press and many politicians preferred malice to magnanimity. 'Hang the Kaiser!' shouted the *Daily Mail*, while exhorting readers to 'Refuse to vote for any Member of Parliament who will not give a definite pledge that he will stand for the total eradication of German influence from our country.' The government eventually surrendered to the monster it had fathered. Eric Geddes signalled the new zeitgeist when he promised that the government would 'squeeze the German lemon till the pips squeak'. As it turned out, hatred cost less than compassion. Xenophobic fury conveniently distracted the electorate's attention away from noble (and expensive) ideals of peace and reconstruction. Churchill wrote in retrospect that the election 'woefully cheapened' Britain – rich comment from the man who built his campaign in Dundee around hysterical references to the Bolshevik menace.[5]

Though the coalition was maintained after the armistice, the election was, in truth, a massive victory for the Conservative Party and the ideals it symbolised. Liberals outside the coalition managed just 28 seats, Labour 63, while the Conservatives won 348. The war had turned the country rightward. Wartime bellicosity harmonised well with the Conservative temper. Though Lloyd George remained Prime Minister of a supposedly national coalition, his government was an electoral abomination that would not survive the first energetic attempt by Conservatives to claim what was theirs.

The election was a reflection of the previous four years and also a harbinger of what was to come. The three-party pattern of British politics, with Conservatives dominant, Labour ambitious and Liberals inconsequential, had been established. It would take a few elections before contemporaries (especially Liberals) accepted this pattern as inevitable, but aside from a few anomalies, it would continue until the present day. Labour would never achieve a sufficiently broad appeal to kill off the Liberals completely, yet that is what it needed in order to thrive. The beneficiary of this untidy arrangement was the Conservative Party, which would profit immensely from a split opposition.[6]

It is commonly assumed that the Great War destroyed liberalism. The ideals of individual liberty were supposedly smashed by the exigencies of war, in particular by the ever-expanding state. While that is true to an extent, the real picture is more complicated. Liberalism did not die. The radical variety, espoused by John Maynard Keynes and William Beveridge, is one of the great success stories of twentieth-century Britain. Instead, it was the Liberal Party, not liberalism, which was crippled. The party never recovered from the divisions exposed by war. Some Liberals found wartime belligerence (especially that of their one-time hero Lloyd George) abhorrent. For others, alienation pre-dated the war – they were agonised by the conundrum that the further extension of liberty required state intervention, which by definition restricted individual liberty. Still others felt too strongly about pacifism, free trade, conscription or other favourite causes to compromise their principles. Stated simply, the war provided too many opportunities for inflexible Liberals to draw a line in the sand. Doctrinal differences were exacerbated by personal rivalries that endured long after the armistice. Thus, the party never capitalised on the return to normality after 1918; old wounds never healed.

Watching Liberals fight was entertaining, but it did not encourage confidence among the voters. They deserted the party in droves. One-time Whigs moved towards the Tories, while social democrats opted for Labour. A rump of hard-core ideologues, with free trade as their battle cry, remained loyal. As a result, the one party genuinely interested in the individual and ideologically committed to social mobility was rendered impotent. Though Labour would adopt many of the causes of the Liberal Party, individualism was not one of them. Labour's *raison d'être* was the advancement of the working-class, an ideal that was by definition divisive.

The British political system accommodated the working-class in a manner unknown before the war. The precarious manpower situation that arose in 1915 had forced the government to deal with trade union representatives on a more equal footing, a change symbolically demonstrated by the inclusion of Labour members in the War Cabinet. This change survived the war, even though mass unemployment eventually emasculated workers. Capital and labour cooperated in constructing mechanisms for the accommodation of their competing interests, at the expense of the nation as a whole. The historian Elie Halevy, who attended the National Industrial Conference (NIC) in February 1919, inadvertently recognised this development. The Conference, he discovered, 'far from denying the idea of class struggle, is organised to permit the struggle to go on, in forms as legal and, so to speak, as "peaceable" as they can be . . . We shall see the class struggle, acclimatised on English soil, adapting itself to the traditional party system.' The NIC was intended to establish consensus between capital and labour, a very different thing from the accommodation that eventually transpired. Though it failed, Halevy's prediction was essentially accurate: class conflict was institutionalised. During the war, Whitley councils provided a harbinger of this development. The councils grew out of the government's desire to establish joint committees of employers and workers that would meet regularly to discuss wages and conditions, in order to minimise strife and eventually establish a national bargaining system. In a similar fashion, the 1919 Restoration of Pre-War Practices Act was an enticement to the main body of workers to join the political mainstream. Radical firebrands complained vociferously of a sell-out, but they were marginalised when the government proved willing to bargain. This trend of accommodation and consolidation continued during the interwar period with national pay awards, collective bargaining and the creation of corporatist behemoths like the Trades Union Congress (TUC) and the Federation (later Confederation) of British Industries.[7]

The Labour Party was hereafter accepted, by both labour and capital, as a legitimate mechanism for working-class expression. As John Hill of the Boilermakers told the TUC in 1917, 'the prejudice of Trade Unionists against politics has hitherto held us back . . . but the events of the last three years have taken the scales from our eyes'. The way forward, it seemed, was a 'strong and intelligent Trade Unionism linked with our political arm, the Labour Party'. The change is illustrated by the inclusion of Clause Four – calling for the common ownership of the means of production, distribution and exchange – in the 1918 Labour Party constitution. On the surface this seems the first salvo in a new class war, but in fact, the clause was a mere symbol. This is revealed in the party's 1918 manifesto, *Labour and the New Social Order*, essentially a plan to tailor capitalism to the needs of the workers. Clause Four expressed the new-found solidarity of the working-class, but the workers' potentially volatile power was restrained by the limiting context of a party committed to the status quo. The clause, intentionally imprecise, was a cheque not intended to be cashed; its importance lay in its ability to inspire, not as a plan destined for implementation. By this means, true socialists were marginalised. They would still be welcome in the party (as long as they behaved), but the thrust of party policy would be towards progressive capitalism. Instead of attempting to destroy capitalism, the party would try to tame it with social welfare reforms. Meanwhile, Labour would give a symbolic nod to socialism once a year when party hacks pretended to sing 'The Internationale' at conferences in Blackpool and Brighton.[8]

After 1918, Labour would never be as formidable an opponent for the Tories as the Liberals had been before 1914. The Great War helped Labour establish itself as a party, but its post-war popularity was never particularly impressive. Its electoral support had increased by nearly two million since 1906, but that is mainly because more constituencies were contested. When it is considered that the electorate had more than doubled and trade union membership had increased during the war from 4 million to 6.5 million, Labour's attractiveness to working-class voters hardly seems striking. During the interwar period 60 per cent of working-class voters consistently refused to support the party.[9]

Labour after 1918 drew its support from the same source it had begun to tap before 1914, namely older skilled workers from the industrial areas of the north, Wales and Scotland, most of whom were already organised into trade unions. With the decline of the Liberal Party and the rise in popularity of trade unions, the voters in these areas grew even more inclined to vote Labour. In contrast, the party, despite its moderation, was conspicuously unsuccessful in attracting former Liberal voters in the suburbs who were disinclined to interpret politics in class terms. Thus, at the hour of its emergence, Labour in its cloth cap already looked old-fashioned.

The chief beneficiary of mass democracy was ironically the party most inclined to elitism. The new voters, both young males and women, leaned toward the Conservatives and would continue to do so for the rest of the century and beyond. It is perhaps understandable that newly enfranchised middle-class voters should behave in this way, but something different might be expected from those of working-class stock. For the workers, however, consciousness was not automatically translated into support for Labour. Competing loyalties pulled them in various political directions, rendering the working-class voter a very fickle animal.

The feminist movement was another casualty of the 1918 Act. Once the vote was granted, female activists went their separate ways. At the risk of oversimplification, women who remained active in gender politics came in two types. The first, concerned about sexual equality, campaigned for legal reform, equal access, equal pay, the removal of the marriage bar to employment, liberalisation of divorce laws, further electoral reform (the removal of the age bar) and the like. The second type consisted of women who still believed in separate spheres. They campaigned for reforms to make the home more comfortable, safe and secure, and to enhance motherhood.

This dichotomy was reflected in the split that divided the National Union of Societies for Equal Citizenship (NUSEC), the successor to the NUWSS. NUSEC was originally established to press for 'all other reforms, economic, legislative and social as are necessary to secure a real equality of liberties, status and opportunities between men and women'. Yet its leader, Eleanor Rathbone, felt that the 1918 Act had rendered women 'virtually free'. 'We can stop looking at all our problems through men's eyes and discussing them in men's phraseology,' she argued. 'We can demand what we want for women, not because it is what men have got, but because it is what women need to fulfil the potentialities of their own natures and to adjust themselves to the circumstances of their own lives.' She specifically sought to enhance 'the occupation of motherhood – in which most women are at some time or another engaged and which no man . . . is capable of performing'. As for employment outside the home, she felt that 'Women working are only birds of passage in their trades. Marriage and the bearing and rearing of children are their permanent occupations.' To old feminists this seemed a regressive step that would breathe new life into the notion of separate spheres.[10]

The showdown within NUSEC came in March 1927 over the issue of legislation designed to protect women in the workplace. Traditional feminists rejected laws of this sort on the grounds that they would provide employers with an excuse not to hire women. They instead proposed a motion that 'legislation for the protection of workers should be based not upon sex, but upon the nature of the occupation'. Protective legislation, Winifred Holtby maintained, 'perpetuates the notion that [women] are not quite persons; that they are not able to look after themselves; to secure their own interests, to judge whether they are fit or unfit to continue employment after marriage, to enter certain trades, or to assume equal responsibility with men in the state. It fosters the popular fallacy that women are the weaker sex, physically and mentally.' Rathbone vehemently disagreed. When the issue was put to a vote, she won by 81 votes to 80. By the narrowest of margins, the conference had essentially given its blessing to any measures designed to discriminate against women in employment. Shortly afterwards, 11 members of the executive resigned, arguing that the decision was 'a betrayal of the women's movement'. Old feminists, by standing still while the rest of Britain moved backwards, found themselves uncomfortably ahead of their time.[11]

*

It fell to the government elected in December 1918 to carry out the reconstruction of British society. During the latter part of the war, discussions of reconstruction focused more on national security than on social improvement. Given the inconclusive fighting on the Western Front, it was generally assumed that a complete military defeat of Germany would be impossible. Since an armistice would leave Germany economically strong, little advantage would come Britain's way and the point of the costly struggle might be called into question. The Allies therefore began formulating plans for how to carry on the war by other means. Cooperation in protecting import and export markets, and supplies of essential raw materials, was discussed, even to the extent of continuing the blockade against Germany. The Paris Economic Resolutions, agreed between the Allies in March 1916, explored these possibilities. Then, during the last year of the war, an even more dismal scenario began to plague British planners. Britain, they feared, would suffer profound turmoil arising from the problems of reintegrating a demobilised army and redundant munitions workers into a peacetime economy ill-equipped to accommodate them. Scarcity of essential commodities, combined with severe economic depression and labour unrest, would create an explosive, potentially revolutionary, situation.[12]

These disaster scenarios shaped the government's planning for the post-war world. Reconstruction was seen primarily in terms of stealing a march on Germany while she lay wounded. This thinking echoed the 'Business as Usual' strategy of 1914; in other words, since competition with Germany on even terms was always difficult, Britain needed to exploit fortuitous opportunities that might arise when Germany was vulnerable. It was further anticipated that in order to take advantage of these opportunities, the government would have to take an active role in directing the economy. Reconstruction would not, therefore, permit an immediate return to laissez-faire economics. Tariffs, cartels and the like would protect British producers. The more dire the scenario, the more comprehensive government intervention would need to be. Under the worst case outlined above, the government anticipated not only trade restrictions, but also constraints upon labour and upon the distribution of goods and services. Wartime rationing and controls would be continued and possibly extended. Sir Edward Carson warned that 'restrictions hardly less drastic' than those already in force would be essential. 'In no other way can the country hope to escape from the perils of hunger, unemployment, social disorganisation, industrial paralysis, and financial chaos'. While the prospect of continued state intervention annoyed businessmen and industrialists, they accepted that it might be a necessary evil in the short term to defend against a rampaging German industrial oligarchy.[13]

All of these discussions were rendered moot by the manner of Germany's defeat. To the great surprise of the British government, her army was beaten, her economy collapsed and her government ruined. The evidence suggested that the post-war world was Britain's oyster. The disaster scenarios suddenly seemed irrelevant and focus instead shifted to social reform – in particular the need to reward those who had made sacrifices during the war. The most prominent advocates of this sort of reconstruction were Edwin Montagu and Christopher Addison, not to mention Lloyd George. The rhetoric was certainly impressive: enthusiasts boasted that reconstruction would be 'not so much a question of rebuilding society as it was before the war, but of moulding a better world out of the social and economic conditions which have come into being during the war'. Yet while those enthusiasts earnestly formulated plans, the government itself moved steadily to the right – away from the ideals implied by Liberal reconstruction.[14]

The great problem with reconstruction was that it meant

different things to different people. To the soldiers it meant reward: a fit land for heroes to live in. To the workers it meant capitalising upon wartime gains. They hoped that their enhanced status could be used to make jobs safer, more secure, with pay and conditions improved. In addition, some hoped that wartime amalgamation of industries like coal would proceed logically toward nationalisation. On the other hand, to radical Liberals within the coalition, and indeed to Lloyd George, reconstruction meant sustaining the mood of cooperation that had supposedly existed during the war. They envisaged a brave new world of consensus and collaboration. Conflict would disappear and with it the rigidity of class distinctions. Thus, within Addison's Ministry of Reconstruction, social reform came to mean not only an amelioration of poverty, but also the development of mechanisms designed to ease conflict. The King's Speech opening the first post-war Parliament set forth this agenda:

> since the outbreak of the war every party and every class have worked and fought together for a great ideal . . . we must continue to manifest the same spirit. We must stop at no sacrifice of interest or prejudice to stamp out unmerited poverty, to diminish unemployment and mitigate its sufferings, to provide decent homes, to improve the nation's health and to raise the standard of well-being throughout the country.

Lloyd George thought that the war had rendered class conflict old-fashioned. The concept of the common good had emerged and, after the war, would remain a beacon for politicians and voters alike. To the economist Arthur Shadwell, this sentiment seemed hopelessly naive: 'The war was generally expected to lead to a sort of Utopia, in which the lion would lay down with the lamb . . . There was no substance in this sanguine vision; it was simply a nebulous hope, born of war excitement and fed by politicians' phrases ... such as the nebulous word "reconstruction". I can remember no such prolific begetter of nonsense as this idea of "reconstruction".' Like Shadwell, the prominent trade unionist Ernest Bevin saw through the misty sentimentality, denying that any profound change in the relationship between labour and management had occurred. He predicted that with the return to a more competitive peacetime economy, workers would need to struggle long and hard to maintain their rights. He therefore wanted reconstruction to be about concrete reforms rather than esoteric ideals.[15]

Conservatives viewed reconstruction as a return to pre-1914 normality. Their vision was clouded by romanticised images of the past: a world where workers were content and obedient, where business was conducted free of government interference and where profits were not prey to voracious tax collectors. They argued, with some justification, that the war had been about international issues, not domestic ones; Britain had fought to preserve and protect, not to change. While they were clever enough not to attack ideals of a land fit for heroes, Tories did cast doubt upon the capacity of Britain to afford those ideals. Progressive reforms, they advised, would have to wait until the stabilisation of Britain's economy and the re-establishment of trade. Groups like the Anti-Waste League warned that a rapacious and uncontrollable 'spendocrat' bureaucracy would destroy fragile prosperity. Dire scenarios of big government running rampant struck a popular chord even among those who supported humanitarian goals. Thus, while the workers wanted the benefits of social reform, they were not so enthusiastic about the large and intrusive government that this implied. A Ministry of Labour official complained as early as 1918 that 'Everybody – employers and workers alike – are saying they don't want the State to act, they want the State to keep out and let them handle their own problems.'[16]

Fears of big government and high taxes eventually overwhelmed honest efforts at reconstruction. In a seminal article published in 1943, R. H. Tawney explained that reconstruction faltered because the instinct to de-control overwhelmed amorphous and disparate desires to create a better world. Governmental controls were easily abolished because intervention had always been ad hoc and temporary. During the war, 'a collectivism was established which was entirely doctrineless. The most extensive and intricate scheme of state intervention in economic life which the country had seen was brought into existence, without the merits or demerits of state intervention being even discussed.' State intervention contradicted Britain's instincts; returning to the status quo was therefore easy and natural. 'Once the war was over, what had been a source of strength became a weakness,' Tawney argued.

> War collectivism had not been accompanied by any intellectual conversion on the subject of the proper relations between the state and economic life, while it did not last long enough to change social habits. With the passing, therefore, of the crisis that occasioned it, it was exposed to the attack of the same interests and ideas as, but for the war, would have prevented its establishment.

The Acts that had established the big wartime ministries like those of food and munitions all had specific deadlines for disbandment, usually one year after the cessation of hostilities. Rolling back the state was therefore a passive action that merely required letting deadlines run.[17]

The government had two choices: it could manage the post-war recovery by continuing and perhaps extending controls, or it could let an inflationary boom set the pace and determine the character of reconstruction. Since powerful capitalists demanded their freedom and workers (particularly those marooned in a now redundant army) were impatient to return to old jobs and old patterns of spending, the second option seemed both attractive and inevitable, thus rendering the first option not really an option at all. The advocates of state control had a tough time demonstrating its continued necessity in what seemed a glorious time of plenty.

Logic suggested that the more profound Germany's defeat, the more promising Britain's post-war economic fortunes would be. The immediate aftermath of war seemed to bear out this assumption. Consumer demand, held in check for over four years, burst forth, producing an insatiable hunger for British goods and, consequently, healthy industrial employment. But in its overwhelming desire to get the economy moving again, government threw caution to the wind. Too much faith was invested in the idea that wartime domestic harmony would inspire capital and labour to cooperate in the construction of a better world. In fact, left alone, labour and capital acted like two pythons trying to swallow one another: the workers demanded rewards which the system was not strong enough to provide, and industrialists engaged in feverish speculation, seriously jeopardising the fragile boom. The government stood idly by, refusing to employ the fiscal mechanisms at its disposal to encourage restraint and to force adversaries to work together in the interests of economic stability.[18]

Having never encountered total war, the government had no idea how to end it. Lloyd George felt that the wartime pattern of spending would need to continue in the medium term. 'I think you have to consider this year [1919] as really almost a war condition year,' he told his Chancellor Austen Chamberlain, who was more inclined to caution. Eric Geddes, agreeing with Lloyd George, warned the Chancellor about the dangers of abruptly cutting spending: 'You must be prepared to spend money on after-the-war problems as you did the during-the-war problems. That must be found, and added to our war-debt if necessary. It is the period of reconstruction, and money has to be spent generously, and on those [social welfare] schemes. If we get over that period I think the trade of the country will revive.' Whether the government spent too little or too much is probably less important than the fact that it lacked a clear sense of what was happening and what to do. When the boom gave way to inflation, as all booms do, the government first reacted with prevarication, then with panic. Boom quickly turned into bust. Unemployment, which stood at just 3.1 per cent in late 1920, rocketed to 13.5 per cent the following year. It would take another war before the number of unemployed again dropped below one million.[19]

The sudden recession seemed to justify the fears of those who had urged restraint. Reconstruction appeared unaffordable – at the very time when it was most essential. Hysterical rantings about squandermania in the Northcliffe and Rothermere press, pressure from the Anti-Waste League, by-election defeats in safe coalition seats and demands from within the government for tax reductions convinced Lloyd George to ask Geddes to set up a committee to carry out sweeping budgetary cuts – the 'Geddes axe'. Against this onslaught, embattled radicals were unable to provide a coherent defence of social welfare programmes. Geddes proposed economies of £87 million, thus driving a bulldozer through the already shaky reconstruction programme. The cuts included a £24 million reduction in social spending, of which £18 million would come from the education budget. Behind the committee's recommendations there lurked something more fundamental than fiscal prudence. The role of the state was itself coming under attack. Intervention might have been necessary in war, but it seemed inappropriate, even dangerous, in peacetime. The economy, it was thought, would recover best by itself. Thus the government responded to recession by taking refuge in orthodox economics, ignoring the fact that these were unorthodox times. Ministers remained confident that producers would on their own lead the country back to abundance, through the gospel of the free market. Government control had become, in the words of one minister, 'a thoroughly abominable thing'. Normal practices would restore normality.[20]

Intervention would not have enabled the government to avoid the slump, which was a worldwide phenomenon. Yet whether one trusts in state intervention or not, it is impossible to deny that hasty de-control was madness. The war had resulted in comprehensive changes in the British economy. In November 1918, factories were operating at full capacity in controlled markets producing goods that had little peacetime utility. Only the foolishly optimistic could believe that producers would be able suddenly to shift to domestic production and adjust smoothly to the return of unbridled competition, without government help. British producers were blithely set loose on a world economy ravaged by war. In no time at all they were mown down by the machine guns of reckless competition or left to drown in shellholes of stagnation. Or, to borrow Tawney's metaphor: 'The patient required to be nursed through a long period of convalescence, and could not be expected, even at the end of this, to lead the same life as before the operation. [The government] thought it sufficient, having removed his bandages, to exhort him to take up his bed and walk.' As a result of wartime reform, the government still retained the power to control labour, prices, distribution and the money markets. Deploying these tools might have alleviated the worst ravages of depression. Unfortunately, the government had lost the will to act.[21]

Lloyd George might have been right. The war might indeed have sown the seeds of post-war consensus. Those seeds, however, needed fertile soil in which to germinate. Reconstruction might have created the conditions for estab-lishing a cooperative spirit in Britain and avoiding the futility of class conflict. It might have weaned both workers and industrialists from their purely sectional interests and encouraged them to think in national terms. Unfortunately, the Geddes axe decapitated consensus. The government's sudden insistence upon fiscal prudence cleaved the nation along class lines. The real problem with reconstruction lay in its ideals. The primary aim was social harmony, not an efficient society. As we saw in the previous chapter, housing and education reforms were not designed to destroy class barriers but rather to make them more tolerable. When a nation is unhealthy, poorly housed and badly educated, it is not just a tragedy; it is also a desecration, since precious talents are wasted.

As an ameliorative, reconstruction was a success. Despite the ravages of the Geddes axe, sufficient social welfare provision survived to cushion the workers from the worst ravages of the slump. Thus it could be argued that Britain avoided the turmoil that occurred on the Continent. Nevertheless, as was the case throughout the twentieth century, social programmes provided relief for society's dispossessed, but did not address the core problems of long-term decline. Politicians lacked either the imagination or the courage to face up to that predicament. In 1917, Lloyd George told a delegation of labour leaders that 'the whole state of society is more or less molten and you can stamp upon that molten mass almost anything so long as you do it with firmness and determination'. That was true, but he failed to act upon his own rhetoric.[22]

Argument rages about the war's long-term effect upon the British economy. Some historians believe that it magnified already inevitable trends, others insist that definite shifts in economic direction are discernible. Those who favour the second view disagree on the balance of good changes versus bad. There were undoubtedly some positive effects. Necessity forced Britain to develop more efficient industrial techniques, which had productive peacetime applications. For instance, dyestuff production (in which Germany had enjoyed a near monopoly) received massive stimulation, rendering Britain much more competitive after the war. Likewise, the aircraft, motor, chemical and food preservation industries, to name but a few, made significant progress.

On the debit side, the coal industry suffered badly from the loss of skilled labour and the exhaustion of valuable seams but more importantly from the collapse of the world market for British coal after the war. The same could be said for shipbuilding and cotton. Britain's competitors absorbed secure markets in Asia and South America while she was preoccupied with war. These markets were never completely recovered. One suspects, however, that this decline was inevitable and was merely hastened by war. Even more profound was the change in Britain's financial position. She entered the war a creditor nation and exited a debtor. Her supreme position at the top of the world financial markets was surrendered permanently to the United States. In order to pay for the necessities of war and to supply these to her allies, Britain had to sell 25 per cent of her overseas foreign investments. She also borrowed at a prodigious rate. Loans of more than £1,350 million accumulated, over £1,000 million from the United States. A greater amount (£1,750 million) was loaned to allies, but afterwards Britain was more faithful in her repayments than her debtors were in theirs. Money loaned to Russia, for instance, was never recovered.[23]

From a position of pre-eminence before 1914, Britain went into persistent decline after the war. The decline should not be confused with the slump – the latter was inevitable and finite, the former avoidable and prolonged. Nor can the decline be blamed on the unfortunate effects of war, since countries more ravaged by the conflict subsequently performed much better. In fact, Britain's decline began well before the Great War, which seems to underline the folly of attempting a return to pre-war practices. Before 1914, Britain's export trade was still concentrated on patterns and products first developed in the eighteenth and nineteenth centuries. The Empire had been bad for business. Instead of embracing competitive continental markets, Britain took refuge in protected imperial trade. As a result, when the Empire ceased to be sustaining, she found herself ill-equipped to compete with her continental rivals. Britain's once great supremacy had encouraged complacency and conservatism. After the war, the long-delayed readjustment of the economy suddenly became urgent, yet politicians and businessmen lacked the humility necessary to learn from their mistakes.

No wonder, then, that the essential readjustment to a fundamentally different world was not embraced with the energy and commitment required. After 1918, the British were remarkably successful at recreating pre-war society. Social and political change was absorbed or contained. The quality of life improved, but class stratification remained solid. One of the most important responsibilities of government is to foster social mobility, yet in this area the government failed miserably. Cautious politicians argued that ambitious housing, health and education programmes jeopardised economic recovery. Yet in conditions of economic decline, Britain could hardly afford not to address the problems of social stasis and national inefficiency. The pre-1914 working-class, in its deference, lack of imagination, fatalism and lack of ambition was ideally suited to the type of war Britain had been called upon to fight. But recovery in the harsh conditions that prevailed after 1918 required a wholly different society in which a dynamic, educated and ambitious workforce was free to pursue its full potential. During discussion of Geddes's proposals for education cuts, Lloyd George had the audacity to argue that 'brighter children would learn as readily and as quickly in a class of seventy as they would in a much smaller class'. That sort of complacency was costly; Britain could no longer afford to allow skills to go untapped because of the dead weight of class stratification. Stability and social harmony were expensive luxuries bought at the cost of growth and prosperity.[24]

It would be easy to blame the Conservative Party for the stagnation that prevailed after 1918. After all, the period of sustained decline was also one of extraordinary domination by the Tories. Yet governments are not alien beings that appear from nowhere and inflict their will upon a defenceless people. Britain is a democracy. If her people have at times failed to act democratically or in their own best interests, that is their fault. There is remarkable similarity between the way the country supported the war from 1914 to 1918 and the way it supported conservative politics afterwards. Similar emotions seem at play. Nationalism, traditionalism and an enduring sense of cultural superiority saw the British through the war and afterwards encouraged acquiescence in their own decline.

Chapter 17

We Shall Remember

> They shall grow not old, as we that are left grow old;
> Age shall not weary them, nor the years condemn.
> At the going down of the sun and in the morning
> We will remember them.[1]

But how should we remember them? 'Though we cannot forget the dead, we must not remember them at the expense of the living,' warned Vera Brittain. She demonstrated better than most just how difficult it was to follow that advice. After the armistice came a battle over memory as bitter as the war itself. The way the war and its victims have been remembered has been shaped by the strident political battles that have dominated British politics over the last century. The past has been formed by the present.[2]

Mourning is supposed to enable closure. Yet never before had the task of coming to terms with devastation been so huge. As a result, in 1918 Britain faced an immediate problem of what to do with the dead – how to give their sacrifice appropriate recognition. The ritual surrounding the burial of fallen soldiers had to be devised anew, to suit this extraordinary war. In the Napoleonic War, the dead were often burned or buried in mass graves to prevent the spread of disease. Instead of being collected together in their own cemeteries, they were honoured (if at all) with a monument or a plaque in a regimental church. With the advent of mass industrialised war, specifically military cemeteries began to appear. It was only after the Great War that these cemeteries gave separate recognition to each individual soldier. The cemeteries impose individual identity upon a vast, depersonalised war – an act of assertion against the machine. According to psychologists who specialise in bereavement, publicly naming the dead is important to the process of recovery.[3]

Early in the war, the dead were usually buried near where they fell, the graves marked with temporary wooden crosses. If the ground was fought over for a considerable time, these could be destroyed and the bodies themselves disinterred. In 1916, it was decided that since it was not practical to bring all bodies home for burial, it was only fair that none should come home. They were therefore disinterred from temporary graves and placed in graveyards located close to where battles had taken place. In 1917, in keeping with the meticulous organisation of huge offensives, long trenches were dug beforehand and filled as the fighting progressed. The graves were still marked with wooden crosses, each labelled with a metal strip. Germans and British, often buried side by side in the temporary graves, were eventually removed to separate cemeteries. The wooden crosses were shipped home, and sometimes buried in churchyards, acquiring, for the bereaved, the status of religious relics.[4]

British cemeteries were deeded in perpetuity to the United Kingdom. Care of around 500 graveyards was given to the Imperial War Graves Commission in 1921. By that time, agreement had been reached upon a uniform pattern. In most there is a Stone of Remembrance with the inscription 'Their name liveth for evermore', taken from Ecclesiasticus and suggested by Kipling. Often a small chapel nearby holds a list of those buried in the cemetery and a symbol of the resurrection. The uniform gravestones are arrayed in neat, evenly spaced rows, suggesting military order but also symbolising equality of sacrifice. Between 1920 and 1923 the shipment of headstones from Britain averaged 4,000 per week. Each man whose body had been found was allotted a stone inscribed with a cross, Star of David, crescent or other appropriate symbol. Above it went the name, rank, regiment and date of death. Below might go an inscription chosen by the family, for which they were charged. The Rosenbergs paid 3s.3d to have their son Isaac memorialised as a poet and artist. Cemeteries were carefully landscaped; each had its own full-time gardener. Where possible, flowers and shrubs readily identifiable as English were planted. 'There is much to be said for the occasional introduction of the English yew (where soil permits) from its association with our own country churchyards,' a War Graves Commission document advised. One is inevitably reminded of Rupert Brooke and his corner of a foreign field that would be forever England. Green pastures and abundant flowers suggested a pre-industrial idyll, a far cry from the urban wasteland from which most of the dead came.[5]

Those whose bodies were not found were usually com-memorated on a plaque in the cemetery. Considerable effort was nevertheless devoted to finding as many as possible. Beginning in 1920, search parties consisting of 4,000 men scoured battlefields looking for corpses. Some 30,000 were found by 1928, but only one quarter of these could be identified. French and Belgian farmers were paid a bounty for every body uncovered. Ploughing still brings them to the surface to this day.[6]

Beginning in 1920, pilgrimages to the graveyards in France and Belgium were organised. The word 'pilgrimage', as they were officially called, was apt. The visits proved very popular; cemeteries became, as they were intended, shrines of remembrance. The first to organise trips was the YMCA, followed soon after by the British Legion, Red Cross and other charitable groups. The cost – £6 in 1920 – was kept as low as possible, but still ruled out the very poor. Before long, sensing a market, the travel agent Thomas Cook began to organise tours, arranging transport and accommodation. Cars could be rented at railway stations and maps to cemeteries were supplied. Entrepreneurs provided tours of battlefields, complete with real trenches.

> Ladies and gentlemen, this is High Wood,
> Called by the French, Bois des Fourneaux,
> The famous spot which in Nineteen-Sixteen,
> July, August and September was the scene
> Of long and bitterly contested strife,
> By reason of its High commanding site.
> Observe the effect of shell-fire in the trees
> Standing and fallen; here is wire; this trench
> For months inhabited, twelve times changed hands;
> (They soon fall in), used later as a grave.
> It has been said on good authority
> That in the fighting for this patch of wood
> Were killed somewhere above eight thousand men,
> Of whom the greater part were buried here,
> This mound on which you stand being . . .
> Madam, please
> You are requested kindly not to touch
> Or take away the Company's property
> As souvenirs; you'll find we have on sale
> A large variety, all guaranteed.
> As I was saying, all is as it was,
> This is an unknown British officer,
> The tunic having lately rotted off.
> Please follow me – this way . . . the path, sir, please,
> The ground which was secured at great expense
> The company keeps absolutely untouched,

And in that dugout (genuine) we provide
Refreshments at a reasonable rate.
You are requested not to leave about
Paper, or ginger-beer bottles, or orange-peel,
There are waste paper baskets at the gate.

'Our war, the war that seemed the special possession of those of us who are growing middle-aged,' complained the war poet R. H. Mottram, 'is being turned by time and change into something fabulous, misunderstood and made romantic by distance.' In truth, this was merely a peacetime manifestation of the gulf in understanding so evident during the war. Civilians tried to comprehend, but inevitably could not. Veterans unfairly scorned their efforts to bridge the gulf.[7]

Since cemeteries in foreign lands could not serve as national shrines of remembrance, demand arose for a suitable monument in Britain. This eventually took the form of the Tomb of the Unknown Warrior and the Cenotaph. In 1920, an unidentified corpse was exhumed and brought across the Channel in the French destroyer *Verdun*. The Unknown Warrior (note the use of 'warrior', not 'soldier') was placed in a coffin made of oak from the royal palace at Hampton Court, in which was also placed a helmet, a khaki belt and Crusader's sword. The coffin was then buried in Westminster Abbey on the same day the Cenotaph was unveiled. Within a week, nearly one million people had paid homage at the tomb. For each grieving relative of a missing son or husband, it provided a point of focus. The historian Adrian Gregory relates the tale of 'a woman carrying a bunch of white heather tied with a tartan knot who had been journeying since the early hours of the morning from a homestead on the slopes of the Pentlands. Her man was one of the "missing" and in her heart was the thought that he might be the "unknown".'[8]

The Cenotaph, designed by Sir Edwin Lutyens and located on

Whitehall, quickly became the spiritual centre of remembrance. On 15 November 1920, the *Daily Mirror* reported a seven-mile queue of mourners waiting to place a wreath at the monument. Each year on Remembrance Day, an ever-declining number of soldiers marched in formation to pay homage at the symbol of the collective dead. Those who could not travel to London took part in similar processions to war memorials erected in the early 1920s in villages, towns and cities across Britain. These memorials evoke the values the British had fought to preserve. Classical designs were popular, with usually a saint or angel, such as St George. If soldiers were depicted, they were presented in a non-threatening manner, often with swords instead of rifles. Equally symbolic was the use of poppies in wreaths and in the lapel buttons sold by the British Legion. They brought to mind not only the flower that grew in abundance on the battlefield, but also, more symbolically, the blood of sacrifice.[9]

The remembrance ceremony inevitably inspires patriotism, but it is above all a ritual of memory, not a celebration of victory. Granted, it did not suit everyone. Some preferred their own private forms of mourning. 'May I remember you/And murmur with serenity,/without intensity,/without virulence,' wrote Ursula Roberts in her poem berating the crowds mobbing the Cenotaph. Some soldiers vowed to have nothing to do with remembrance ceremonies and avoided them for the remainder of their lives. For most, however, the ritual was an essential part of the process of coming to terms with the war without forgetting it. Many former soldiers, including those deeply embittered by their experiences, took part. That they did so surely suggests that they perceived it as a fitting way to honour comrades. For one day at least, the ritual brought together the living – both veteran and civilian – in solemn homage to the dead.[10]

Deciding upon how to remember the dead was considerably easier than deciding how to remember the war. Granted, in the immediate aftermath, the subject was not open to debate. With suffering so recent and emotions so raw, most people needed to see the conflict as worthwhile, noble and efficiently conducted. Doubts, being impediments to closure, were banished. Victory was seen as sufficient proof of the righteousness of the British people, the worthiness of their cause and the competence of their leaders. That sense of certainty lasted about ten years. In 1928, misgivings began to surface.

On 29 January 1928, Douglas Haig died of a sudden heart attack. A few days later, huge crowds lined the streets as the funeral procession made its way to Westminster Abbey, where the memorial service was held. 'The crowds were large everywhere,' a reporter for *The Times* remarked.

They had come to do honour to the chief who had sent thousands to the last sacrifice when duty called for it, but whom his war-worn soldiers loved as their truest advocate and friend. Little details in the arrangements appealed to the minds of all. The gun-carriage which bore the Field-Marshal to the Abbey was the same which had borne the Unknown Warrior to his grave, chosen for that honour because it had also carried the gun from which the first

British shell was fired in the War. Twice yesterday the two were again close together, the Field-Marshal and the unnamed soldier, the Known and the Unknown . . .

Thousands had earlier paid tribute at St Columba's (Church of Scotland), where his body lay in state. *The Scotsman* commented:

> Slowly the unending stream of people passed in front of the coffin. Many of the firstcomers were women, some of them wearing the medals of the husband or the children they had lost. Some, too, were women who had served in France themselves, nurses, and other women who had decorations of their own. There were ex-Service men who limped and other old soldiers who instinctively sprang to attention as they stood for a moment before the coffin. The man from the City, smartly dressed and carrying his silk hat, was once again in the same long line as men in mufflers.
>
> Nor did the blinded ex-Service man feel himself unable to pay a last tribute to his dead leader. One man who had lost his sight in the war was led in the procession by two friends, and as he reached the coffin was heard to ask, 'Where is he?'

A train then took Haig's body to Edinburgh, where a second service was held at St Giles. The scene was repeated. The High Street was packed with solemn mourners including, again, old soldiers.[11]

Within a few years, Haig the hero became Haig the butcher. According to the accepted narrative, it was not machine guns, artillery and gas that killed the cream of Britain. It was, instead, Haig, whose stubbornness and incompetence rendered him ill-suited to modern war. Among his most strident detractors were the veterans who had once admired him. Their memories of the war evolved to suit the hatred and betrayal they now felt. Thus the Great War that is remembered today is not the same as the war fought many years ago. The past is what happened, history the method of recollection. History is something fluid, buffeted by the experiences and emotions that occur after an event. An editorial in *The Scotsman* on the eighty-second anniversary of the armistice described the war as 'a pointless, static conflict over strips of earth, which achieved nothing other than the slaughter of millions of young men from both sides'. Today, the vast majority of Britons accept that view without qualification. Yet that image was an invention of the 1930s. The 'war to end all wars' had produced unemployment, depression and political instability across Europe. No wonder, then, that the sacrifice began to seem meaningless.[12]

The transformation of the war came about in large part because of a sudden boom in war books around the time of Haig's death. Writing in the *Times Literary Supplement* in 1929, the military historian Cyril Falls remarked that 'until about two years ago no one wanted to hear about the War, or, if they did, the publishers and book-sellers had not realised the fact'. The books had in common a tendency to question the sacred truths to which the British had adhered so diligently, namely that their cause was just, that the commanders were competent and that the sacrifice was noble. One of the first books to break the dam that held back doubt was Lloyd George's *War Memoirs*, in which he suggested that lives would have been saved if the incompetent Haig had been sacked. Originally published in six volumes, it was repackaged for a mass market into two weighty, but very readable, books. Unable to best Haig during the war, Lloyd George managed to crucify him in print after his death. There then followed a flood of war memoirs and novels that reinforced the message of futility and incompetence. Falls wrote: 'The writers have set themselves, not to strip the war of its romance – for that was pretty well gone already – but to prove that the Great War was engineered by knaves or fools on both sides, that the men who died in it were driven like beasts, without their deaths helping any cause or doing any good'.[13]

According to Falls, the soldier was invariably represented in this literature 'as a depressed and mournful spectre helplessly wandering about until death brought his miseries to an end'. That was the lament eloquently advanced by the 'war poets' – men like Siegfried Sassoon and Wilfred Owen. The term 'war poets' has come to imply a specific genre of ardent negativity, to the exclusion of all the other poems that were written during the war. These poems worked like acid on noble conceptions of the war. Sacrifice and duty gave way to devastation and regret. Of the commanders, Sassoon wrote:

> 'Good-morning; good-morning!' the General said
> When we met him last week on our way to the Line.
> Now the soldiers he smiled at are most of 'em dead,
> And we're cursing his staff for incompetent swine.
> 'He's a cheery old card,' grunted Harry to Jack
> As they slogged up to Arras with rifle and pack.
> But he did for them both by his plan of attack.

Sassoon obviously felt deeply betrayed by the high command, yet as we know, his cynicism was unusual. The most popular poet during the war was Jessie Pope whose patriotic doggerel, printed in *Punch*, remained a constant right up to Armistice Day. For every bitter critic like Sassoon, there were thousands of irrepressible cheerleaders like Pope. Yet Sassoon and those of his ilk are remembered because they harmonise so perfectly with the way the British now want to view the war. It is virtually impossible to escape from the British school system without at some point being required to read Sassoon or Owen. Today's students, conditioned to believe in the gospel according to St Wilfred, think that Pope's honeyed sentimentality must be clever satire. They can't imagine that anyone could have written positively about the war in 1917. Yet we forget that the war poets were themselves propagandists, though in this case for the cause of futility. Exaggeration is the tool of the persuader, as Robert Graves admitted:

> the memoirs of a man who went through some of the worst experiences of trench warfare are not truthful if they do not contain a high proportion of falsities. High-explosive barrages will make a temporary liar or visionary of anyone; the old trench-mind is at work in all overestimation of casualties, 'unnecessary' dwelling on horrors, mixing of dates and confusion between trench rumours and scenes actually witnessed.

Sassoon agreed that 'nearly all war books fall into that trap [of] pitching the story too strong and forgetting the decent element'.[14] Owen certainly did that, and after his death, his executors distilled his message further by destroying contradictory evidence, the better to create a new type of war hero – the combatant conscientious objector.

The way the war is remembered, particularly on Remembrance Day, has evolved according to political circumstance. In 1924, the Labour Party unveiled a simple election poster showing Tommy facing a starlit no-man's-land. Underneath was a message of entreaty: 'YESTERDAY THE TRENCHES'. The unwritten subtext was that the workers should use their votes to prevent a repeat of the slaughter. The eleventh of November has frequently been used for ulterior purposes – the war dead deployed to punctuate political debate. During the Depression, unemployed veterans attached pawn tickets to their medal ribbons – a potent demonstration of their feelings of betrayal. In the 1930s, the Peace Pledge Union introduced the white poppy to symbolise rejection of war, a sentiment in keeping with the mood of appeasement. During the Second World War, the idea of noble sacrifice resurfaced. Hitler's undoubted evil restored respectability to the idea of fighting Germans. Before long, however, the differences between the two wars reflected badly on the earlier contest. The Second World War came to be seen as the antithesis of the Great War, proof that wars can be heroic and commanders competent.

In the 1980s, remembrance reflected Thatcherite divisions. Mass unemployment again gave weight to feelings of betrayal, even if the victims were the grandchildren of the veterans. The war provided the left with potent ammunition, given that it illustrates the iniquities of class so profoundly. In addition, during that stridently antagonistic decade, fears of militarism encouraged a suspicion of all things military. Those worried by missiles on Greenham Common or by Thatcher's Cold War belligerence judged remembrance rituals excessively militaristic. The white poppy returned, this time sold by CND activists, who could never quite explain the logic of expressing one's opposition to war by denying sustenance to those who had the misfortune to fight. Meanwhile, Tories pilloried the Labour leader Michael Foot for wearing a donkey jacket while laying a wreath at the Cenotaph. His lack of respect for the dead of past wars was taken as proof that he could not be trusted to defend Britain in a future contest.

The 1930s version of the war has remained resilient to this day, despite the efforts of revisionists to spin a more positive account. The predominant image relies upon caricature: representations of the war are peopled with crudely drawn victims, heroes and malefactors. For nearly a century, books, films, plays, poetry, comedies and television documentaries have presented two contrasting images: the noble Tommy in his wretched trench and the inept senior commander living in luxury miles from the front. According to the widely accepted version of events, the insane orders of the latter resulted in the mass slaughter of the former. 'Field Marshal Haig is about to make yet another gargantuan effort to move his drinks cabinet six inches closer to Berlin,' Captain Blackadder famously remarks in *Blackadder Goes Forth*. That series perfectly illustrates the way the British have remembered the war. In the first episode, General Melchett, Captain Darling and Blackadder discuss a 'secret plan' that has arrived from GHQ:

MELCHETT: Field Marshal Haig has formulated a brilliant new tactical plan to ensure final victory in the field.

BLACKADDER: Now, would this brilliant plan involve us climbing out of our trenches and walking slowly towards the enemy, sir?

DARLING: How can you possibly know that, Blackadder? It's classified information.

BLACKADDER: It's the same plan that we used last time, and the seventeen times before that.

MELCHETT: E-E-Exactly! And that is what is so brilliant about it! We will catch the watchful Hun totally off guard! Doing precisely what we have done eighteen times before is exactly the last thing they'll expect us to do this time! There is however one small problem.

BLACKADDER: That everyone always gets slaughtered in the first ten seconds.

In recent years, Blackadder has been incorporated into the history syllabus at British schools. That is perfectly acceptable if the series is used as evidence of how the war has been judged. Perhaps inevitably, however, it occasionally gets mistaken for reality itself. Fiction has become fact.[15]

Objecting to this representation of the war, a determined band of revisionists have, over the years, presented a different account, one in which the war retains meaning and British commanders are competent and sagacious. These revisionists feel that popular images are ill-informed, unrealistic and excessively emotional – in other words, dangerously detached from the cruel reality of modern war. They have fought a rearguard action against the mammoth weight of popular opinion. Hopelessly outnumbered, they veer to the opposite extreme, transforming the senior commanders from butchers into genuine heroes. A website obsessively devoted to Haig argues with impressive certitude that he was the best commander in British history. The passage of time has not cooled tempers nor significantly altered the terms of engagement. Thus, the arguments of John Terraine, who led the efforts to rehabilitate Haig in the 1960s, sound remarkably similar to those of Gary Sheffield, who doggedly ploughs the same furrow today. The battle is as polarised as it has ever been, and the middle ground as sparsely populated as no-man's-land. Argument has been reduced to ritual, generating a great deal of heat, but little light. It is all, quite frankly, rather boring.

The popular view holds stubbornly to the 'lions led by donkeys' plotline. The reasoning is easy to chart. The Great War, it is argued, was the worst disaster in British military history. Since the heroism of Tommy Atkins is beyond doubt, blame must rest with the senior commanders, specifically with Haig – the supreme donkey. Out of this evolves a comfortably monochromatic picture consisting of heroes and villains who are easy to judge. The more incompetent Haig seems, the more noble Tommy becomes.

This school of thought rests on a steadfast confidence in man's ability to shape his destiny. At the core of the argument lies an assumption that slaughter occurred because genius was unavailable or went unnoticed. In other words, better tactics or strategies would have resulted in a less costly war. A Napoleon would have discovered them; Haig did not. This scenario is preferable to that of a war of limited options – a monstrous Leviathan beyond the control of any man. It is difficult for some to accept that the technologies man created eventually oppressed him, forcing upon him a terrible war immune to his genius. How much easier, instead, to focus blame on a single individual, a group of individuals or a class. By this means blame is easily apportioned and man's agency is restored.

Haig's critics argue from the war to the man: the legions of dead are evidence of incompetence. His champions take the opposite approach, arguing that his values were the same as those that made Britain great. They glide smoothly to the assumption that if a man of such stature could not limit the slaughter, no one could have. In other words, no attempt is made to deny that this was a horrible war, but its horror becomes a measure of Haig's greatness. His heroism lies in his ability to endure its ghastliness and in his determination to find a way to victory. Lesser men would have crumbled. There is some merit to this argument, but the ability to endure should not be confused with martial prowess.

Over the years, champions and critics have shouted their arguments across the vast expanse that divides them. The scholarly landscape has become, in consequence, as barren and blasted as the Western Front. The periodic raids of revisionists and counter-revisionists do nothing to alter the stalemate. The argument is irresolvable because it is, essentially, political. Interpretations of the war are hopelessly entangled with arguments about tradition, class, wealth, consciousness and privilege. What matters passionately to one side matters little to the other.

Haig was not a genius. He was, in truth, a third-rate general with a second-rate mind and a first-class sense of entitlement. Nor were his senior commanders any more impressive. They were men out of their depth, soldiers of another era who adjusted awkwardly to modern war. Their shortcomings should not, however, influence judgement of the men they commanded. Among the ordinary soldiers there were heroes and saints aplenty but also, in a mass army so perfectly reflective of wider society, a fair number of cowards, thieves, sadists, murderers and rapists. In other words, when judging the way the British reacted to war, it is important to avoid absolutes. Britain from 1914 to 1918 was a nation at war. Like any nation, there was virtue and iniquity, sacrifice and selfishness, all held together by a dogged determination to carry on. Enlightenment does not easily emerge from cardboard characterisations.

It matters not if students today learn about the war from *Blackadder, Birdsong* or the *Horrible Histories*, as long as they understand that those representations reveal more about the post-war mood than about the war itself. History should not be constructed from a few bitter poems. We have come to believe that the war was foolish and have consequently pitied those who had the misfortune to fight or to lose loved ones. Yet that generation does not need our pity. They did not wish to become martyred symbols of past folly. 'We may have been naive,' wrote the nurse Beryl Hutchinson, 'but we all had the feeling that we really were keeping the world fit to live in, that our many sacrifices had been worthwhile.' For them, the war was necessary, and duty sublime. At that precise moment, the war seemed a noble cause, worthy of sacrifice. The nation responded. That response deserves immense admiration.[16]

Endnotes

Chapter 1: A Lovely War

1   Playne, pp.19, 329–30. Hamilton, *Dead Yesterday*, p.43. *Manchester Guardian*, 12 November 1918.

2   http://www.firstworldwar.com/source/scrapofpaper1.htm.

3   Kennedy, *War Plans*, p.101. James, p.412.

4   Garvin, p.302.

5   Howard, *Continental Commitment*, p.14.

6   Wilson, *Policy of the Entente*, pp.79–80. Wilson, *Empire and Continent*, pp.38–9.

7   Roynon, p.20. *Manchester Guardian*, 1 August 1914.

8   http://www.firstworldwar.com/source/scrapofpaper1.htm. *Hansard*, 6 August 1914.

9   *Hansard*, 6 August 1914. *Daily News*, 25 March 1913. http://www.firstworldwar.com/source/scrapofpaper2.htm.

10 David Lloyd George, 'Honour and Dishonour', 19 September 1914, Queen's Hall, London.

11 *Daily Mirror*, 5 August 1914.

12 Eksteins, p.119.

13 Ibid., p.124. *Daily Mail*, 31 December 1914.

14 Wilson, *Empire and Continent*, p.38.

15 Roynon, p.5.

16 Eksteins, p.131. J. M. Bourne, p.230. Montague, p.3. Cross, p.55. Englund, p.54.

17   Braybon, *Evidence*, pp.76–7. Roynon, p.5.

Chapter 2: Gentlemen and Amateurs

1   Englund, p.53.
2   A. Summers, 'Militarism', p.108. Wavell, p.138. Keegan, p.220.
3   Keegan, p.197.
4   Harries-Jenkins, p.44.
5   Bond, 'Late Victorian Army', p.623.
6   Howard, *Soldiers and Governments*, p.29.
7   Summers, 'Militarism', p.111.
8   Brodick, pp.526–7.
9   Ibid. Maxwell, p.1063.
10   Low, pp.390–2.

Chapter 3: Muscular Christians

1   Keegan, pp.139, 224.
2   Eksteins, p.120. Mangan and Walvin, pp.55–6.
3   *Field Service Regulations*, Part I (Operations), p.11. Travers, 'Technology, Tactics and Morale', p.286.
4   Bradley and Simon, pp.134–5, 142, 157. Newbolt, *Poems Old and New*, pp.78–9.
5   R. Wilkinson, p.83.
6   Waugh, p.90. Harrison, p.227.
7   Diver. Newsome, p.258. Vachell, pp.242–3.
8   Springhall, pp.55, 57.
9   Mangan and Walvin, pp.176–7. Travers, 'Technology, Tactics and Morale', p.280.
10   Steiner, p.159. Beckett and Simpson, p.5. Howard, *Studies in War and Peace*, p.92. Travers, 'Technology, Tactics and Morale', p.280.
11   Springhall, p.58.
12   Ibid., p.59.
13   Ibid., pp.67, 69.
14   Englund, p.54.
15   Roynon, p.13.

16   Beckett and Simpson, p.134.

17   Ibid., p.130.

18   Ibid., p.197. Vansittart, p.35. Cross, p.55. Summers, 'Militarism', p.120.

19   Vansittart, p.44.

20   Ibid., pp.261–2.

21   *The Times*, 26 August 1914.

22   Beckett and Simpson, pp.9–10, 103. Turner, *Britain and the First World War*, p.104.

23   Beckett and Simpson, p.197. http://www.spartacus.schoolnet. co.uk/FWWdisembark.htm.

24   D. Winter, p.33. Reilly, p.87. http://www.spartacus.schoolnet. co.uk/FWWrecruit.htm.

25   *The Times*, 11 February, 9 April, 23 June, 4, 7 September 1915. *The Scotsman*, 3 September, 30 November 1914.

26   Waites, p.158. *The Times*, 9 January, 6 February 1915.

27   Reader, pp.112–13. *The Times*, 7 July, 3 September 1915.

28   Reader, p.116. Reilly, p.88. Simkins, p.124. *The Times*, 20 January 1915.   http://www.spartacus.schoolnet.co.uk/FWWfeather. htm.   http://www.bbc.co.uk/history/british/britain_wwone/ women_combatants_01.shtml.

29   *The Times*, 16 January, 8 July 1915. http://www.spartacus. schoolnet.co.uk/FWWwomenrecruit.htm. Haste, pp.56–7.

30   Reader, pp.120–1. Beckett and Simpson, p.102. *The Times*, 7 August 1914. http://www.spartacus.schoolnet.co.uk/FWWfeather.htm.

31   http://www.spartacus.schoolnet.co.uk/FWWrecruit.htm. J. Winter, *The Great War and the British People*, pp.50–3. Beckett and Simpson, pp.103, 110. Reader, p.119. *The Scotsman*, 16 October 1914.

32   Coppard, p.1. *The Observer*, 20 September 2009.

33   http://www.spartacus.schoolnet.co.uk/WthomasH.htm.

Chapter 4: Lions and Donkeys

 1   Younghusband, pp.187–8. Beckett and Simpson, p.168. Watson, p.44.

2 Beckett and Simpson, pp.172–4.

3 Ibid., p.200.

4 Ibid., p.104. D. Winter, p.55. http://www.spartacus.schoolnet. co.uk/FWWcamps.htm. Beckett and Simpson, pp.118, 195, 200. J. Winter, *Great War and the British People*, pp.50–3, 59.

5 Beckett and Simpson, p.225. Turner, *Britain and the First World War*, p.87.

6 D. Winter, p.18. Keegan, pp.224–5. Silkin, *Poetry*, pp.187–8.

7 Watson, pp.22–3.

8 Vaughan, p.193. Beckett and Simpson, p.85. Graves, pp.66, 82, 192. Chapman, *Passionate Prodigality*, p.58. Sheffield, p.98.

9 *The Times*, 5 February 1915. *The Observer*, 20 September 2009. Graves, p.97. http://www.bbc.co.uk/history/worldwars/ wwone/humanfaceofwar_gallery_02.shtml.

10 Beckett and Simpson, p.85. Graves, p.107. Keegan, p.243.

11 Petter, pp.127–52. Beckett and Simpson, p.78.

12 H. Milward to Lady Haig, 6 June 1929, Haig Papers (National Library of Scotland). D. Winter, pp.53–4. http://www.spartacus. schoolnet.co.uk/Jbuchan.htm.

13 DeGroot, *Haig*, pp.173, 184, 234–5, 277.

14 *The Scotsman*, 13–20 August 1958.

15 Silkin, *Prose*, p.27. Beckett and Simpson, p.47.

16 Graves, p.188. Keegan, pp.274–84. Montague, p.142.

17 Ellis, p.185. Englander and Osborne, p.595.

Chapter 5: Business Not Quite as Usual

1 McDermott, p.274.

2 French, *British Economic and Strategic Planning*, p.92.

3 Ibid., p.34.

4 Roynon, p.6. *The Scotsman*, 4 August 1914.

5 *The Scotsman*, 19 August 1914.

6 French, *British Economic and Strategic Planning*, p.88. *Hansard*, 8 August 1914.

7 Roynon, pp.18, 71. Money, p.482. *The Scotsman*, 31 August 1914.

8   Roynon, p.2.

9   *The Times*, 6 August 1914. Jenkins, p.342. Royle, p.254.

10 Magnus, p.339.

11 Hazlehurst, p.528. Grey, pp.68–9.

12 French, 'The Meaning of Attrition', p.388. Magnus, p.349.

13 Magnus, p.348. Haldane, *Autobiography*, pp.278–80. French, *British Economic and Strategic Planning*, pp.127–8. Beckett and Simpson, p.102.

14 Roynon, p.16.

15 Wilson, *Myriad Faces*, p.151.

16 Winter, *War and Economic Development*, pp.152–61.

17 Haig to Leo Rothschild, 17 April 1915, Haig Papers.

18 Wilson, *Myriad Faces*, p.163. Jenkins, p.338. Roynon, p.93.

19 Magnus, pp.378, 340. Lloyd George, p.298. Hankey, p.221.

20 *The Nation*, 21 October 1916. Klein, p.54. Brittain, *Chronicle of Youth*, p.244. S. Sassoon, *Collected Poems*, p.78.

21 Lloyd, pp.26, 32. French, *British Economic and Strategic Planning*, p.134.

22 *The Times*, 12 August 1915. McDermott, p.277.

23 Waites, p.69. Wilson, *Myriad Faces*, pp.150–1.

24 Dutton, p.117. *The Times*, 14 May 1915.

25 Jenkins, p.348. Grieves, p.15. *Punch*, 26 May 1915. *The Times*, 23 June 1915. Roynon, p.136.

Chapter 6: Building a War Machine

1   *The Times*, 16 March 1915.

2   *The Observer*, 20 September 2009.

3   J. Bourne, pp.177–8. D. Winter, pp.236–7.

4   Burk, p.37.

5   Adams, *Arms and the Wizard*, pp.53–4.

6   Wilson, *Myriad Faces*, p.237.

7   Wrigley, *Lloyd George*, pp.42, 47.

8   Wilson, *Myriad Faces*, p.238.

9   Lloyd George, pp.389–90. Adams, *Arms and the Wizard*, pp.172–3,

244–5. Wilson, *Myriad Faces*, p.232.

10 Dewey, 'Food Production', p.84. Dewey, 'Agricultural Labour Supply', pp.100–9.

11 Burk, p.138. Taylor, *English History*, pp.122–4. Hankey, pp.648–50. Newbolt, *Naval Operations*, Vol. IV, p.385. Wilson, *Myriad Faces*, p.537.

12 Hardach, p.44.

13 Dewey, 'Food Production', p.81. Dewey, 'British Farming Profits', pp.378, 387. Horn, p.57.

14 Milward, p.25. Horn, p.55. Hardach, pp.126–7.

15 Dewey, 'Food Production', pp.72–3.

16 Burk, pp.140, 148. Roynon, p.207.

17 Horn, p.50.

18 *The Observer*, 24 February 1918. Burk, pp.135, 144. Lloyd George, p.788. Roynon, p.207.

19 Beckett and Simpson, p.8.

20 *The Times*, 6 May 1915. Fraser, p.7. Grieves, pp.21–2.

21 *Manchester Guardian*, 7 October, 17 November 1915. Adams, 'Asquith's Choice', p.254. Churchill, p.193. Roynon, p.144.

22 Grieves, pp.24–5. Robertson to Haig, 31 December 1915, Haig Papers. Fry, p.617.

23 Adams, 'Asquith's Choice', pp.251–2.

24 Grieves, pp.32–3.

25 Dewey, 'Military Recruiting', p.215.

26 Grieves, p.56.

27 Ibid., pp.73, 82.

28 Ibid., p.110.

29 Dilks, pp.218, 237. Grieves, p.113.

30 *The Times*, 13 December 1917.

31 Haig to Lady Haig, 21 March 1918, Haig Papers. DeGroot, *Haig*, p.374.

32 Grieves, p.192.

33 Burk, pp.111–19.

34 Wilson, *Myriad Faces*, pp.646–7. Milward, p.28.

35   Whiting, pp.896–7, 902, 911, 914. Milward, p.38.

36   Whiting, p.908. *The Times*, 6 February 1915. *The Scotsman*, 13 October 1915.

37   Pearce, pp.35–6. Burk, p.91. Milward, p.46.

Chapter 7: Shoulders to the Wheel

1   Hinton, *Labour and Socialism*, p.107. Hinton, *First Shop Stewards' Movement*, p.14.

2   Hardach, p.204. Cook and Stevenson, p.153. Turner, *Britain and the First World War*, p.95. E. Woodward, p.477.

3   Webb, pp.10–11. Waites, p.196.

4   Hardach, p.205.

5   McLean, pp.18–20.

6   Hinton, *Labour and Socialism*, p.106. Middlemas, *The Clydesiders*, p.61.

7   Lloyd George, p.177. Middlemas, *The Clydesiders*, p.63.

8   McLean, p.30.

9   Wolfe, p.127. Liddle, p.180.

10   Taylor, *Lloyd George*, p.87.

11   Hinton, *First Shop Stewards' Movement*, p.136. Grieves, p.127.

12   Hinton, *First Shop Stewards' Movement*, p.210. Braybon, *Women*, p.69. Wilson, *Myriad Faces*, p.526.

13   Hinton, *Labour and Socialism*, p.98. Liddle, p.17.

14   Waites, p.208. Wilson, *Myriad Faces*, p.522.

15   Waites, p.232. Wilson, *Myriad Faces*, pp.654–5. Middlemas, p.69.

16   Waites, p.232. Wilson, *Myriad Faces*, p.656.

17   Rubin, *War, Law and Labour*, p.17. Tawney, pp.2–3. Turner, *Britain and the First World War*, p.79.

18   Pearce, p.39. Clegg, p.161. Whiteside, p.313. Lloyd George, p.209.

19   Cook and Stevenson, p.153.

20   Braybon, *Women*, p.44. Cole, *Labour in War Time*, pp.229, 234. *The Times*, 18 September 1914; 3 February 1915. Pugh, *Women and the Women's Movement*, pp.18–19. Pankhurst, p.54.

21 http://www.spartacus.schoolnet.co.uk/FWWrecruit.htm.
    Common Cause, 7, 14 August 1914.

22 http://www.spartacus.schoolnet.co.uk/FWWrecruit.htm.
    Klein, p.23. Englund, p.210.

23 Englund, pp.27, 153, 155.

24 *The Guardian*, 11 November 2008. Klein, p.40. Englund, pp.37–8.

25 Balfour, p.144.

26 Roynon, p.49. Reilly, pp.88–90. *The Times*, 28 August 1914; 18
    November 1918.

27 *The Times*, 16 January 1915. Reilly, p.12.

28 http://www.firstworldwar.com/diaries/storyofawaac.htm

29 Lloyd George, p.174. *The Times*, 8 July 1915.

30 Pugh, *Women and the Women's Movement*, pp.19–21. *The Times*,
    30 March 1915. Cole, *Labour in War Time*, p.241. *The Times*, 8
    February, 17 March 1915.

31 Wilson, *Myriad Faces*, p.716.

32 Braybon and Summerfield, p.76. Braybon, *Women*, pp.162–3.

33 Drake, p.17. Pugh, *Women and the Women's Movement*, p.25.

34 *The Times*, 23 April 1915. Cole, *Labour in War Time*, p.228. Boston,
    pp.112–13, 115, 117.

35 Pugh, *Women and the Women's Movement*, p.25. Braybon and
    Summerfield, p.50.

36 Braybon, *Women*, p.79. Boston, p.112.

37 Smith, 'Equal Pay', p.45. Pugh, *Women and the Women's Movement*,
    p.28. Boston, p.110.

38 Winter, *The Great War and the British People*, pp.207–8.

39 Klein, p.83. Braybon and Summerfield, p.85. Whiteside, p.313.

40 McFeely, p.141.

41 Boston, p.127. Braybon and Summerfield, p.73. Pugh, *Women and
    the Women's Movement*, p.27.

42 Watson, p.119. Dakers, p.150. Dewey, 'Agricultural Labour
    Supply', p.104.

43 Strachey, p.344. Reilly, p.90. *The Times*, 8 February 1915.

44 Reilly, p.7.

45 Braybon and Summerfield, p.47. *Daily Mail*, 30 March 1916.

46 Klein, p.84. *The Times*, 8, 17 Febuary 1915. Watson, p.82.

47 Roynon, p.210.

Chapter 8: Outlaws and Dissenters

1   *The Times*, 10 December 1914; 8, 15 January 1915.

2   Levine, pp.43–5, 54.

3   Marwick, *Deluge*, p.76. Pankhurst, pp.36, 375.

4   *The Times*, 21 November 1914; 6 March 1915; 26 February, 13 April 1917. *The Scotsman*, 29 March 1917. Horn, pp.66–7.

5   Horn, p.438. Boswell and Johns, pp.428–9. *The Scotsman*, 17 March 1915. *The Times*, 13 February 1915.

6   http://www.guardian.co.uk/world/2008/nov/11/ed-morel-anti-war-movement.

7   Carsten, p.25. Bennett, p.98.

8   Morel. http://www.spartacus.schoolnet.co.uk/FWWudc.htm. Hinton, *Protests and Visions*, pp.48–9.

9   Carsten, p.54. Hinton, *Protests and Visions*, pp.44–5.

10 Hinton, *Protests and Visions*, p.42. Pankhurst, p.147.

11 Hinton, *Protests and Visions*, p.44. Wilson, *Myriad Faces*, pp.155–6. Doyle, p.1217. Taylor, *Lloyd George*, p.81.

12 Pugh, *Women and the Women's Movement*, p.11. Pankhurst, p.149.

13 Pankhurst, pp.150–1, 153. Wiltsher, pp.89, 96. Pugh, *Women and the Women's Movement*, p.10. Hinton, *Protests and Visions*, p.43.

14 Haste, p.150. Hynes, p.147. Wallace, p.114.

15 http://www.spartacus.schoolnet.co.uk/FWWudc.htm. Wrigley, *Lloyd George and the British Labour Movement*, p.181. Carsten, p.170.

16 Hinton, *Protests and Visions*, p.59. Wilson, *Myriad Faces*, p.522.

17 Wilson, *Myriad Faces*, p.525. Haste, p.165. Stubbs, p.737.

18 Hinton, *Protests and Visions*, p.69.

19 Carsten, pp.170–1, 201.

20 Stubbs, pp.718, 728, 739. Douglas, 'The National Democratic Party', p.536.

21 Wrigley, *Lloyd George and the British Labour Movement*, p.181. Hynes, p.217. Haste, p.171. http://www.spartacus.schoolnet. co.uk/FWWudc.htm.

22 *Daily Telegraph*, 30 June 1917.

23 http://www.spartacus.schoolnet.co.uk/FWWncf.htm. Carsten, p.67. Wiltsher, p.146. Marwick, *Deluge*, p.128.

24 Hinton, *Protests and Visions*, p.52. Marwick, *Deluge*, pp.120–1.

25 Carsten, p.68. Hinton, *Protests and Visions*, p.53.

26 Rae, p.131.

27 Hinton, *Protests and Visions*, p.52.

28 Pankhurst, pp.314–15, 336. Graham, pp.322, 347–52. http://www. spartacus.schoolnet.co.uk/FWWncf.htm. *Manchester Guardian*, 27 June 1916.

29 *The Times*, 17 October 1916. Wallace, p.84. Hinton, *Protests and Visions*, pp.53–4.

30 French, 'Spy Fever in Britain', p.360. Panayi, pp.47–8, 50. *The Scotsman*, 24 August 1914.

31 *The Scotsman*, 3, 8 September 1914.

32 Panayi, p.72.

33 *The Guardian*, 11 November 2008. Panayi, pp.72, 114–15, 125.

34 Hiley, *Failure*, pp.858–9. Panayi, p.181. *The Times*, 21 August 1914. Haste, p.113.

Chapter 9: Thinking the Right Thoughts

1 Messinger, pp.208–9. Rawlings, pp.42–8.

2 Lasswell, p.40.

3 Haste, p.105. Wilson, *Myriad Faces*, p.170.

4 Haste, p.25.

5 Wilson, *Myriad Faces*, p.740.

6 Ibid., *Myriad Faces*, p.734. Haste, p.59.

7 http://www.spartacus.schoolnet.co.uk/FWWrecruit.htm. Messinger, pp.208–9. Rawlings, pp.42–8.

8 Sanders and Taylor, p.68. Messinger, p.130.

9 *Hansard*, 5 August 1918.

10 Haste, pp.40–1.

11 Sanders and Taylor, p.105.

12 Ibid., p.68.

13 Englund, pp.90–1, 332.

14 Lasswell, p.32.

15 Haste, p.29. Wilson, *Myriad Faces*, p.402.

16 Wilson, *Political Diaries of C. P. Scott*, p.142.

17 Sanders and Taylor, p.20. Hiley, 'Lord Kitchener Resigns', p.27. Koss, p.245. Haste, p.37.

18 Sanders and Taylor, p.23. Haste, pp.32, 34. http://www.spartacus. schoolnet.co.uk/FWWwarpress.htm. Wilson, *Myriad Faces*, p.195. *The Times,* 16 November 1914.

19 Hiley, 'Lord Kitchener Resigns', p.33. Sanders and Taylor, pp.21–2.

20 Roynon, pp.23, 95. Sanders and Taylor, p.24. Messinger, p.115. *The Times,* 8 November 1915.

21 Wilson, *Myriad Faces*, p.510.

22 http://www.spartacus.schoolnet.co.uk/Jgibbs.htm.   http:// www.spartacus.schoolnet.co.uk/FWWjournalism.htm.

23 Wilson, *Myriad Faces,* p.30. L. Masterman, p.296. Haste, pp.68–9. http://www.spartacus.schoolnet.co.uk/FWWjournalism.htm.

24 http://www.spartacus.schoolnet.co.uk/FWWjournalism.htm. http://www.spartacus.schoolnet.co.uk/FWWaccredited.htm. Wilson, *Myriad Faces*, p.31.

25 Lasswell, p.82.

26 Haste, p.88. Marquis, p.487.

27 Haste, pp.22–3. http://www.firstworldwar.com/source/ brycereport.htm.

28 Wilson, 'Lord Bryce's Investigation', pp.373–5, 379–82.

29 Haste, pp.113, 125. Panayi, p.233. Wilson, *Myriad Faces*, p.198.

30 Panayi, pp.199–200. *The Scotsman,* 12 November 1914; 7 January, 16 September, 8 October 1915. *The Times,* 2 September, 2 October 1914.

31 Panayi, pp.243, 257. *The Times,* 17 August 1914.

32 http://www.spartacus.schoolnet.co.uk/FWWblackbook.htm. Barker, pp.154–5. Wilson, *Myriad Faces*, pp.402–3.

33 Panayi, pp.243, 257. *The Times*, 12 May 1915. http://www. spartacus.schoolnet.co.uk/FWWantigerman.htm.

34 *The Times*, 9 February, 5 March 1917. Wrigley, *Warfare, Diplomacy and Politics*, p.104. Rubinstein, pp.129–48.

35 Wilson, *Myriad Faces*, p.643.

36 Panayi, p.286. Wilson, *Myriad Faces*, pp.160–1.

Chapter 10: Home Fires

1 Hinton, *Protests and Visions*, p.44.

2 Marwick, *Deluge*, p.65.

3 Ibid., pp.244–5. Braybon and Summerfield, pp.23, 98. Burnett, p.217. Winter, *The Great War and the British People*, p.243. Bowley, p.12.

4 Winter, *The Great War and the British People*, p.243.

5 Reilly, p.120. Wilson, *Myriad Faces*, p.390. *The Times*, 4 January, 7 June 1915. Roynon, p.73.

6 Wilson, *Myriad Faces*, p.509. Marwick, *Deluge*, p.238. Braybon and Summerfield, p.97.

7 Reiss, p.3.

8 Wilson, *Myriad Faces*, pp.150, 404–5. Marwick, *Women at War*, p.137. *The Times*, 18 November 1914.

9 Peel, pp.96–7. Marwick, *Women at War*, p.141. *The Times*, 15 January 1915. Hardach, p.128.

10 *The Times*, 12 July, 14 August 1915; 9 January 1919. Reilly, p.113.

11 Braybon and Summerfield, p.103. Marwick, *Deluge*, p.239.

12 Beveridge, pp.238–9. *The Times*, 12 March 1918.

13 Pugh, *Women and the Women's Movement*, p.13. *The Times*, 8, 14 August 1914; 9 January, 6 July, 25 August 1915.

14 Braybon and Summerfield, p.99.

15 Winter, *The Great War and the British People*, pp.215, 229–31. *The Times*, 28 February 1917. Whiting, pp.897, 908.

16 http://www.bbc.co.uk/history/trail/wars_conflict/home_

front/the_home_front_02.shtml. *The Times*, 16 December 1914; 26 January 1915. Hardach, p.124.

17   Pedersen, 'Gender', pp.99, 1003. Winter, *The Great War and the British People*, p.241.

18   *The Times*, 23 November 1914. http://www.spartacus.schoolnet. co.uk/FWWalcohol.htm. *The Guardian*, 11 November 2008. Jones, p.35. Pedersen, 'Gender', pp.997–9. *Evening Times*, 26 November 1914.

19   Marwick, *Women at War*, p.137. Pankhurst, p.28. Pedersen, 'Gender', p.993.

20   Reilly, p.69. Waites, p.51.

21   Burk, p.138. *The Times*, 16 October 1914. Pugh, *Women and the Women's Movement*, p.14. Marwick, *Deluge*, pp.240, 242. Wilson, *Myriad Faces*, p.405. Roynon, p.211. Meyer, p.128.

22   Winter, *The Great War and the British People*, pp.105–6, 117. Winter, 'Aspects', p.718.

23   Bryder, p.143. Harris, pp.349–51. Winter, 'Public Health', p.168.

24   Winter, *The Great War and the British People*, pp.161, 170, 179, 186. *The Times*, 6 November 1918. Loudon, pp.27–41.

25   Winter, 'Aspects', pp.728–9. Pedersen, 'Gender', p.1002. Woollacott, 'Maternalism', p.33. Dewey, 'Food Production', pp.73, 78.

26   Braybon and Summerfield, p.83.

27   *Daily Telegraph*, 2, 18 July 1917. Fawcett, *What I Remember*, p.218. Lewis, p.29.

28   Jones, p.40. Braybon and Summerfield, p.107. Pugh, *Women and the Women's Movement*, pp.18–19. *The Times*, 21 April 1915.

29   Braybon, *Women*, p.117. Whiteside, p.315. Lewis, p.202. Weeks, p.45.

30   Koven and Michel, pp.1076–1108. Pedersen, 'Failure of Feminism', p.91. Kent, p.241.

31   http://www.spartacus.schoolnet.co.uk/FWWalcohol.htm. Lewis, p.29. Braybon, *Women*, pp.124–5. Wall and Winter, pp.376, 378.

32 Braybon, *Women*, pp.124–5. Lewis, p.93. Wall and Winter, p.314.

33 Jones, p.41. *The Times*, 8 September 1915. Braybon, *Women*, p.126.

34 Lewis, pp.34, 96. Winter, *The Great War and the British People*, p.192. Jones, p.41.

35 Lewis, pp.30, 69, 100. Winter, *The Great War and the British People*, p.203–4.

36 *The Times*, 14 December 1914. Winter, *The Great War and the British People*, p.210.

37 Wilson, *Myriad Faces*, p.815. Waites, p.266.

38 Marwick, *Deluge*, pp.156–7. *The Times*, 6 August 1915. Jones, p.45.

39 Marwick, *Women at War*, pp.143–4. Marwick, *Deluge*, p.159. *The Times*, 23 April 1915; 12 March 1918.

40 Braybon and Summerfield, pp.100–1. *The Times*, 24 June 1916.

41 Braybon and Summerfield, p.106. Braybon, *Women*, p.124. Lewis, pp.79–80.

42 Braybon and Summerfield, p.105.

43 http://www.spartacus.schoolnet.co.uk/FWWrelationships. htm. Peel, p.172.

44 Winter, *The Great War and the British People*, p.257. Reilly, p.15. *The Times*, 5 October 1916. Kent, p.245. Braybon, *Women*, p.166.

Chapter 11: Having Fun

1 Wilson, *Myriad Faces*, pp.164–5.

2 Ibid., pp.164, 405. Repington, Vol. 2, p.3.

3 Walvin, p.130.

4 Roynon, p.21. Wilson, *Myriad Faces*, p.164. *The Times*, 24 November 1914. Walvin, p.129. 'The Subaltern' (by O. N. E. More), *College Echoes*, 30 October 1914.

5 *Stratford Express*, 2 December 1914. Marwick, *Deluge*, p.90. *The Scotsman*, 5 January 1915. *The Times*, 23 November 1914. Walvin, p.129.

6 *The Times*, 25 November 1914. *Athletic News*, 7 December 1914.

7 *The Times*, 26 November 1914; 26 January, 4, 9 March, 26 May 1915.

8   *The Times*, 15, 31 July, 13 September 1915; 26 January 1917.

9   Braybon and Summerfield, p.90. *The Times*, 13 October 1914. Woollacott, 'Khaki Fever', pp.329, 331.

10   *The Guardian*, 11 November 2008. Pankhurst, p.98. Braybon and Summerfield, pp.108–9. Braybon, *Evidence*, p.129.

11   Pugh, *Women and the Women's Movement*, p.32. http://www. spartacus.schoolnet.co.uk/Wpatrols.htm. Levine, pp.44, 49. Jones, p.36. Woollacott, 'Khaki Fever', p.336. *East Grinstead Observer*, 13 November 1915.

12   http://www.spartacus.schoolnet.co.uk/Wpatrols.htm. Hamilton, *Our Freedom*, p.251. Englund, p.124. http://www. spartacus.schoolnet.co.uk/Wswanwick.htm. Braybon, *Evidence*, p.121.

13   http://www.firstworldwar.com/diaries/storyofawaac.htm. Beckett and Simpson, pp.175–6. Pankhurst, p.182.

14   Simkins, p.176. *The Times*, 21 April, 18 June 1915. Jones, p.36.

15   Simkins, p.185. Weeks, pp.215–16. Marwick, *Deluge*, p.150. Jones, p.37. Meyer, p.158.

16   http://www.spartacus.schoolnet.co.uk/FWWunseen.htm. Weeks, p.214.

17   Marwick, *Deluge*, p.147. Weeks, pp.187–8. Wilson, *Myriad Faces*, p.724. Braybon and Summerfield, p.113.

18   *The Times*, 3 October, 14 December 1914. Pedersen, 'Gender', p.998. Braybon and Summerfield, p.70. Watson, pp.35, 37.

19   *The Times*, 13 March 1917; 16 December 1918. Marwick, *Deluge*, pp.104, 345.

20   Marwick, *Deluge*, p.181.

21   *The Times*, 1, 2, 5 September 1916; 13 January 1917. Taylor, *Lloyd George*, p.112. Mosse, p.149. *St Andrews Citizen*, 14 October 1916.

22   Reeves, pp.465, 472, 480. Haste, p.45. Wilson, *Myriad Faces*, p.738.

23   *The Times*, 23 January 1915. Walvin, p.133. *The Scotsman*, 21 October 1914.

24   *The Times*, 25 January, 27 February 1915.

25   *The Times*, 26 December 1914; 5 February 1915; 22 January 1917.

26   Marwick, *Deluge*, p.185.

27   *The Scotsman*, 1 October 1915.

28   *The Spectator*, 12 August 1916. *College Echoes*, 12 February 1916.

29   *The Guardian*, 11 November 1918. Silkin, *Prose*, p.289. Eksteins, p.229. Reilly, p.100.

Chapter 12: And Then, Suddenly, It Was Over

1   Englund, p.248. http://www.spartacus.schoolnet.co.uk/FWWdisembark.htm.

2   Roynon, p.218.

3   D. Winter, p.245. Woodward, *Lloyd George and the Generals*, Ch.12 and p.238.

4   *Manchester Guardian*, 8 November 1918. Weintraub, p.252.

5   Sitwell, pp.1, 3–4. *Manchester Guardian*, 12 November 1918. Weintraub, p.263.

6   Chapman, *Vain Glory*, pp.705, 707. D. Winter, p.235. Montague, p.129.

7   Chapman, *Vain Glory*, p.706. Mosley, p.19. Weintraub, p.261. Roynon, p.277.

8   Weintraub, p.257. Brittain, *Testament of Youth*, pp.327–8. Vansittart, p.253. Roynon, p.277.

9   *Manchester Guardian*, 12 November 1918. Silkin, *Poetry*, p.197.

Chapter 13: Back to Blighty

1   http://www.firstworldwar.com/diaries/storyofawaac.htm.

2   Graubard, pp.297–311.

3   Ibid., p.299; Coppard, p.133; D. Winter, p.239.

4   Graubard, p.301. D. Winter, p.240. Coppard, p.134.

5   Graubard, p.303.

6   DeGroot, *Haig*, pp.401–2.

7   Beckett and Simpson, p.213. Graubard, p.311.

8   Koven, p.1185. D. Winter, p.253.

9   DeGroot, *Haig*, p.398. J. Winter, *The Great War and the British People*, pp.273–6. Koven, p.1191.

10   Koven, p.1201.

11   Winter, *The Great War and the British People*, pp.265, 273–8. Jones, p.52.

12   Koven, p.1200.

13   Coppard, p.133.

14   Ibid., p.133. Petter, p.150.

15   Rubin, 'Law as a Bargaining Weapon', pp.933, 936–7.

16   Braybon, *Women*, pp.179, 187. Braybon and Summerfield, pp.122–3. Boston, p.151.

17   Braybon and Summerfield, p.121.

18   Kent, p.238. Braybon, *Women*, p.189. Pugh, *Women and the Women's Movement*, p.82.

19   Pugh, *Women and the Women's Movement*, pp.81–2. *The Times*, 18 December 1918.

20   Braybon and Summerfield, p.120.

21   Pugh, *Women and the Women's Movement*, p.81.

22   Haig to Lord Derby, 3 October 1917, Haig Papers. S. Ward, p.179.

23   Englander and Osborne, p.619.

24   S. Ward, p.182.

25   Ibid., p.184.

26   DeGroot, *Haig*, pp.403–4. Barr, p.112.

27   Kendall, pp.187, 194.

28   *The Times*, 15 March 1917.

Chapter 14: The Dead, the Living and the Living Dead

1   Mowat, p.142.

2   Winter, *The Great War and the British People*, pp.68–9, 72–3. D Winter, p.261.

3   Winter, *The Great War and the British People*, pp.83, 266–70.

4   Ibid., pp.91–3.

5   Ibid., pp.84, 98. D. Winter, p.254.

6   Wilson, *Myriad Faces*, pp.751–2.

7   Brittain, *Testament of Youth*, p.608.

8   Silkin, *Poetry*, p.89. Reilly, p.22. Jameson, p.179. Englund, p.406.

Montague, p.136.

9   Stapledon, p.225. Chapman, *Passionate Prodigality*, p.276. Silkin, *Poetry*, pp.115, 124. Sassoon, *Memoirs of an Infantry Officer*, p.280. Panichas, p.157. Ford, p.181. Fussell, p.325.

10 Chapman, *Passionate Prodigality*, p.346. D. Winter, pp.243, 262–3. Coppard, pp.134–5. Watson, p.268.

11 D. Winter, pp.248, 252. Hynes, p.307. Englander and Osborne, p.599. Jones, p.51. Silkin, *Poetry*, p.195. Gibbs, pp.547–8.

12 http://www.hellfire-corner.demon.co.uk/holman.htm.

13 *The Guardian*, 11 November 2008. http://www.guardian.co.uk/world/2008/nov/13/disabled-wilfred-owen-poem.   Gregory, p.52. D. Winter, pp.251–2, 254. Reilly, p.31.

14 Koven, p.1188. Silkin, *Poetry*, p.131.

15 Aldington, p.201. Silkin, *Poetry*, pp.89–90. http://www.spartacus. schoolnet.co.uk/FWWletters.htm. Englund, pp.130–1. *Daily Express*, 11 November 1919.

16 Wilson, *Myriad Faces*, pp.751–3. Tylee, p.229. Lauder, pp.184–5. D. Winter, p.255. Gregory, p.39. Oxford and Asquith, Vol. 2, pp.158–9. http://www.guardian.co.uk/world/2008/nov/14/for-the-fallen-laurence-binyon. Silkin, *Poetry*, pp.135–6.

17 D. Winter, pp.255, 258. *The Times*, 3 January 1919. *The Guardian*, 14 November 2008.

18 Reilly, pp.1–2, 64. Wilson, *Myriad Faces*, p.753. Klein, p.56.

Chapter 15: 'Daddy, What Did You Do in the Class War?'

1   *Daily Telegraph*, 29 November 1917.

2   Waites, p.98.

3   Wilson, *Myriad Faces*, p.772.

4   A. Sinclair to M. Sinclair, 5 September 1918, personal collection. DeGroot, *Liberal Crusader*, p.54.

5   Turner, *Britain and the First World War*, p.97. *The Times*, 30 January, 21 February 1917. Boswell and Johns, p.432.

6   Roynon, p.44. C. Masterman, pp.34, 79.

7   Cole, *Trade Unionism and Munitions*, p.4. Waites, p.195. Wilson,

     Myriad Faces, p.770. Whiteside, p.93. E. Woodward, pp.475–7. Whiting, pp.900, 904.

8   Melling, p.213. Englander and Osborne, p.615.

9   Liddle, p.181. Wilson, *Myriad Faces*, p.529. Boswell and Johns, p.442. Whiting, p.912.

10 Waites, pp.256–7.

11 Pearce, p.38. Liddle, pp.188–9.

12 Gleason, p.250.

13 Englander and Osborne, pp.602–3. Sheffield, p.98. Wilson, *Myriad Faces*, p.769.

14 Petter, pp.130–43.

15 Abrams, pp.43–64.

16 Wilson, *Myriad Faces*, p.800.

10 Swenarton, pp.85–6. *The Times*, 2 April 1919; 21 June 1921.

10 Wilson, *Myriad Faces*, pp.817–18.

10 Watson, p.65. *The Guardian*, 11 November 2008. Silkin, *Poetry*, p.132. Jameson, p.211.

20 Pugh, *Women and the Women's Movement*, p.21.

21 *The Pioneer and Labour Journal*, 4 February 1916. A. Holmes. http://allpoetry.com/poem/8610777-Women_at_Munition_Making-by-Mary_Gabrielle_Collins.

22 http://www.spartacus.schoolnet.co.uk/FWWnurses.htm.

23 http://www.spartacus.schoolnet.co.uk/FWWnurses.htm. Jones, p.39.

24 Mitchell, p.266. Pugh, *Women and the Women's Movement*, pp.29–30. Kent, 'Sexual Difference', p.238. Strachey, p.371.

25 Wall and Winter, p.313. Kent, p.236. http://www.bbc.co.uk/history/british/britain_wwone/women_employment_01.shtml. Braybon and Summerfield, p.130.

26 Pugh, *Women and the Women's Movement*, pp.16–17. Kent, p.244. Wall and Winter, p.313. http://www.bbc.co.uk/history/british/britain_wwone/women_combatants_01.shtml.

27 Smith, *British Feminism*, pp.68, 74. Marwick, *Explosion*, p.26. Wilson, *Myriad Faces*, p.723. *The Times*, 1 July 1915.

28   *The Times*, 2 December 1918.

29   Tylee, pp.65, 218. Reilly, p.15. Pugh, *Women and the Women's Movement*, pp.11, 79.

30   Braybon and Summerfield, p.131.

Chapter 16: The Triumph of the Hard-Faced Men

1   *Manchester Guardian*, 12 November 1918.

2   Wilson, *Myriad Faces*, p.820.

3   Pugh, *Women and the Women's Movement*, pp.34, 40–1. Pugh, *Electoral Reform*, p.180.

4   Fawcett, *Women's Victory*, p.141. Fawcett, *What I Remember*, pp.243–53.

5   Haste, , pp.178, 181, 188–9.

6   R. Lowe, 'Failure of Consensus', p.650. Rubin, 'Law as a Bargaining Weapon', pp.926, 940. Waites, p.30.

7   McKibbin, p.105.

8   Pugh, *Making of Modern British Politics*, pp.255–6.

9   Pugh, *Women and the Women's Movement*, p.50. Kent, pp.240–1.

10   Kent, pp.243–4.

11   Burk, pp.160, 163.

12   Ibid., p.173.

13   Marwick, *Deluge*, pp.279–80.

14   *Hansard*, 11 February 1919. Waites, p.73.

15   Lowe, 'Erosion of State Intervention', p.286.

16   Tawney, p.7.

10   Dowie, p.447.

10   Cline, pp.167, 169.

10   Morgan, *Consensus and Disunity*, pp.289–90, 293. Tawney, p.17.

20   Tawney, p.27.

21   Lowe, 'Erosion of State Intervention', p.270.

22   Hardach, p.290. Wilson, *Myriad Faces*, p.792.

23   Morgan, *Consensus and Disunity*, p.292.

Chapter 17: We Shall Remember

1   http://www.guardian.co.uk/world/2008/nov/14/for-the-fallen-laurence-binyon.

2   Brittain, *Testament of Experience*, p.92.

3   Mosse, pp.45, 50. Gregory, p.23.

4   Mosse, p.91; Hynes, p.271.

5   Eksteins, p.255. D. Winter, pp.259–60. Mosse, p.84.

6   D. Winter, pp.260–1.

7   Chapman, *Vain Glory*, pp.710–11. Mottram, p.44.

8   Gregory, p.27.

9   Ibid., p.26; Eksteins, p.255.

10   Reilly, pp.93–4.

11   *The Times*, 4 February 1928. *The Scotsman*, 2 February 1928.

12   *The Scotsman*, 11 November 2000.

13   *The Times Literary Supplement*, 31 October 1929. Watson, p.212.

14   http://www.bartleby.com/136/12.html. Watson, pp.212, 227.

15   *Blackadder Goes Forth*, episode 1, http://www.suslik.org/Humour/FilmOrTV/BlackAdder/ba4–1.html.

16   Watson, p.271.

Bibliography

Abrams, Philip, 'The Failure of Social Reform', *Past and Present* (1963)

Adams, R. J. Q., and Poirer, P., *The Conscription Controversy*, 1987

Adams, R. J. Q., 'Asquith's Choice, the May Coalition and the Coming of Conscription, 1915–1916', *Journal of British Studies* (1986)

Adams, R. J. Q., *Arms and the Wizard*, 1978

Adams, Tony, 'Labour and the First World War, Economy, Politics and the Erosion of Local Peculiarity?', *Journal of Regional and Local Studies* (1990)

Aldington, Richard, *Death of a Hero*, 1984

Andreski, Stefan, *Military Organization and Society*, 1968

Angell, Norman, *The Great Illusion*, 1909

Balfour, F., *Elsie Inglis*, 1918

Barker, Pat, *The Eye in the Door*, 1994

Barlow, Adrian, *The Great War in British Literature*, 2000

Barnett, L. M., *British Food Policy During the First World War*, 1985

Barr, Niall, 'Service not Self, The British Legion 1921–1939'. unpub. PhD thesis (St Andrews 1994)

Beckett, Ian and Simpson, Keith, eds., *A Nation in Arms*, 1985

Bennett, Arnold, *Journal 1896–1926*, 1954

Bet-El, Ilana, *Conscripts: Lost Legions of the Great War*, 1999

Beveridge, William, *British Food Control*, 1928

457

Bond, Brian, 'The Late Victorian Army', *History Today* (1961)

Bond, Brian, *The Victorian Army and the Staff College*, 1972

Boston, Sarah, *Women Workers and the Trade Unions*, 1980

Boswell J., and Johns, B., 'Patriots or Profiteers? British Businessmen and the First World War', *Journal of European Economic History* (1982)

Bourne, J. M., *Britain and the Great War, 1914–1918*, 1989

Bourne, Kenneth, *The Foreign Policy of Victorian England*, Oxford, 1970

Bowley, M., *Housing and the State 1919–1941*, 1945

Bradley, M. J., and Simon, B., *The Victorian Public School*, 1975

Braybon, Gail and Summerfield, Penny, *Out of the Cage, Women's Experiences in Two World Wars*, 1987

Braybon, Gail, *Women Workers in the First World War*, 1981

Braybon, Gail, ed., *Evidence, History and the Great War*, 2003

Brittain, Vera, *Chronicle of Youth: War Diary 1913–1917*, 1981

Brittain, Vera, *Testament of Experience*, 1980

Brittain, Vera, *Testament of Youth*, 1944

Brodick, George, 'A Nation of Amateurs', *The Nineteenth Century* (1900)

Bryder, L., 'The First World War, Healthy or Hungry?', *History Workshop Journal*, 24 (1987)

Buitenhuis, Peter, *The Great War of Words*, 1989

Burk, Kathleen, *War and the State*, 1982

Burnett, J., *A Social History of Housing 1815–1970*, 1978

Carrington, C., *Soldier from the Wars Returning*, 1945

Carsten, F. L., *War Against War*, 1982

Chapman, Guy, *A Passionate Prodigality*, 1933

Chapman, Guy, *Vain Glory*, 1937

Churchill, Randolph, *Lord Derby, King of Lancashire*, 1959

Clegg, H., *The System of Industrial Relations in Britain*, Oxford, 1956

Clegg, H., Fox, A., and Thompson, A. F., *A History of British Trade Unions Since 1889*, 1985

Cline, Peter, 'Reopening the Case of the Lloyd George Coalition and the post-War Economic Transition, 1918–19', *Journal of British Studies* (1970)

Cole, G. D. H., *Labour in War Time*, 1915

Cole, G. D. H., *Trade Unionism and Munitions*, 1923

Cole, G. D. H., *Workshop Organization*, 1923

Constantine, Stephen, ed., *The First World War in British History*, 1995

Cook, Chris, and Stevenson, John, *The Longman Handbook of Modern British History 1714–1980*, 1983

Coppard, George, *With a Machine Gun to Cambrai*, 1969

Cross, Tim, ed., *Lost Voices of World War I*, 1988

Dakers, Caroline, *The Countryside at War*, 1987

Dallas, Gloden, and Gill, Douglas, *The Unknown Army*, 1985

Davidson, Roger, 'The Myth of the "Servile State"', *Bulletin of the Society for the Study of Labour History* (1974)

DeGroot, Gerard, 'Educated Soldier or Cavalry Officer?, Contradictions in the pre-1914 Career of Douglas Haig', *War and Society* (1986)

DeGroot, Gerard, *Douglas Haig, 1861–1928*, 1988

DeGroot, Gerard, *Liberal Crusader, The Life of Sir Archibald Sinclair*, 1993

Demm, E., 'Propaganda and Caricature in the First World War', *Journal of Contemporary History* (1993)

Dewey, P. E., 'Agricultural Labour Supply in England and Wales During the First World War', *Economic History Review* (1975)

Dewey, P. E., 'British Farming Profits and Government Policy During the First World War', *Economic History Review* (1984)

Dewey, P. E., 'Food Production and Policy in the United Kingdom, 1914–1918', *Transactions of the Royal Historical Society* (1980)

Dewey, P. E., 'Military Recruiting and the British Labour Force During the First World War', *Historical Journal* (1984)

Dilks, David, *Neville Chamberlain*, 1984

Diver, Maud, *Desmond's Daughter*, 1916

Douglas, Roy, 'The National Democratic Party and the British Workers' League', *Historical Journal* 27 (1984)

Douglas, Roy, 'Voluntary Enlistment in the First World War and the Work of the Parliamentary Recruiting Committee', *Journal of Modern History* 42 (1970)

Dowie, J., '1919–20 is in Need of Attention', *Economic History Review* (1975)

Doyle, Barry, 'Who Paid the Price of Patriotism? The Funding of Charles Stanton during the Merthyr Boroughs By-Election of 1915', *English Historical Review* (1994)

Drake, Barbara, *Women in the Engineering Trade*, 1915

Dutton, David, *Austen Chamberlain, Gentleman in Politics*, 1985

Eksteins, Modris, *Rites of Spring*, 1989

Ellis, John, *Eye-Deep in Hell*, 1976

Englander, D., and. Osborne, J., 'Jack, Tommy and Henry Dubb, The Armed Forces and the Working Class', *Historical Journal* 21 (1978)

Englund, Peter, *The Beauty and the Sorrow*, 2011

Fawcett, Millicent, *What I Remember*, 1925

Fawcett, Millicent, *The Women's Victory – And After, Personal Reminiscences, 1911–1918*, 1920

Ford, Ford Madox, *Parade's End*, 1950

Fraser, P., 'British War Policy and the Crisis of Liberalism in May 1915', *Journal of Modern History* (1982)

French, David, 'Spy Fever in Britain, 1900–1915', *Historical Journal* (1978)

French, David, 'The Meaning of Attrition', *English Historical Review* (1988)

French, David, *British Economic and Strategic Planning, 1905–1915*, 1982

French, David, *British Strategy and War Aims, 1914–1916*, 1986

Fry, M., 'Political Change in Britain, August 1914 to December 1916, Lloyd George Replaces Asquith, The Issues Underlying the Drama', *Historical Journal* 31 (1988)

Fussell, Paul, *The Great War and Modern Memory*, 1977

Garvin, J. L., *The Life of Joseph Chamberlain*, 1932

Gauldie, Enid, *Cruel Habitations*, 1974

Gibbs, Philip, *Now It Can Be Told*, 1920

Gilbert, Bentley, 'Pacifist to Interventionist, David Lloyd George in 1911 and 1914. Was Belgium an Issue?', *Historical Journal* (1985)

Gill, Douglas, and Dallas, Gloden, 'Mutiny at Etaples Base in 1917', *Past and Present* (1975)

Gleason, Arthur, *What the Workers Want*, 1920

Gordon, M., 'Domestic Conflict and the Origins of the First World War, The British and the German Cases', *Journal of Modern History* (1974).

Graham, John, *Conscription and Conscience*, 1969

Graubard, S. R., 'Military Demobilization in Great Britain Following the First World War', *Journal of Modern History* (1947)

Graves, Robert, *Goodbye to All That*, 1929

Gregory, Adrian, *The Silence of Memory*, 1994

Grey, Edward, *Twenty-Five Years, 1893–1916*, 1925

Grieves, Keith, *The Politics of Manpower*, 1988

Guinn, Paul, *British Strategy and Politics 1914 to 1918*, 1965

Gullace, N., 'White Feathers and Wounded Men: Female Patriotism and the Memory of the Great War', *Journal of British Studies* (1997)

Haldane, R. B., *Autobiography*, 1929

Haldane, R. B., *Before the War*, 1927

Halsey, A. H., *British Social Trends Since 1900*, 1972

Hamilton, Mary Agnes, *Dead Yesterday*, 1916

Hamilton, Mary Agnes, *Our Freedom*, 1922

Hankey, Maurice, *The Supreme Command*, 1961

Hardach, Gerd, *The First World War 1914–1918*, 1987

Harries-Jenkins, Gwyn, *The Army in Victorian Society*, 1977

Harris, B., 'The Demographic Impact of the First World War, An Anthropometric Perspective', *Journal of the Society for the Social History of Medicine* (1993)

Harrison, Jane, *Alpha and Omega*, 1915

Hart, Michael, 'The Liberals, the War and the Franchise', *English Historical Review* (1982)

Haste, Cate, *Keep the Home Fires Burning*, 1977

Hazlehurst, Cameron, 'Asquith Gas Prime Minister, 1908–1916', *English Historical Review* (1970)

Henty, G. A., *With Kitchener in the Soudan*, 1903

Hiley, N., '"Lord Kitchener Resigns", The Suppression of the Globe in 1915', *Journal of Newspaper and Periodical History* (1992)

Hiley, N., 'The Failure of British Counter-Espionage Against German, 1907–1914', *Historical Journal* (1985)

Hinton, James, *Labour and Socialism*, 1983

Hinton, James, *Protests and Visions*, 1989

Hinton, James, *The First Shop Stewards' Movement*, 1973

Holmes, Alec, 'The Munition Worker: A Play in One Scene', *The Englishwoman* (March 1917)

Holmes, Richard, *Firing Line*, 1987

Horn, Patricia, *Rural Life in England in the First World War*, 1984

Horne, John, and Kramer, Alan, 'German "Atrocities" and Franco-German Opinion, 1914, The Evidence of German Soldiers' Diaries', *Journal of Modern History* (1994)

Howard, Michael, ed., *Soldiers and Governments*, 1957

Howard, Michael, *Studies in War and Peace*, 1970

Howard, Michael, *The Continental Commitment*, 1972

Hunt, Barry, and Preston, Adrian, eds., *War Aims and Strategic Policy in the Great War 1914–1918*, 1977

Hyman, A., *The Rise and Fall of Horatio Bottomley*, 1972

Hynes, S., *A War Imagined*, 1990

James, Robert Rhodes, *Rosebery*, 1963

Jameson, M. Storm, *No Time Like the Present*, 1933

Janowitz, Maurice, *The Professional Soldier*, 1960

Jenkins, Roy, *Asquith*, 1964

Jones, Helen, *Health and Society in Twentieth-Century Britain*, 1994

Keegan, John, *The Face of Battle*, 1976

Kendall, W., *The Revolutionary Movement in Great Britain*, 1969

Kennedy, Paul, ed., *The War Plans of the Great Powers*, 1979

Kennedy, Paul, *The Realities Behind Diplomacy*, 1981

Kent, Susan Kingsley, 'The Politics of Sexual Difference, World War I and the Demise of British Feminism', *Journal of British Studies* (1988)

Klein, Yvonne, *Beyond the Home Front: Women's Autobiographical Writing of the Two World Wars*, 1997

Koss, Stephen, *The Rise and Fall of the Political Press*, 1984

Koven, Seth, and Michel, Sonya, 'Womanly Duties, Maternalist Politics and the Origins of Welfare States in France, Germany, Great Britain and the United States, 1880–1920', *American Historical Review* (1990)

Koven, S., 'Remembering and Dismemberment, Crippled Children, Wounded Soldiers, and the Great War in Britain', *American Historical Review* (1994)

Laslett, Peter, *The World We Have Lost*, 1971

Lasswell, Harold, *Propaganda Technique in the World War*, 1938

Lauder, Harry, *Roamin' in the Gloamin'*, 1928

Levine, Philippa, '"Walking the Streets in a Way No Decent Woman Should", Women Police in World War I', *Journal of Modern History* (1994)

Lewis, Jane, *The Politics of Motherhood*, 1980

Liddle, P., ed., *Home Fires and Foreign Fields*, 1985

Lloyd, E. M. H., *Experiments in State Control*, 1924

Lloyd George, David, *War Memoirs*, 1938

Loudon, I., 'Deaths in Childbed from the Eighteenth Century to 1935', *Medical History* (1986)

Low, S., 'The Future of the Great Armies', *The Nineteenth Century* (1899)

Lowe, Rodney, 'The Erosion of State Intervention in Britain, 1917–24', *Economic History Review* (1978)

Lowe, Rodney, 'The Failure of Consensus in Britain, the National Industrial Conference, 1919–1921', *Historical Journal* (1978)

McDermott, J., '"A Needless Sacrifice", British Businessmen and Business as Usual in the First World War', *Albion* (1989)

McDonald, A., 'The Geddes Committee and the Formulation of Public Expenditure Policy, 1921–1922', *Historical Journal* (1989)

McFeely, Mary, *Lady Inspectors,* Oxford, 1988

McKibbin, Ross, *The Evolution of the Labour Party 1910–1924,* 1973

McLean, Iain, *The Legend of Red Clydeside,* 1983

Magnus, Philip, *Kitchener, Portrait of an Imperialist,* 1958

Mangan J. A., and Walvin, James, ed., *Manliness and Morality,* 1987

Mangan, J. A., *Athleticism in the Victorian and Edwardian Public School,* 1981

Marquis, A. G., 'Words as Weapons, Propaganda in Britain and Germany During the First World War', *Journal of Contemporary History* (1978)

Marwick, Arthur, *The Deluge,* 1991

Marwick, Arthur, *The Explosion of British Society 1914–62,* 1963

Marwick, Arthur, *Women at War,* 1977

Masterman, C. F. G., *England After the War,* 1922

Masterman, Lucy, *C. F. G. Masterman,* 1939

Maxwell, Herbert, 'Are We Really a Nation of Amateurs?', *Nineteenth Century* 48 (1900)

Melling, Joseph, '"Non-Commissioned Officers": British Employers and the Supervisory Workers, 1880–1920', *Social History* 5 (1980)

Melman, Billie, ed., *Borderlines: Genders and Identities in War and Peace, 1870–1930*, 1998

Messinger, G. S., *Propaganda and the State in the First World War*, 1992

Meyer, Jessica, ed., *British Popular Culture and the First World War*, 2008

Middlebrook, Martin, *Your Country Needs You*, 2000

Middlemas, R. K., *Politics in Industrial Society*, 1979

Middlemas, R. K., *The Clydesiders*, 1965

Miliband, Ralph, *Parliamentary Socialism*, 1972

Milward, A. S., *The Economic Effects of the Two World Wars Upon Britain*, 1970

Mitchell, David, *Women on the Warpath*, 1966

Money, Leo Chiozza, 'British Trade and the War', *Contemporary Review* (October 1914)

Montague, C. E., *Disenchantment*, 1922

Morel, E. D., *Truth and the War*, 1916

Morgan, K. O., *Consensus and Disunity*, 1979

Morgan, K. O., *Lloyd George*, 1974

Mosley, Nicholas, *Rules of the Game*, 1983

Mosse, G., *Fallen Soldiers*, 1990

Mottram, Rolto, *Journey to the Western Front Twenty Years After*, 1936

Mowat, C. L., *Britain Between the Wars*, 1968

Newbolt, Henry, *Naval Operations (Official History of the Great War)*, 1931

Newbolt, Henry, *Poems Old and New*, 1912

Newsome, David, *Godliness and Good Learning*, 1961

Oxford and Asquith, *Memories and Reflections*, 1928

Pakenham, Thomas, *The Boer War*, 1982

Panayi, Panikos, *The Enemy in Our Midst*, 1991

Panichas, V. A., *Promise of Greatness*, 1968

Pankhurst, Sylvia, *The Home Front*, 1987

Parker, P., *The Old Lie, The Great War and the Public School Ethos*, 1987

Pearce, R., *Britain, Industrial Relations and the Economy 1900–1939*, 1993

Pedersen, Susan, 'Gender, Welfare, and Citizenship in Britain during the Great War', *American Historical Review* (1990)

Pedersen, Susan, 'The Failure of Feminism in the Making of the British Welfare State', *Radical History Review* (1989)

Peel, C. S., *How We Lived Then*, 1929

Petter, Martin, '"Temporary Gentlemen" in the Aftermath of the Great War, Rank, Status and the Ex-Officer Problem', *Historical Journal* (1994)

Phelps Brown, Henry, *The Origins of Trade Union Power*, 1986

Playne, Caroline, *The Pre-War Mind in Britain*, 1928

Ponsonby, Arthur, *Falsehood in War-Time*, 1928

Porter, Bernard, *The Lion's Share*, 1975

Pugh, Martin, *Electoral Reform in War and Peace*, 1978

Pugh, Martin, *The Making of Modern British Politics*, 1982

Pugh, Martin, *Women and the Women's Movement in Britain, 1914–1959*, 1992

Rae, John, *Conscience and Politics*, 1970

Rawlings, G., 'Swindler of the Century', *History Today* (July 1993)

Razzell, P. E., 'Social Origins of Officers in the Indian and British Home Army, 1758–1962', *British Journal of Sociology* (1963)

Reader, W. J., *At Duty's Call*, 1988

Reeves, N., 'Film Propaganda and Its Audience, The Example of Britain's Official Films during the First World War', *Journal of Contemporary History* (1983)

Reilly, Catherine, ed., *Scars Upon My Heart, Women's Poetry and Verse of the First World War*, 1981

Reiss, R., *The Home I Want*, 1918

Repington, Charles, *The First World War 1914–1918*, 1920

Robertson, William, *From Private to Field Marshal*, 1921

Royle, Trevor, *The Kitchener Enigma*, 1985

Roynon, Gavin, ed., *Home Fires Burning*, 2006

Rubin, G. R., *War, Law and Labour*, 1987

Rubin, G. R., 'Law as a Bargaining Weapon, British Labour and the Restoration of Pre-War Practices Act 1919', *Historical Journal* (1989)

Rubinstein, W. D., 'Henry Page Croft and the National Party 1917–22', *Journal of Contemporary History* (1974)

Sanders, Michael, and Taylor, Philip, *British Propaganda during the First World War*, 1982

Sassoon, Siegfried, *Collected Poems*, 1947

Sassoon, Siegfried, *Memoirs of an Infantry Officer*, 1930

Sassoon, Siegfried, *Sherston's Progress*, 1936

Sheffield, Gary, 'The Effect of the Great War on Class Relation in Great Britain, The Career of Major Christopher Stone DSO MC', *War and Society* (1989)

Silkin, John, ed., *The Penguin Book of First World War Poetry*, 1979

Silkin, John, ed., *The Penguin Book of First World War Prose*, 1990

Sillars, S., *Art and Survival in First World War Britain*, 1987

Simkins, Peter, *Kitchener's Army*, 1988

Sitwell, Osbert, *Laughter in the Next Room*, 1949

Smith, Angela, *The Secret Battlefield: Women, Modernism and the First World War*, 2000

Smith, Harold, 'The Issue of "Equal Pay for Equal Work" in Britain, 1914–19', *Societas* (1978)

Smith, Harold, *British Feminism in the Twentieth Century*, 1990

Spiers, Edward, *Haldane, An Army Reformer*, 1980

Springhall, John, *Youth, Empire and Society*, 1977

Stapledon, O., *Last Men in London*, 1963

Steiner, Zara, *Britain and the Origins of the First World War*, 1986

Strachey, Ray, *The Cause*, 1928

Stubbs, J. O., 'Lord Milner and Patriotic Labour', *English Historical Review* (1972)

Summers, Anne, 'Militarism in Britain Before the Great War', *History Workshop Journal* (Autumn 1976)

Summers, Anne, *Angels and Citizens, British Women as Military Nurses*, 1988

Back in Blighty

Swenarton, M., *Homes Fit for Heroes*, 1981

Tanner, Duncan, 'The Parliamentary Electoral System, the "Fourth" Reform Act, and the Rise of Labour in England and Wales', *Bulletin of the Institute of Historical Research* (1983)

Tanner, Duncan, *Political Change and the Labour Party, 1900–1918*, 1990

Tate, Trudi, *Modernism, History and the Great War*, 1998

Tawney, R. H., 'The Abolition of Economic Controls, 1918–1921', *Economic History Review* (1943)

Taylor, A. J. P., ed., *Lloyd George, A Diary by Frances Stevenson*, 1971

Taylor, A. J. P., *English History 1914–1945*, 1965

Terraine, John, *The Smoke and the Fire*, 1980

Thomas, Helen, *World Without End*, 1931

Travers, T. H. E., *The Killing Ground*, 1987

Travers, T., 'Technology, Tactics and Morale, Jean de Bloch, the Boer War, and British Military Theory, 1900–1914', *Journal of Modern History* (1979)

Travers, T., 'The Hidden Army, Structural Problems in the British Officer Corps, 1900–1918', *Journal of Contemporary History* (1982)

Travers, T., 'The Offensive and the Problem of Innovation in British Military Thought 1870–1915', *Journal of Contemporary History* (1978)

Turner, John, *British Politics and the Great War*, 1992

Turner, John, ed., *Britain and the First World War*, 1988

Tylee, Claire, *The Great War and Women's Consciousness*, 1990

Vachell, H. A., *The Hill*, 1905

Vansittart, Peter, *Voices from the Great War*, 1981

Vaughan, E. C., *Some Desperate Glory*, 1981

Veitch, Colin, '"Play up! Play up! and Win the War!" Football, the Nation and the First World War 1914–15', *Journal of Contemporary History* (1985).

Waites, Bernard, *A Class Society at War*, 1987

468

Wall, Richard, and Winter, Jay, *The Upheaval of War*, 1988

Wallace, Stuart, *War and the Image of Germany*, 1988

Walvin, James, *Leisure and Society 1830–1950*, 1978

Ward, Paul, '"Women of Britain Say Go": Women's Patriotism in the First World War', *Twentieth Century History* (2001)

Ward, S. R., 'Intelligence Surveillance of British Ex-Servicemen, 1918–20', *Historical Journal* (1973)

Watson, Janet, *Fighting Different Wars*, 2004

Waugh, Alec, *The Loom of Youth*, 1929

Wavell, Archibald, *Soldiers and Soldiering*, 1953

Webb, Sydney, *The Restoration of Trade Union Conditions*, 1918

Weeks, Jeremy, *Sex, Politics and Society*, 1989

Weinroth, H., 'Norman Angell and The Great Illusion, An Episode in Pre-1914 Pacifism', *Historical Journal* (1974)

Weintraub, S., *A Stillness Heard Round the World*, 1985

Whiteside, Noelle, 'Industrial Welfare and Labour Regulation in Britain at the Time of the First World War', *International Review of Social History* (1980)

Whiting, R. C., 'Taxation and the Working Class, 1915–24', *Historical Journal* (1990)

Wilkinson, Alan, *The Church of England and the First World War*, 1978

Wilkinson, G., '"Soldiers by Instinct, Slayers by Training", The Daily Mail and the Image of the Warrior, 1899–1914', *Journal of Newspaper and Periodical History* (1992)

Wilkinson, Rupert, *The Prefects*, 1964

Wilson, Keith, *Empire and Continent*, 1987

Wilson, Keith, *The Policy of the Entente*, 1985

Wilson, Trevor, 'Britain's "Moral Commitment" to France in August 1914', *History* (1979)

Wilson, Trevor, 'Lord Bryce's Investigation into Alleged German Atrocities in Belgium, 1914–15', *Journal of Contemporary History* (1979)

Wilson, Trevor, ed., *The Political Diaries of C. P. Scott*, 1970

Wilson, Trevor, *The Myriad Faces of War*, 1988

Wiltsher, Anne, *Most Dangerous Women*, 1985

Winter, Denis, *Death's Men*, 1979

Winter, J. M., ed., *War and Economic Development*, 1975

Winter, J. M., *The Great War and the British People*, 1985

Winter, J. M., *Remembering War*, 2006

Winter, J. M., 'Aspects of the Impact of the First World War on Infant Mortality in Britain', *Journal of European Economic History* (1982)

Winter, J. M., 'Public Health and the Political Economy', *History Workshop Journal* (1988)

Wolfe, Humbert, *Labour Supply and Regulation*, 1923

Woodward, David, 'Did Lloyd George Starve the British Army of Men Prior to the German Offensive of March 1918?', *Historical Journal* (1984)

Woodward, David, *Lloyd George and the Generals*, 1983

Woodward, E. L., *Great Britain and the War of 1914–1918*, 1967

Woollacott, Angela, 'Khaki Fever and its Control, Gender, Class, Age and Sexual Morality on the British Homefront in the First World War', *Journal of Contemporary History* (1994)

Woollacott, Angela, 'Maternalism, Professionalism and Industrial Welfare Supervisors in World War I Britain', *Women's History Review* (1994)

Wrigley, C., *David Lloyd George and the British Labour Movement*, 1976

Wrigley, C., ed., *Warfare, Diplomacy and Politics, Essays in Honour of A. J. P. Taylor*, 1986

Younghusband, George, *A Soldier's Memories*, 1917

Index

Scarborough and Hartlepool 244,
256; spies 197, 219, 220–2, 234–5, 249,
250, 251; use of poison gas 244, 250;
Zeppelin raids 244, 256, 257, 317
Gibbs, Philip 235, 239, 240, 241, 339, 357
Gish, Lillian 310
Glasgow 51, 68, 100, 160, 163–4, 165, 210,
256, 270, 271
Glasgow Labour Party Housing
Committee 160
Gleason, Arthur 378
Globe 236, 238
gonorrhea 301
'good form' 48, 87
Good Housekeeping 393–4
Goschen, Sir Edward 9, 16–17
Gotha bombers 257, 317
Goudge, Ansell John 198
Grace, W. G. 290
Grant, Ulysses 28
Graves, Robert 85, 86, 420
Great Illusion, The (Angell) 9, 200
Great Love, The (film) 310
Greene, Graham 62, 249
Grenfell, Julian 62, 63
Grey, Sir Edward 104, 107–8
grief 273, 349, 352, 353, 354–5, 362–6, 421
Griffith, D. W. 309–10
Gurney, Ivor: 'To His Love' 354

Haggard, H. Rider 54
Hague Conferences, 1901 and 1907 9
Haig, Sir Douglas 139; Allied victory and
169, 319; blames German counter-
offensive, 1918 on Lloyd George 149–
50, 318; British Legion and 344, 345;
cavalry and 32; censorship and 239;
Churchill scheme for demobilsation
and 331, 332; conscription and
341; death 426; decline in power of
148; Lord Derby and 147; disabled
soldiers and 333; gambles on
loyalty of working-class soldiers
93; government refusal to increase
amount of troops available to him
149–50, 151; gratuity 330; luxurious
wartime lifestyle of 89–91; munitions
crisis and 112; post-war reputation
of 89, 427–8, 432–3, 434; Somme
and 141, 143; volunteers make more
dependable soldiers, argues that 39

Haldane Reforms 34, 35–7, 42, 58, 59,
108–9
Haldane, Richard Burdon 35–6, 54, 108–9
Halevy, Eric 403–4
Halfpenny Marvel, The 57
Hall, Isaac 216
Hamilton, Mary Agnes 7, 8, 299
Hamilton, Sir Ian 92
Hampshire 127–8
Hanbury-Sparrow, A. A. 85
Hankey, Maurice 99, 109, 129–30, 287–8
Harcourt, Lewis 104
Hardie, Keir 102, 199, 203
Hardinge, Sir Charles 21
Hardy, Thomas 225
Harris, Bernard 271
Harrison, Jane 48–9
Harrow School 49–51
Headmistresses' Association 280
Health of Munitions Workers Committee
170
Heart of the World 310
Henderson, Arthur 140, 144, 199, 208,
209, 213
Henry, Sir Edward 250
Henty, George Alfred 54, 55, 57, 62
Herald, The 329, 330
Hill, John 404
Hills Committee, The 390
Hindenburg Line 319
Hinton, James 156
Hirschfield, Magnus 392
Hitler, Adolf 431
Hobhouse, Stephen 217
Hobson, J. A, 205, 206
Hockey Association 290
Holman, Private Charles 358
Holmes, Alec: *The Munitions Worker* 387
Holtby, Winifred 390–1, 392, 407, 408
Home Army 145, 146, 149
home front 253–86; babies/'cult of the
child' 273–82; birth control 274–5;
childcare 281–2; children as workers
264–5; children's education 279–80;
coal rationing 263–4; disability
allowances 268; employment of
children 280–1; enemy action and
housing problems 256–7; eugenicists
275–6, 278; greater freedom of some
women 285; grief 273, 285; health
standards/mortality rates 270–3;